George William Cox

An Introduction to the Science of Comparative Mythology and Folklore

George William Cox

An Introduction to the Science of Comparative Mythology and Folklore

ISBN/EAN: 9783744778466

Printed in Europe, USA, Canada, Australia, Japan

Cover: Foto ©Thomas Meinert / pixelio.de

More available books at **www.hansebooks.com**

COMPARATIVE MYTHOLOGY AND FOLKLORE

BY THE SAME AUTHOR.

A HISTORY of GREECE from the EARLIEST PERIOD to the end of the PERSIAN WAR. New Edition. 2 vols. Demy 8vo. 36*s.*

The MYTHOLOGY of the ARYAN NATIONS. New Edition. Demy 8vo. 16*s.*

TALES of ANCIENT GREECE. New Edition. Small crown 8vo. 6*s.*

A MANUAL of MYTHOLOGY in the form of QUESTION and ANSWER. New Edition. Fcp. 8vo. 3*s.*

POPULAR ROMANCES of the MIDDLE AGES. By the Rev. SIR G. W. COX, M.A., Bart., and EUSTACE HINTON JONES. Third Edition. Crown 8vo. 6*s.*

London : KEGAN PAUL, TRENCH, & CO.

AN INTRODUCTION TO THE SCIENCE OF COMPARATIVE MYTHOLOGY AND FOLKLORE

BY THE

REV. SIR GEORGE W. COX, BART., M.A.

AUTHOR OF
'THE MYTHOLOGY OF THE ARYAN NATIONS' ETC.

SECOND EDITION

LONDON
KEGAN PAUL, TRENCH, & CO., 1 PATERNOSTER SQUARE
1883

(The rights of translation and of reproduction are reserved)

PREFACE.

MY PURPOSE in this volume is to give a general view of the vast mass of popular traditions belonging to the Aryan nations of Asia and Europe, and of other tribes so far as the conditions of the subject may render necessary.

Its starting point is the principle that the popular traditions of no one Aryan people can be really understood except in their relation to those of other tribes and nations of the same family, and that the epical and dramatic literature of those races has been constructed from materials common to all branches of the Aryan stock and furnished by popular sayings, stories, and tales, many of which have never had the good fortune to be more than the talk of nurses and children.

The Greek term *mythology* scarcely expresses, indeed, the fact that the traditions, on which the epic, lyric, and dramatic poetry of the Aryan nations has sprung up, really constitute what in strict speech we may speak of as the whole learning of the people in early stages of thought and civilisation, and sum up their thoughts on the origin and constitution of the outward world. Folklore, in short, is perpetually running into mythology; and there are few myths which do not exhibit in some of their features points of likeness to the tales usually classified under the head of folklore.

In my 'Manual of Mythology' I dealt with the Greek and Latin myths in the form of a catechism designed for children who have to make their first acquaintance with the subject. My effort in that little volume was to give the outlines of Greek and Roman mythology in their simplest possible shape, yet so that the children using that book might not only have nothing to unlearn, but should become fairly grounded in the method of the science. I venture to hope that this primary catechism may continue to serve as a useful and necessary introduction to the present volume, the purpose of which is to impart to the student a more complete knowledge of the nature and character of Aryan popular tradition or folklore generally, and to carry him to a point from which, if he desires to extend his researches further, he may, with the aid of my volumes on the 'Mythology of the Aryan Nations,' make himself acquainted with many parts of the subject (some of them of the utmost importance) which in the present volume I could do no more than glance at, while not a few I have been obliged to leave altogether unnoticed. To these volumes I must, further, refer the reader for the full evidence of many assertions which in the present work I am compelled to regard as proved.

I make no pretension of treating systematically the popular traditions of non-Aryan nations or tribes. But I am fully aware of the dangers involved in attempts to explain Teutonic, or Greek, or Latin, or Scandinavian myths, solely from Aryan sources. The Greeks of lesser Asia, in particular, were brought into close contact with

Semitic peoples, who exercised over them a most powerful religious influence; and the theology and ritual of this portion of the Greek world, which after a severe struggle worked their way into Western Hellas, teem with difficulties and perplexities for the student who tries to exhibit them as belonging wholly to an Aryan stock. The worship of Poseidon, Dionysos, Aphroditê, and some other deities, may have been derived bodily from Semitic races; but beyond all doubt it was largely affected and modified by Semitic ritual and belief. A presumption, therefore, is raised that to this source we may trace the many mysterious, or uncouth, or grotesque beings who come before us in Greek stories in the shape of Korybantes, Kabeiroi, Kouretes, Idaian Daktyls, Telchines, and others. In this part of the subject I gladly acknowledge my obligations to Mr. Robert Brown's very valuable work on 'The Great Dionysiak Myth.'

The examination of the vast storehouse of Aryan popular tradition points in every part to the one conclusion, that it owes its existence to words and phrases which expressed the sensations and thoughts awakened in primitive generations of mankind by the sights and sounds of the outward world. Of these phenomena some would be more important and impressive than others; and in proportion the sayings applied to them would be more numerous or striking. Among these the sun, moon, and stars would stand out with special prominence; but when the myths or sayings related to these have been put aside, there remains a multitude of legends which are neither solar, lunar, nor sidereal, and which describe with singular exactness the phenomena of clouds and water, of forests and mountains, of the upper and the nether world, of winds, and dew, and storms. The myth is a parasite which is ready to twine round any stem ; and in each case it is the business of the mythologist to ascertain the nature of the stem, if he would account satisfactorily for the peculiar forms of its vesture.

G. W. C.

BEKESBOURNE: *Feb.* 16, 1881.

CONTENTS.

CHAPTER I.

THE MATERIALS OF POPULAR TRADITION.

	PAGE
Popular stories of ancient and modern times	1
Self-moving and self-guiding ships	2
Antiquity of popular stories	3
Materials for epic poems	4
Varying fortunes of popular stories	6
Question of the origin of popular traditions	7
Organic or Primary, and Inorganic or Secondary, Myths	9
Effects of the dispersion of tribes	10
Conditions needed for the development of myths	11
Mythical names	13
Polyonymy	—
The Fatal Children	14
Mythical robes and weapons	15
Greek tribal legends	16
Common elements of popular tradition	17
Modes of transmission of popular stories. Hypothesis of borrowing	18
Cases of lateral transmission	20
Conditions determining the course of the development of myths	23
Alleged connexion of mythology with primitive revelation	24

CHAPTER II.

THE HEAVENS AND THE LIGHT.

Manifold aspects of mythical tradition	27
Question of the priority of myths	28
Language of the Hymns of the Rig Veda	29
Hymns to the Dawn	—
I. The Vedic VARUNA	31
II. DYAUS	32
III. MITRA	33
IV. INDRA	—
V. BRAHMA	34

	PAGE
VI. The Hellenic ZEUS	35
Zeus and Prometheus	36
The Olympian Zeus	37
The physical and spiritual Zeus	39
The Olympian hierarchy	—
Zeus and Lykosoura	40
Zeus the judge	41
Lykaon	42
The Teutonic gods of the heaven	—
VII. ODIN. Genealogy of Odin	44
Odin and Wish	45
Odin, the one-eyed, and Hakol-berend	46
Odin and Tyr	47
VIII. THOR. Thor and his hammer	—
IX. FRO. Friuja	48
X. HEIMDALL. Himinbiorg	49
XI. BRAGI. Œgir	—
XII. The Latin JUPITER. Characteristics of Latin mythology	50
The Latin deities	—
Jupiter and Juno	52
Myths of the Dawn and the Sun	53
Framework and materials of these myths	54
XIII. URVASÎ	55
Eros and Psyche	—
Northern sun and dawn myths	56
XIV. USHAS. Ushas and the Panis	57
XV. AHANÂ and SARAMÂ	58
XVI. SARANYÛ. Erinyes, Harpies, Atê	59
The doctrine of Necessity. Moirai, Weird Sisters, Norns, Adrasteia, Nemesis, the Parcæ, Fates, and Aisa	61
The horses and chariot of the sun	62
XVII. ARUSHA, the Greek Eros	63
The Muses and the Camenæ	64
XVIII. Eos. Tithonos	65
XIX. HÊBÊ. Ganymedes	—
XX. EUROPA. Kadmos (Cadmus), Agênôr, Telephassa	66
XXI. ALTHAIA. Meleagros, Olger the Dane	68
XXII. ATHÊNÊ. Athênê and Ahanâ	70
Athênê Koryphasia and Akria	71
Athêne Tritogeneia	—
Athene Glaukôpis	—
Athênê mother of Lychnos and Phœbus	72
XXIII. The Latin MINERVA	—
XXIV. APHRODITÊ	74
Aphroditê and Hephaistos	—
The children of Aphroditê	75
Aphroditê and Adonis	—
Aphroditê and Dionysos	76
XXV. VENUS	77
XXVI. HÊRÊ	—
Relations of Hêrê with Zeus	78
The children of Hêrê	—
XXVII. The Latin JUNO	80
XXVIII. SURYA and SAVITAR	—

	PAGE
XXIX. SOMA	81
Correlative deities. Soma and Uma	82
The Asvins	83
Yama	—
XXX. PHŒBUS APOLLO	84
The Delian legend	85
Mythical geography	—
Phœbus and Telphoussa	86
Apollon Delphinios	87
Apollo and Daphne	88
Apollo, the life-giver and healer.—Asklepios	89
Apollo and Hermes	91
The oracle of Delphi	92
Iamos and the Iamidai	—
Amphiaraos and Alkmaion	—
XXXI. HELIOS and PHAETHON. Class of Secondaries	93
Endymion and Narkissos (Narcissus)	95
Hesperos	96
Ixion	—
Tantalos	98
Stories of drought	99
The gardens of Midas	100
XXXII. HERAKLES (Hercules)	101
The labours of Herakles	102
The apologue of Prodikos	—
The weapons of Herakles	103
Herakles and Kerberos (Cerberus)	104
Herakles and Laomedon	—
Herakles and Deianeira	105
Herakles and Admetos	106
Herakles in bondage	107
The death of Herakles	108
The comic Herakles	109
The children of Herakles, and their fortunes	—
Herakles and Hercules	110
XXXIII. PERSEUS	—
Perseus and Polydektes	111
Perseus and the Gorgons	112
Perseus and Akrisios	114
Perseus and Herakles	115
XXXIV. THESEUS	116
Theseus and the tribute children	117
Theseus and the Amazons	118
Theseus and Peirithoös	119
Theseus and the Athenian Commonwealth	—
XXXV. ŒDIPUS	120
Œdipus and Theseus	121
Moral aspect of the myth of Œdipus and Iokastê	122
Œdipus and the Sphinx	123
Œdipus and the Eumenides	125
The children of Œdipus	126
Œdipus and Telephos	127
Paris and his kinsfolk	128

		PAGE
	Pelias and Neleus	130
	Romulus and Remus	—
	Cyrus	131
	Minos and Manu	132
	Sarpêdôn and Glaukos	133
	Kephalos (Cephalus) and Prokris	134
	Vitality of the Aryan gods	136
XXXVI.	BALDER	137
	Cloudeslee and Tell	138
XXXVII.	VISHNU. The Dwarf Incarnation	139
	Vishnu and Indra	141
	The worship of Vishnu	—
	Eastern and Western Mysteries	144
XXXVIII.	KRISHNA	145
	The birth and infancy of Krishna	—
	Krishna and the Gopias	147
	Krishna and Kalinak	148
	Osiris	—
	Neith and the Phenix	151
	The moon and stars	—
	Io and Argos	—
	The wanderings of Io	153
	Io, Epaphos, and Apis	—
	Hipponoös Bellerophontes	155
	Bellerophon and Anteia	156
XXXIX.	HECATE	157
XL.	ARTEMIS	158
	Artemis Tauropola, Iphigeneia, Britomartis, and Diktynna	---
	Kirke (Circe) and Kalypso	160
	Tanhaüser and Thomas the Rimer	161
	The Seven Sleepers and the Seven Rishis	162
	The hunter Orion	—
	Aktaion	163

CHAPTER III.

THE FIRE.

I.	AGNI	164
	The parentage and birth of Agni	—
	Agni and Hestia	166
	Agni, Bhuranyu, and Phoroneus	167
II.	HESTIA. Vesta	—
	The Latin Lares and Penates	169
III.	HEPHAISTOS	—
	The home of Hephaistos	170
	Hephaistos and Thetis	—
	Hephaistos and Daidalos (Dœdalus)	171
IV.	VULCAN	—
V.	LOKI.—Fenris	172
VI.	PROMETHEUS. The Hesiodic Ages	—
	Prometheus and Epimetheus	175
	Prometheus and Deukalion	176
	Ramifications of the myths of Prometheus	177

CONTENTS. xiii

	PAGE
VII. The TITANS	178
The Kyklopes (Cyclopes)	179
Myths of the lightning. Schamir, Sassafras, Sesame	180

CHAPTER IV.

THE WINDS.

I. VAYU : the MARUTS : RUDRA.	182
II. HERMES. The story of the Hymn	183
Hermes and Saramâ.	185
The Hermes of the Iliad.	187
Hermes the Master-Thief	188
Hermes and Perseus	189
Hermes and the Latin Mercurius	—
III. ORPHEUS	190
Orpheus and the Argonauts.	191
Orpheus and the Seirens.	—
Teutonic and other versions of the myth	192
IV. PAN	193
Pan and Boreas	194
V. AMPHION.—Zethos	195
Linos, Zephyros, and the Harpies	196
VI. AIOLOS (Æolus)	197
VII. ARÊS. Mars; Enyo	198
Mars and Romulus	200

CHAPTER V.

THE WATERS.

I. POSEIDON.—Proteus and Nereus	202
Nereids and Apsaras	204
Thetis	—
The kinsfolk of Triton	205
Skylla and Charybdis	—
The name Poseidon	206
Poseidon, Hêrê, and Athênê.	207
Introduction of the worship of Poseidon into Hellas	208
Poseidon, the horse and the bull	209
II. INO and MELIKERTES	211
III. OKEANOS : The Ocean Stream.	212
IV. NEPTUNUS	—
Danaos and Aigyptos (Egyptus)	213

CHAPTER VI.

THE CLOUDS.

The children of Nephele.	216
The Phaiakians and Odysseus	217
Niobê and Chionê	218
The nymphs and the cattle of the sun	219
The Hyades and Pleiades	220
The Graiai and the Gorgons. The Muses and the Pierides.	221

CHAPTER VII.

THE EARTH.

	PAGE
Difference of Aryan from Semitic mythology.	223
I. DIONYSOS	225
Dionysos and Semelê	226
Dionysos and the Tyrrhenian sailors	—
Dionysos the Wanderer	228
Dionysos and Bacchus	—
Dionysos a cosmical deity.—Zagreos.	230
Priapos	231
II. DÊMÊTÊR. Ceres	—
Dêmêtêr and Persephonê.	232
Dêmêtêr in the house of Keleos	233
Dêmêtêr and Demophoôn	234
Eleusis, the trysting place	—
Teutonic versions of the myth of Persephonê	235
III. HOLDA and BERCHTA	237
Earth deities of the Latins	—
IV. SATURNUS. Ops	238
The Latin Genii and Dii Indigetes	—
Pilumnus, Picumnus, Semo-Sancus	239
Pomona and Anna Perenna	—
V. CONSUS	240
VI. ERICHTHONIOS and his kinsfolk	—
Terra, Tellus, and Mars	241
VII. RHEA	—
The Kabeiroi (Cabiri) and Idaian Daktyloi.	242
The Satyrs and Seilenoi (Sileni) .	243

CHAPTER VIII.

THE UNDER-WORLD AND THE DARKNESS.

I. HADES	244
Hades and the Olympian gods	245
Hades Polydegmon	—
Erebos and Charon	246
II. ELYSION	247
The conflict of light and darkness	248
The shutting up of the waters	249
III. TYPHON and Typhoeus	250
Hercules and Cacus	251
Belleros and the Sphinx	252
Persian dualism	254
IV. ORMUZD and AHRIMAN	—
Devas and Asuras	255
The Teutonic devil	256

CHAPTER IX.

THE EPICAL TRADITIONS AND POEMS OF THE ARYAN WORLD.

Materials for epical poems	259
The stolen treasures	260

… CONTENTS. …

		PAGE
I.	The Argonautic Expedition	260
	Iason and Medeia	261
	The materials of the myth	262
II.	The Tale of Troy	264
	The judgment of Paris	265
	Agamemnon and Iphigeneia	—
	Sarpêdôn and Memnon	266
	The wrath of Achilles	267
	Achilles and Patroklos	269
	Achilles and Agamemnon	270
	The arming of Achilles	271
	Achilles and Priam	272
	The death of Achilles	—
	The fall of Ilion	273
	Paris and the Panis	—
	Achilles and the Myrmidons	274
III.	The Return of the Heroes from Troy	276
	The Odyssey	—
	Odysseus and Polyphemos	277
	Kirkê (Circe), the Seirens, Skylla, Charybdis, Kalypso	279
	The land of the Phaiakians	280
	Odysseus and the suitors	281
	Parallel between the stories of the Iliad and the Odyssey	282
	Materials of Aryan epic poems	283
IV.	The Volsung Tale	284
	Sigmund and Sinfjötli	285
	Sigurd and Regin	287
	Brynhild and Gudrun	288
V.	The Nibelungenlied	291
	The vengeance of Kriemhild	292
VI.	Walter of Aquitaine	294
VII.	Hugdietrich	296
VIII.	The Gudrun Lay	297
IX.	The Fritiijof Saga	298
X.	The Grettir Saga	299
XI.	The Story of Roland	300
XII.	Olger the Dane	302
XIII.	Havelok the Dane	304
	Havelok and Goldborough	305
	The loves of Argentile and Curan	306
	Havelok and Hamlet	307
	The genealogy of Hamlet	308
XIV.	The Saga of Beowulf	309
XV.	The Romance of Arthur	310
	Early years of Arthur	314
	The loves of King Arthur	315
	Arthur's sword	316
	The scabbard of Arthur's sword	317
	Arthur and the Fatal Children	318
	The story of Balin	—
	Arthur and Guenevere	319
	The Round Table and the Sangreal	320
	The wanderings of Arthur	321

	PAGE
Gawaine and Lancelot	322
The weird sisters	323
Mythical cycles in the Arthur Romance :—	
I. Arthur	—
II. Balin	—
III. Lancelot	—
IV. Gareth	324
V. Tristram	326
Tristram and Marhaus	327
Tristram and the two Isoltes	328
Tristram as a warrior	329
Tristram and Arthur	330
Talismanic tests	—
The Sangreal	332
Guenevere and Elaine	333
Arthur and Mordred	336
Arthur in the Vale of Avilion	337
Merlin	338
XVI. BEVIS OF HAMPTON	340
XVII. GUY OF WARWICK	341
XVIII. The MAHÂBHÂRATA	343
The Pandavas and Draupadi	345
Yudhi-shthira and the Kauravas	—
Nala and Damayanti	346
XIX. The RAMAYANA	347
Results of the analysis of Aryan mythical tradition	348
APPENDIX I. Mythology and Primitive Revelation	351
II. The Historical Value of the Nibelungenlied	361
III. The Tristram Story	365
IV. Composition of the Arthur Romance	367
V. The Historical Arthur	368
INDEX	371

INTRODUCTION

TO THE SCIENCE OF

MYTHOLOGY AND FOLKLORE.

CHAPTER I.

THE MATERIALS OF POPULAR TRADITION.

FEW things are more strange than the persistency with which impressions received in early youth remain fixed in the mind, although they may have no founda- *Popular stories of ancient and* tion whatever in fact. We are, or were, generally *modern times.* led as children to look on Greek and Latin as dead languages, and to regard all the books written in those languages as the literature of a dead world. Between ancient and modern times we place an iron barrier, although where the line is to be drawn we cannot say; and so we learn the forms of the ancient speech without seeing that those forms are still quick and living in our own, and read the poems which delighted Athenian hearers or readers without perceiving that they have any materials in common with the poems and stories which have come to us in a distinctively Teutonic or English dress. Of these two wonderful facts it would be hard to determine which is the more astonishing. Things may be somewhat changed now-a-days; but until within the present generation boys read the Iliad and Odyssey and worked their way through

B

the dramas of the Greek tragic poets under the fixed impression that they contain nothing with which children in our nurseries are familiar in other shapes.

Under this impression some have gone on to suppose that the stories told to English children were never told to children in Athens or Rome two thousand years ago; and a few perhaps have tried to find reasons for the fact that the Iliad and the Odyssey, the Odes of Pindar, and the plays of Æschylus or Sophokles should be made up of materials wholly different from those which have furnished our nursery tales. That these poems and dramas, the works of the highest human genius, should contain anything like the stories of Cinderella or Bluebeard, of Beauty and the Beast, of Big Bird Dan or the Shifty Lad, was a thought not to be entertained for a moment. The dignity of the Homeric poets would not have stooped to use such materials, even if they had known them; but our common impression is that they did not know them. In so thinking or speaking we are no wiser than the learned men who set to work to explain why a jar of water weighed no heavier with a fish in it than it weighed without the fish. The fish, of course, added to the weight of the jar; and the familiar tales of English nurseries are to be found in the Iliad and Odyssey, in the Greek drama, and in the pages of Greek historians or mythographers. It would be almost within the bounds of truth to say that scarcely one is wanting, and that the only matter for astonishment is that the forms of these stories were so much more beautiful then than they are now.

We may take the story of Big Bird Dan.[1] Here we have a boat which sails of itself, if you only say, 'Boat, boat, go on.' The wanderer who is to go in it is told that in the boat there is an iron club, which he is to lift when he sees before him the ship which is bearing away the maiden whom he loves, and the raising of

Self-moving and self-guiding ships.

---

[1] Dasent, *Popular Tales from the Norse.*

MATERIALS OF POPULAR TRADITION.

the club will add force to the wind until it becomes a tempest. He is further told, 'When you've got to land, you've no need to bother yourself at all about the boat; first turn it about and shove it off and say, "Boat, boat, go back home."' The boat of this old Norse story matches the mysterious ships of the Phaiakian king Alkinoös in the Odyssey.[1] These vessels have neither rigging nor tackling, helmsmen nor rudders; but they know the thoughts and minds of men, and dread no disaster as they pass from one land to another, for not one of them has ever been stranded or wrecked, or failed to reach the point which it was seeking. But it is not here only that we come across these marvellous ships. The bark Skidbladnir can carry all the Æsir, the gods of the Teutonic Olympus, and yet it may be folded up and borne in the hand like a garment. In another Norse story[2] the ship becomes bigger and bigger as soon as the voyager steps into it, and when he leaves it becomes again as small as it was before. These ships are the fleets which sail across the blue seas of heaven. They are the clouds which swell and shrink, which go straight to their mark with unerring instinct without failure and without hurt. They are to be seen everywhere; and so we find the meaning of the lines in which the poet of the Odyssey tells us that there is not a city or a cornfield throughout the wide earth which the barks of the Phaiakians fail to visit.[3] Ships do not sail commonly either on the dry land or over it; but the phrase stamps the character and reveals the nature of all these wonderful vessels.

We may take, next, the familiar tale of the Master Thief.[4] The main incidents of this story we find in the legend related by Herodotos[5] of the Treasures of the Egyptian king Rhampsinitos. This tale is repeated in the Hindu legend of Karpara and Gata,[6] in

Antiquity of popular stories.

---

[1] *Od.* 8. 557. [2] That of Shortshanks, Dasent. [3] *Od.* 8. 560.
[4] Grimm, *Household Tales*; Dasent, *Norse Tales*; Campbell, *Popular Tales of the West Highlands.*
[5] 2. 121. [6] *Mythology of the Aryan Nations,* book i. ch. viii.

the Highland story of the Shifty Lad,[1] in that of Ali Baba and the Forty Thieves in the Arabian Nights. But it was also told in Europe in days long before those of Herodotos. It is found in the ancient Hymn to Hermes, who expressly receives as his reward the title of the Master Thief.[2] So, again, the slipper of Cinderella is the slipper of Rhodôpis, which an eagle drops into the lap of the Egyptian king at Memphis, and thus brings about the discovery of the owner;[3] and we find it again in the Deccan tale of Sodewa Bai.[4] In the legend of the Argonautic voyage, Phrixos and Hellê are borne away by a ram with a golden fleece; but this golden fleece is the carpet of Solomon in the beautiful story of the Pilgrim of Love, related by Washington Irving in his Tales of the Alhambra.[5] In this story we have also the enchanted horse, the rider of which is carried on in an unbroken career of victory until the sun reaches the zenith. The magic spell then resumes its power, and the steed, scouring across the plain, plunges into the Tagus, hurries to the cavern from which it had issued in the morning, and becomes fixed as a statue beside the iron table. The story of the horse is the story of the stone which Sisyphos has to roll daily to the summit of the hill, from which it begins immediately to roll down again to the unseen land of darkness.

Among the most striking incidents in the Odyssey are the visits of the Ithakan chief to the land of the lotos-eaters and the palace of Kirkê (Circe).[6] The fruit on which they feast makes all who taste it forget their homes, their honour, and their duty. Similar incidents are favourite features in Hindu stories. In one tale the rajah who marries the Queen of the Five Flowers[7] tastes some food over which the nautch-people, or con-

_{Materials for epic poems.}

---

[1] Campbell, *Tales of the West Highlands.*
[2] Ἀρχὸς φηλητέων. Hymn. Herm. 292.
[3] Strabo, xvii. p. 808.   [4] Frere, *Old Deccan Days.*
[5] *Mythology of the Aryan Nations*, vol. i. p. 157.   [6] *Od.* 9. 84; 10. 210.
[7] Frere, *Old Deccan Days*, Panch Phul Ranee.

jurors, have sprinkled a powder. No sooner had he done so than 'he forgot about his wife and little child and all that had ever happened to him in his life before; and when the conjuror said to him, " Why should you go away? stay with us and be one of us," he willingly consented.' Here the effect of the lotus is produced by the evil charms of Kirkê;[1] and when at length the wanderer is found after an absence of eighteen years, he is clad in the garb of a fakeer, and his face is thin, wrinkled, and seamed with age. But he is restored to all his ancient beauty, like Odysseus, and his wrongs are amply avenged. In this popular Hindu tale we have the framework of one of the greatest epics of any age or country; and of many another tale it may be said that in them are stored materials for epics not less great, although they have never been used. In the Indian stories, the radiant maiden, who becomes the raja's wife, dwells commonly in a house surrounded by seven wide ditches, each defended by seven great hedges made of spears. The tradition is one which belongs to a climate very different from that of Hindustan. The maiden is the summer-child of the great earth-mother, and the house in which she is shut up is the abode of winter. The seven hedges are the seven coils of the dragon Fafnir, who lies twined round the sleeping Brynhild on the Glistening Heath,[2] and her deliverance by Sigurd is the theme of the Volsunga Saga, which in its turn has furnished the materials of the Nibelungenlied, or the Lay of the Children of the Mist. We may descend into minute details even of incidents which may seem the most far-fetched. When the raja is dead in the story of Paneh Phul Ranee, a jackal, talking to his wife, says: 'Do you see this tree? If its leaves were crushed, and a little of the juice put into the raja's two ears and upon his upper lip, he would come to life again and be as well as ever.' Here we have the Snake Leaves[3] of the German story, in which

[1] Κακὰ φάρμακα, Od. 10. 213.
[2] *Mythology of the Aryan Nations*, i. 273.   [3] Grimm, *Household Tales*.

a prince is buried alive with his dead wife. A snake approaches her body, and he cuts it into three pieces. Another snake then comes with three green leaves in its mouth, and putting one leaf on each wound, restores the dead serpent to life. The prince applies the leaves to his wife's body, and she too lives again. The story is told by Apollodoros and by Ælian. 'When Minos said that Polyidos must bring Glaukos to life, Polyidos was shut up with the dead body; and, being sorely perplexed, he saw a dragon approach the corpse. This he killed with a stone, and another dragon came, and, seeing the first one dead, went away and brought some grass, which it placed on the body of the other, which immediately rose up. Polyidos, having beheld this with astonishment, put the same grass on the body of Glaukos and restored him to life.'[1] This remarkable tale is thus proved to have been known to Greek writers upwards of two thousand years ago; and we have not the least warrant for supposing that it was less ancient than the story of the Master Thief as given in the Hymn to Hermes.

Without going further, we have here ample evidence that the popular traditions of Germany, Norway, and India at the present day were well known in Greece and elsewhere for centuries before the Christian era, and that a large number of these stories are to be found in the Homeric poems, and in the great treasure-house of the Athenian drama. The fate of these stories has been anything but uniform. Many with which Greek children were familiar have probably been lost altogether: some have been preserved in the pages of historians and geographers; others have grown into epic poems which will never die. But between these and the rest there is absolutely no difference of kind. The epic poem is a popular tale to which the highest human genius has imparted a peculiar charm; and the same genius might have

Varying fortunes of popular stories.

---

[1] Apollodoros, iii. 3. 1.

handled in like manner other tales which perhaps may never have passed out of the range of common story-tellers. They must all, therefore, be regarded and treated as belonging to the vast stores of popular tradition. They form, indeed, in the strictest sense of the words, and have formed for thousands of years, the folklore or learning of the people, embodying practically their whole knowledge of the outward or sensible world. If any distinction is to be drawn between them, we might say that the tales which have been imbedded in the literature, written or unwritten, of the several nations form the Folklore, while those which are preserved only in the common speech of everyday life belong to the Folkrede, or popular talk.[1] But, in truth, the distinction is scarcely needed; and we have only to deal with the vast mass of popular traditions, and find, if possible, the source of the mighty river.

In this task the prudent course seems to be to take those tales which have come to us in the simplest form. Such a tale is that of Sisyphos, who, as we have seen, is condemned daily to roll a stone to the top of a hill from which it begins at once to roll down. Now if we look at the outward world, we see each day a great sphere or ball pushed up to a summit or zenith, and then descending from the height which it had reached. This sphere or ball is the Sun. But it is needless to say that the image of the sun suggests directly the idea of a light from which nothing is hid. In the story of Demeter and Persephone,[2] and again in that of the Cattle of the Sun in the Odyssey, the Sun, or Helios, is the being

Question of the origin of popular traditions.

---

[1] It is, perhaps, open to doubt whether the terms Mythology and Folklore are likely to retain permanently their present relative meanings. Neither term is altogether satisfactory; but the distinction between tales susceptible of philological analysis and those which are not must nevertheless be carefully maintained, as indispensable to any scientific treatment of the subject. In his Introduction to the Science of Language, Mr. Sayce admits 'that it is often difficult to draw the line between folklore and mythology, to define exactly where the one ends and the other begins, and there are many instances in which the two terms overlap one another.' Vol. ii. p. 276.

[2] Hymn to Demeter, 70.

who sees all things; and the thought of this all-searching eye suggests inevitably the thought of wisdom. Wisdom, therefore, is the inherent property of the Sun-god, and thus belongs to Apollo by birthright.[1] Hence Hermes, who, as we shall see, represents the air in motion, begs the boon of this wisdom from Phœbus, who tells him that his request can be granted only in part.[2] But the Greek name Sisyphos is simply a reduplicated form of Sophos, the wise; and so we have the image of a wise being compelled to ascend the heaven or mountain, and compelled, in spite of his wisdom, his strength, and his power, to come down as he had gone up. The idea of compulsion may soon pass into that of toil, and the latter into the thought of punishment; and thus the Sun becomes a criminal under sentence. This is perhaps one only among a thousand modes in which he may be regarded; but the essential point for our notice is that the story of Sisyphos represents one popular notion of the functions of the Sun, or, in other words, embodies a popular thought respecting the outward or sensible world. A presumption is therefore at once raised that such thoughts are embodied in other traditions also; and it becomes at the least conceivable that these popular stories generally may be of the same nature, and may spring ultimately from this source. The work before us is therefore one strictly of comparison and analysis, and the conditions under which this work must be done are laid down by the Science of Comparative Mythology, the science which compares the stories, as the science of comparative philology compares the speech, of tribes or nations which exhibit any tokens of affinity. The science proposes, in short, to examine popular traditions generally, beginning with the only basis which may be surely trusted, the basis of language. The Greek mythos, or myth, is simply a word or a saying; and in the story of Sisyphos we have nothing more than a word or saying about the sun. But it is a saying

---

[1] Hymn to Apollo, 132. [2] Hymn to Hermes, 533.

which may be traced through countless stories belonging to the most distant lands, and thus we cannot treat the folklore or the mythology of any people as a peculiar possession. The measure in which their special characteristics may have developed or shaped it can be ascertained only when the work of comparison is done.

It is obvious that what was done for the Sun, as in the story of Sisyphos, might be done for any other object of thought in the outer world, for the moon or the stars, for summer and winter, for light and darkness, for heat and cold; and the few traditions of which we have already spoken are common, as we have seen, to Greeks, Norwegians, Germans, Hindus, and perhaps Egyptians also. We must therefore treat their stories as one vast body of popular tradition, for which the presumption is that it expresses the thoughts of mankind on the mighty multitude of things which they saw, heard, or felt in the world around them. But one great lesson of history is that nations and tribes will throw out shoots and branches, these branches often preserving no political connexion with the parent stem. The popular stories or folklore belonging to them may thus be divided at once broadly into two classes, (1) those which were known to the yet undivided tribe or race, and (2) those which sprang up after the division, and were developed by the offshoots severally, or were borrowed by one from any other. The stories or myths of the first kind are called Organic or Primary,[1] those of the other kind being Inorganic or Secondary. The tale of Sisyphos belongs to the former class, and resolves itself, in fact, into one or two short sayings, 'The wise being is rolling the ball up the heaven;' 'The great ball is rolling down the heaven.' But after the separation Sisyphos became for the Greeks a proper name, and Sisyphos himself took his place amongst

Organic or primary, and inorganic or secondary, myths.

---

[1] Professor Max Müller defines these as myths 'which were known to the primæval Aryan race, before it broke up into Hindus, Greeks, Romans, Germans, and Celts.'

the mythical kings of Corinth. The story, therefore, ran that he was very wise and very wicked, and that in the unseen world his punishment was the performance of the task which the sun each day accomplishes in the heaven.

Such a result was the inevitable consequence of separation : and we can now begin to form some idea of the mighty changes which would come over the common talk or folklore of the undivided Aryan race, when, starting from their home in Central Asia, one set or branch started to find their way into India, another into Persia, another into Greece and Italy, and another again into the regions of Northern Europe. It is easy to see that so long as they remained in their original home, the members of the family, or tribe, or nation, would all attach the same meaning to all the words which they used. If they had, as we know that all nations have, a great many names for the same sights and sounds in the outward world,[1] for the sun, moon, and stars, for night and day, for sea and land, for summer and winter, there was no one who would not know, when he heard these names, that they denoted the sun, moon, and stars or other objects, and not something else of which he was ignorant. But after the separation names and words would begin gradually to change their meaning, while the old safeguards which prevented them from being misunderstood would no longer exist; and thus at length the meaning of many or most of the old words or names would be either partially or wholly forgotten. The proof of this fact is furnished to us by the comparison which we are now able to make be-

Effects of the dispersion of tribes.

---

[1] The Greek word for this usage is Polyonymy. Thus the sun might be the wise being, the all-seeing, the wanderer, the toiler, the healer, the poisoner, the slayer, the shortlived, the beautiful, the malignant, the conqueror, the slave, the charioteer, the faithful, the faithless, the husband of the dew, the child or the destroyer of the night, the darkness, or the morning. The words used in speaking of him under any of these aspects would serve as the basis of a separate story, and this story might or might not be made the groundwork of an epic poem, of a lyric ode, or of a drama.

tween the several cognate languages in which any of these names or phrases are found. This comparison shows us that many names which in some one or more of a group of dialects have no meaning are perfectly intelligible in other kindred languages; or, to put it in another way, that words which in the one look only like proper names of human beings or of gods with human forms and human appetites appear in the other as names of clouds or storms, light or darkness, mountains, trees, waters, or other objects of the outward world. Thus, in Greek, the words Argynnis, Phorôneus, and Erinys, are names which do not explain their own meaning, as do Selênê and Helios, Eos and Asterodia. They cannot be interpreted by any words in the Greek language, or at least the old Greeks were quite unable to find the clue. But in the earliest traditions of India we still find them retaining their original force, and serving simply as names for visible things in heaven and earth. Erinys is thus found to be Saranyû, a name for the dawn as it creeps along the sky;[1] Argynnis appears as Arjuni, a name denoting the brilliancy of the morning or early day;[2] and Phorôneus becomes intelligible as the god of fire Bhuranyu.[3]

But this process of change would not go on at the same rate with all names. The meaning of some might be forgotten altogether in the course of a few generations; and this would happen when of two, three, or more names for a single object one

Conditions needed for the development of myths.

[1] The root of the name is *Sar*, to creep. It gives us not only the name Saranyû, but Sarama, who in the Rig Veda is likewise the dawn, as the guardian of the cows of Indra, which she rescues from the Panis, the robbers of the night. The child of Sarama is Sarameyas, which in Greek is transliterated into Hermeias, or Hermes, the air in motion, or wind. The name Sarama itself is reproduced in the Greek Helenê. From this same root we have also the name of the Lykian chief Sarpêdôn, the serpent or creeper. *Mythology of Aryan Nations*, book ii. ch. ii.

[2] From this root *arj, raj*, we have the Hindu raja, the Latin rex, reg-is, a *king*, argentum, *silver*, the Norse god Bragi, and the Greek Argos, with its large family of kindred words.

[3] The Greek had, of course, the correlative word πῦρ, the German *Feuer*, our *fire*; but there was nothing to guide him to this comparison.

was retained as the name for that object, while the others were flung aside. The name which was kept would remain, as we may say, transparent; that is, everyone would know what it meant when they heard it. But they would not know the meaning of the others; and if any phrases ascribed to things so named the actions or feelings of living beings (as the phrases of savages still ascribe these actions and feelings to every object of the outward world), these would grow into stories which might afterwards be woven together, and so furnish the groundwork of what we call a legend or a romance. This will become plain, if we take the Greek sayings or myth about Endymion and Selênê. Here, besides these two names, we have the names Protogeneia and Asterodia. But every Greek knew that Selênê was a name for the moon, which was also described as Asterodia because she has her path among the stars, and that Protogeneia denoted the first or early-born morning. Now Protogeneia was the mother of Endymion, while Asterodia was his wife; and so far the names were transparent. Had all the names remained so, no myth, in the strict sense of the word, could have sprung up; but as it so happened, the meaning of the name Endymion, as denoting the sun when he is about to plunge or dive into the sea, had been forgotten, and thus Endymion became a beautiful youth with whom the moon fell in love, and whom she came to look upon as he lay in profound sleep in the cave of Latmos. But Latmos, again, was a word which told its own story to the Greek, who knew that it meant only forgetfulness. The myth of Endymion may thus be said to have been arrested in its first, or organic, stage. It could not have gone farther, until the meaning of the other names had been to the same extent forgotten. Had they been so forgotten, we should have had a story about them all not less stirring, perhaps, than that which tells us of the loves of Paris and Œnone, of Brynhild and Sigurd.

MATERIALS OF POPULAR TRADITION. 13

Hence the measure in which the old meaning of names was remembered or forgotten determined the growth of the popular stories; and in these stories we may find portions of which the dullest among those who heard them could not fail to catch their real significance, while in other parts the names have so far lost their early force, that at first sight they look like names applied arbitrarily to ordinary men and women. Thus the Greeks knew that Helios was the sun, because the word remained the common name for the sun; and although they had forgotten what was meant by the cattle of Helios in the Odyssey, they would still understand that the names of Phaethousa and Lampetie, the nymphs who fed them, denoted simply their splendour and brightness.[1] They knew also that Phœbus was the lord of life and light, and the idea of him was closely connected in their minds with that of the sun. Hence they cannot have altogether failed to see why he should be born in Delos, the bright land; why he should be Lykêgenês, the being who springs up in glory; and why his mother should be Leto, the dark night from which he comes, and whose name we have already seen in that of the cave at Latmos.

Mythical names.

Having advanced thus far, we begin to see the practical working of the system of Polyonymy,[2] and to mark how names of the same meaning, and often the same names, are given both to the men and women who appear as actors in these popular stories. Thus in the Theban legend, the mother of Kadmos (Cadmus) and Europa is Telephassa, the being who 'shines from far;' but this is only the feminine form of the name of the Argive hero Telephos, who is also a child of Augê, another of the representations of the light. We have, indeed, a vast family of names, all denoting the rushing light of the dawn across the sky, or the blaze of splendour which spreads suddenly from one end of the heaven to the other. To this family

Polyonymy.

[1] *Od.* 12. 132.   [2] See note, p. 10.

belong Eurytos and Europa, Euryganeia, Euryphassa, Euryanassa, Eurymedousa, Eurybates, Eurydike, Eurykleia.

But in these stories the correspondence is by no means confined to the names of the actors only. The likeness invariably extends to the incidents of the tales, and not merely to separate incidents, but to the series and order of events, and generally to the whole framework of the tale or myth. One large class of stories relates the fortunes of the fatal children, whose life involves the destruction of their parents. Sometimes the latter are warned by an oracle of the doom which awaits them at the hands of their offspring, whom accordingly they expose, and who are always saved by some beast and brought up by some herdsman. The children so rescued always grow up beautiful, brave, generous, and strong; but either unconsciously or against their will they fulfil the warnings given before their birth. This is the fate of Perseus, who kills Akrisios in the Argive story; of Œdipus, who smites his father, Laios, the Theban king; of Cyrus, who slays the Median king Astyages; and of Romulus and Remus, who slay Amulius. These heroes are all brought up in great simplicity and poverty; but their real rank is in each case made known by the splendour of their countenances and the dignity of their bearing. Not unfrequently the birth of the child involves the death of the mother; and in all these cases the children are destined to be heroes of popular tradition,[1] whose career is as short as it is glorious. Thus the mother of Volsung, in the northern saga, dies as soon as she has beheld the face of her babe. In the Hindu tale, the mother of Vikramaditya is already dead when her child, the offspring of Indra, comes into the world. In the Arthur story, Tristram, like Macduff in the Scottish, and Sigurd in the Teutonic tradition, is

[marginal note: The fatal children.]

---

[1] Grimm had long ago remarked that all the children brought into the world like Macduff were in popular story born to be great. *Deutsche Mythologie.*

MATERIALS OF POPULAR TRADITION.   15

the son of sorrow,[1] and like them is the avenger of his parents' wrongs.

In tale after tale, again, we have garments which gleam like gold or dazzle like flame, and which are sometimes as destructive as fire. Such is the robe which Helios (the sun) gives to Medeia, and by which she brings about the death of her rival, the Corinthian Glaukê. In the Theban story, this robe, smeared with the blood of the Kentaur (Centaur) Nessos, eats into the flesh of Herakles, who immolates himself on the summit of Oita; and it reappears as the golden fleece in the story of Phrixos and Helle. Heat glows and destroys, but the rays of light go always straight to their mark; and thus the heroes of popular tales are always armed with weapons which never fail to hit the point at which they are aimed. Like the robe of Medeia, these weapons are sometimes poisoned; but in no case do any escape whom the bearers of these weapons seek to smite down. In spite of their weapons and their strength, the life of these heroes is little more than a long endurance of suffering and unwilling labour, for the interests of others and not in their own. They are often slaves and bondmen, like Apollo with the Trojan Laomedon and the Pheraian Admetos, and like Herakles with the tyrant Eurystheus. Like Herakles also, they are compelled to perform a series of impossible tasks, and the quarrels in which they fight are commonly not of their own making.[2] They are, moreover, slayers of monsters or of beasts which ravage fruitful lands or otherwise afflict mankind. Thus Kadmos (Cadmus) slays the dragon which chokes up the well of Ares; and his descendant Œdipus destroys the Sphinx who plagued the Thebans with drought and pestilence. So Perseus rescues Andromeda from the Libyan dragon, and slays the mortal Gorgon Medousa, while Bellerophon, the destroyer of the Chimera,

Mythical robes and weapons.

---

[1] *Popular Romances of the Middle Ages,* p. 41.
[2] This is emphatically asserted by Achilleus, *Il.* i. 154.

is also, as his name tells us, the bane of the monster Belleros.

If these resemblances were confined to Greek stories only, their occurrence would be a remarkable and even an astonishing fact, because no conviction, perhaps, was more deeply impressed upon the several Hellenic tribes than that their own traditions were independent of those of other tribes, and that they recorded a veritable history which had run always in its own distinct channel. We shall find as we go on that no delusion could well have been greater. The Argives boasted of their hero Perseus, the child of the Golden Shower,[1] who is doomed to be the slayer of his grandsire, Akrisios. He is girded with the sword of Apollo, and the golden sandals of the Nymphs bear him like a bird through the air. From the dim land of the Graiai he goes to the desolate abode of the Gorgons, where the woes of the mortal Medousa are ended by the stroke of his sword. On the shores of Libya he rescues Andromeda from the dragon's jaws, and he returns to Argos in triumph with his mother, who still retains all her ancient beauty. The Theban tale related the fortunes of Oidipous (Œdipus), like Perseus, one of the fatal children, and destined to slay his father, Laios. It told how, by a wisdom peculiar to himself, he understood the language of the Sphinx, how he solved her riddles, and delivered his country from the plague of drought and sickness caused by the presence of the hated monster. In reward of his prowess, he received a bride not less lovely than Andromeda; but Iocastê, the wife of Laios, was also his own mother, and the story, thus taking a new departure, assumed an ethical form, which exercised the genius of one of the greatest poets of any age or country. To this point, however, the Theban and the Argive tales were made up on the same framework, and the men of Thebes and Argos prided themselves on the distinctive characters of legends which

Greek tribal legends.

---

[1] Horace, *Od.* 3. 16.

had all their essential features in common. The names are changed, and the local colouring is altered, but nothing more. In one case the myth may come out glorified by the touch of the highest human genius; in others it may remain tame by comparison, or uncouth, or rough. But wherever we go, in the west, the north, or the east, we are confronted by fabrics of popular tradition built up of the same materials. Everywhere we find the conflict of the bright heroes with dark demons, dragons, and monsters.

Thus the great theme of the Vedic hymns is the mighty conflict of the Sun-god Indra with the huge serpent Vritra, who has stolen his cows, and shut them up in his stifling prison-house. In the Volsung story,[1] Sigurd rescues the maiden Brynhild by slaying the snake Fafnir, who lies coiled around her golden treasures on the Glistening Heath. In Rustam the Persian story has a hero as mighty as Herakles, to whose career his own presents a marvellous resemblance. All these, again, are armed with the same impenetrable mail, all have weapons which never miss their mark, and most of them are invulnerable, except in one spot of their body. The astonishing likeness seen in this bright band of warriors and heroes is not confined to the character of their lives; it extends to their persons and their features. Amongst the dark as well as amongst the fair races, amongst those who are marked by black hair and dark eyes, they exhibit the same unfailing type of blue-eyed heroes whose golden locks flow over their shoulders, and whose faces gleam as with the light of the new-risen sun. Nay, in the general course of their lives we see the same moral outlines. Each starts with the desire of doing a benefit to those who may need it; each is ready to sacrifice his own ease and to undergo hard toil for the sake of those who are weaker and meaner than himself. In all or most of them this bright promise is clouded by a change, which shows them in

Common elements of popular tradition.

---

[1] Thorpe, *Edda of Sæmund.*

capricious, or indolent, or even malign aspects. In the spendour of their beauty they love maidens as radiant as themselves; in a little while they either forsake them or slay them. Death is thus the fate of Korônis, the mother of Asklepios; of Daphne, another darling of Apollo; of Prokris, the bride of Kephalos. A hundred legends tell the story of the desertion which befell Ariadne at the hands of Theseus, or Brynhild at those of Sigurd. The stories of Achilleus, Meleagros, and Herakles bring these heroes before us in their strange fits of gloom and sullenness. When they are absent from the fight, their followers or countrymen are powerless; but though they are doomed to early death, their death is to be preceded by brilliant victory—a victory in which they take unsparing vengeance over the enemy who has done them wrong. Then follows the time in which the maidens, or the mothers, who had loved and cheered them at the outset of their career, return to them with the lustre of their beauty undimmed, and without malice for the faithlessness which had so long left them desolate.

It is impossible to suppose that such resemblances as these, extending to the very core as well as to the frame-work of the stories, can be accidental. That Greeks and Romans, Hindus, Germans, and Norsemen can have borrowed them from one another after they became settled in the homes in which we find them at the beginning of history, is a notion scarcely less wild and absurd. The Homeric Hymn to Hermes is, as we have seen, sufficient evidence that the title of the Master Thief and his chief exploits were known to Greek poets perhaps a thousand years before the Christian era. Yet the story has come down from generation to generation in the wilds of Scotland, Germany, and Scandinavia. Even more striking, perhaps, is the comparison between the story of the Dog and the Sparrow in Grimm's Household Tales, and that of Champa Ranee in the Hindu legend of the

Modes of transmission of popular stories. Hypothesis of borrowing.

MATERIALS OF POPULAR TRADITION. 19

wanderings of Vicram Maharajah.[1] In both these stories a bird vows to bring about the ruin of a human being for injuring a helpless and unoffending creature; and in both the offender is made to bring about the catastrophe by his own voluntary acts. In the German story the wrong is done by a carter to a dog, which he deliberately crushes beneath the wheels of his waggon. The dog's friend, a sparrow, warns him that his deed shall cost him his horses and his cart. The bird contrives to force out the cork from the bunghole of one of the casks in the waggon, and the wine is lost. She then perches on the head of one of the horses, and picks out his eye. The carter, hurling his hatchet at the bird, slays the horse. The same incidents are repeated with the other casks and the remaining horses. Hastening home, the carter bewails his disasters to his wife, who tells him that a wicked bird had brought a vast army of birds, which were eating every ear of corn in their wheat fields. The carter moaned over the poverty which had come upon him; the bird, hearing him, says that he is not poor enough yet. His deed shall cost him his life. After desperate efforts he catches the bird, and when his wife asks if she shall kill it, he replies that that would be too merciful. He therefore swallows her alive; but the bird flutters about in his stomach, and coming into his throat, cries out again that she will have his life. The carter, in despair, bids his wife bring an axe, and smite the bird in his mouth. Missing her aim, she kills her husband, and the predictions of the sparrow are fulfilled. In the Deccan tale the place of the sparrow is taken by a parrot, and that of the carter by a dancing-girl, while a wood-cutter, whom the girl tries to cheat, represents the dog of the German story. The case is brought before the raja, who determines to abide by the sentence of a wise parrot belonging to a merchant in the city. The bird is enabled to prove the false dealing of the nautch-girl, who declares that she will get the parrot

[1] Frere, *Old Deccan Days*, 103. *Myth. of Ar. Nations*, book i. ch. viii.

into her power, and then bite off its head. The vow of the parrot is now made once for all, and the story runs to its issue with a cleverness and simplicity for which we look in vain in the German tale. Summoned to the merchant's house, the maiden dances so well that she is bidden to name her own reward. She asks only for the parrot, which she gives to her servant to be cooked, ordering that its head may be grilled and brought to her, that she may eat it before tasting anything else. The parrot is plucked, having escaped the wringing of its neck by pretending to be dead, and, during a momentary absence of the servant, wriggles itself into the hole which carries off the kitchen sewage. A chicken's head is placed before Champa Ranee, who exults over the success of her scheme of vengeance. But the nautch-girl is one who fears death exceedingly, and her prayer to the god whose image stood in a neighbouring temple was, that she might be translated to heaven without the process of dying. The parrot, placing itself behind this image, tells the girl when next she comes that her prayer has been heard, and that, if she wishes to attain her desire, she must sell all her goods and give them to the poor, and having levelled her house to the ground, must return to the temple, whence she should be bodily taken up into heaven. Champa Ranee does as she is bidden; but when she hastens to the shrine with the women whom she has brought to witness her glorification, the parrot flies up from behind the image, and bids her farewell. 'You ate a chicken's head,' she says. 'Where is your house now? Where are your servants and all your possessions? Have my words come true, think you, or yours?' Cursing her folly, the nautch-girl dashes herself down on the floor of the temple, and is killed.

The leading ideas of both these tales agree exactly; the ways in which they are worked out are entirely different. *Cases of lateral transmission.* What opportunity has the German had of borrowing from the Hindu, or the Hindu from the German, since the days when Hermann[1] crushed the legions

[1] Arminius. Tacitus, *Ann.* i. 61.

of Varus? Clearly none; and it would probably be true to say that no borrowed story ever differed so widely from its original as that of Champa Ranee differs from the German tale of the Dog and the Sparrow. If there is absolutely no evidence of borrowing, and indeed no possibility of it, the notion must be given up, and it should be given up with good will. The argument which ascribes to conscious borrowing even those fables which are common to all the branches of the Aryan Family has been deservedly called sneaking.[1] It seems to afford an explanation, when it is a mere surmise which furnishes none. But it is none the less impossible that the Hindu and the German should each for himself have hit on the idea which makes a bird the avenger of wanton wrongs, and brings about the ruin of the wrongdoer through his own acts, while in each case the criminal swallows or thinks that he has swallowed his persecutor. The framework of the story belongs, therefore, to that distant time when the forefathers of the Hindu, the German, and the Englishman had still their common home in Central Asia. In these two tales we have a case of lateral transmission. The framework remains in each; the materials worked into it differ wholly. But when we have traced the stories back to a common source, there remains the task of discovering the nature of that source, if it be possible to do so. Unless the traditions exhibit common names in cognate languages (as Saranyu and Erinys, Arjuna and Argynnis, are admitted to be), we are not justified in ascribing them to phrases denoting the phenomena of the outward world. In these two stories the leading idea, it can scarcely be doubted, was a moral one—the idea that wrong-doers will be punished, and that beings of no repute may be made the means of punishing them, or, to adopt the language of St. Paul, that weak things of the earth may be chosen to discomfit the strong, and the foolish to confound the wise. The case is altered when we come to deal with a

---

[1] Max Müller, *Chips from a German Workshop*, ii. 233. *Myth. of Ar. Nations*, book i. ch. viii.

story like that of Kephalos and Prokris. Here Prokris is the child of Hersê, a word which for the Greek denoted dew as clearly as Selênê denoted the moon. Kephalos is the head of the sun, the sun-god rising in his majesty. He sees Prokris on the Hymettian hill, and loves her, and Prokris returns his love. The dewdrop reflects the sunlight. But the dawn also loves the sun, and therefore Eos, another word as transparent to the Greek as Selênê, loves Kephalos, and is jealous of Prokris. Then follows the sad story of deception, which leads Prokris to obtain from Artemis the spear which never misses its mark. This spear she gives to Kephalos, and with it she is smitten by him while she lurks hidden in the inmost thicket of the forest. Of course it is precisely here that the last dewdrop would linger, until even in this secret spot it would be reached by the spear of the sun as he rose higher in the heavens. In this tale, then, we have a series of names, the analysis of which guides us straight to the root of the story and brings before us the phrases relating to the sun, the dawn, and the dew, out of which it sprang. We see our way clearly, therefore, when we are confronted with the legend of Krishna, the sun-god of later Hindu theology. Amongst the foes whom he conquers is the giant Naraka, who has imprisoned vast multitudes of women, elephants, horses, and other creatures. All these are rescued by Krishna, who at one and the same moment becomes the husband of sixteen thousand one hundred maidens, whose hands he receives at the same time according to the ritual in separate mansions. Into so many forms, we are told, the son of Madhu multiplied himself that every one of the damsels thought that he had wedded her in her single person.[1] To suppose that this is the arbitrary invention of a poet living in a polygamous society, is beyond measure ludicrous. The essence of the story lies in the simultaneous marriage of a countless multitude to one single being; and thus we see that it is

[1] *Vishnu Purana*, II. II. Wilson, p. 589.

simply the tale of Prokris in another form. The black giant Naraka is the night which throws its veil over all earthly things. The dew cannot become visible until the darkness has been dispelled; and when the shades have been driven away, the same sun is reflected in the thousands of sparkling drops. At this point with the Hindu the myth ended. Had the same notion been presented to the Greek, he would probably have worked out a series of incidents leading up to a catastrophe in which the sun slays them all.

In these two stories of Prokris and of Krishna we have two phases in the development of myths in the inorganic or secondary stage. In the former some of the names are still transparent, and the incidents are so closely in accordance with the meaning of the words that the narrators must have been to a certain extent conscious of the nature of the materials with which they were dealing. In the latter there was little in the names to furnish a clue to the origin of the tale, although the incidents, as in the other, speak for themselves. But the law of mythical development guides the poet as surely as in the myths of the primary or organic stage. The parts of Krishna and Naraka cannot be reversed; and it is Prokris, not Kephalos, who must fall by the spear of Artemis. The same may be said of the great Theban legend already noticed. The names Oidipous (Œdipus), Laios, Iokastê, Antigonê, had ceased to convey their original meaning to the Greek; and the explanations which they offered for some of them were wrong and far-fetched. But the poets who told their story found themselves compelled to move within certain lines, and to adhere to the ancient framework of the myths. The myths so worked out became stories full of action and suffering, which are human in their character, although, it may be, superhuman in their grandeur and intensity. But we shall find that although the Greeks were in most cases unable to interpret the names

Conditions determining the course of the development of myths.

of their mythical personages, the old tradition effectually prevented any confusion of their parts. Sophokles could not, indeed, interpret the names Laios or Sphinx; but it was nevertheless impossible for him to make Laios the conqueror of the Sphinx, or the slayer of Oidipous. Without going further, therefore, we begin to see the nature of the framework provided for the epic, lyric, and tragic poets of the Aryan world. We catch glimpses of the sentences which were gradually crystallised into a coherent tale, and we see that these sentences, when traced back to their earliest form, resolve themselves into sayings about outward and sensible objects or phenomena. Oidipous slays his father Laios. The great dragon shuts up the rain, and brings plague upon the city. The Sphinx can be conquered only by him who can expound her riddles. Oidipous interprets them, and discomfits the dragon. The hero wins the wife of Laios as his bride. Such were the chief phrases which furnished the framework of the Theban story; but Oidipous was the slayer of his father, and he becomes therefore his mother's husband. In the language of the Vedic hymns this is the marriage of the sun with the dawn from which he springs, and the saying is thus seen to be of precisely the same kind and of much the same meaning as the phrase, 'Selênê loves Endymion.' But for the Greek the union of the son with the mother was a disaster unspeakably terrible, and none the less awful because the guilt was incurred unconsciously. For the Greek poet it became thus a moral problem, which he worked out with marvellous power.

But if the Theban myth, turned into this channel, became shocking and awful, there were others which by a *Alleged connexion of mythology with primitive revelation.* like process were rendered simply horrible and loathsome. The light thrown on the story of Oidipous by the imperfect analysis already made may justify the suspicion that the coarsest and grossest of these tales may, in their earliest shape, have been as harmless and innocent as the myth of Iokastê. No room, therefore, is left for the theory that they are simply fruits of a corrupt imagination deliberately bent on multiplying images of impure horrors; and with this theory must fall also the idea that these old stories contain the corrupted and misinterpreted fragments of a divine revelation once granted to the whole race of mankind.[1] To suppose that these tales embody a number of beliefs capable of being stated in the form of propositions, and that a series of propositions should be laid before men which they could not fail to misunderstand, and which, it is admitted, are contained in the earliest records only by a dim and feeble foreshadowing,[2] is to involve ourselves in a labyrinth of perplexities. Some of these tales, it has been well said, are as hideous and revolting as any which we find among the lowest tribes of Africa and America; and in order to prove that they had a direct and close connexion with a primitive religion, we should have to show that with the corruption of belief the moral character of the people underwent a corresponding debasement. But this picture seems to be the very reverse of the facts. If we take the Iliad and Odyssey, we shall find a number of gods who inhabit Olympos, and interfere in greater or less degree with the affairs of men. The descriptions given of these deities, if not absolutely and designedly immoral, certainly cannot be regarded as moral. Some of them are repulsive, some even revolting and foul. Along with these, we have a society which, however great may be its faults and vices, is still vastly better than that of the Olympian hierarchy; and this fact seems to be wholly inconsistent with the idea that a plan of redemption divinely imparted to man should have been constantly travestied until it assumed the form of society under which the gods live in the Iliad and Odyssey, as in other Hellenic literature. Of these deities Hermes is the messenger; but the story of Hermes is that

---

[1] Max Müller, *Chips from a German Workshop*, ii. 13.
[2] Gladstone, *Juventus Mundi. Myth. Ar. Nat.* i. 24.

of the Master Thief. In other words, it is a story which belongs to the class of popular tales which includes those of Sisyphos and Tantalos. One or two of these we have already traced to the phrases or sayings on which they grew up; and we have seen that these sayings referred simply to the sights or the sounds of the outward world. Our task, therefore, is to ascertain whether the stories told of Zeus, Apollo, Athênê and other deities, whether Olympian, or called by any other name, have not grown up in precisely the same way. If it should be proved that they have, the theory that the Olympian gods are an anthropomorphic representation of a series of truths divinely revealed to man falls to the ground. Both processes could not go on at the same time; and if the tales can in every instance be traced to phrases denoting sensible phenomena, the effort to assign them to any other source must be labour thrown away. The examples already examined may suffice to show that the wonderful changes which they underwent were due not to any wilful corruption of religious or moral truths, not to any weakness or disease of language,[1] but solely to failure of memory, caused by the disruption of tribes from their ancient home. So long as names retained their original meaning, anything like a story with a series of incidents could not be put together. When the Greek had either partially or wholly forgotten what his forefathers in Central Asia had meant by such words as Prokris, Erinys, Hephaistos, Hermes, the growth of tales which spoke of them as beings of human form with human feelings was inevitable; but although his memory was weakened, his language was as healthy and strong as ever.[2]

[1] The term Mythology was explained by Professor Max Müller as diseased language; but as he added that this result was brought about only when the steps which led to the original metaphorical meaning of a word had been forgotten, and artificial steps had been put in their place, it is clear that the change is attributable not to language, but strictly to the defective memory of the speaker. There is, therefore, no controversy on the subject.

[2] See Appendix I.

CHAPTER II.

THE HEAVENS AND THE LIGHT.

THE impression that comparative mythology resolves everything into the sun is very widely spread, and maintains itself with singular pertinacity. Few impressions are more thoroughly groundless. The science proves conclusively that the popular traditions which have come down to us in the form whether of myths strictly so called or of folklore generally, embody the whole thought of primitive man on the vast range of physical phenomena.[1] There is scarcely an object of the outward world which has not been described or figured in these popular stories. We have myths and mythological beings belonging to the heavens and the light, to the sun, the moon, and the stars, to the fire and the winds, to the clouds and the waters, to the earth, the under-world, and the darkness. Under all these heads we have a crowd of myths

Manifold aspects of mythical tradition.

[1] Mr. Sayce, in his *Introduction to the Science of Language*, has dealt summarily with the objections commonly urged against the method and results of comparative mythology. These objections fall for the most part under two heads: (1) That there is no warrant for endowing primitive man with the high imagination of a poet; and (2) that the mythopœic ages must have been marked by dull stupidity, if 'the phenomena of the atmosphere engrossed the whole attention of men who were yet too witless to understand the language in which they were described.' These objections, he remarks, are mutually destructive. The imagination of primitive man was neither too high nor too feeble. 'The gods they worshipped were the gods that brought them food and warmth, and these gods were the bright day and the burning sun. . . . It was not stupidity, but the necessities of his daily existence, the conditions in which his lot was cast, that made man confine his thoughts and care to the powers which gave him the good gifts he desired. Winter, according to the disciples of Zoroaster, was the creation of the evil one, and among the first thanksgivings lisped by our race is praise of the gods as "givers of good things"'[1] (ii. 268).

which fall into distinct groups; but the phenomena of the universe do not all leave the same impression on the mind. Some are immeasurably more prominent than others, and more striking. Some are connected immediately and closely with the life and the well-being of man; others scarcely affect them at all. The most important of all are necessarily those of the seasons, and these are dependent directly on the sun, so that of the whole body of myths an immensely large proportion relates to the action of that brilliant orb which even we can seldom mention without running into mythology ourselves. But the myths belonging to other groups are not less marked and distinct, and we shall find in the clouds and water sources of popular stories as rich in thought and colouring as any which relate to the bridegroom who comes forth daily from his chamber in the East and rejoices as a giant to run his course.

We can, then, only take these traditions under their several heads, without attempting to determine the exact order in which the conceptions set forth in them arose in the human mind. It is the ethereal heaven, and not the sun, which has been chosen in the language of myths as the abode of the supreme God, the dwelling of the All-father; but it would be rash, perhaps, to assign priority in order of time to myths of the heaven over those of the sun, or to the latter over the former. The Hesiodic Theogony, which gives a long ancestry to Zeus, the supreme god of the Hellenic tribes, and seems to make him younger than Aphroditê, is the growth of a later age which had acquired a love of systematic arrangement; and it is impossible to determine the order in which the ideas of the several beings springing from Chaos and Gaia took shape.[1]

Question of the priority of myths.

---

[1] We have a parallel case in what are called *roots* in language. We find that many groups of Aryan words can be reduced to a root *mar* or *mal*, this root denoting a gradation of ideas from grinding, crushing, and destroying, to those of languor, decay, softness, and sweetness; and we are apt to suppose that this root was used as a word in something like its naked shape before the several words of which it is regarded as the foundation took shape. The

But of the mode in which these ideas were formed we are left in no doubt. The book known as the Rig Veda in the sacred literature of the Hindus exhibits perhaps in their oldest shapes the thoughts of men on the phenomena of the outward world. It contains a multitude of hymns addressed to living powers on the earth and in the heavens; and to these powers the worshipper prays under names denoting what we call natural forces—wind, storm, frost, cold, heat, light and darkness. But for him all these are beings capable of hearing and understanding what he says. They can feel love and hatred; they may be cruel or merciful; and he may win from them by devout service the happiness for which he yearns, or he may ward off with their aid the evils which he dreads. On some he looks with awful fear; to others he can speak almost with affectionate familiarity. He pours out before them all the thoughts of his heart, and the words by which he gives expression to these thoughts describe with marvellous exactness all that they noticed in the world around them.

Language of the hymns of the Rig Veda.

Thus for him Ushas,[1] the Dawn, is a bright being whom age cannot touch, but who makes men old as she returns day after day and year after year in undiminished beauty. She is full of love, of gentleness, and compassion. She thinks on the dwellings of men, and she

Hymns to the Dawn.

notion is a mere guess, and, it can scarcely be doubted, an erroneous one. The root *mar* or *mal* is found also in the forms *mardh*, *marg*, *mark*, *marp*, *mard*, *smar*. It is thus safe to say that, as 'the vocables that embodied these roots underwent the wear and tear of phonetic decay, many of them passed out of the living speech and were replaced by others, and there was left at last a whole family of nouns and verbs, whose sole common possession was the syllable *mar*. That alone had resisted the attacks of time and change' (Sayce, *Introd.* ii. 17). Thus the words are necessarily older than the roots contained in them, these being 'due to the reflective analysis of the grammarian' (*ib.* p. 18). In the same way it is likely that the attention of primitive men was directed to the objects seen in the heavens before it was fixed on the heaven itself.

[1] The name Ushas is in Latin Aurora. In the Græco-Italian dialects it assumed the form *ausos*. In Latin a secondary noun was formed from the primary one, *ausosa*. But both Greeks and Latins disliked the sound of *s* between vowels; and so with the former Ausos became Auos, Eos, the goddess of the morning; with the latter it became Aurora, the verb appearing in Greek as

smiles on the small and the great. In short, it is impossible to mistake the meaning of the words addressed to her. We see that she is the dawn, and no mere personification of the morning light; but she is as completely a conscious being, moved by the emotions that may stir the human heart, as any woman whom the greatest of epic poets has immortalised in his song. She is bright, fair, and loving —the joy of all who behold her.

'She shines upon us like a young wife, rousing every living being to go to his work.

'She rose up, spreading far and wide, and moving towards everyone. She grew in brightness, wearing her brilliant garment. The mother of the cows, the leader of the days, she shone gold-coloured, lovely to behold.

'She, the fortunate, who brings the eye of the god, who leads the white and lovely steed, the dawn was seen revealed by her rays. With brilliant treasures she follows everyone.

'Shine for us with thy best rays, thou bright dawn, thou who lengthenest our life, who givest us wealth in cows, horses, and chariots.'[1]

Still more exact in its description of the phenomena of the morning and the day is the hymn in which the worshipper addresses her as leading on the sun and going before him, preparing practicable paths and expanding everywhere.

'Lucidly white is she, occupying the two regions[2] and manifesting her power from the east; she traverses the path of the sun, as knowing his course, and harms not the quarters of the horizon.

'Ushas, the daughter of heaven, tending to the west, puts forth her beauty. Bestowing precious treasures on the offerer of adoration, she, ever youthful, brings back the light as of old.'

aľw, in Latin as *uro*. The Lithuanian form is Ausera. (Peile, *Introduction to Greek and Latin Etymology*, xii.)

[1] R. V. vii. 77.
[2] The upper and middle firmament.

VARUNA.

1. The Vedic Varuna.

This is not personification, nor is it allegory. It is simply the language of men who have not learnt to distinguish between subject and object, and in it we have the key to expressions with which the hymns of the Rig Veda are filled. Nor need we be surprised if in these hymns the phrases suggested by outward phenomena run into a meaning purely spiritual. This is especially the case with Varuna and Dyaus, the supreme gods of the earliest Vedic ages. The former is simply the heaven which serves to veil or cover Prithivî, the broad or flat earth, which is his bride,[1] and who in the Theogony of Hesiod reappears as Gaia. As such, Varuna is a creation of mythical speech, and is embodied in visible form. He sits on his throne, clothed in golden armour, and dwells in a palace supported on a thousand columns, while his messengers stand round to do his bidding. But in many of the hymns we also find language which is perpetually suggesting the idea of an unseen and almighty Being, who has made all things and upholds them by his will. In these hymns Varuna dwells in all worlds as sovereign. The wind is his breath. It is he who has placed the sun in the heavens, and who guides the stars in their courses. He has hollowed out the channels of the rivers, and so wisely ordered things that, though all the rivers pour their waters into the sea, the sea is never filled. He has a thousand eyes: he knows the flight of birds in the sky, the paths of the ships on the seas, and the course of the far-sweeping wind. Such language may pass easily into that of the purest worship of the One Maker and Father of all men; and thus we have the prayer:

'Let me not yet, O Varuna, enter into the house of clay; have mercy, Almighty, have mercy.

[1] The name Varuna corresponds to the Greek Ouranos, and is built up on the same root which gives the names of the Hindu Vritra, the veiling demon of darkness, the Greek Orthros, who with Kerberos (Cerberus), the Vedic Çarvara, guards the gates of Hades. Prithivî transliterated into Greek becomes Plateia, our *flat*.

'If I go along trembling like a cloud driven by the wind, have mercy, Almighty, have mercy.

'Through want of strength have I gone to the wrong shore; have mercy, Almighty, have mercy.

'Whenever we men, O Varuna, commit an offence before thy heavenly host, whenever we break thy law through thoughtlessness, have mercy, Almighty, have mercy.'

But although the name of Varuna has a common element with that of Vritra, the dark enemy of Indra, there is no likeness of character between them. Varuna is armed, indeed, with destructive nooses; but these are prepared for the wicked only. They ensnare the men who speak lies, passing by the man who speaks truth. He holds the unrighteous fast in prison, but he does so only as the punisher of iniquity, which cannot be hidden from him who 'numbers the winkings of men's eyes,' and not as the gloomy Hades of the nether world.

The true greatness of Varuna belongs seemingly to one of the earliest stages of Hindu thought. In Greece he **II. Dyaus.** reappears as Ouranos; but as there Zeus became the name of the supreme God, Ouranos lost his importance, and almost faded out of sight. The same fate befell Varuna, who gave way first to the correlative of Zeus, the Vedic Dyaus, the god not of the veiling or nightly heaven, but of the bright and gleaming canopy of the day. The name is widely spread among the Aryan tribes. It reappears not only in the Greek Zeus (Zen-os), but in the Latin Juno, answering to a form Zenon, in Diana, Dianus, Janus, and many more. In Teutonic dialects we find it in the form Tiu, the God of light, a name still familiar to us in Tivsdag, or Tuesday. Dyaus was invoked commonly as Dyaus-Pitar, the Zeus Pater, or father Zeus of the Greeks, the Jupiter of the Latins. But although some mythical features entered gradually into the conceptions of this deity, the word retained its original meaning far too clearly to allow it to hold its ground in Hindu mythology. Dyaus, therefore, gave way to his child Indra, who, in a land which under its scorching sun depends wholly on the bounty of the benignant rain-god, was worshipped as the fertiliser of the earth, and was naturally regarded as more powerful than his father.[1] But although his greatness is obscured by that of his son, he still wields the thunderbolt, and is spoken of as the father of the Dawn, who is invincible by all but Indra.

In Mitra, the brother of Varuna, we have another god of the heaven, who, like Dyaus, represents the firmament of noontide. Thus the two represent the phases which pass over the sky by night and by day. Hence it is not strange that in the Zendavesta Mithras should occupy a place between the two powers of light and darkness, of good and evil.

III. Mitra.

In Indra we have the god whose special office it is to do battle with the demon of drought, and let loose the life-giving waters. He is the son of Dyaus, the gleaming heaven, and he is seen in the dazzling orb which seems to smite the thunder clouds, and compel them to give up their prey. His golden locks flow over his shoulders, and his unerring arrows have a hundred points and are winged with a thousand feathers. In his hand he holds a golden whip, and he is borne across the heaven in a flaming chariot drawn by the tawny or glistening steeds called the Harits. His beard flashes like lightning, and as his eye pierces to every part of the universe, he is possessed of an inscrutable and unfathomable wisdom. As the bringer of the rain, and therefore also of the harvest, he is the god whose power is most earnestly invoked by his Hindu worshippers; but no purely spiritual prayer, such as those which were offered to Varuna, was ever addressed to him. The only work for which he was supposed to exist was to

IV. Indra.

---

[1] The name Indra, which is that of the great stream Indus, denotes moisture or sap.

do battle with, and to conquer, the demons who were in revolt against him. The chief of these demons is Vritra, the hiding thief; Ahi,[1] the strangling snake; or Pani, the marauder. But he is also known as Namuki, the Greek Amykos, as Sushna, Sambara, Bala, Chumuri. The victory of Indra over these rebels brings plenty of corn, wine, oil; but there is nothing moral or spiritual in the struggle. He is the rescuer of the cows (the clouds), whose milk is to refresh the earth, and which have been hidden away in the caves of the robbers. As driving these before him he is Parjanya, the rain-bringer; and the poet says: 'The winds blow strong, the lightnings flash, the plants spring up, the firmament dissolves. Earth becomes fit for all creatures when Parjanya fertilises the soil with showers.'[2]

V. Brahma. The name Brahma is associated with a much later stage of Hindu thought; but it denoted at first simply the self-existent being, whose mythical acts are susceptible of a spiritual interpretation, and are so interpreted in all the Hindu comments on the sacred literature of the country. As in the Orphic Theogony, the generation of Brahma begins with the great mundane egg; but in it Brahma produces himself, and becomes the progenitor of all creatures. Along with Vishnu and Siva, he forms a later Hindu Trimurtti or trinity, being himself the creator, while Vishnu is the preserver, and Siva the destroyer. The older trinity had consisted of Agni, Vayu, and Surya—the fire, the air, and the sun. The name Mahâdeva, *great god* (Greek, Megas Theos), is applied to all these deities and to many others; but it was especially used in speaking of the destroyer Siva—to destroy, according to Indian philosophy, being only to reproduce under another form.

The evidence already before us shows that in the most

[1] Ahi reappears in the Greek Echis, Echidna, the dragon which crushes its victim with its coil. It is, in short, anything that chokes, whether as *Anhas*, sin, or the Latin *angor*, anguish.
[2] The name Indra is sometimes used as a physical equivalent of Dyaus, the heaven, the clouds being said to move in Indra, as the Maruts, or winds, are described as coursing through Dyaus.

ancient hymns and prayers of the Hindus the supreme
Creator and Ruler of all worlds was invoked VI. The Hel-
under many names, all of which were regarded lenic Zeus.
as denoting his power or his goodness. The entreaty for
deliverance from sin and guilt is made to Varuna, and the
worshipper finds comfort in the thought that he is the child
of Dyaus-pitar, his father who is in heaven. However it
may have been in earlier times with the ancestors of the
Greek tribes, the Achaians spoken of in the Iliad and
Odyssey had in like manner learnt to look upon Zeus,
whose name represents the Sanskrit Dyaus, as the Father
of gods and men; and in like manner the Zeus Pater of
the Greeks reappears as the Jupiter of the Latins, and the
All-father of the Teutons. But in Greece, as in India,
there was growth, and therefore change, in the character of
the deities; and according to the Theogonies or poems
which trace the descent of the gods, there had been a time
when Zeus was inferior to his father Kronos, and when even
Kronos had not yet come into being. In the origins thus
assigned to them there are, as we might well expect, the
widest differences between one narrative and another.
These mythical genealogies, which certainly do not belong
to the earliest mythopœic ages, could but express the thought
of the time in which they grew up, as to the mode in which
the outward world took shape and form. Thus in one
version the first beings are Chaos and Gaia[1] (earth), from
whom springs Ouranos (Uranus), the Varuna of the Rig
Veda, together with the Long Mountains and Pontos (the
sea).[2] In another, Gaia, or Gê, is the wife of Ouranos; and

---

[1] This name clearly contains the root of a vast number of words denoting the power or the fact of production, this root being perhaps *ga* or *gen*; hence the Greek verbal form γέγαμεν, and the nouns γένος, L. gens, γυνή, queen, quean, &c. It can scarcely be doubted that the reference in this family of words explains the Latin phrase in the form of marriage known as Coemptio, in which the wife says to her husband, 'Ubi tu Caius, ego Caia.' Cicero (*pro Mur.* 12) supposes the choice of name to be a mere accident (as with the English Doe and Roe); but this is a matter on which the judgment of a man who could deal practically with only one language was worth nothing.

[2] Iles. *Theog.* 129.

their children, Hyperion, Iapetos, and many others, are born before Kronos, the father of Zeus. These legends go on to tell us that Ouranos hunted the Kyklôpes (Cyclopes) with Brontê and Steropê (thunder and lightning), and other children of Gaia, into the seething abyss of Tartaros, and that Gaia, in her grief and anger, urged her other children to mutilate their father, and to set up Kronos instead upon his throne. Henceforth Kronos swallowed his children soon after each was born; nor could any have been saved had not Rhea, the mother of Zeus, anxious to preserve her child, given to her husband a stone to swallow, while Zeus was born and nourished in the care of Diktê, or Lyktos, or, as some said, on Ida.[1]

In the strict meaning of his name, Zeus, who to the Teutonic tribes was known as Tiu, Tuisco, Zio, and Tyr, was the god who dwelt in the pure blue sky, the abode of light, far above the clouds or the mists of the lower atmosphere, which might sully its purity.[2] As such, he is naturally born in the cave of Diktê, or Lyktos, a phrase as transparent as that which tells us that Phœbus sprang to

Zeus and Prometheus.

---

[1] That this story, strange and coarse as it is, has reference to the consumption and reproduction perpetually going on in nature, is beyond all doubt. The hymn-writers of the Rig Veda were perfectly aware that a series of mornings and days made men old, although the mornings and days remained as young and fresh as ever; and for mere savages the passing away of months or moons would be a fact as indisputable as that of their continuance. Hence the being who consumes or swallows the moons (and this might be made to mean months, weeks, or days) must be regarded as reproducing, *i.e.* disgorging them. In other words, the story would refer to time and the effects of time; and as the impressions which would embody themselves in those stories might spring up in the minds of any tribes capable of thinking at all, the tales would belong to the province not of mythology but of folklore. The notion of time once given, the features of these tales would be determined by the modes of measuring time which might be in use in any given country. Thus in Grimm's German story of the wolf and the seven little goats, the wolf, which is the night or darkness, tries to swallow the seven kids, and actually swallows six. The seventh is hidden in the clockcase. In other words, the week is not quite run out; and before its close the mother of the goats, ripping the wolf's stomach, substitutes stones for the kids, who come trooping out, as the days of the week begin again to run their course. Here we have the Hesiodic notion of the stone swallowed by Kronos, with an idea distinctly suggested by the clocks of modern times; but the reference to the clock-case furnishes proof conclusive that the narrator of the story knew well the nature of the materials with which he was dealing. [2] *Il.* 14. 288.

ZEUS.

life in Delos, or that Endymion slept in the cave of Latmos. No sooner, we are told, had he come to his full strength than he delivered the Kyklôpes (Cyclopes) from Tartaros, and obtained the aid of the hundred-handed giants, the Hekatoncheires, in his war against the Titans. In this struggle, according to the story followed by Æschylus, he had the help of Prometheus, son of Deukalion, and was thus able to dethrone his father, Kronos. But his gratitude was afterwards turned into hatred, from a cause which shows how completely the mythical Zeus was distinct from the Zeus whom the swineherd Eumaios worshipped, and of whom the Hesiodic poet thought when he spoke of the righteous ruler and judge of all mankind. Under the sway of Zeus, the lord of the glistening firmament, Prometheus, it is said, found the race of men grovelling in the lowest depths of misery, without clothing, without dwellings, without fire.[1] From him they learnt the use of fire, which he stole from heaven, and brought to them in the hollow of a reed ; and so began the new order of things in which they gradually groped their way into a condition more befitting creatures who have the power of thought and speech. For these great deeds done for the benefit of beings whom he hated or despised, Zeus condemned Prometheus to be chained on the rugged crags of Caucasus, where a vulture gnawed his liver, which grew as fast as it was devoured.

So soon as, in accordance with the meaning of the name, Zeus was regarded as the lord of the upper air, it became certain that the same process would go on in reference to other parts or aspects of the material world. Thus the story grew up that the Kyklôpes (Cyclopes) gave to Zeus a thunderbolt, to his brother Hades a helmet which made the wearer invisible,[2] and to Poseidon a trident, and that, having received these gifts, the three gods cast lots, and

The Olympian Zeus.

---
[1] Æsch. *Prom.* v. 450 *et seq.*
[2] This is the Tarnkappe of the popular Teutonic stories.

the sovereignty of heaven fell to the portion of Zeus, that of the sea to Poseidon, and that of the lower regions to Hades. That there was no such chance in the distribution of their offices it is scarcely necessary to say: but it may be noted that this assignment of functions is based purely on physical considerations; and thus as the god dwelling on the heights of Olympos with the subordinate deities around him, Zeus, although invested with a majesty not to be invaded by others, is a being moved by very earthly appetites and emotions. It cannot, indeed, be said with truth that the Zeus of the Olympian hierarchy, whether in the Iliad and Odyssey or elsewhere, is the Zeus to whom prayer is addressed. Men could not seek for justice against those who wronged them in their persons or their families from a being whose actions exhibited the most ruthless disregard for the rights of others. The Zeus of the Olympian courts is partial, unjust, fond of rest and pleasure, changeable in his affections and unfaithful in his love, greedy, wrathful, and impure. The Zeus to whom the people pray is not only irresistible in might, but also just and righteous. Here, as in India, the religious convictions of the worshippers rose into a region immeasurably higher than that of their mythology. To both the name for the bright heaven had become a name for the One only God; but the old meaning of the word still clung to it,[1] and brought up images of the visible sky in its relation to the earth and its products, of its clouds, vapours, and storms. The phrases which described these changes might easily come to denote vile or shameful actions when applied to a being with human form and human feeling. Thus the earth had been spoken of as the bride of the sky, while the heaven was said to overshadow the earth with its love in every land. The necessary out-

---

[1] This is strikingly shown in the Athenian prayer for rain, ὖσον, ὦ φίλε Ζεῦ, κατὰ τῆς ἀρούρας τῶν Ἀθηναίων; and even more plainly in the words of the Latin poet, 'Adspice hoc sublime candens quem invocant omnes Jovem.' With the Latins 'malus Jupiter' remained an expression for bad weather, and the phrases 'sub dio vivere,' 'sub Jove frigido,' denoted time spent in the open air or in the cold.

growth from such phrases was a multitude of stories of strange and lawless licence.

The antagonism thus caused between the physical and the spiritual Zeus was at first acquiesced in as a fact which must be accepted, and on which the people did not care to fix their thoughts. Thus in the Hesiodic poems the descent of the gods, their earthly loves and their gross actions, are brought out even more prominently than in the poems to which we give the name of Homer. Yet the poet can turn seemingly without an effort from the thought of such things to the idea of the pure and holy Zeus, who looks down from heaven to see if men will do justice and seek after God. As time went on, the contrast was felt more and more strongly. By some the thought that the gods must be good was regarded as a sufficient reason for disbelieving all stories to their discredit; by others these tales were considered to disprove their divinity, as Euripides said: 'If the gods do aught unseemly, then they are not gods at all;'[1] others, again, rested content with the conviction that Zeus was a mere name by which they might speak of Him in whom we live and move, but which was utterly incapable of expressing, as our mind is of conceiving, His infinite perfection. *The physical and spiritual Zeus.*

As the deity, therefore, of the visible heaven, Zeus has his brides and his children in all lands. The greatest among those are Apollo and Artemis, Ares, Hermes, and Athênê. These, with Poseidon, Hêrê, Hephaistos, Hestia, Dêmêtêr, Aphroditê, and Zeus himself, formed the body which in the days of the historian Thucydides was worshipped as the twelve gods of Olympos.[2] This ordering of the gods is not found in the Greek tragic or lyric poets or in our Iliad or Odyssey. In these poems many of the deities are not nearly so important as they appear elsewhere, while in other traditions some are described as lower in character. This systematic arrangement of the heavenly *The Olympian hierarchy.*

---

[1] Fragment. *Belleroph.* 300. [2] Thuc. vi. 64. 6.

hierarchy was the necessary result of the poems called Theogonies, which relate the birth and recount the attributes of the gods.

Of the sanctuaries dedicated to Zeus, the most celebrated were the temple on the Arkadian mount Lykaios (Lycæus), a word denoting, like Delos, merely brightness; that of Dodona, which at first was in Thessaly and afterwards in Epeiros; and that of Olympia in Elis, where the great Olympic games were celebrated at the end of every fourth year. Zeus, indeed, must of necessity have his abode on the Lykaian heights, just as Phœbus must be lord of the Lykian kingdom or realm of light, for this is only saying that the gods of the clear heaven must dwell in the unclouded ether. But the Arkadian legend is remarkable as showing the strange growths which spring up from mythical phrases when either wholly or partially misunderstood. The blue sky is seen first in the morning against the highest mountain tops, on which the rays of the sun rest awhile before they can light up the regions beneath. Accordingly the Arkadians insisted that their own Lykosoura (Lycosura) was the most ancient of all cities, and the first which Helios, the sun, had ever beheld, and that Zeus had been nourished by the nymphs on the Lykaian hill hard by the shrine of Despoina, the lady. We are even told that the hill was also called Olympos, that in it there was a spot named Kretea, and that here Zeus was born and not in Crete, the island of the Egean Sea.[1] The truth is that in the strict meaning of the words Zeus had his Olympian and Lykaian hills, his Crete, his Diktê or Lyktos, his Arkadia, his Phoinikian or Phenician home, wherever the sun sent forth his long train of light[2] across the

marginalia: Zeus and Lykosoura.

---

[1] Pausanias, viii. 38. 1.

[2] Λυκόσουρα. The Kynosoura, or Cynosure, has the same meaning, the association of the word with a dog being the result purely of a false etymology. The same remark applies to Kynosarges, Kynossema, &c.; and the epithet of Kunôpis, applied by Helen to herself, receives an explanation very different from that which seems to be applied to it in the *Iliad*. Emile Burnouf, *La Légende Athénienne*, p. 111.

sky. But more than this, the Arkadian, when he spoke of this Lykaian sanctuary, averred not only that all living things which might enter it would die within the year, but that not a single object within it ever cast a shadow. With unquestioning faith the geographer Pausanias declared that the huntsman, who from regard to his own life drew back from the inclosure when a hunted beast entered it, failed not to see that its body cast no shadow after it had come within the charmed circle. He tells us that, when the sun is in the sign of Cancer or the Crab, there are no shadows at midday in the Ethiopian Syene; but here, he adds, the marvel was that there were no shadows the whole year round. As to this he was mistaken; but he could scarcely know that in the real Lykosoura there could be no shade, since this Lykosoura was not to be sought in the Peloponnesos, or in any earthly land. In the bright heaven, through which travels the unclouded sun, there can be no darkness at all. Zeus is also nursed by Ida; but the incident is at once explained when we find that in the eastern myth Idâ is a name for the earth, and that she is assigned as a wife to Dyaus.

The god worshipped in these sanctuaries was invoked under a multitude of titles. He was named sometimes from places, and was thus known as Dodonaian, Pelasgic, Cretan; but more commonly the worshipper approached him as the fountain of order, justice, law and equity. As guarding the sanctities of family life, he was Ephestios. He was Pistios and Horkios, as watching over the fulfilment of covenants and contracts, and Xenios as the protector of strangers. But between these offices and his character as a strictly mythical judge there is a sharp and strong contrast. As such, he passes sentence on Ixion and Tantalos, on Lykaon and Sisyphos; but in all such cases the penalty is one which has a direct reference to the mythical actions of the offenders, while it has nothing more to do with absolute justice than has the punishment of

Zeus the judge.

Prometheus. Whether the doom which according to Æschylus is to overtake Zeus after the liberation of the Titan has any connexion with the Teutonic notion of the twilight of the gods, which is to be brought about by Loki, a being closely resembling Prometheus, it might perhaps be rash to affirm positively.

The shadowless sanctuary of Lykosoura is said to have been built by Lykaon, who is called a son of Pelasgos. His own story is one of horror, suggested by the equivocal use of words which had lost their earlier significance. When Zeus came to visit Lykaon, he and his twenty or fifty sons set before him, it is said, a meal of human flesh; and Zeus in his anger at this offence turned them all into wolves. The change is easily accounted for. Like Delos, Phenicia, Lykia, and Argos, the name Lykaon denoted brightness or splendour. Hence he is placed in Arkadia, which also means the bright land. But the Greek words for light and for wolves were the same or nearly the same in sound, and closely allied by their origin; and the Arkadian chief and his sons were easily regarded as changed into beasts with which the Myrmidons of Achilles are carefully and exactly compared.[1]

<small>Lykaon.</small>

The Teutonic belief in the final extinction of the gods might lead us to suppose that the mythology of the German and Scandinavian nations belongs to an earlier stage of thought than that of the Hindu or the Greek. The gods of the latter seem to be essentially free from decay or death; and even the Æschylean myth of Prometheus says no more than that Zeus should be put down and a more righteous ruler set up in his place. In the Teutonic legends Odin himself falls, and Thor dies, and the body of the beautiful Baldur is consumed in the flames. But the links which connect the belief of the one race with that of

<small>The Teutonic gods of the heaven.</small>

---

[1] *Il.* 16. 156. The equivocations of words denoting spears, flowers, and poison, will be noticed hereafter, together with the confusion of words which converted the Rishis or sages into bears, and the seven stars into oxen, Charles's Wain.

the others may be traced readily enough. The Vedic gods, like the Hellenic, live for ever. The Soma inspires them with fresh vigour, as the soul of Zeus is refreshed and strengthened by the ambrosia and nectar of his heavenly banquets. So the Soma draught becomes in Northern Europe the cup of honey mingled with the blood of Qvasir, the wisest of all beings, who during his life had gone about the world doing the work of Prometheus for the wretched children of men. In other respects also the Teutonic deities exhibit the closest likeness to the Greek. The rapidly acquired strength and might of Zeus, Phœbus, and Hermes, simply express the brief period needed to fill the heaven with light, to give to the sun its scorching heat, to the wind its irresistible force; and the same idea is expressed by the myth of Vali, the son of Odin and Rind, who, when only a night old, comes with his hair untouched by a comb, like Phoibos Akersekomes,[1] to take vengeance on Hödr for the death of Baldur, and again in the story of Magni, who, when three days old, rescued his father Thor as he lay crushed beneath the foot of the gigantic Hrungnir. Thus, also, as Hêrê lays one hand on the earth and the other on the sea so Thor drinks up no small part of the ocean with his horn which reaches from heaven to its surface. The very expressions used in speaking of these gods are transparent. The flowing locks of the Wish-god and of Baldur are those of Zeus and Phœbus. The golden-haired Dêmêtêr of the Greek reappears as the fair-haired Lif of the Teuton. The power of Zeus is seen again in that of Thor; and the golden glory which surrounded the head of Phœbus or Asklepios (Æsculapius), is not less a mark of the German deities, and appears on the head of Thor as a circlet of stars.

But we can as little doubt that the theogony or descent of the gods set forth in the Völuspa Saga marks a comparatively late stage of thought, as that the Hesiodic

[1] *Il.* 20. 39.

theogony is later than the simpler myths which tell us of Prokris or Persephonê or Endymion. The myth of Baldur, at least in its cruder forms, must be far more ancient than any classification resembling that of the Hesiodic ages. Such a classification we find in the relations of the Jötun or giants, who are conquered by Odin or Wuotan, as the Titans are overthrown by Zeus; and this sequence forms part of a theogony which, like that of Hesiod, begins with Chaos. From this chaos the earth emerged, made by the blood and bones of the giant Ymir, whose name denotes the dead and barren sea.[1] The Kosmos so brought into existence is called the Bearer of God, a phrase which finds its explanation in the world-tree Ygg-drasil. This mighty tree, which in Odin's Rune Song becomes a veritable tree of knowledge, and whose roots are undermined by Hel or death, and by the Hrim-thursen or frost-giants, rises into Asgard, the highest heaven, where the Æsir[2] or gods dwell, while men have their abode in Midgard, the middle garden or earth, embraced by its branches. The giant Ymir was nourished by the four streams which flow from the cow Audhumla, from whom there came forth a perfect man Buri, the fashioner of the world, whose son Bor had as his wife Besla or Bettla, the daughter of the giant Bölthorn. From Buri proceeded apparently Odin or Wuotan himself, and also the race of the Æsir who dwell in Asgard or Ether,[3] while the middle air is Vanaheim, the home of the Vanen,[4] or spirits of the breathing wind. To this race belong Freyr and Freya, the deities of beauty and love, the children of the sea-god Mördur.[5] But all this visible Kosmos is doomed to undergo a catastrophe, the results of which will be not its de-

<small>VII. Odin. Genealogy of Odin.</small>

---

[1] Lat. *mare*, Fr. *mer*, a word to be referred to the root *mar*. See note, p. 28.
[2] The Teutonic æsir are the Vedic asuras (the Zend ahura), the root of the word being *as*, the foundation of the primary verbs, Sansk. *asmi*, Gr. εἰμί, Lat. *sum*, Lith. *esmi*, Eng. *am*.
[3] *Il.* 15. 192.
[4] The Sansk. Pavana, Gr. Pan, Lat. Favonius, and perhaps Faunus.
[5] See note, p. 28.

struction, but its renovation. The whole world will be consumed by fire; the life and the reign of the Æsir themselves will be brought to an end; but a new earth, rising from the second chaos, will resemble that of the golden age in the Hesiodic tradition.

The name Odin, Wuotan, is closely connected with the German *Wuth*, in which the notion of energy has been exaggerated into that of impulse uncontrolled by will.[1] Odin and Wish. Wuotan, Odin, thus became essentially the armed deity, the god of war and battles, the father of victory. As such, he looks down on the earth from his heavenly home through a window, sitting on his throne with Freya by his side, as Hêrê sits by Zeus in Olympos. As the giver of victory, the greatest of all blessings in Teutonic eyes, he was necessarily the giver of all other good things, like the Hermes of the Greeks.[2] As such, he is Osci, Oski, the power of wish or will, the Wunsch to whom the poets of the thirteenth century assign hands, eyes, knowledge, blood, with all the appetites and passions of humanity. This power of Wuotan or Odin is seen in the Oska-stein or Wishing-stone which the Irish localise in Blarney, in the Osk-mayjar, or Wish-maidens or Valkyries, who guide to Valhalla all heroes slain in battle, and who are the wish or choice children of Odin, and more especially in the Oska-byrr or Wish-wind, in which we recognise, both in the name and in the thing, the Ikmenos Ouros of our Iliad.[3] It is beyond doubt this power which is denoted by the Sanskrit Kama, as the force which first brought the visible Kosmos into being,[4] and by the Eros of the Hesiodic theogony.

[1] In the same way the Hindu Brahm denoted originally the active force in creation; and the same idea was set forth still more fully under the name Atman, the breath or spirit which becomes the Atmos, atmosphere, of the Greek, the *Athem* of the Germans. Odin, Brahma, and Atman are thus, all, names of the self-existent being.
[2] Grimm assigns this meaning to Gibicho, Kipicho, titles of Odin. *Teutonic Mythology*, i. 137, translated by Stallybrass.
[3] The attempt to explain this Ikmenos by a reference to the verb ἰκνέομαι is mere labour lost.
[4] Max Müller, *History of Sanskrit Literature*, p. 561.

The single eye of Odin is the sun, the one eye which all day looks down from heaven upon the earth. But when he was figured as an old man with a broad hood and a wide-flowing robe, the myth necessarily sprang up that he had lost an eye, a story which answers to that of Indra Savitar, who is said to have cut off his hand at a sacrifice, and to have received a golden hand from the attendant priests.[1] But as the sun is his eye, so his mantle is the vapour which, like Zeus Nephelegeretes, the cloud-gatherer, Odin wraps around himself, and thus becomes Hakol-berend, the wearer of the veil, or Harbard, the bearded god. By his side are the two wolves Gari and Freki, with whom he hunts down his victims; and on his shoulders sit the two ravens, Huginn and Muninn, who whisper into his ears all that they see and hear. As the bearded god, Odin becomes the giver of the rain, the Zeus Ombrios of the Greeks, the Indra Parjanya of the Hindus, the Jupiter Pluvius of the Latins. As such he is Hnikar, the old English Nicor or water-god, whose offspring are the Nixes or water sprites. All these names, like those of the Naiads and Nereids, come from the same root with the Sanskrit *sna*, the Greek nêchô, the Latin nare, to float or swim.[2] In this character Odin is the Biblindi, or the drinker, of the Eddas. Like Phœbus, again, or Asklepios

Odin the one-eyed, and Hakol-berend.

---

[1] The Teutonic Tyr is also one-handed. Compare the story of Nuad of the Silver Hand (Fergusson, *Irish before the Conquest*) and Grimm's tale of the Handless Maiden, who is separated from the king her husband, but who, when she is restored to him, has hands as beautiful as ever. We have to note the contrast between the expression of Saxo, which speaks of Odin as, 'Armipotens uno semper contentus ocello,' and the myth which explains the fact by saying that he was obliged to leave his eye in pledge when he wished to drink at the fountain of Mimir. The reflexion of the sun in the water would be Odin's second eye; and as soon as the sun passed away from the water, this second eye would be no longer visible. So Ushas, the Dawn, is spoken of in the Vedic hymn as bringing the eye of the god. With these myths we may compare the legends of the one-eyed Kyklops (Cyclops) and the one-handed Savitar and Tyr.

[2] Old Nick, it is scarcely necessary to say, is merely an abraded form of Nicor. Another name, denoting a water-god from the same root which has given us the names of many streams, Taff, Tavy, Taw, Tay, Tagus, &c., is seen in the phrase, 'Davy Jones's locker.'

(Æsculapius), he is the healer and restorer; and as the Muses are the daughters of Zeus, so is Saga the daughter of Odin, the source of all poetry, the inspirer of all bards. In his hunts he rides the eight-footed horse Sleipnir. Lastly, he is the All-father, and the Psychopompos, who takes all souls to himself, when their earthly journey is done.

For the nations of Northern Europe, Odin or Wodin has become a mere name; but the mark of this name is impressed on many places, and it survives in our Wednesday and Wednesbury. The close connexion of the name Tyr or Tiw with the several forms developed from or containing the root *dyu*, to shine, would lead us to expect that it would remain a mere epithet of gods whose names might again betray a relation to the same root. Thus we meet with Sigtyr, the victorious Tyr, as a name for Odin, and Reidartyr or Reidityr, the riding or driving Tyr, as a name for the thunder-god Thor. Odin and Tyr.

Through the forms Donar and Thunor the name of Thor, which survives in our Thursday, has passed into our later English *thunder*. The consonant introduced into this word answers simply to the change which converted the Latin *tener* into the French *tendre* and the English tender. The name itself had at the first no reference to noise or din. It denoted merely extension, whether of sound or of anything else; and from its source we have the Greek *teino*, reappearing in the Latin *tendo*, to stretch; *tonos*, tone or the stretching and vibration of chords; the Latin *tonitru*, thunder, as well as *tenuis*, Sanskrit *tana*, which reappears in the English *thin*. As the lord of the lightning, the thunder, and the rain, Donar or Thor is as closely allied and as easily identified with Odin, as Vishnu with Indra, or Indra with Agni. But although most of their characteristics are as interchangeable as those of the Vedic gods generally, each has some features peculiar to himself. Thus, although Thor is sometimes said to move in a chariot, he is never represented VIII. Thor.
Thor and his hammer.

as riding like Odin. He is essentially, like Vishnu,[1] the walking or striding god, who moves amid the lightnings. As wielding the thunderbolt, he is Thor Miölnir or Tydeus,[2] the kinsman of the Aloadai and the Molionids,[3] the crushers or pounders; but the well-known hammer of Thor meant not only a mallet but a rock, and thus we are brought to the weapons employed in Greek myths by the giants and the Titans. This *hamar* is stolen by the giant Thrym, who according to one story buries it eight miles beneath the surface of the earth. Rising a mile each year, it ascends into heaven again at the end of eight years. In Sæmund's Edda, Loki, learning the theft, asks Freyja to lend him her feather garment, that he may go and find it. Thrym will not surrender it unless Freyja consents to become his wife; but Loki cheats the thief by bringing Thor disguised as Freyja. The hammer is brought in to consecrate the bride, and Thor, taking the weapon, smites down the giant and discomfits the dwellers in Jötunheim.

In the oldest Teutonic mythology we find a god Fro or Friuja, who is, like Odin, worshipped as the lord of all created things. Fro is the power which imparts to human life all its strength and sweetness, sanctioning all righteous efforts and all honest motives. To this deity belongs the wonderful ship Skidbladnir, which can be folded up like a cloth when the seafarers have reached the end of their voyage.[4] In our Friday we retain his name, as well as that of Freyja, to whom he stands in the relation of Liber to Libera in the Latin cultus of Ceres.

IX. Fro.— Friuja.

In the mythology of Northern Europe, the Hellenic

---

[1] See p. 34.

[2] The relation between the forms Tydeus and Tyndareus is much the same as that between Thunor and Thunder, and between the present and aorist of the Latin verb *tundo, tutudi*.

[3] The affinity of Miölnir with Molion is manifest. In the name of the Aloadai the labial has dropped away, as it has dropped away from Aleuron, originally Maleuron, *ground corn*. All these words must be referred to the root *mar*. See note p. 28.

[4] See p. 3.

Iris, the messenger of the gods, is represented by Heimdall, who guards Bif-rost, the waving bridge or resting place, which joins heaven and earth. As such, he dwells in Himinbiorg, the hill of heaven, the Mons Cœlius of the Latins. He needs less sleep than a bird. He hears the corn growing on the earth, and the wool lengthening on the sheep's back. His warder's horn rests on the root of Yggdrasil,[1] his teeth are of gold, and he rides a horse with a golden mane.

<small>x. Heimdall.—Himinbiorg.</small>

Another Teutonic god of the heavens is Bragi,[2] the brilliant, who, like Donar or Baldur, is the son of Odin. As the god of poetry and eloquence, he is the guardian and patron of bards and orators. Thus Bragr-Karla came to denote an eloquent man, and a further step degraded the name of the chief among the gods, and left it as an epithet of vain boasters. The name of the god Œgir, with whom Bragi is sometimes associated, has shared a like fate. Originally a name for the sea, it carries us directly to the Okeanos or ocean stream of the Greeks, of which Ogen and Ogyges seem to be variations. In modern times it has come to denote the ogres with which nurses frighten children. In Grimm's belief the word belongs to or contains the root of the Gothic *agas* or *ôg*, the Old English *ege, egera*, the Old High German *aki, eki*, all denoting fear, dread, and horror. If it be so, the later meaning has not been arbitrarily imported into the word; and this conclusion seems to be justified when we remember that the *Oegishialm* is the helmet of dread, which the dragon Fafnir wears as he lies coiled round the golden treasures on the glistening heath; and again that Eckesax or Uokesahs is the fearful sword tempered by the dwarfs in the Vilkina Saga.

<small>xi. Bragi.— (Egir.</small>

Between the Latin Jupiter and the Greek Zeus Patêr,

---

[1] See p. 44.
[2] This word may be referred to a root braj, *to shine*, which gives us the Latin *rex, reg-is*, the Hindu *raja*, the Latin *argentum*, and the Greek *argyros*, silver.

there is as close an affinity of names as between the latter and the Dyaus-pitar of the Rig Veda; but practically the mythology of the Latin tribes introduces us almost into a new world. We are, indeed, apt to confuse under the term two wholly distinct things. We read, in the Æneid of Virgil, for instance, a story which may be fairly regarded as a pendant to the Iliad. We find Jupiter, Juno, Venus, and other deities described much as Zeus, Hêrê, and Aphroditê would be described by Greek poets, and in the odes of Horace we have expressions of thought and feeling such as the idea of these gods would naturally evoke in the minds of the Hellenic worshipper. We also come across notices of strange beings, as, for instance, Consus, Anna Perenna, Muttunus, Mana, Semo Sancus, which for us at least are associated with no very definite images; and we include both these beings and the deities spoken of by Virgil or Horace under the one head of Latin gods, and treat what is said about them as Latin mythology. No two things could well be more entirely distinct. The great poets of the Augustan age simply borrowed at will from the vast storehouse of Greek tradition, and set before their countrymen a mythology towards which they had no natural attraction, and for which they never acquired any genuine liking. The Greek myths thus bodily imported became fashionable at Rome and perhaps in the great cities of the empire generally; but on the people of the country far removed from town influences they seem never to have made any deep or permanent impression. It would be almost nearer the truth to say that they failed to make on them any impression at all.

The gods of the country population, which had at one time been the only gods worshipped by the Latin tribes, were practically nothing more than natural powers and processes called by the names which naturally expressed them. The seed time, the harvest, the changes of

XII. The Latin Jupiter.—Characteristics of Latin mythology.

The Latin deities.

the seasons, the periods of human and other life, the garnering and grinding of grain, all these, with other incidents in the history of the revolving year, were marked by a particular name; and this name passed for that of the god by whom these processes were supposed to be wrought. But so thin was the disguise, that the growth of a Latin mythology, strictly so called, became almost impossible. We might as well imagine the growth of the infinitely complex mythology of the Greeks, if their minds had had to work only on such beings as Helios, Selênê, Astraios, Eos, Hersê, and others of a like transparent sort. For the Latins, their gods, although their name was legion, remained mysterious beings without human forms, feelings, or passions; and they influenced human affairs without sharing or having any sympathy with human hopes, fears, or joys. Neither had they, like the Greek deities, any society among themselves. There was for them no Olympos where they might gather to take counsel with the father of gods and men. They had no parentage, no marriage, no offspring. They thus became a mere crowd of oppressive beings, living beyond the circle of human interests, yet constantly interfering within it; and their worship was thus as terrible a bondage as any under which the world has yet suffered. Not being associated with any definite bodily shapes, they could not, like the beautiful creations of the Greek mind, promote the growth of the highest art of the sculptor, the painter, and the poet. A spear or a stone might serve as the sign or emblem of their majesty or their presence; an inclosed space with an altar would be all that they would need as a temple. Thus, between them and their worshippers there was no real and direct connexion. Of the Eupatrid families among the Greeks the greater number, perhaps, traced their descent from Zeus himself or from some other god; no Roman patrician ever thought of proclaiming himself as the offspring of the cold and colourless beings who in solitary state presided over the processes and working of the visible world. Nay, even in Rome itself the Greek deities remained only a fashion, and were honoured with an exotic worship. The true Roman ritual was that which had for its object the worshipping of the household gods; and these were practically the spirits of the founder of the house, and of those who had followed him in true hereditary succession. The religion of Roman life was influenced by the worship, not of the bright and joyous Phœbus, or of the virgin daughter of Zeus, but of the Lares and the Penates before that altar of Vesta, the goddess of the hearth, which was the common heritage of the whole Aryan race. But in the literature of Rome the genuine deities of the country are so strangely confused or even jumbled up with the importations from the East, that it becomes difficult sometimes to assign each portion of material to its proper place. In some cases the characteristics of a Greek god have been fitted on to a Latin god with whose character they are inconsistent; but it is probable that even in the days of Ovid or Horace this confusion never troubled the country folk of Samnium or Calabria.[1]

For these the omnipotent Jupiter remained, what he had always been, the god of the heaven or sky;[2] but of the vast mass of mythology which had grown up round his name elsewhere, the Latin peoples of the Italian peninsula knew nothing. His Oscan name Lucerius or Lucesius (corresponding to the Greek Lykios, and Lykeios, as epithets of Phœbus) marks the bright shining firmament as his habitation. But the Latin tribes had, like the Greeks, a great aptitude for the multiplication of names; and thus in calling down lightning Jupiter was invoked under the name of Elicius; as giving rain, he was Jupiter Pluvius; as protecting boundaries, he was Jupiter Terminus, the Zeus Horios of the Greeks. In Latin literature he has for a wife Juno, with whose name (which answers to a Greek form Zenon) was coupled that of

Jupiter and Juno.

---

[1] See further, Ihne's *History of Rome*, book i. ch. xiii.   [2] See note, p. 38

Regina, as marking her sovereignty. As Juno Jugalis she presided over marriage; as the guardian of money and treasure, she was Juno Moneta, a name which gives us our *money* and *mint*, and which probably contains the same root with Minerva. The mythology for Juno in Virgil is not Italian; but her name is akin to that of Diana, which again is only the feminine form of Dianus or Janus. When the fashion for fitting all Greek mythology to Latin names came in, the little that is told of Artemis was transferred to Diana, with thus much of justification in this case that both are, like Janus or Dianus, the gods of the clear bright heaven. The name of the latter was mistakenly connected with the words *dis, duo*, two; and thus he was represented as having two faces which looked opposite ways.[1]

It is more than possible that the idea of the Dawn as the herald of the sun before his rising, and as the bride who remains in the heaven mourning his early death,[2] took definite shape before that of the glistening firmament of day or of the nightly sky which descends upon the earth which it loves. The phenomena of the Dawn and the Evening Twilight soon suggested the thought of the great tragedy of nature. The Dawn appears, full of light, life, and love. For a few moments she seems to rejoice in the love of the newly-risen sun; but his splendour then becomes fatal to her, and she is seen no more, while he goes on his weary way, mourning for the love which he has lost, toiling for the benefit of weak and worthless men, and hurrying on to his home in the west where he knows that he shall behold the face of the radiant maiden whom he had deserted or driven away at the beginning of his career. She too has had her troubles. Her love has been sought

Myths of the Dawn and the Sun.

---

[1] The gate of Janus at Rome (and it should be remembered that it was a gate, not a temple) was kept open in time of war, and shut in time of peace, and it is said to have been closed only six times in eight hundred years.

[2] In the *Iliad* Eos ends as well as begins the day. Eos is the shining and burning goddess (see note, p. 29); and the word Dawn has precisely the same meaning. It belongs to the same family with the Sanskrit Dahanâ, the Greek Daphne, and Daïs, Lat. tæda, *a torch*.

by those who would make her faithless to her husband; but she comes forth scatheless from the ordeal, only to see the being to whom her heart is given smitten down by the blackness of death almost as soon as she is reunited to him. There seems to be little but woe everywhere. The glance of both the Dawn and the Sun is fatal. The latter looks upon the dew, and the sparkling drops vanish away. The former gazes on him after his day's journey is ended, and he is snatched away from her sight.

We have here an outline which might be filled in with a marvellous variety of forms and details, and it is more <small>Framework and materials of these myths.</small> than possible that the framework of many of the stories which have grown up from them may have been shaped before any clear ideas of the sky, the heaven, and the sun, as gods, presented themselves to the human mind. The separation of the Sun from the Dawn and his reunion with her would probably be marked by primitive men, before they reached any notion of the deity whose abode is the blue vault of the sky. The imagination might work the materials thus presented into a thousand shapes. The bride of the sun was seen with him at the end of his journey: she was seen again before he rose in the east. The union had therefore lasted during the hours of the night; but as his glance was fatal to her in the morning, it could have so lasted only because he was disguised or because he had assumed some other form. Hence would spring up the notion that the Dawn-maiden had been given in marriage to some unsightly monster; or that she had been frightened by her kindred into the belief that she had been wedded to a loathsome being. A fact being given, a cause must be found for it; and the explanation might be that the mother of the Dawn-maiden was dead, and that her father's new wife shared the jealousy felt by her elder sisters for the good fortune of the youngest and the loveliest. The attempt to verify their suspicions would reveal to her the majesty and the beauty of her husband; but she would make the discovery only to see him vanish from her sight. Now would remain for her the weary search, in which she would find herself oppressed by a series of impossible tasks laid on her by her stepmother. But her kindliness to all living things gains for her the gratitude of birds and beasts, which enable her to accomplish them; and her undaunted devotion is at length rewarded.

Among the most beautiful versions of the tale thus suggested is the story of Urvasî as given in the drama of Kalidasa,[1] entitled Vikramorvasî. The name is XIII. Urvasî. as transparent as that of Selênê or Asterodia. In the Vedic hymns the dawn is spoken of both as Urukî, the far-going, and as Uruasî, the wide-spreading; and these names have their counterpart in the Greek Euryanassa, Euryphassa, Europê, and many others. As such, she is the mother of Vasishtha, the son of Mitra and Varuna.[2] Urvasî, then, is wedded to Pururavas, the gleaming one,[3] on the condition that she is never to see him unclothed. Tempted by the Gandharvas, Pururavas rises from his couch; a flash of lightning reveals the splendour of his form; and Urvasî vanishes away, to be united to him again on the last day of the year.

In this story the sun has to seek for the dawn. The beautiful tale of Eros and Psyche brings before us the search of the dawn for the sun; but there is little difference in the framework of the story. The name Psyche denotes simply the breath of all living things; and, as such, she is naturally the bride of Eros, the lord of love, whose unveiled splendour would be too dazzling even for her eyes to rest upon. She believes that she is wedded to the most glorious of all living beings; but a doom is laid on her by Aphroditê, and she brings about her own punishment. Being assured by her sisters that her husband, whom she never sees except when he comes to

Eros and Psyche.

---

[1] A Hindu poet of the first or second century B.C.   [2] See p. 33.
[3] The name answers to the meaning of the Greek Polydeukes.

visit her at night, is a hideous monster, she takes a lamp and, gazing upon her lover, sees before her the perfection of beauty. A drop of oil falls on the sleeping god, and the brief happiness of Psyche is ended. Eos has looked on Helios, and Helios has plunged beneath the sea. If she would be united with him again, she must seek him amidst many perils and at the cost of vast labour. At last she finds him in the dwelling of Aphroditê, at whose bidding she accomplishes some hard and degrading tasks, under which she must have sunk had it not been for the love of Eros, who, though invisible, still consoled and cheered her. By his aid she at length made her peace with his mother, and becoming immortal, was united with her lover for ever. Thus the stories of Urvasî and Psyche exhibit the same leading features which are common to the German stories of Grimm's collection entitled the Soaring Lark, the Twelve Brethren, the White Snake, the Golden Bird, the Queen Bee, to the Norse tale of East of the Sun and West of the Moon, and many others.

This myth may be referred to the succession either of night and day or of the seasons. In the former case we should have a series of tales, more or less in accordance with the two just mentioned; in the latter they would agree with the general spirit of the legend of Dêmêtêr and Persephonê. All receive a local colouring and local features according to the climate of the countries with which they are associated. In the north, before the Dawn or Summer child can be won, there must be a battle with the powers of frost and snow; mountains of glass must be scaled, castles of ice must be thrown down, and huge icebergs moved out of the way. In these tasks the seeker is aided by bears, wolves, or foxes, by ducks or swans, eagles or ants, who are grateful to him for past kindness; but all these are names which in the old mythical language denoted the clouds, the winds, or the light. In Eastern and Western traditions alike, the clouds assume

Northern sun and dawn myths.

the forms of eagles and swans; and these creatures soon remove the huge heaps of grain, stones, and ice, and thus bring about the meeting of the lovers.

In the glowing land of the East these tales are necessarily less prominent than in the West. Their place was taken by those pictures of the daily phenomena of dawn and sunlight, which were gradually overloaded with the cumbersome details of later Hindu mythology. But in their earlier shapes they bring before us forms closely corresponding to those of the chief inhabitants of the Greek mythical world. How thoroughly Ushas was the morning, and how at the same time she was a being greeted with the affection and love of mankind, we have already seen;[1] and it is only necessary to add that in all that is said of her we can scarcely be said to advance beyond the stage of primary or organic myths.[2] The phrases addressed to her for the most part state facts which it is impossible to dispute.

XIV. Ushas.
Ushas and the Panis.

'Ushas, nourishing all, comes daily like a matron, conducting all transient creatures to decay.'

'The divine and ancient Ushas, born again and again, and bright with unchanging hues, wastes away the life of a mortal, like the wife of a hunter cutting up the birds.'

'Those mortals who beheld the pristine Ushas dawning have passed away; to us she is now visible, and they approach who will behold her in after times.'

'Unimpeding divine rites, although wearing away the ages of mankind, the Dawn shines the likeness of the mornings that have passed, or that are to be for ever, the first of those that are to come.'[3]

We still have before us the primeval mythical speech, when we read the plain and artless statements that 'the night prepares a birthplace for her sister, the day, and having made it known to her departs,' and that the night and dawn

---
[1] See p. 29. [2] See p. 9.
[3] R. V. Sanhita, i. 129, 274, 298; ii. 8. 10. H. H. Wilson.

'of various complexions, repeatedly born but ever youthful, have traversed in their revolutions alternately from a remote period earth and heaven—night with her dark, dawn with her luminous limbs.'[1] But the germs of the first myths are seen in the phrases which tell us that, as the daughter of Dyaus, she goes before Indra, Savitar, and Sûrya ; that she opens the ends of heaven, where the thievish Panis had hidden away the cows of which she is the mother ; that she shows the Angiras where they are to be found, and drives her own herds to their pastures. The conception of Ushas thus approaches nearly to that of the Greek Athênê or the Latin Minerva. She brings light, and she is the possessor of knowledge.[2] Hence she is said to enable men to cross the frontier of darkness, and, as the seer, to give light far and wide. She is also the mother of the Divine Night, who reveals her splendours after she has driven away her sister the Twilight ; and lastly, like Athênê, she is spoken of as sprung from the forehead of Dyaus, the sky.

But Ushas is also Ahanâ, the burning light, which reappears in Athênê and Daphnê.[3] She is also Saramâ, and Saranyu, the being who creeps along the heaven.[4] In the Rig Veda, Saramâ is the keeper of the cows of Indra, the clouds ; and as his messenger she is sent to the Panis, who have stolen them. Like Ushas, she is first to spy out the cleft in the rock where the robbers had hidden them, and, like Herakles in the story of Cacus, the first to hear their lowings. It is only, therefore, what we might expect, when we are told that, like Ushas, Saramâ is followed by Indra ; that both go to the uttermost ends of heaven ; that both break the strongholds of the robbers ;

XV. Ahanâ and Saramâ.

[1] R. V. Sanhita, ii. 12 ; i. 169. H. H. Wilson.
[2] The Sanskrit *budh* (Gr. οἶδα, Lat. vidi, Eng. wit) means both to make clear and to know.
[3] Referred to a root *da*, to burn, which is found also in Gr. δαίς, Lat. tæda, *a torch*.
[4] These names contain the root *sar*, to creep, round which are grouped the Greek Erinys and Sarpedon. The verbal forms are in Greek ἕρπω, in Latin *repo* and *serpo*. The transliteration of Saramâ into Greek gives us Helenê.

and that both are the mothers and deliverers of the cows. In the Vedic hymns the Panis try to bribe her by the offering of part of the cattle which they have stolen; but Saramâ steadily refuses. In the later Anukramanika, or index to the Veda, Saramâ is spoken of as the dog of the gods who is sent to seek for the stolen herds, and who, although she refuses to share the booty with the Panis, yet drinks a cup of milk which they give her, and, returning to Indra, denies that she has seen the cows. It is possible that we have here the germ of the notion which took a more definite shape in the Western traditions of the faithlessness of Helen, in whom the name of Saramâ is reproduced,[1] although the interpretation given by Helen herself to her epithet Kunôpis in the Iliad is clearly wrong.[2]

Ushas, again, is Saranyû, the feminine of Saranyu, the horse; and, like Ushas, Saranyû is the mare, and the mother of the twin Asvins or steeds, who represent the Hellenic Dioskouroi, Kastor and Polydeukes (Pollux). Thus with Saranyû she takes her place by the side of the two Ahans or Dawns, of the two Indras, the two Agnis, the two Varunas, and the rest of the great company of correlative deities. But Saranyû, transliterated into Greek, is Erinys; and we have to mark the astonishing difference which these two beings exhibit in the East and in the West. There would in the form of thought of the Vedic hymns be no euphemism in speaking of the Erinyes as Eumenides or gentle beings; and we may be sure that it was not euphemism which first led the Greeks to give them that title. It was assigned to them as naturally as to Dyava-Matar, or Demeter; and it must not be forgotten that these beings, fearful as they were to others, were always benignant to Œdipus, and that to him their sacred grove was as the Hyperborean gardens, into which grief and anguish could never enter. There is nothing astonishing in the change. In the Iliad and Odyssey the

XVI.
Saranyu.
Erinyes;
Harpies: Atê.

[1] See *Myth. Ar. Nat.*, vol. i. Appendix E.   [2] See note 2, p. 40.

Harpies are the beautiful daughters of Thaumas and Elektra; in the Æneid of Virgil they are foul monsters who do the work of vultures. The Ara, which had once been the prayer of the longing heart,[1] became the curse which the weak imprecated on their tyrants. As seeing all things, the sun gods would become the avengers of iniquity, and we have already seen that the nooses of Varuna pass by those who speak truth and ensnare only the liars. In like manner it could not fail to be said of sinners that their evil deeds would be laid bare by Saranyû, the morning light, just as in the Hesiodic Theogony Nyx (the night), which is the mother of Eris (strife), and of all the evils which come of strife, is also the mother of Nemesis, or righteous recompense. The direction thus given to the thought of these once beautiful beings could not fail to issue in the awful picture of the snake-haired avengers of blood which is brought before us in the drama of Æschylus. In the same way, the Atê of the Iliad is simply the spirit of mischievous folly, hurled by Zeus from Olympus, because she postpones the birth of Herakles to that of Eurystheus; the Atê of Æschylus is the fearful power which broods over a house until it has exacted a full penalty for the shedding of innocent blood. But in thorough fidelity to the old mythical speech, the Erinys of the Iliad [2] still wanders in the air, and hears the summons addressed to her from the land of darkness.[3]

The thought which colours these myths gave shape to a doctrine of Necessity more powerful than the will of Zeus himself. All things are within its grasp. The sun must rise in the heavens, and must be hurled down from his lofty place. He must be united again in the evening to the mother from whom he was parted in the morning; and hence the awful marriage of Œdipus with Iokastê, which

---

[1] Herod. vi. 63.   [2] x. 571.
[3] At Athens there were statues of only two Erinyes. This perhaps may point to the notion of correlative deities, which have already come before us in the Asvins or Dioskouroi, in the two Indras, Agnis, &c.

filled his house with woe and brought his lineage to an end in blood. Iphigeneia must die that Helen may be brought back, for the evening twilight must vanish away if the dawn is to return. But Iphigeneia has done no wrong; and there must be condign vengeance for the shedding of her innocent blood. This vengeance is exacted by the Erinyes, who in this aspect appear with writhing snakes instead of hair, and with blood dripping from their eyes. Being now referred to the stages of man's life, they became three in number, and were known as Allekto, Megaira, and Tisiphone (names which denote endless hatred, jealousy, and revenge), as the three Moirai, called Klotho, Lachesis, and Atropos, weave, deal out, and cut short the thread of human life. This later mythology is, it must be confessed, thoroughly artificial. The course of human life is summed up in the past, the present, and the future; and it only remained to assign each of them to one personal being. The three fatal sisters are thus rather an ethical or theological than a mythical growth; but their functions were only gradually determined, and the offices usually assigned to Klotho, Lachesis, and Atropos are sometimes reversed. Still, in whatever order we take them, they answer to the Teutonic Vurdh, Verdhandi, and Skuld, arbitrary names denoting the past, the present, and the future. These are the weird sisters whom Macbeth encounters on the desolate heath; the Thriai, with whom Hermes is bidden to take counsel; the Norns, who guard the ash tree Yggdrasil. The same ethical or theological process gave birth to the idea of Adrasteia, the inexorable power which assigns to each man the recompense due to his work; and of Nemesis, whose business it is to redress the inequalities caused by human injustice, and to make all whose well-being passes beyond certain limits feel the meaning of pain and suffering. The fatal sisters reappear in the Latin Parcæ, if we assume that this name was given to them merely for the sake of euphemism.

The doctrine of Necessity. The Moirai; Weird Sisters; Norns; Adrasteia; Nemesis; the Parcæ, Fates, and Aisa.

It is, however, possible that, as in the case of the Eumenides, the word may have been used at first in all sincerity; nor is this surmise weakened by the fact that the Parcæ were also known as the Fata, or fates, a word answering to the Greek Aisa, the spoken word of Zeus.

These myths attest conclusively the superabundant wealth of primitive language. They spring from the multitude of names which might designate one and the same object,[1] and any point of likeness between the object thought of and that with which it was compared would lead to the identification of the former with the latter. The sun moved rapidly; so did the horse. The clouds nourished the earth with their rain; so cows nourished men with their milk. The name of the one might, therefore, be used, and was used, to denote the other. Thus from their attribute of speed the sun was *asvan* and the horse was *asvan*;[2] but when *asvan* became a name specially for the horse, the sun also became the steed who hurries across the broad heaven. As the bearer of burdens, the horse was called *vahni*;[3] but the flame of fire carried its materials into the air, and the rays of the sun brought his light to the earth. These, therefore, were also *vahni* and they likewise became horses, like the twin steeds or Asvins. From this point the idea of the sun as a being drawn in a chariot by winged steeds was soon reached; and thus Indra is drawn by the Harits, whose name denotes the glistening surface produced by anointing with fat or oil. We say now-a-days, 'The sun is rising,' or 'The sun is high in the heaven,' when the Vedic poets would have said, 'The sun has yoked his steeds for his journey,' or that 'his horses have borne his chariot to the house of Dyaus.' These steeds are also known as Rohits, from their gleaming brown hue; and under both names a distinct personality was

(margin note: The horses and chariot of the Sun.)

---

[1] This is, of course, polyonymy. See p. 13.
[2] Gr. ὠκύς, ἵκκος, ἵππος, Lat. equus.
[3] Compare the Latin *vehere* with the Gr. ἔχω, and the compound cervix, the neck, as carrying the head.

growing up, which made it easy to speak of the Harits as sisters who fly on beautiful wings. We can thus understand how in the West the Harits should become the lovely Charites of the Greeks, whom the Latins called the Gratiæ, and we the Graces.[1]

But the horses of the sun in the Veda are also Arushi, and the sun himself is frequently called Arusha, but only at his rising. The name, therefore, is applied to him strictly as the Asvan or horse stepping forth with irresistible power on his appointed pathway. He is Arusha, we are told, when 'Night goes away from her sister the Dawn, and the dark one opens the path for the bright god.' But with all his strength Arusha is also a child. 'The seven sisters have nursed him, the joyful, the white one, as he was born, the Arusha with great might. As horses go to the foal that is born, so did the gods bring up his son when he was born.'[2] He has the eyes of a man, and he is also called Saparnas, as having beautiful wings. We have thus both the picture and the name of the Hellenic god of love. Arusha is the bright and winged Eros; he is also the young child of Dyaus, the offspring of heaven, the sun of strength, who awakens the earth with his rays. He is the first of the gods, as coming at the point of the days, and of his two daughters the one is clad with stars, and the other is the wife of Svar, the sun.[3] He moves swift as thought, longing for victory; he is Kama, the love or desire of all men; and as being irresistible in his strength, he is Ushâpati, lord of the dawn. These phrases explain all that is told of Eros in Greek mythology, for, although, according to later poets, he is a son of Zeus and of Gaia, or Aphroditê, or Artemis, in the Hesiodic Theogony,

<small>XVII.
Arusha, the Greek Eros.</small>

---

[1] The name Charis belongs to the same group of words with the English grease. Compare the widely differing shades of meaning exhibited by words containing the root *mar* or *mal*. See note, p. 28.

[2] It is precisely thus that the Muses nurse the infant Phœbus in the Homeric hymn.

[3] In these two beings we can scarcely fail to see the Snow-white and Rose-red of the German popular story. Grimm.

as in the Veda, he is the first of the gods, since with Chaos, Gaia, and Tartaros, he makes up the number of self-existent deities. Appearing thus in the awful silence of a formless universe, he is said to be the most beautiful of all the gods, and to conquer the mind and will both of gods and men. The transition was easy to the thought of Eros, ever bright and fair, the companion of the Charites, and the child of the Charis Aphroditê.

The seven sisters who nurse the infant Arusha are represented, we can scarcely doubt, by the Muses, who, in Hellenic mythology, are called the nurses of the new-born Phœbus, whose body they swathe in pure white linen.[1] But the light of day is the emblem and earnest of peace, harmony, and love; and the Muses, whose voice is song, became naturally the goddesses of music, poetry, art, and science. They seem at first, like the Thriai, the Gorgons, and many others, to have been three in number, and afterwards to have been increased to nine. They were also, according to some traditions, called Pierides, from the fountain of Pieria, near Olympus; but another legend says that the Pierides were daughters of Pieros, king of Emathia, who, entering into a contest with the Muses, were beaten by them and changed into birds.[2] The names of the nine, as given by later mythographers, are Kleio (Clio), the proclaimer; Euterpe, the charmer; Erato, the lovely; Thalia, the joyous; Melpomene, the singer; Terpsichore, the enjoyer of dances; Polymnia, the lover of songs; Ourania, the heavenly; and Kalliope, the beautiful-voiced. But neither the names nor the functions of these nine are known to the great epic and lyric poets, or to the tragedians of Greece. Beings in some respects answering to these Muses are found in the Latin Camenæ, whose name in the forms Carmentes and Carmenæ connects them with *carmen*, song. One of these, Egeria, is said to have been the secret counsellor of Numa, the second of the seven kings of Rome.

The name Ushas, as we have seen, reappears in the Greek Eos; and Ushas is a being who, ever young herself, makes others old. Eos is a daughter of Hype- rion, the soaring sun, and a sister of Helios and Selênê; and it is perhaps a reminiscence of the old Vedic tradition which represents her as forgetting to ask for youth when she obtained immortality for Tithonos, whose couch she leaves every morning to spread light over the world of men. Tithonos is thus oppressed by a perpetual old age; but Tithonos is not the only one who has the love of Eos. In the legend of Kephalos she is the rival of Prokris.[1] She is also the lover of Orion, of Kleitos, and of Asterios; and among her children are Heosphoros, the light-bringer; the ill-starred Phaethon; and the Ethiopian chieftain Memnon, whom her prayers and tears constrain Zeus to recall to an endless life.

<small>XVIII. Eos. Tithonos.</small>

In Hêbê, the ever young,[2] the daughter of Zeus and Hêrê, we have another dawn goddess, whose transparent name prevented the growth of much mythical tradition around her person. Like Ushas, she cannot grow old, and she ministers to the gods the life-giving nectar and ambrosia. She is spoken of as Ganymêdê, the brilliant; and thus the relation of Iris to Hermes is that of Hêbê to Ganymedes, the lovely Trojan youth who becomes in Olympos the cupbearer of the gods. In the Hesiodic Theogony she is a sister of the Harpies; according to others, she was the wife of Zephyros, and mother of Eos, the morning.

<small>XIX. Hêbê. Ganymedes.</small>

In the story of Eurôpê[3] we see the dawn, not as fleeing from the pursuit of the sun, but as borne across the heaven by the lord of the pure ether. It is, however, only one of the many forms assumed by the myth that the sun and the dawn are soon parted. The scene is here laid in the

---

[1] See p. 22.
[2] The name Hêbê is akin to the Latin juvenis, Sanskr. yavan, *young*. In Hephaistos we have the same word in the superlative.
[3] For the meaning of the name, see p. 55.

Phenician or purple land, a region belonging to the same aerial geography with Lykia, Delos, and Ortygia. Her father Agênôr is, according to some traditions, the son of the Argive Phorôneus, the representative of the Vedic Bhuranyu, or god of fire. But in some versions Agênôr is her brother, and therefore Phorôneus himself becomes her father—a parentage corresponding closely with that of Athênê in the myth which makes the fire-god Hephaistos cleave the head of Zeus, to allow the dawn to leap forth in its full splendour. From fire, however, come also smoke and vapour, and Phorôneus is thus the father not only of Eurôpê but of Niobe, the snow-cloud, who weeps herself to death on Mount Sipylos. In the more commonly received story Agênôr is the husband of Telephassa, the feminine form of the name Telephos, a word conveying precisely the same meaning with Hekatos, Hekatê, Hekatebolos, well-known epithets describing the far-reaching action of the solar or lunar rays. His children are Kadmos (Cadmus), Phœnix, Kilix, and Eurôpê, although some made Eurôpê herself a daughter of Phœnix. On this maiden Zeus looks down with love, and in the form of a white bull comes to bear her away to a new home in Crete, the western land. She becomes the mother of Minos, Rhadamanthys, and Sarpêdôn. But in the house from which the bull has borne her away all is grief and sorrow. There can be no rest until the lost one is found again. The sun must journey westwards until he sees again the beautiful tints which greeted his eyes in the morning. Kadmos is therefore bidden to go in search of his sister, with strict charge not to return unless he finds her. With him goes his mother, and a long and weary pilgrimage brings them at length to the plains of Thessaly, where Telephassa, worn out with grief and anguish, lies down to die. But Kadmos must journey yet farther westwards; and at Delphi, where he finds his sister, he learns that he must follow a cow, which he would be able to distinguish

xx. Europa.
Kadmos,
Agênôr,
Telephassa.

by certain signs; and where she should lie down for weariness, there he must build his city. The cow lies down on the site of Thebes; but before he can offer the animal in sacrifice to Athênê, he has to fight with the dragon offspring of Ares,[1] which slays the man whom he sends to bring water from the fountain. Kadmos alone can master it; but his victory is followed by another struggle or storm. He sows in the earth the dragon's teeth, which produce a harvest of armed men, who slay each other, leaving five only to become the ancestors of the Thebans. Kadmos has now, like Phœbus, to serve for a time as a bondman; and after this servitude, Athênê makes him King of Thebes, and Zeus gives him Harmonia as his bride. Harmonia becomes the mother of Ino, wife of Athamas, of Semelê, the mother of Dionysos, and of Agavê, who tore her child Pentheus to pieces for opposing the introduction of the Dionysiac worship. There are few other features in this Theban legend. The wars in which Kadmos fights are the wars of Kephalos and Theseus, with fewer incidents to mark them; and the spirit of the old myth is better seen in the legend that, when their work here was done, Kadmos and his wife were changed into dragons, and so taken away to Elysion. Whether the Semitic names[2] found in these Bœotian legends furnish evidence for the colonisation of that country by the Phenicians, it might be rash to say; but it seems to show with sufficient clearness the large influence exercised by Phenician thought, ritual, and even theology

[1] See Appendix I.
[2] Kadmos is simply the Semitic Kedem, the east; Athamas is the god Tammuz; Melikertes, the son of Ino, and therefore grandson of Cadmus, is undoubtedly the Phenician Melkarth (Moloch). The sacrifices of children in his honour, and the horrid nature of his worship generally, are thus at once explained. Adonis is the Semitic Adonai. With these undoubtedly Semitic names before us, it would be imprudent to deny the possibility that other names in the myth, which have an Hellenic or Aryan look, are not, after all, Semitic also. This may be the case with Europê herself, and probably is so with Palaimon. Agenor, which is indubitably Greek, may yet, in this instance, represent the Semitic Chnas. It would be merely an example of the process which turned the French 'chaude mêlée' into the English chance medley.' See Brown, *Great Dionysiak Myth*, i. 247.

in this part of Western Hellas. The precise limits of this influence remain an open question; but the fact that Semitic names and Semitic rites found their way into the territories of some Greek tribes may, perhaps, enable us to account for some strange beings in Greek mythology, which cannot be explained by referring them to any Aryan sources.

Among the less pleasing forms assumed by the dawn myth is the story of Althaia, the nourisher, as the mother of a child whose life is bound up with a burning brand. This story is recited to Achilles in the Iliad by Phœnix, the teacher of his childhood, the dweller in that purple land of the East from which Europa was taken to her western home. His purpose in telling it is that Achilles may see in Meleagros, the fated son of Althaia, a reflexion of himself; and the parallel is closer than the poet imagined it to be. The chief point is that the existence of Meleagros is bound up with the preservation of a piece of wood which was burning away. As the child lay sleeping in his cradle, the Moirai (Mœræ), who shape the fortunes of men, stood suddenly, it is said, before his mother, and pointing to a log burning on the hearth, told her that as soon as the brand had burnt itself out, her child would die. The phrase declared simply that the light of the sun must disappear when he sinks below the western horizon; but from failure of memory the notion might arise that it was possible to interrupt the waste of life, and that the burning brand might be quenched in water and stored away. This work is therefore done by Althaia; and like the multitude of heroes, who share his divine origin, Meleagros grows up strong, brave, and beautiful. Like them he achieves great exploits, taking part especially in the Argonautic expedition and the great Kalydonian boar hunt. This last enterprise was undertaken to destroy a monstrous boar which Artemis had sent to punish Œneus, the father of Meleagros, for neglecting to give her her portion

<small>XXI. Althaia. Meleagros. Olger the Dane.</small>

of a sacrifice. Foremost among those who were gathered together for this chase was Atalantê, the daughter of the Arkadian chieftain Schœneus. This beautiful maiden first pierced the boar, which was afterwards slain by Meleagros. But the sequel brought disaster. Meleagros wished to have the head, and the Kourêtes (Curetes) of Pleuron, who had aided the Kalydonians in the hunt, were not content to have the skin only. Thus a strife arose, in which Meleagros slew the chief of the Kourêtes, who was also a brother of Althaia. This was followed by a war between the peoples of Pleuron and Kalydon, in which, after a little while, Meleagros refused to take part, because Althaia in her grief for the loss of her brother laid her curse upon her son. No sooner had he withdrawn himself from the contest than the men of Kalydon lost ground, and remained utterly dismayed until his wife Kleopatra induced him to go forth. As soon as he reappeared, the enemy was routed. But the men of Kalydon would give him no prize, and Meleagros again withdrew to his secret chambers. As he refused altogether to give further aid to his countrymen, Althaia, enraged at his sullenness, brought out the brand and flung it into the fire. As the wood burnt away, the strength of Meleagros decayed, and as the last spark flickered out, he died. His death was by a mythical necessity soon followed by that of Kleopatra and Althaia. The twilight cannot long survive the setting of the sun. So passes away the hero who can only thus be slain; and his sisters, who are changed into guinea-hens, weep for his death, as the sisters of Phaethon shed tears of amber over their brother's grave. His short and chequered life is one of the many forms which the course of the sun may take in any land. He is capricious and sullen; and periods of complete inaction alternate with others of vehement and violent energy. Sometimes he reappears in wonderful splendour; at others he is hidden away and refuses to be seen. It is the career of the sun on a day when the clouds and vapours are hurrying across the sky, and moments of glaring brightness are followed by intervals of heavy gloom. But in whatever way the time may be spent, the hours are hurrying on; and if the brand is allowed to burn itself out, his life must end with its last spark. This torch reappears in the Danish legend of Olger,[1] the mighty hero who rescues the land of the Franks, after spending generations with Morgan le Fay in the enchanted valley of Avilion. It is this fairy queen who delivers to him the fatal torch with the charge, 'See that you kindle it not, so shall you live for ever; but if by mischance it should break out and burn, cherish the fire with care, for the measure of your days is the last spark of the torch.' But these possibilities of deathless life are never realised, and as long as we are speaking of the phenomena of the outward world, they never can be. The Danish Olger is saved from the doom of Meleagros, only because at the moment of his marriage with the Frank queen he is snatched away by Morgan le Fay, who bears him off to her charmed paradise.

We now approach a group of heaven-inhabiting deities, whose forms were invested by the Greeks with a majesty greater even than that of the Vedic Ushas. In Athênê we have, in one form of the myth, a being who comes into existence without a mother, springing armed from the forehead of her father Zeus, when, according to some versions of the legend, Hephaistos had split it open with an axe. Translated into the old phrases, the story tells us simply of the dawn as it bursts forth from the dark forehead of the broad heaven, of which it was easy to speak as cloven by an axe of fire. We find the name itself in the hymns of the Rig Veda, where it still bears its old meaning of the morning light. 'Ahanâ comes near to every house, she who makes every day to be known.'[2] As springing thus from the forehead of the heaven, this dawn-

XXII.
Athênê.
Athênê and Ahanâ.

---

[1] See Popular Romances of the Middle Ages, *Olger the Dane*.
[2] Compare the names Dahana and Daphnê, p. 58.

goddess remains fresh, pure, and undefiled for ever. Like the sun who follows her, she searches out the dark corners and fills all with her light. This idea of her penetrating scrutiny must pass readily into that of profound wisdom; and for the Greek, as he thought of the virgin goddess, the notion of light became inseparably connected with that of knowledge. So too in a hymn of the Rig Veda, the Dawn, as waking every mortal to walk about, receives praise from every thinker; and Ushas also is here spoken of as born without a mother from the head of Dyu.[1] The Hesiodic Theogony,[2] it is true, assigns Metis, another name denoting wisdom, as a mother to Athênê; but this story is reconciled with the other myth by saying that by the counsel of Ouranos and Gaia Zeus swallowed Metis before her child was born.

It is possibly from the supposed incidents of her birth that Athênê was known as Koryphasia[3] in Messene, and as Akria[4] in Argos, while Minerva was called Capita or Capta[5] in Rome. But even if this was the idea present to the minds of Greek or Latin worshippers of later ages, these epithets pointed probably in earlier times simply to the way in which the morning light must first strike the highest peaks before it reveals the lower lands, just as in the Arkadian myth Lykosoura is said to be the most ancient of earthly cities, and the first that was ever beheld by Helios, the sun.[6] *Athênê Koryphasia and Akria.*

With the myth of her birth the idea which found expression in the epithet Tritogeneia, as applied to this goddess, seems to have been closely connected. There were some who took it as meaning that she was born on the third day; but this explanation explains nothing;[7] nor is anything gained by tracing it to the Libyan lake Tritonis, or even to the Bœotian stream Triton, *Athena Tritogeneia.*

---

[1] See p. 58.   [2] Line 886.   [3] From κορυφή, a head or summit.
[4] *Topmost.*   [5] Lat. *caput,* a head.   [6] See p. 41.
[7] The quantity of the first syllable would be a grave, if not an insuperable, difficulty in the way of this interpretation.

on the banks of which we may note that towns sprang up called Athens and Eleusis. We are on firmer ground, when we remember that Trita was the Vedic god of the water and the air. We thus see that Tritos had been a name or an epithet of Zeus, forgotten probably in the long migration which brought the ancestors of the Greeks from their home in Central Asia to the coasts of the Egean Sea, and we can understand the relations of Athênê to Triton, Amphitrite, and the Tritopatores or lords of the winds.

The first work of the Vedic Ushas or Ahanâ is to rouse men from their slumbers: that of Athênê is precisely the same. Hence next to the owl, the cock, the bird of the morning, is specially sacred to her. The epithet by which she is best known in the Iliad and Odyssey is Glaukôpis; and the word denotes simply her bright and gleaming countenance. With us the full grey eye is properly an eye which has not a dearth but an excess of light; and the owl was called Glaux, either from the flashing whiteness of its plumage, or from the brilliancy of its eyes. But in truth the word Glaukopis points to a radiance almost too intense for mortal eyes to rest on, just as Glaukos, the bright hero of the Lykian land, the sun in his noonday strength, is the avenger of Sarpedon, who was slain in the first promise of his youthful beauty. In the same way she is called Optiletis, Oxyderkes, Ophthalmitis —all of them signifying the overpowering glory of her countenance.

Athênê Glaukôpis.

It is, however, not difficult to look at the dawn goddess from other points of view. Regarded as the pure light of morning springing from the bright blue heaven, she is the virgin who can know nothing of the tumults and the agitations of love. But she may be looked upon not only as the child of the dark night, but as the precursor of the sun. In the former case we find her spoken of as a child, not of Zeus, but of the winged giant Pallas or of Poseidon or Hephaistos. In the latter, the deity,

Athênê mother of Lychnos and Phœbus.

ATHENE.

whom the Athenians worshipped as the maiden who knows no earthly love, becomes the lover of Prometheus and the mother of the sun-god Phœbus Apollo. Assuredly, he may be her son, as following the dawn; but as springing from the darkness of the night, he is the child of Leto, whom the Delians welcomed to their island as the mother of the god who was to make them wealthy and famous. Another myth makes her the mother of Lychnos, who reappears elsewhere as Phaethon. Inconsistencies of a similar kind may be seen in the character of perhaps all the Olympian gods. One by one, they may have a strong reluctance to interfere with the majesty of Zeus; and generally the relation of Athênê to her father is that of perfect harmony and submission. But, for whatever reason, she shares the conspiracy of Poseidon and Hêrê to dethrone or imprison Zeus,[1] and she aids Prometheus in stealing fire from heaven against the will of the father of gods and men. In the Iliad and Odyssey she is the deity who knows most deeply the mind of Zeus, and is the guide, comforter, and counsellor of Achilles, Odysseus, and other heroes; but in the legend of Pandora we find her taking part in the plot by which Zeus seeks to add to the misery of mankind. Her task is to teach Pandora the skilful use of the loom, while Aphroditê is to bestow on her all the allurements of physical beauty, and Hermes is to give her a crafty and thievish disposition. In Athenian painting and sculpture, Athênê always appears fully clothed, having on her ægis or cloak the face of the mortal gorgon Medusa which turned all who looked on it into stone. Thus arrayed, her colossal statue, carved in gold and ivory by the great sculptor Pheidias, the friend of Perikles, stood in front of the Parthenon or the Acropolis of Athens; and as the sun rose, the flashing light of her spear and shield was distinctly seen at a distance of twelve miles by the mariners who might be rounding Cape Sounion (Sunium).

[1] *Il.* i. 400.

The genuine Latin goddess of the dawn is, beyond doubt, Minerva; and, as such, she must be compared with the Greek Athênê. The language of the Vedic hymns, which we have already cited, enables us to understand the connexion of the name Minerva with the old Latin verb *promenervare*, used in the Carmen Saliare as equivalent to the kindred verb *monere*, to admonish; and again, with the Latin *mens*, the Greek *menos*, and the Sanskrit *manas*, mind, with the Latin *mane*, morning, with Mania, an old name of the mother of the Lares, and Matuta, another name for the dawn. To the same source we must refer the name Moneta, applied to Juno as the guardian of the Capitoline mint.

Marg. XXIII. The Latin Minerva.

The story told of Aphroditê in the Hesiodic Theogony is clearly a comparatively late form of the legend; yet it resolves itself, none the less certainly, into the early mythical phrases. The life-blood of Ouranos shed over the sea calls forth from the waters the goddess of love and beauty. By her side walked Eros,[1] and Himeros, *longing*, followed after her.[2] It has been doubted whether her name is Greek, and whether it belongs to any of the Aryan languages; but although the Greeks believed that she was so called because she sprang from the seafoam, this of itself goes for very little.[3] For the same reason she is also called Anadyomene, the being who rises from the waters—a name which it would be absurd to assign to a Semitic origin. In the Iliad she is known as the daughter of Zeus and Diônê; according to others she was the child of Ouranos and Hemera, the heaven and the day. The difference here is one of names only. In either case she is the image of the dawn; and as the dawn is the

Marg. XXIV. Aphrodite.

---
[1] See p. 63. [2] Hes. *Theog.* 194-201.
[3] The Greek ἀφρός, foam, seems certainly to contain the same root with our word *froth*; but Aphroditê may nevertheless be referred to it by a false analogy. Agenor is undoubtedly Greek, so is Palaimon. But in the story of Kadmos the one may represent the Semitic Chnas, the other Baal Hamon. See note 2, p. 67.

APHRODITÊ.

most lovely of the sights of nature, Aphroditê became to the Greek, as she was to the Hindu, the goddess of perfect beauty. On her was lavished all the wealth of words denoting the loveliness of the morning; and thus the Hesiodic poet, having spoken of her birth, goes on at once to say that the grass sprang up under her feet as she moved, and that all earthly things rejoiced to look upon her. She is also spoken of as Enalia and Pontia, the deity who sheds her glory on the deep sea; and, again, Ourania and Pandemos, as the goddess, in the one case of pure, in the other of gross and sensual, love.

In the Odyssey she is the wife of Hephaistos, the fire-god; and in this poem she is attended by the Charites,[1] who wash her and anoint her with oil at Paphos. In the Iliad the wife of Hephaistos is Charis; and thus we are brought back to the old myth in which both Charis and Aphroditê are mere names for the glistening dawn. Between the language addressed by the Greek poets to Aphroditê and the phrases applied in Vedic hymns to Ushas there is a close correspondence. The latter is Duhitâ Divah, the daughter of Dyaus, just as Aphroditê is the daughter of Zeus. Another Sanskrit name for the morning was Arjuni,[2] the brilliant; but of this word the Greek in his westward journeyings had forgotten the meaning, and Argynnis became for him a beautiful maiden loved by Agamemnon.

Aphroditê and Hephaistos.

The idea of the morning embodied in Aphroditê exhibits none of the severity which marks the character of Athênê. She is the dawn, not as unsullied by any breath of passion, but as preserving and fostering all creatures in whom is the breath of life. She would thus be associated with those forms under which the phenomena of reproduction were universally set forth. She is, therefore, the mother of countless children, not all of them beautiful like herself, for the dawn twilight may be

The children of Aphroditê.

[1] See p. 63. [2] See p. 11.

regarded as sprung from the darkness, and that of the evening as the parent of the night. Hence Phobos and Deimos, fear and dread, are among the children born by Aphroditê to Ares, while Priapos and Bacchus are her children by Dionysos. As rising from the sea, she was loved by Poseidon; and as the lover of Anchises, she became the mother of Aineias, Æneas, whom Latin poets arbitrarily chose as the mythical progenitor of the Roman people. As such, she takes part in the action of the Iliad, throwing her influence, such as it is, on the side of the Trojans; and when the body of Hector has been dragged in the dust behind the chariot of Achilles, it is Aphroditê who cleanses it from all that is unseemly, and brings back to it the beauty of death, anointing it with the ambrosial oil which makes all decay impossible. Of this war she may, indeed, be regarded as the cause. Her beauty led Paris to adjudge to her the golden apple, flung on the table by Eris [1] at the marriage of Thetis and Peleus, as a gift for the most fair; and the poison instilled into his soul by her promise that he should have the loveliest of women as his wife made him steal Helen from her home, and kindle the strife which ended in the downfall of Ilion.

But Aphroditê is more particularly the lover of Adonis. This name is clearly the Semitic Adon, Adonai, *lord*.[2]

Aphroditê and Adonis. The influence of Asiatic thought in the later outgrowths of the myth cannot be denied, and the consequences of the admission may be indefinitely important; but the myth itself is one which must spring up wherever there is any visible change or alternation of the seasons. Adonis, as denoting the fruitfulness and fruits of the earth, must spring from its plants; and so the story went that he was born from the cloven body of his mother, who had been changed into a tree, as Athênê sprang from the cloven head of Zeus. The babe, anointed by the Naiads with his mother's tears (the dews of spring-time),

[1] See p. 60.   [2] See note 2, p. 67.

was placed in a chest and put into the hands of Persephone, the queen of the under-world, who, seeing his loveliness, refused to yield up her charge to Aphroditê. The latter carries her complaint to Zeus, who decides that the child shall remain during four months of each year with Persephone, and for four he should be with his mother, while the remaining four were to be at his own disposal. In a climate like that of Greece the story would as certainly relate that these four months he chose to spend with Aphroditê, as on the fells of Norway it would run that he must spend them in Niflheim. Still the doom is upon him. He must beware of all noxious and biting beasts. The savage boar was ready to pierce him with his tusk; and, as some said, this boar was Ares disguised.

The myth of Adonis links the legends of Aphroditê with those of Dionysos. Like the latter, Adonis is born only on the death of his mother, while, like Adonis, Dionysos is placed in a chest which carries him to the spot where the body of his mother is buried. But like Adonis or the Syrian Tammuz, Semele is raised from the under-world, and, receiving the name of Diônê, becomes the mother of Aphroditê. _{Aphroditê and Dionysos.}

Of the Latin Venus it is unnecessary to say more than that her name is not borrowed from the Greek. It is the genuine growth of Italian speech, being connected with *venia*, grace, favour, or pardon, with the verb *venerari*, to venerate, and with the English winsome. But so far as the Latin tribes were concerned, it remained a mere name, to which, as to Fortuna or others, any epithet might be applied according to the taste or the wants of the worshipper. Thus she might be Venus Cloacina, or the purifier; *barbata*, the bearded, *militaris, equestris*, and many more. The stories told about her by later Latin poets were simply borrowed from the traditions of the Greek Aphroditê; and as the latter was said to be the mother of Æneas, the an-

xxv. Venus.

cestor of Romulus, so was Venus supposed to be the special protector of the Roman state.

In the mythology of the Greeks Hêrê is the queen of heaven; but, in spite of her majesty, she belongs to the class of beings of whom Kronos may be taken as a type. Zeus had been Kronion, the ancient of days; but the word had a patronymic form, and so Kronos was assigned to him as a father. In like manner he must have a wife, and her name must denote her abode in the brilliant ether. The word belongs probably to the same group with the Sanskrit Svar, the gleaming heaven, and the Zend Hvar, the sun, which in Sanskrit reappears in the kindred form Surya, the Greek Helios, the sun. Little is told about her beyond the story which she tells of herself in the Iliad,[1] namely, that like the rest of his progeny she was swallowed by her father Kronos, and that she was placed by Rhea in the charge of Okeanos[2] and Tethys, who nursed and tended her after Kronos had been dethroned and imprisoned by Zeus beneath the earth and sea. But Greek tradition had different versions for almost every tale; and according to some Hêrê was brought up by the daughters of the river Asterion, while others gave to her as nurses the beautiful Horai (the hours as meaning the seasons), who guard the gates of heaven. When she became the bride of Zeus, she brought him the golden apples which had been guarded by the hundred-headed offspring of Typhaon and Echidna.[3]

<small>XXVI. Hêrê.</small>

Although compelled to submit to Zeus, Hêrê is by no means always in harmony with his will. Her love is given exclusively to the Argives; and the story of the judgment of Paris was devised to furnish a reason for this exclusive favour. According to this tale, when the gods were assembled at the marriage board of Peleus, Eris flung on the table a golden apple to be given to the fairest of the fair. In the trial which followed, Hêrê,

<small>Relations of Hêrê with Zeus.</small>

---

[1] 14. 202. [2] See p. 49. [3] Apollod. ii. 5. 11.

Aphroditê, and Athênê appear before Paris, the Trojan shepherd, as claimants of the apple, which is given to Aphroditê as the embodiment of the mere physical loveliness of the dawn, apart from the ideas of wisdom and power which underlie the conceptions of Athênê and Hêrê. From that time forth Hêrê and Athênê are said to have hated the city of Priam. But the way was not so clear to Zeus as it seemed to be to Hêrê. Hektor himself was the darling of Apollo; and this of itself was a reason why Zeus could not eagerly wish to bring about the victory of the Achaians; but, beyond this, there were among the allies of Priam some in whose veins his own blood was running—the Ethiopian Memnon, the child of the morning; Glaukos, the brave chieftain of Lykia, and, dearest of all, Sarpedon. Here were ample causes of strife between Zeus and his queen; and in these quarrels Hêrê wins her ends partly by appealing to his policy and his fears, and in part by obtaining from Aphroditê her girdle of irresistible power. Once only we hear of any attempt to use force; and this is in the strange story which tells us of the plot of Hêrê with Poseidon and Athênê to put Zeus in chains—a tale which seems to point to the struggles consequent on the attempt to introduce the foreign worship of Poseidon into the west.[1] The pendant to this story may be found in the legend which says that Zeus once hung up Hêrê in the heaven, with golden handcuffs on her wrists and two heavy anvils suspended from her feet. In the same way she quarrels with Herakles, and is wounded by his arrows. Otherwise she is endowed with attributes equal to those of Phœbus himself. Thus she imparts to the horse Xanthos the gifts both of human speech and of prophecy, and sends the unwilling sun, Helios, to his ocean bed, when Patroklos falls beneath the spear of Hektor.

[1] Brown, *Great Dionysiak Myth*. I do not wish to commit myself to Mr. Brown's conclusions; but I am bound to admit the great ability with which he has brought together all the evidence bearing on this very important subject.

The few myths related of her point clearly enough to her office as the queen of the pure heaven. This idea is specially brought out in the story of Ixion (the sun on his flaming noontide cross), who, after being purified by Zeus from the guilt of blood, seeks to win her love, and is cheated by Zeus with a cloud, which is made to assume her shape.

Among the many names by which Hêrê was known is the epithet Akraia. This word was supposed to describe *The children of Hêrê.* her as the guardian of citadels; but it was applied, we have seen, to Athênê as denoting the bright sky of morning. Thus viewed, Hêrê is the mother of Hêbê, the embodiment of everlasting youth. But, as the source of like convulsions with those of Ouranos, from whom sprang the giants, Thunder and Lightning,[1] Hêrê is the mother also of Ares,[2] the crusher, and of Hephaistos, the forger of the thunderbolts. By the Greeks she was especially regarded as instituting marriage and punishing those who violate its duties. In these functions she is practically identical with the Latin Juno.

The Latin deities seldom correspond with the Greek; but the affinity of Hêrê and Juno is manifest; for as the *XXVII. The Latin Juno.* Sanskrit Dyavan represents the Greek Zeus, so the latter answers to the Latin Dianus or Janus, while the feminine forms, Diana and Juno, would correspond to the Greek Zenon. The Latin Juno, however, not only presides over marriage, but is the special protectress of women from the cradle to the grave, and, as such, is both Matrona and Virginalis.

Without attempting to decide the order in which the *XXVIII. Surya and Savitar.* conceptions of the several gods arose in the human mind, we advance from the survey of the dawn maidens and the inhabitants of the ether or air to

---

[1] Brontê and Steropê. Hes. *Theog.* 140.
[2] Like the Greek ἄλευρον for μάλευρον, ground corn, Ares has lost its incipient consonant which reappears in the Latin *mars*. See note, p. 28.

that of the beings who have their habitations in the bodies which are seen moving in the heavens—the sun, moon, and stars. Of these some remain inseparable from the orbs with which they are associated, while some, like the Vedic Indra and the Hellenic Phœbus, simply show in their general characteristics the sources from which they derive their personality. In the Rig Veda the actual sun-god is Surya or Savitar, the former name denoting the splendour of the luminary, the latter his irresistible energy.[1] Surya, we are told, sees all things, and notes the good and evil deeds of men. He is the husband of the dawn, but the dawn is also his mother; and here we have the germ of the myth which in Greece grew into the terrible history of Œdipus and Iokaste. The most active of all the gods, he is the third in the earlier Trimurtti, or trinity, in which he is associated with Agni and Vayu. Savitar, when distinguished from Surya, is especially the glistening or golden god; and the story went that once when Savitar cut off his hand at a sacrifice, the priests gave him instead of it a hand of gold.[2] His power is irresistible. Age cannot touch him, and nothing can withstand his will.

'Shining forth, he rises from the lap of the Dawn, praised by singers: he, my god Savitar, stepped forth who never misses his place.'

The chariot of the sun-god is drawn, as we have seen, by the immortal horses, who are called Vahni or Harits.[3] His strength is said to come from his parent or generator, Soma, which in the Vedic mythology takes the place of the nectar and ambrosia of the Greeks. But flexible and indefinite though it may be, Soma has a sensible personality. Of the phrases applied to him in the Vedic hymns, some have led interpreters to identify him with the rain: others relate strictly to the juice of the Soma plant, and the mode of preparing it as an intoxicating

XXIX. Soma.

---

[1] It contains the root *su*, to drive or stimulate.
[2] See p. 46. [3] See p. 62.

drink: and others, again, speak of him as a god higher even than Varuna or Indra. The word thus denotes not merely the gladdening power of wine, but the life-giving force from which the sky and the sun derive their strength and splendour, and which is embodied in the Greek Dionysos.[1] It becomes even the beatific vision for which the pilgrims of this earth yearn.

'Where there is eternal light, in the world where the sun is placed, in that immortal, imperishable world, place me, O Soma.

'Where there is happiness and delight, where joy and pleasure reside, where the desires of our desire are attained, there make me immortal.'[2]

In some of the hymns all creatures are said to spring from his divine seed, and like Varuna and Indra, Soma is called Skambha, the sustainer of the world. In the later mythology Soma, as the supreme spirit, with Uma, as divine knowledge, falls into the ranks of the correlative deities. This idea of correlated gods is one which arose very early in the human mind, and it seems especially to have impressed itself on the mind of the Hindu. It is easy to see a dualism in nature until knowledge assumes a strictly scientific form. The earth reposes under the heaven, therefore she is his bride; and this relation the Vedic poets expressed, as we have seen, in the single word Dyâvaprithivi.[3] It is the same with the morning and the evening, day and night, light and darkness. We cannot by a sharp line mark where one begins and the other ends. Hence the dawn and the gloaming may be easily described as twin-brothers or sisters standing side by side, and having the same home.

Correlative deities,— Soma and Uma.

Such a twin we find in the Asvins or horsemen, the Hindu representatives of the Greek Dioskouroi, or sons of Zeus. Difficult though it may be to interpret all that is said

---

[1] Brown, *Great Dionysiak Myth*, ch. iv. sect. 5.
[2] R. V. ix. 113. 7.   [3] See p. 31.

about them, their general character seems to be shown with sufficient clearness in the statement that their time is after midnight, whilst the break of day is yet delayed. *The Asvins.* The two Ahans, or dawns, are born, it is said, when the Asvins yoke their horses to their car. The twain are born 'when the Night leaves her sister the Dawn, when the dark one gives way to the bright.' After them comes Ushas, followed by Suryâ, the sister of the sun, then by Saranyû, and lastly by Savitar. As to the meaning of this sequence there can be no question; and when we are told that the Asvins are *ihchajâte*, born here and there, as appearing in the east, and again at eventide in the west, we have a clue to that notion of alternate manifestation which marks the Hellenic myth of Kastor and Polydeukes (Pollux). As such, they are called children of Prajâpati, or of Savitar, and as ushering in the light, they are healers and physicians, like Asklepios, the son of Phœbus. So also like Proteus, and other beings of Western tradition, they can change their shape at will.

'The twain adopt various forms; one of them shines brightly, the other is black.' These, it is possible, may be connected with the white and black eagles mentioned in the Agamemnon of Æschylus.[1]

The impulse being once given, the multiplication of Gemini, or couples, might be carried to almost any length. We have already had the two Indras, the two *Yama.* Agnis, and others. These are in the Veda Yama or Yami,

---

[1] Line 113. It is worth noting that in the Norse tale of Dapplegrim we have the Asvins in their original form of horses, for when the lad who has won his wonderful victories on his unearthly steed is told that he must produce its match or die, he tells his steed in despair, 'Your match is not to be found in the wide world.' The horse answers that he has a match, although it is not easy to get at him, for he abides in Hell. Here, again, we have the alternate manifestations of the Asvins and the Dioskouroi.

It is impossible not to notice the coupling of brothers in Western tradition. In many of these instances the dualism involves complete antagonism; in others, there is the closest harmony. Such couples are seen in Achilleus and Patroklos, Theseus and Peirithoos, Phaethon and Helios, Pelias and Neleus, Prometheus and Epimetheus, Romulus and Remus, Odysseus and Telemachus, Eteokles and Polyneikes, with many others.

twin-brothers or twin-sisters. The one who represented the evening would naturally become the guide or judge of the departed in the regions of Sutala. Thus Yama is said to have crossed the waters, showing the way to many, and first making known the paths on which our fathers crossed over. He thus becomes specially the god of the blessed in the paradise where he dwells with Varuna, while his messengers summon the children of men from the world when their time for departure is come.

Answering to Surya and Savitar, Phœbus Apollo and Helios represent the sun-god, the latter being inseparably connected with his orb. The name of the former cannot be explained with certainty. The word Phoibos has been connected with the Greek Phôs, light. It may, perhaps, more plausibly be compared with the Sanskrit Bhava and Bhavani, names which denote life and the producing powers of nature. The epithet Apollon has been generally interpreted as the destroyer, because the sun's rays, when too powerful, can destroy the life of animals and plants; but some have also asserted that the genuine form was Apellon, and have connected it with other epithets which express his powers of healing disease and averting disaster.[1] It is possible that at first Phœbus may have been, as Helios remained, a god who had his dwelling in the solar orb; but in the earliest Greek traditions we find him regarded as the god of light, who was not confined to the habitation of the sun. He is usually called the son of Zeus and of Leto; of Zeus, because the sun, like the dawn, springs in the morning from the sky; and of Leto, because the night, as going before the sun, may be considered as his mother. Her name, denoting the oblivion of night, reappears in that of Lethe, the river of the underworld, which makes men forget the past; as well as in that of Latmos, the land of shadows, in which Endymion sinks to

[marginal note: XXX. Phœbus Apollo.]

---

[1] Preller, *Griechische Mythologie*, i. 182. Welcker, *Griechische Götterlehre*, i. 460.

sleep; and of Leda, the mother of the twin Dioskouroi (Dioscuri).

The Ionian legend of his birth, embodied in the hymn addressed to the god,[1] tells us the simple tale that Leto, when about to become the mother of Phœbus, could find no resting-place until she came to Delos. To wealthier and more fertile lands she made her prayer in vain; and when she addressed herself to the little stony island with its rugged cliffs and hills, Delos trembled with mingled joy and fear. The unborn child, she knew, would be a being of mighty power, and she dreaded lest he should despise his sterile birthplace, and spurn it with his feet into the sea. It remained only for Leto to make a solemn covenant with Delos, that here should be the sanctuary of her child for ever, and that here his worshippers, coming from all lands to his high festival, should lavish upon her inexhaustible wealth of gold and treasures. Here, then, Phœbus was born, and at his birth the earth laughed beneath the smile of heaven, and Delos, though in itself a hard and stony land, covered itself with flowers. The nymphs wrapped him in a spotless robe, and placed a golden band round the body of him who, though now weak and helpless, was to be Chrysaor, the lord of the golden sword. But no sooner had Thetis touched the child's lips with the drink and food of the gods than, like the striding Vishnu,[2] he became possessed of irresistible strength, and his swaddling bands fell off him like flax, as, taking harp in hand, he proclaimed his office of declaring the will of Zeus to men. *The Delian legend.*

He is, then, born in Delos merely because the word Delos denotes the bright land. For the same reason he is Lykeios and Lykêgenes, born in Lykia, the realm of light; and in some legends Ortygia is mentioned as the birthplace both of Phœbus and of his sister Artemis. But Ortygia is merely the land of the quail,[3] *Mythical geography.*

[1] Hymn, 1-178. [2] See p. 34. [3] Gr. ὄρτυξ, ὄρτυγ-ος, Sansk. vartika.

the earliest bird of spring, and thus of the early morning; and the names of mythical geography refuse to be confined within the borders of any one country. There might be an Ortygia in the Egean, another near Ephesus, and another close to the Sicilian Syracuse; but the true Lykia and Ortygia of the myth belong to the regions of cloudland, like the wonderful Lykosoura of Pausanias.[1] But the sojourn of Phœbus in Delos was necessarily short. The sun cannot linger long in the east after his rising; and thus to the hymn which related his birth was added another hymn speaking of his westward wanderings,[2] telling us how he went from land to land, and how he loved the tall sea-cliffs and every jutting crag, and the rivers which hasten to the broad sea, although he came back with ever fresh delight to his native Delos, as the sun reappears morning after morning, glorious as ever, in the east.

As soon as he burst the bonds of his cradle (the white mists which are swathed round him when he first becomes visible), Phœbus is armed with irresistible weapons, and his quiver is filled with arrows which never miss their mark. These are the unerring weapons which belong to all the heroes who share his nature—to Herakles and Philoktetes, to Achilles and Odysseus, to Perseus, Bellerophon, and many others in Greek tradition; to Rustem in Persian story; to Sigurd and Siegfried in the Volsunga Saga and the Nibelungenlied. So armed, he goes on his westward journey, which brings him to the fountain of Telphoussa, where he wished to build himself a home; but Telphoussa, saying that her broad plain, filled with horses and cattle brought to her for their daily supply of water, could give him no peaceful abode, urged him to go on to the more favoured land of Krisa. Thus warned, he betook himself to Parnassos, where Trophonios and

Phœbus and Telphoussa.

---

[1] See p. 40. Lykia, it is almost needless to say, contains the same root with the Gr. λευκός, white, and the Lat. lux, luc-eo, and luc-na, luna, the moon.

[2] This second hymn begins with line 179.

Agamedes[1] raised his world-renowned home. But, like Kadmos (Cadmus) and Indra, Phœbus must have his Vritra or Ahi to fight with and to slay;[2] and it is at this point that the author of the second hymn introduces the slaughter of the worm or dragon to account for the name of Pytho, as given to the sanctuary from the rotting of its carcase in the sun. Thence he takes him back to Telphoussa, to wreak his vengeance on the beautiful fountain which had cheated him of a bright home beside her glancing waters.

The temple which rose in his honour beneath the twin summits of Parnassos became the greatest of all the oracles in Greece, and its fame was extended through all lands. When Xerxes invaded Greece, the force which he sent to plunder the sanctuary at Delphi is said to have been smitten and destroyed by the god, who hurled on them great rocks from the sides of the mountain.[3] The first priests of this shrine were furnished by the crew of a Cretan ship sailing with merchandise to Pylos. In the guise of a dolphin,[4] Phœbus urges the vessel through the

Apollon Delphinios.

---

[1] These two builders also raise the treasury of Hyrieus, placing one of the stones so that they could remove it from the outside. Astonished at the lessening of his wealth, Hyrieus sets a snare, in which Agamedes is caught, and Trophonios cuts off his head to save him from torture and himself from discovery. This precaution seems in this instance superfluous, since Pausanias, ix. 37, 3, adds that the earth opened and received Trophonios, as it received Amphiaraos. But the incident recurs not only in the Arabian Night's story of Ali Baba and the Forty Thieves, but in that of the Treasury of Rhampsinitos, related many centuries before by Herodotus, and in the West Highland tale of the Shifty Lad.

[2] See Appendix I.   [3] Herod. viii. 37.

[4] He thus becomes Apollon Delphinios. Whether the name of the sanctuary suggested that of the fish, or the latter suggested the former, we do not know; but apart from the name, we see Phœbus here invested with the power of changing his shape, which is possessed by Proteus as well as by the Syrian fish-god Dagon or Onnes. If it could be proved that this idea is an importation from Semitic mythology, we could have no motive for resisting the conclusion; but we need not travel away so far from Aryan sources for comparisons of the sun to creatures which belong to the waters. By the Hindus the sun resting on the horizon was called Bheki, or the frog, which squats by the water-side; and Bhekî was spoken of as a maiden who marries a king on condition that he never shows her a drop of water. Bhekî reappears as the Frog Prince in the German popular tale. In that of the Sick Queen in Campbell's collection of West Highland stories, it is the Frog alone which can heal her with the water of life. In the Vishnu Purana the demon Sambara

waters, while the mariners sit still on the deck in terror, as the ship moves on without either sail or oar along the coasts of Peloponnesos. As they entered the Corinthian gulf, a strong zephyr carried them eastward till the ship was lifted on the sands of Krisa. Then Apollo leaped from the vessel like a star, while from him flew sparks of light till their radiance reached the heaven, and hastening to his sanctuary he showed forth his weapons in the flames which he kindled. This done, he hastened with the swiftness of thought back to the ship, now in the form of a beautiful youth, with his golden locks flowing over his shoulders, and asked the seamen who they were and whence they came. In their answer, which says that they had been brought to Krisa against their will, they address him at once as a god, and Phœbus tells them that they can hope to see their home, their wives, and their children again no more. But a higher lot awaits them. Their name shall be known throughout the earth as that of the guardians of Apollo's shrine, and they shall have all their hearts' desire, if only they will avoid falsehood in word and violence in deed.[1]

Between Phœbus and Helios there is essentially no distinction. Both are beings of unimaginable brightness; both have irresistible and unerring weapons, and the power of awakening and destroying life; both have inexhaustible wealth and treasures; and both can mar the work which they have made. Each of these qualities might and would furnish groundwork for separate stories. But although the sun may have unbounded power, he may also be regarded as a being compelled to do his work, even against his will.[2] He must perform his daily journey; he must slay the darkness which is his mother; he must be parted from the dawn which cheered him in his course; and after a few hours he must sink into the dark-

Apollo and Daphne.

---

casts Pradyumna, the son of Vishnu, into the sea, where he is swallowed by a fish, from whose belly he is born anew. *Myth. Ar. Nat.* i. 400; ii. 26.

[1] *Hymn. Apoll.* 540.
[2] See p. 7. The punishment of Sisyphos.

ness from which he had sprung in the morning.[1] In strict accordance with these ideas, we see the sun in the myth of Daphne as the lover of the dawn, to whom his embrace is, as it must be, fatal. As the delicate tints fade before the deepening splendour of the sun, so Daphne flies from Apollon as he seeks to win her. The more eager his chase, the more rapid is her flight, until in her despair she prays that the earth or the waters may deliver her from her persecutor. So the story went that the laurel tree grew up on the spot where she disappeared, or that Daphne herself was changed into the laurel tree, from which Apollo took his incorruptible wreath. That Apollo himself has to submit to an irksome yoke is shown by the myths relating to Poseidon.[2] Not only is he compelled with that god to build the walls of Ilion, but he is constrained to serve for a year as a bondsman in the house of the Thessalian Admetos, whose wife, Alkestis, is the devoted bride who dies for her husband, and is brought back to him from the under-world in undiminished beauty.

From the lot of Endymion, Apollo is freed only because he is regarded not as the visible sun who dies when his day's journey is done, but as the living power who kindles his light afresh every morning. The one idea is as natural as the other; and we still speak of the tired or the unwearied sun, of his brief career and his everlasting light, without any consciousness of inconsistency. Phœbus is then the ever bright sun, who can never be touched by age. He is emphatically Akersekomes, that is, the being whose golden locks no razor may ever touch. He is at once the comforter and healer, the saviour and the destroyer, who can slay and make alive at will, and from whose piercing glance no secret can remain hid. But although these powers are inseparable from the notion of Phœbus Apollo, they are also attributed sepa-

Apollo, the life-giver and healer.— Asklepios.

---

[1] Hence the doctrine of Anankê, or Necessity. Eurip. *Alk.* 965. See p. 61.
[2] See p. 39, and Appendix I.

rately to beings who are closely connected with him, and whose united qualities make up his full divinity. Thus his knowledge of things to come is given to Iamos; his healing and life-giving powers to his son Asklepios (Æsculapius). The story of the latter is another of the countless instances in which the sun is faithless to his love, or his love is faithless to him; and the doom of Korônis, the mother of Asklêpios, only reflects the fate which cuts short the life of Daphne. Her child, like all other fatal children,[1] is born at the moment of her death amidst a blaze of light, and rescued from the flames. The dawn cannot long survive the birth of the sun. Hence, in the Northern Saga, the mother of Volsung dies as soon as she has kissed her child; and the same lot befalls the mother of little Snowwhite, and of other dawn maidens in the popular stories of Germany. Like Œdipus, Romulus, and other heroes, the child Asklepios is discovered by the splendour which surrounds him, and he is hence called Aiglaêr, the shiner, a mere name for the sun. The wonder is noised abroad, and over land and sea the tidings were carried that Asklepios healed the sick and raised the dead.[2] But, like almost all the other beings to whose kindred he belongs, Asklepios must soon die. Either Zeus feared that man might conquer death altogether, or Hades complained that his kingdom would be left desolate. So the thunderbolt smote down the benignant son of Phœbus, and the sun-god in his vengeance slew the Kyklôpes (Cyclopes), the fashioners of the fiery lightnings for the lord of heaven, and thus

---

[1] See p. 14.
[2] Pausanias, ii. 26. 4. The notion of his healing powers is found in germ in many legends. The sun was regarded naturally as the restorer of all vegetable life after the sleep or death of winter; and as such, his power was extended over all human ailments, and finally to the restoration of the dead to life. With the exception of Hestia, there were few divine personages more widely honoured than this son of Apollo or Paiêôn. His most celebrated temple was perhaps that at Epidauros; and all his temples were practically large hospitals where something like the aid of Christian charity was given to the sick and afflicted by physicians, whose knowledge raised them far above the general run of empirics during the Middle Ages.

brought down upon himself the sentence which made him a bondman first of the Trojan Laomedon, and then of the Thessalian Admetos.

But Apollo is not merely Hekatos and Hekaergos,[1] the god whose rays reach to the furthest corners of the earth; he is also the lord of song. But the Greek knew well that the sun must live in a world of absolute stillness without mist and without clouds, until the breath of the wind stirs the stagnant air. We might, therefore, pronounce it simply impossible that the power of song and the mastery of melody assigned to Phœbus could have originated with himself, or have been his from the first; and when we turn to the Hymn to Hermes, we find that this expectation is fully justified. Hermes in that hymn is the god of the moving air, and it is Hermes who is the maker of the lyre and the true lord of song. The power is born with him, and is in fact himself,[2] and the main object of the hymn is to account for the harmony existing between Hermes and Phœbus, from whom he receives charge over the bright and radiant clouds which float across the blue seas of heaven. It is impossible to lay too great stress on this difference of inherent attributes, as showing the rigid conditions which the primitive mythologic speech imposed on the poets of later generations. Hermes may yield up his lyre to Phœbus, asking in return the boon of that wisdom in which Phœbus has no rival; but willing though the latter may be to grant the prayer so far as he can, he tells him that it is impossible for him to give to the god of the air a share in the secret councils of Zeus.[3]

Apollo and Hermes.

Next, perhaps, to that of Hestia,[4] the worship of Apollo had the greatest influence in forming the Greek character.

---

[1] See p. 62.   [2] See p. 4.
[3] It is useless to assign a place in the text to the so-called Latin god, Phœbus Apollo. He is not a Latin god at all. The name of his mother Latona was only a Latinised variation of the Greek Leto. The true Latin god of light is Jupiter Lucerius or Lucesius.   [4] Vesta.

Under the shadow of his temple at Delphi, the Amphiktyonic Council, the greatest religious association of the Greeks, held its meetings; and the answers given by the Delphian priestess are said to have changed more than once the current of Greek history.

The oracle of Delphi.

We have seen in Phœbus the destroyer of the serpent, or worm, or dragon at Pytho. But the myths related of him bring before us serpents of a very different kind, the serpents who bestow wisdom, and who are as beneficent as the others are deadly.[1] These serpents appear in the story of Iamos, a son of Phœbus and Evadne, born on the banks of the Alpheios. On his birth, Evadne, fearing the wrath of her father, Aipytos, chief of Phaisana, fled away, and Phœbus sent two serpents, who guarded the child and fed him with honey. Aipytos, after a long search, found the babe lying in a bed of violets; and the child soon showed himself possessed of a marvellous wisdom, for Phœbus, touching his ears, made him understand the voices of birds, and underneath the waters of Alpheios Iamos[2] had gained a knowledge of things hidden from the minds of men. His children, the Iamidai, became, it was said, the famous seers or prophets of Olympia.

Iamos and the Iamidai.

Like Iamos, Amphiaraos, a descendant of the wise seer Malampous, was a being whose ears, being cleansed by serpents, were enabled to catch the utterances of birds. He took part, we are told, in the Kalydonian boar hunt and the Argonautic expedition, and finally in the war at Thebes, waged by Polyneikes against

Amphiaraos and Alkmaion.

---

[1] The snakes which Herakles strangles in his cradle are the demons of darkness. But the word dragon, Gr. δράκων, denotes simply any keen-sighted thing, as the word Dorkas or Zorkas, belonging to the same group, denoted a gazelle. It may be noted that the names of many of the mythical lawgivers have a similar meaning. The Athenian Drakon, Draco, is merely one who sees; the Spartan Lykourgos is the light-bringer, and the Lokrian Zaleukos is the gleaming and dazzling one.

[2] The name Iamos seems to belong to the group of words which includes Iole, Iason, Iasion, Iokaste, Ion, Iolaos, and others, pointing to the violet tints of morning.

his brother Eteokles. With this strife Amphiaraos wished to have nothing to do; but his wife, Eriphyle, bribed by the necklace which Cadmus gave to Harmonia, betrayed her husband's lurking-place. When, in the fight which followed the death of the two sons of Œdipus, Amphiaraos found himself hard pressed, he prayed to Zeus, who caused the earth to open and swallow up his chariot. But he had taken care to leave with his son Alkmaion commands enjoining him to avenge his death. Eriphyle was accordingly killed by Alkmaion, who, after long wanderings, found rest in the islands at the mouth of the river Acheloôs. Alkmaion was afterwards the leader of the Epigonoi (the sons of the chiefs who had fought in the war of Eteokles and Polyneikes) in that attack upon Thebes which ended in the destruction of the city.

Of myths which describe the perpetually varying phenomena exhibited by the course of the sun throughout the year, there is, in truth, an inexhaustible wealth. Even we can speak of the angry or the threatening, the kindly or deadly, the young, the strong, or the tired sun; and if we can do so in spite of scientific knowledge, which tells us that these impressions do not correspond to or represent the facts, we can well understand the exuberant energy with which the human imagination would work on these phenomena, when such science as the primitive Aryans possessed was itself founded upon these impressions of their senses. The sun to them might be a deceiver of those whom he loves, a fugitive from the bride whom he deserts, or the destroyer of his parents. He might be the wanderer or the bondman, he might be wise or he might be mad, or in times of raging drought he might have suffered some one to take his place who was incapable of controlling his fiery steeds. This last idea is fully drawn out in the story of Phaethon, who becomes in it a being distinct from Helios, although his name, like Phanaios,[1] was

XXXI. Helios and Phaethon. Class of Secondaries.

---

[1] From the same root with φαίνω

originally nothing more than an epithet of the sun-god. But the same process which made Helios a son of Hyperion, though, as we have seen, he was Hyperion himself, made him also the father of Phaethon. In the Iliad we have both Helios Phaethon and Helios Hyperion; but elsewhere Phaethon is a son of Helios and Klymene, and the word which had now come to denote a distinct personality served to account for some of the phenomena of the year. The hypothesis of madness was brought in to explain the slaughter of Eunomos the son of Œneus by Herakles; but it was at the least as reasonable to say that if the sun scorched up the fruits and flowers which his genial warmth had called into life, it must be because an unskilled hand was holding the reins of his chariot. So the story grew up that in an evil hour Phaethon asked his father to let him drive his horses for a single day. Helios, much against his will, suffered him to take the reins. After rising for a little while into the heaven, the horses, becoming conscious of their driver's weakness, plunged down towards the earth, and the ground, with all its fruits and streams and rivers, was parched and dried up. Seeing that unless his course was stayed all living things must soon die, Zeus smote Phaethon with his thunderbolts, and the daughters of Hesperos, the evening star, built his tomb on the sea-shore where he fell. But as a distinct person and not as a mere epithet, Phaethon is simply a reflexion of his father. He has some of his brightness, but he lacks his power and his wisdom. In this respect he answers precisely to Patroklos, who in the Iliad is described as clothed in the armour of Achilles and placed in his chariot, which is drawn by the immortal horses Xanthos and Balios (the golden and speckled), the same steeds, indeed, which were harnessed to the car of Helios. Patroklos, like Phaethon, receives directions which he neglects to obey, and, like Phaethon, he is slain. In the Odyssey, Telemachos is to his father what Patroklos is to Achilles, or Phaethon to

Helios. With others they form a class known as Secondaries.

The image of the tired sun, sinking to sleep in the west and facing the rising moon, is embodied in the myth of Endymion, which, as we have seen,[1] can scarcely be said to have passed beyond its primary stage. *Endymion and Narkissos (Narcissus).* The story was localised in Elis merely because Elis was the most westerly region of the Peloponnesos, just as Kephalos is said to sink into the sea from the cliffs of Leukas, the most westerly point of northern Hellas. But although there were slight variations of detail, none were apparently of any importance. By some he is said to be the father of fifty daughters by Asterodia, the moon, whose pathway lies among the stars, and who thus answers to the Teutonic Ursula with her band of virgin followers; others gave him Neis and Iphianassa as his wives, or made him the father of Eurydike, the bride of Orpheus. The simplest form of the myth is that of Apollodoros,[2] who merely says that when Zeus offered him anything that he might desire, he chose an everlasting sleep in which he might remain youthful for ever.[3] The same idea is embodied in the transparent story of Narkissos, who is described as the beautiful son of the stream Kephisos, loved by the nymph Echo, who, failing to win his love, died of grief. As a punishment, Nemesis[4] made Narkissos fall in love with his own image reflected in the waters, and the youth in his turn pined away from unsatisfied longing. On the spot where he died the flower sprang up which is called by his name. Later versions said that he was himself turned into a narcissus, as they also said that Daphne was changed into a laurel. This story the geographer Pausanias rejects on account of the absurdity of the notion that Narkissos was unable to distinguish between a man and his shadow, or

[1] See p. 9.   [2] I. 7. 5.
[3] We have here a contrast to the blunder of Eôs, who asks immortality for Tithonos without adding the condition of youth.
[4] See p. 60.

the reflexion of his form. Hence he prefers the other but less known legend, that Narkissos loved his own twin sister, and that on her death he found a melancholy comfort in noting the likeness of his own face and countenance to those of his lost love. But in truth, as in the myth of Endymion, we have here hardly crossed beyond the borders of mythology. As Endymion sleeps in Latmos, so the name Narkissos denotes the numbness or deadness of profound sleep; and the sun, as he looks down upon his own face reflected in a lake or sea, sinks or dies at last still gazing on it.

Like Selênê and Endymion, Hesperos is a being without a mythical history. He was so clearly the evening star, *Hesperos.* that there was nothing to say of him except that he was the father of the Hesperides, whose beautiful gardens are in an island which no earthly ship ever approaches, and where the ambrosial stream always flows by the couch of Zeus. It is the land of the evening twilight; and so the myth goes on to tell us that this enchanted region is hard by the land of the Gorgons, and near the bounds of that everlasting darkness which is the abode of Ahi and the Panis, of Vitra and Echidna.

The myth of Ixion exhibits the sun in another aspect. He is here seen bound to the four-spoked wheel which is *Ixion.* whirled round everlastingly in the sky, a punishment answering to that of Sisyphos.[1] By some he is called a son of Phlegyas, the flaming; but he is himself Phlegyas, as much as Helios is both Hyperion and Phaethon. As the son of Phlegyas he is the brother of Koronis, the mother of Asklepios. He is said to have married Dia,[2] the daughter of Hesioneus, to whom he promised rich gifts, which after the marriage he refused to send. To show his sense of the wrong, Hesioneus stole the undying horses which bore the

---

[1] See p. 7.
[2] A name belonging to the same group with Zeus, Dios, Dyaus, Dyu, Tyr, &c.

gleaming chariot of Ixion, who thereon bade him come and take the gifts if he wished to have them. Hesioneus went accordingly; and when he insisted on seeing the treasure-house in which the gifts were stored, Ixion opened the door, and Hesioneus fell into a pit full of fire.[1] This crime was followed by a time of drought and wretchedness, until Zeus purified Ixion from his guilt. But Ixion is hurried on from one offence to another by the necessity which suggested to a Greek the idea of a moral destiny.[2] He now offers his love to Hêrê, the queen of heaven, and to meet this new danger Zeus made a cloud assume the likeness of his wife, and thus deceived Ixion, who became the father of the Kentaurs (Centaurs).[3] To punish him still further, he bound him to a four-spoked wheel, which bears him round for ever and ever.[4] This wheel of the sun is mentioned in many of the Vedic hymns, which speak of the battle waged by Dyaus, the heaven, to snatch it from the grasp of night. His wife Dia is one of the company of dawn-maidens, for all of whom there is the early lover and the speedy parting in a drama which is perpetually presenting itself in new aspects. In Hesioneus we have the counterpart of Laios,[5] the darkness from which the light springs, and which is utterly unable to withstand the blinding splendour of the treasure-house in which Ixion kept his much-coveted gifts. But forsaking Dia, Ixion loves Hêrê, because the sun, as it rises in the heavens, may be said to woo the blue sky, which was specially her abode. At this point of the myth Ixion is said to be sojourning in the house of Zeus, and this sojourn is the long pause which the sun seems to make

---

[1] See Diod. iv., 69.   [2] See p. 61.
[3] The name Kentaur certainly cannot be explained by referring it to any Greek word, or to any word belonging to the western Aryan dialects. But in the Rig Veda we have a class of beings called Gandharvas, who are manifestly the bright sunlit clouds, probably cumuli with their heads illuminated, while the other parts are in shade. M. Bréal, in his analysis of the myth of Œdipus, has no doubt that the two names Kentaur and Gandharva are identical. See *Myth. Ar. Nat.* ii. 35, note 3.
[4] *Tales of Ancient Greece*, p. 52; Pind. *Pyth.* 2. 74.   [5] See p. 14.

in the highest heaven at noontide. The phantom which cheats him in the guise of Héré is the beautiful cloud which reposes on the deep blue sky, and the Kentaurs or Gandharvas are its children, the vapours which expand from the solitary cloud and float across the heaven. The four-spoked wheel, which Zeus had snatched from the powers of darkness in the morning, becomes the instrument of torture to which Ixion is bound at noontide, the fiery cross which is seen in the sky by those who look on the noonday sun.[1] There seems to be good reason for thinking that the name itself bears out the meaning of the story, if it be only another form of the Sanskrit word Akshanah, denoting one who is bound to a wheel. The word Ixion would thus be akin to the Greek axon, the Latin axis, and the English axle.

The treasure-house of Ixion reappears in the Palace of the Lydian or Phrygian Tantalos, blazing with gems and gold, which is placed beneath the Sipylan mount, where Niobe wept herself to stone. He was as widely known for his wisdom and power as his wife Euryanassa, whose name corresponds with a crowd of names for the morning or the dawn,[2] was for her beauty. Indeed, Tantalos was admitted to share the secret counsels of Zeus, and thus gained a knowledge beyond the reach of mortals. In short, he is pre-eminently Sisyphos,[3] the wise man; and the idea of transgression and punishment is brought into his story as it is into that of Sisyphos. In course of time he stole some of the food and drink of the gods, and gave them to his people; and he also refused to give up the dog Pandareos, which had guarded Zeus as an infant in the cave of Dikté. Finally, when Zeus and all the gods came down to feast in his banquet hall, he cut up his own child Pelops, and placed his roasted limbs before them as a repast.

Tantalos.

---

[1] This wheel reappears in the Gaelic story of the Widow and her Daughters, Campbell, ii. 165, and in Grimm's German tales of the Iron Stove and the Nix of the Mill-pond. *Myth. Ar. Nat.* ii. 302.
[2] See p. 14.   [3] See p. 7.

Pelops was restored to life by Zeus, who doomed Tantalos to gaze on beautiful fruits which he might not touch, and on clear waters which he might not taste. If he bowed his head to drink, the waters fled away; if he put forth his hand to pluck the fruit, the branches which bore them vanished, and a huge rock appearing above his head threatened to crush him to powder.

This myth is one of the most transparent in the whole range of Greek mythology. The palace of Tantalos is the golden house of Helios, from which Phaethon goes forth on his luckless journey. Tantalos,[1] in fact, is Phœbus, for he has the wisdom which Phœbus alone possesses. His frequent converse with Zeus represents the daily visits of Helios to the heights of heaven. His theft of nectar and ambrosia answers to the theft of fire by Prometheus, for the benefit of mortal men; and the wealth which he bestows on his people is the wealth which the warmth of the sun draws forth from the earth. But as the sun, when the heat becomes too great, burns up these fruits, so, when such drought came, men said, 'Tantalos is slaying and roasting his own child.' The restoration of Pelops to life is the action of that mighty power which restores freshness to the earth after drought, and which is wielded specially by Asklepios, the healer. The sentence passed on Tantalos agrees closely with the same idea. His stooping to drink the water which shuns his approach, and to eat the fruits which elude his grasp, points to the drying up of streams and the withering of herbage by the fierce rays of the sun. The rock which threatens to crush him is the dark storm cloud which rises, beetling like a crag above the sun into the highest heaven, or broods like the Sphinx over the mountain summit. As the earth is the more scorched in proportion as the sun may be said to stoop nearer down to it, the expression 'to be tantalised' is applied to all dis-

Stories of drought.

---

[1] His name is a reduplication of the syllable which appears in the words Atlas and Atalanta. It denotes the ideas of strength and endurance.

appointments when the prize sought seems to be within our grasp.

But the palace of Tantalos is seen again in the rose-gardens of the Phrygian King Midas, whose wisdom is said to come from Seilenos. Being told by the latter that he shall have anything for which he may express a wish, Midas asks that everything which he touches may be turned into gold. The phrase may almost from the first have had the double meaning which is expressed by it in later times. The connexion of gold and wealth is close enough, and early rising is a condition for acquiring it. The common English couplet is, however, not so significant as the German, which says: 'Morgenstunde Hat Gold im Munde,' and which points as much to the early flush of morning as to the benefits which she is supposed to confer on man. But the granting of the wish of Midas would not add to his happiness, if he be regarded as a being of human form with human appetites; and accordingly he finds to his dismay that it is as impossible for him to swallow his food as the dishes on which it is laid. To his prayer for deliverance, the answer is that he must go and wash in the stream of Paktôlos, which has ever since retained a golden hue. This is but one of the almost countless forms of the myth as given in popular stories, which speak of the quenching of the sun's light on his coming into contact with water.[1] His ass's ears are accounted for as a punishment for adjudging the prize to Marsyas in his contest with Phœbus. The deformity now becomes a mysterious secret; but his servant discovers it, and being unable to keep it to himself, digs a hole and whispers into it that Midas has ass's ears. A reed growing up on the spot repeats the words; and the rushes all round take up the strain and publish the fact to the world. In all likelihood the Eastern version of the myth described his pos-

The gardens of Midas.

---

[1] See p. 79.

session of ass's ears as the symbol of his wisdom, and therefore as his glory, not as his disgrace.[1]

The legend of Sisyphos exhibits the sun as an unwilling toiler under a penal sentence. Apart from the notion of punishment, the idea of enforced labour is that which underlies and runs through the whole career of Herakles, the greatest, or at the least the most conspicuous, of all the Hellenic solar heroes.[2] He is said to be a son of Zeus and Alkmene, born according to some in Argos, according to others in Thebes. A few hours before his birth, Zeus, we are told, boasted to Hêrê that the child then to be born to the family of Perseus should be the mightiest of men. On hearing this, Hêrê, urged on by Atê, the spirit of mischief, caused Eurystheus to be born before Herakles, who was thus doomed to be the servant of his kinsman. So wroth, it is said, was Zeus when Hêrê told him that Eurystheus must according to his oath be king of Argos, that he seized Atê by the hair of her head, and, swearing that she should never again darken the courts of heaven, hurled her from Olympos. The whole life of Herakles thus became a long servitude to a master meaner and weaker than himself, and one continued self-sacrifice for the good of others, his most marked characteristic being an irresistible bodily strength, which is always used to help the weak and suffering, and for the destruction of all noxious things. The great harvest of myths which has sprung up round his name may be traced to the old phrases which had spoken of the glorious sun as toiling for so poor and weak a creature as man; as born to a life of toil; as entering on his weary tasks after a brief but happy infancy, and as sinking finally to his rest after a fierce battle with the storm clouds which had sought to hinder his journey.

XXXII. Herakles.

---

[1] Brown, *Great Dionysiak Myth.* vol. i. p. 65.
[2] The first part of his name is the same as that of Hêrê, and is, therefore, connected with Helios and the Vedic Surya.

His labours may be said to have begun in his cradle; but the toils known as the twelve labours of Herakles[1] are assigned to later periods of his life. In the Iliad and Odyssey, however, no attempt is made to classify his toils or his exploits. The stories of his infancy tell us that as he lay sleeping in his cradle, two snakes coiled themselves around him, and that the child on waking placed his hands round their necks, and gradually tightened his grasp until they fell dead upon the ground. These snakes are the serpents of the night, on which the sun may be said to lay his hands as he rises, and which he slays as he climbs higher into the heavens.[2] Exposed by his mother Alkmene on a barren plain, he is picked up by the dawn goddess Athênê, who beseeches Hêrê, the queen of the blue heaven, to suckle it. The child bites hard, and Hêrê flings it back to Athênê, who carries him to his mother. The boy grows up in the perfection of human strength and power. His teachers are Autolykos and Eurytos, the harper Linos, Kastor the twin brother of Polydeukes (Pollux), and the wise Centaur Cheiron, who is also the teacher of Asklepios, Iamos, and other heroes.

The labours of Herakles.

Thus far we have a time answering to that in which Phœbus is tended by the nymphs in his infancy, when his face is unsoiled and his raiment all white. We can readily understand that the myth may at this point be made to assume the moral aspect of self-denial. The smooth road of indulgence is the easiest for men to travel on, or it may seem to be so at first. But he who takes the rugged path of duty must do so from deliberate choice; and thus Herakles, going forth to his long series of labours, suggests to the sophist Prodikos the beautiful apologue in which Aretê and Kakia, virtue and vice, each claim his obedience. The one promises endless pleasures

The apologue of Prodikos.

---

[1] The idea of the twelve labours is not improbably Semitic.
[2] These snakes must be distinguished, therefore, from the serpents which impart wisdom to Iamos. See p. 92.

here and hereafter: the other holds out the prospect of hard days followed by healthful slumbers, and warns him that nothing good was ever won without labour, nothing great ever done without toil. The mind of Herakles is made up at once; and the greatest of all mythical heroes is thus made to enforce the highest lessons of human duty, and to present the highest standard of human action.

With this high heroic temper Herakles set forth on his great career. His great fight is with the lion of Kithairon (Cithæron), from whose carcase (or from that of the lion of Nemea) he obtains the skin with which he is commonly represented. *The weapons of Herakles.* In many of the tales which are told of his later career the idea of lofty moral purpose is lost in the notion of constant wanderings in which the toil-worn hero gives himself to any enjoyments of the passing hour, but throughout which he is guarded by invulnerable armour. The coat of mail is brought to him by Athênê, as the armour of Achilles is brought to him by Thetis, and that of Sigurd in the Teutonic epic by his mother Hjordis. His bow and arrows he receives from Phœbus, the lord of the spear-like sunbeams; and from Hermes he obtains his sword, whose stroke may split the forest trees. The arrows, it must be especially noted, are poisoned: and these poisoned barbs are used by Philoktetes, who receives them from Neoptolemos, the son of Achilles, and also by Odysseus. But we have no historical evidence that poisoned arrows were used by any Hellenic tribes, or that they would not have regarded the employment of such weapons with horror. How then comes it to pass that the Iliad and Odyssey can attribute to any Achaian heroes practices from which their kinsmen would, so far as we can form a judgment, have shrunk with disgust? The mystery is easily solved. The equivocation which turned the violet-tinted rays of morning into spears was inevitable: the change of the spears or arrows into poisoned barbs was, at the least, as natural and necessary, the words Ios and Ion, which furnished a name for the violet hue, for a spear, and for poison, being really homonyms, traceable to two or three roots. Nor are these the only derivatives from these roots which occur in the myths of Herakles. His stoutest ally is Iolaos, the son of Iphikles:[1] his earliest love is Iolê, the daughter of Eurytos, from whom, like Apollo from Daphne, he is parted in the spring-time of life, to see her again once more just when his career is ended.

As the conquest of the lion of Kithairon is the first great exploit, so, according to the later mythographers, who took delight in classifying his labours, the bringing up of the dog Kerberos (Cerberus) from Hades is the last. This story is mentioned in the Odyssey, in which Herakles tells Odysseus that his sufferings are but a reflexion of the toils which he had himself undergone through the tyranny of the mean Eurystheus, and that this task of bringing up the hound of Hades had been achieved by the aid of Athênê and Hermes, the dawn and the breeze of the morning.[2] The dog of Yama,[3] the Indian Hades, thus brought back is, of course, carried down again by Herakles to the lowest world.

Herakles and Kerberos (Cerberus).

But the sun, as he rises in the heavens, acquires a fiercer power; and hence Apollon becomes Chrysaor, and Herakles becomes mad. The raging heat burns up the fruits of the earth which the genial warmth had fostered; and so, in accordance with the idea which underlies the myths of Tantalos and Phaethon, Herakles slays his own children by Megara, and two also of the sons of Iphikles. On Laomedon, King of Ilion, who had refused to pay the promised recompense to Poseidon and Phœbus for building the walls of his city, and then cheated Herakles by giving him mortal horses in the place of the deathless steeds for which he had covenanted, the hero takes ven-

Herakles and Laomedon.

---

[1] Iphikles is the twin brother of Herakles. He belongs thus to the class of Secondaries, or correlative deities. See p. 93.
[2] *Odyssey*, 11. 623.   [3] See p. 83.

geance in the first Trojan war mentioned in the Iliad, which relates how, coming with six ships and a few men, he shattered its towns, and left its streets desolate.

Of the other exploits of Herakles the greater number explain themselves, although of some it would be rash to venture on an interpretation. The vast mass of tradition which has gathered round his name contains probably a certain amount of Semitic material, and some of the myths seem to reflect the feeling expressed in such legends as those of Pentheus and of Orpheus. The Nemean lion is the offspring of Orthros[1] or Echidna.[2] Another child of the same horrid parents is the Lernaian Hydra, a monster who, like Ahi, Vritra, the Sphinx, or the dragons of Pytho and Thebes, shuts up the waters and causes drought. The stag of Keryneia is, according to some versions, slain, in others only seized by Herakles, who bears it with its golden antlers and brazen feet to Artemis and Phœbus. The story of the Erymanthian boar is in some accounts transferred from Argos to Thessaly or Phrygia; the monster itself, which Herakles chases through the deep snow, being closely akin to the Chimera slain by Bellerophon. In the myth of the stables of Augeias, Herakles appears simply to play the part of Indra when he lets loose the imprisoned waters and sweeps away the filth accumulated on the land. The myth of the Cretan bull brings before us a dark and malignant monster driven mad by Poseidon; but Crete lay within the circle of Phenician influence, and the bull may be the savage and devouring Moloch of Semitic theology. Although Herakles carries this monster home on his back, he is obliged to let it go again; and it reappears as the bull which ravages the fields of Marathon, till it is slain by the hands of Theseus, who is also the slayer of the Minotauros. In the noisome birds which take refuge in the Stymphalian lake because

Herakles and Deianeira.

---

[1] The Greek form of the Vedic Vritra. See p. 32.
[2] The representative of the Vedic Ahi. See p. 34.

they are afraid of the wolves, we have perhaps a picture of the dark storm clouds dreading the rays of the sun,[1] which can only appear when they themselves have been defeated. The fertilising rain clouds appear yet again as the cattle stolen by Geryon, and recovered by Herakles in the story of Cacus. The legend of the golden apples guarded by the Hesperides is only a repetition of a like idea, the same word, Mêla, denoting in Greek both apples and sheep.[2]

The bondage of Apollo connects the story of Herakles with that of Admetos, the chieftain of the Thessalian Pherai, *Herakles and Admetos.* the happy husband of Alkestis, the most beautiful and the most loving of wives, and the lord of a house enriched by the labours of Phœbus, who has brought him health and wealth and all good things. One thing alone is wanting, and this even Apollo cannot grant to him. On the day of his marriage Admetos has made Artemis angry by neglecting her in a sacrifice. The goddess, however, promised that when the hour of his death came, he should escape his doom, if his father, mother, or wife should die for him. Alkestis agreed to do so; and it was her life that he could not win even from Phœbus himself. Thus in the very prime of her beauty she is summoned by Thanatos, death, to leave her home and children, and to cross with him the dark stream which severs the land of the living from the region of the dead; and although Phœbus intercedes for a short respite, the gloomy being whose debtor she is lays his icy hands upon her, and will not let her go until the mighty Herakles grapples with him, and, having by main force rescued her from his grasp, brings her back to her husband. Here, as in the myth of Orpheus, the disaster is brought about or portended by serpents; and

---

[1] The same root or word furnished a name for wolves, λύκοι, and for the rays of the sun. The growth of a myth converting the rays into wolves, would thus be inevitable. The connexion of these ideas is prominent in the story of Lykaon, see p. 42. The comparison of the Myrmidons of Achilles to wolves is especially striking. See p. 42.

[2] We shall see, later on, that a similar equivocation turned the seven stars into seven sages or seven bears.

when Admetos enters his bridal chamber on the day of his marriage, he sees on the bed a knot of twisted snakes. But although Alkestis may die, Death cannot hold her in his keeping; and the story thus resolves itself into the simple phrases which said that the dawn or twilight, which is the bride of the sun, must die, if she is to live again and stand before her lord in all her ancient beauty.

The narratives of these greater exploits are interspersed with numberless incidents of more or less significance, some of which plainly interpret themselves. Thus in his journey to the land of the Hesperides, he is tormented by the heat of the sun,[1] and shoots his arrows at Helios, who, admiring his bravery, gives him his golden cup wherein to cross the sea. It is a time of many changes, which crowd on each other during the season of his madness, from which he is told that he can be loosed only if he consents to serve for a time as a bondman. He is now sold to Omphalê, and assumes a half-feminine guise. But even with this story of subjection a vast number of exploits are interwoven, among these being the slaying of a serpent on the river Sygaris, and the hunting of the Kalydonian boar. His union with Deianeira, the daughter of the chief of Kalydon, brings us to the closing scenes of his troubled and tumultuous career. He unwittingly slays the boy Eunomos; and refusing to accept the pardon which is freely offered to him, he departs into exile with his wife. At the ford of a river he entrusts her to the charge of the Kentaur (Centaur) Nessos, who acted as ferryman,

Herakles in bondage.

---

[1] In reference to such incidents as these, Mr. Paley says: 'A curious but well-known characteristic of solar myths is the identification of the sun both with the agent or patient, and with the thing or object on or by which the act is exercised. Ixion is the sun, and so is Ixion's wheel. . . . Hercules is the sun, who expires in flame on the summit of Mount Œta; but the fiery robe which scorched him to death is the sun-cloud. Now this, so far from being an objection to the theory, goes far to confirm it. It is the unconscious blending of two modes of representation—the sun as a person, and the sun as a thing. To construct a story, there must be both agents and subject-matter for action; and both, from different points of view, may be the same.' ('On the Origin of Solar Myths,' *Dublin Review*, July 1879, p. 109.)

and who, for attempting to lay hands on Deianeira, is fatally wounded by the hero. In his last moments Nessos bids her preserve his blood, as the sure means of recovering her husband's love if it should be transferred to another.

When at length the evening of his life was come, Deianeira received the tidings that her husband was returning in triumph from Œchalia, not alone, but bringing with him the beautiful Iolê, from whom he had long been parted. Remembering the words of Nessos, Deianeira steeps in his blood the white garment which, at the bidding of Herakles, Lichas comes to fetch from Trachis. The hero is about to offer sacrifice to the Kenaian Zeus, and he wishes to offer it up in peace, clad in a seemly robe of pure white, with Iolê standing by his side. But so it is not to be. Scarcely has he put on the robe, when the poison begins to course through his veins and to rack every limb with agony unspeakable. Once more the suffering hero is lashed into madness, and seizing the luckless Lichas, he hurls him into the sea. Borne at last to the heights of Œta, he gathers wood, and charges those who are round him to set the pile on fire, when he shall have laid himself down upon it. Only the shepherd Poias ventures to do the hero's will; but when the flame is kindled the thunder crashes through the heaven, and a cloud comes down which bears him away to Olympos, there to dwell in everlasting youth with the radiant Hêbê[1] as his bride. It is the last incident in what has been called the Tragedy of Nature—the battle of the sun with the clouds, which gather round him like mortal enemies at his setting. As he sinks, the fiery mists embrace him, and the purple vapours rush across the sky, like streams of blood gushing from the hero's body, while the violet-coloured evening clouds seem to cheer him in his dying agony.

The death of Herakles.

There is, however, a comic as well as a tragic side to

[1] See p. 65.

the career of Herakles. The sun may be spoken of as one who toils for us; but he may also be said to enjoy in every land the fruits which he has ripened. Hence in many stories Herakles is a being fond of eating and drinking; and thus when in the house of Admetos[1] he learns that his host has just lost his wife, he regards this as no reason why he should lose his dinner. The same burlesque spirit marks the conflict with Thanatos (death), in which Herakles rescues Alkestis (Alcestis) from his grasp. The comic Herakles.

After the death of Herakles, his tyrant Eurystheus insisted, it is said, on the surrender of his sons. Hyllos, the son of Deianeira, hastily fled away with his brothers, and after wandering to many places, found a refuge in Athens. This was only saying in other words that on the death of the sun the golden hues of evening are soon banished from the sky, but that after many weary hours they are seen again in the country of the Dawn,[2] as indeed they could be seen nowhere else. Eurystheus now marches with his hosts against Athens; but the Athenians are led on by Theseus, by Iolaos, and by the banished Hyllos. Eurystheus is slain, and Hyllos carries his head to Alkmene. After his death the Herakleids return to the Peloponnesos, but after a year they are driven out again, and are forced to retreat once more to Athens. Their next return ends in the slaughter of Hyllos by Echemos, and the children of Herakles are bound by a compact to forego all attempts at return for fifty or a hundred years. At the end of this time preparations for regaining their old home are made on a scale almost equal to that of the armaments which were to assail and destroy Ilion. The narrative which follows resembles in many of its most important incidents the story of the Trojan expedition, and the result is a success not less complete. The Herakleids share the Peloponnesos between them—Argos The children of Herakles and their fortunes.

[1] See p. 89. [2] Attica, the land of Athênê.

falling to the lot of Temenos, Sparta to the sons of Aristodemos, and Messênê to Kresphontes.

Of the Latin god Hercules it may be enough to say here that Livy tells of him a story in which, undoubtedly, Herakles and Hercules. he has all the characteristics of the Hellenic Herakles. But it is not less certain that the Latin Herculus or Hercules answers strictly to the Greek Zeus Herkeios, and is in short Jupiter Terminus, or the god of inclosures and boundaries. With this fact before him, Niebuhr insisted that the story must at the first have been told not of the genuine Latin Hercules, but of some god into whose place his name had been intruded, from the phonetic resemblance between it and that of the Greek Heracles. The introduction of the name is, therefore, simply a result of that wholesale system of borrowing which extended practically to the great mass of Greek mythology; but the story of Hercules and Cacus is nevertheless a Latin myth, and we shall see its importance when we deal with the traditional legends of drought and darkness.

The myths relating the fortunes of the Herakleids show us how easily myths might be made to go round in cycles. XXXIII. Perseus. The children of the sun-god are expelled from their home in the west only to reappear in the dawn city of the east, from which they repeat their efforts to gain possession of their western inheritance. But the repetition seems never to have left the impression of sameness. Differences of names and of local colouring invariably sufficed to maintain the conviction that legends substantially identical were wholly independent; but we might be tempted to suppose that the faith of the Argives must have been sorely strained when they were called upon to believe that the myth of Herakles was not a reflexion of the career of his mythical ancestor Perseus. The measure of correspondence between the two may perhaps be best seen by taking the story of the latter after that of his more conspicuous descendant. But we are justified on other grounds in reversing the Argive order. Herakles is sprung from Perseus only in the mythology of Argos; and the names which occur in both the myths furnish conclusive evidence that we have in them a history of phenomena connected with the sun in its daily course, and in the revolution of the seasons. In either case we have a hero whose life, beginning in disaster, is a long series of labours undertaken at the behest of one who is in every way his inferior, and who comes triumphantly out of his fearful ordeals because he is armed with the invincible weapons of the dawn, the sun, and the winds.

Like Œdipus, Romulus, and a host of others, Perseus is one of the fatal children.[1] Akrisios, the King of Argos, was accordingly warned by the Delphian oracle that if his daughter Danaê had a son, he would be slain by that child. So he shut her up in a dungeon; but Zeus entered it in the form of a golden shower, and Danaê became the mother of Perseus. Akrisios thereon placed Danaê and her babe in a chest, which the waves of the sea carried to the island of Seriphos. There she with her child was rescued, and kindly treated by Diktys, the brother of Polydektes, king of the island.[2] Like all other fatal children, Perseus grows up with marvellous beauty and strength. His gleaming eyes and golden hair made him like Phœbus, the lord of light; but the doom which was on him was as heavy as that of Herakles, and his troubles began through the sufferings of his mother, who refused the love of Polydektes. On this refusal the tyrant shut her up in prison, saying that she should never come out until Perseus brought back the head of Medusa, the youngest of the three Gorgon sisters, the daughters of Phorkos and Keto. Medusa, a mortal maiden, dwelt with

Perseus and Polydektes.

[1] See p. 14.
[2] The name Diktys seems clearly to be connected with that of the Diktaian cave, see p. 36. The word Polydektes is only another form of Polydegmon, an epithet of Hades.

her immortal sisters Stheino (or Stheno) and Euryale, in the distant west, far beyond the gardens of the Hesperides, where the sun never shone, and where no living thing was ever to be seen. Yearning for human love and sympathy, she visited her kinsfolk the Graiai; but they could give her no help. So when Athênê came from the Libyan land, Medusa besought her aid. But Athênê refused it, saying that men would shrink from the dark countenance of the Gorgon; and when Medusa answered that in the light of the sun her face might be as fair as that of Athênê herself, the goddess in her anger told her that henceforth all mortal things which might look upon her face should be turned into stone. Then her countenance was changed, and her hair was turned into snakes, which coiled and twisted themselves round her temples.

Only through the aid of the gods was Perseus enabled to find her dwelling. When he slept once more upon Argive soil, Athênê stood before him, and gave him a mirror in which he might see the face of Medusa reflected, and thus know where to strike, for upon Medusa herself he could not gaze and live. When he awoke he saw the mirror by his side, and knew that it was not a dream. So with a good hope he journeyed westwards, and on the following night he saw in his sleep Hermes, the messenger of the gods, who gave him the sword which slays all mortal things on which it may fall, and bade him obtain the aid of the Graiai in his further search. When he awoke he took up the sword, and went to the land of the Graiai, where Atlas[1] bears up the pillars of the high heaven. There, in a cave, he found the three sisters, who had but one eye between them, which they passed from one to the other. This eye Perseus seized, and thus compelled them to guide him to the dwelling of Medusa. By their advice he went to the banks of the Ocean stream which flows round all the earth, and there the nymphs gave him

Perseus and the Gorgons.

[1] See p. 99.

the helmet of Hades,[1] which enables the wearer to move unseen, and a bag into which he was to put Medusa's head, and the golden sandals of Hermes, which should bear him more swiftly than a dream from the pursuit of the Gorgon sisters. Thus armed, Perseus drew nigh to the dwelling of the Gorgons, and then, while the three sisters slept, the unerring sword fell, and the woeful life of Medusa was ended. On waking the two sisters saw the headless body, and rushed in mad chase after Perseus; but with the cap of Hades he went unseen, and the golden sandals bore him like a bird through the air. Onwards he went, until he heard a voice asking him whether he had brought with him the head of Medusa. It was the voice of the old man Atlas, who bore up the pillars of heaven on his shoulders, and who longed to be released from his fearful labour. On his entreaty Perseus showed him the Gorgon's face, and his rugged limbs soon grew stiff as ridges on a hill side, and his streaming hair looked like the snow which covers a mountain summit. Thence Perseus rose into the land of the Hyperboreans, who know neither day nor night, nor storm, nor sickness nor death, but live joyously among beautiful gardens where the flowers never fade. In spite of all its bliss, he could not tarry here long. He remembered his mother in her prison-house at Seriphos, and once more, on his winged sandals, he flew to the Libyan shore, where he saw a fair damsel chained on a rock, while a great dragon approached to devour her. But before he could seize his prey, the unerring sword smote him; and, taking off his cap, Perseus stood revealed before Andromeda. In a little while there was a marriage feast, where the maiden sat as his bride. But among the guests was Phineus, who

---

[1] Ἄιδος κυνέη, *Il.* 5. 845. The Teutonic *tarnkappe*. The powers of this cap may have led to the notion which explained the name Hades from the invisible world. This explanation might suit the form Ἄϊς, Ἄιδος; but it is not easy to apply it to Hades, for which probably there is no Greek comparison. The name may perhaps be connected with that of Hodr, the slayer of the Teutonic sun-god Baldur.

had wished to marry Andromeda, and this man reviled the bridegroom until Perseus, unveiling the Gorgon's face, turned him and all his followers into stone.

There remained no more enemies to trouble him, and Kepheus, the father of Andromeda, would gladly have kept the hero with him; but the work of Perseus was not done until he had freed his mother from her prison. He must, therefore, hasten back to Seriphos, where Danaê was brought forth from her dungeon, and the glance of the Gorgon's face turned Polydektes and his abettors into stone. Thus his task was at length accomplished. The gifts of the gods were no longer needed, and so Perseus gave back to Hermes the helmet of Hades and the sword and sandals, and Athênê took the Gorgon's head and placed it upon her Ægis.[1] On this follows the return of the hero with his mother to Argos, whence Akrisios, remembering the warning of the Delphian god, had fled in great fear to Larissa, where he was received by the chieftain Teutamidas. Thither also came Perseus, to take part in the great games to be held on the plain before the city. In these games Perseus was, throughout, the conqueror; but while he was throwing quoits, one turned aside and killed Akrisios. The sequel is given in two versions. In the one Perseus returns to Argos, and dies in peace; in the other, grief and shame for the death of Akrisios drive him to abandon his Argive sovereignty for that of the huge-walled Tiryns, where his kinsman Megapenthes is king. Thus, as the unwilling destroyer even of those whom he loves, as the conqueror of monstrous beasts and serpents, as toiling for

Perseus and Akrisios.

---

[1] By the Greeks the Ægis was regarded as a buckler or shield covered with the skin of a goat, αἴξ, αἰγός, or a mantle of the same material, borne by the virgin-goddess Athênê. But the *Iliad* speaks also of Zeus Aigiochos, who was first the Storm-bringer (the idea of tempest being expressed in the word καταΐξ, καταιγίς) and then the Ægis-bearer. The Homeric poet, M. Bréal remarks, 'semble se souvenir de la première signification, quand il nous montre, au seul mouvement du bouclier, le tonnerre qui éclat, l'Ida qui se couvre de nuages, et les hommes frappés de terreur.'—*Hercule et Cacus*, p. 116. Compare also the Ægis-hialm of northern myths, p. 49.

a mean and cruel master, yet as coming forth in the end victorious over all his enemies, Perseus is at once the forefather and the counterpart of Herakles.

It is scarcely necessary to say much in explanation of this legend. In the warning given to Akrisios, in the exposure of the child and his rescue, in his subjection to Polydektes, we have the main features of all the myths relating to the career of solar heroes. The name Polydektes is but an epithet of Hades, and the tyrant is only another Hades, who greedily seizes all that comes within his reach. To his brother Diktys, who necessarily befriends Danaê, he stands in the relation of Hades to Zeus. In Medusa, the mortal Gorgon, we have probably an image of the starlit night, solemn in its beauty, but doomed to die when the sun rises. Her immortal sisters represent the absolute darkness which it was supposed that the sun could not penetrate. The journey of Perseus to the land of the Graiai is manifestly the counterpart of the journey of Herakles to the land of the Hesperides. The Graiai represent the twilight or gloaming, the region of doubtful shadows and dim mists. The Libyan dragon is only another form of Python killed by Phœbus, of the dragon of the well of Arês slain by Cadmus, and of Vritra or Ahi pierced by the spear of Indra. The marriage of Andromeda, we have to mark, follows immediately on the slaughter of the monster who threatens her life; and we have already had evidence enough to show that these incidents are common to a large number of legends of all the Aryan nations. The weapons with which Perseus is armed have already come before us in Vedic and other traditions; and Perseus, so armed, is pre-eminently, as his name seems to denote, the destroyer of evil and noxious things. He is the counterpart of Indra, who is Vritrahan, or the bane[1] of Vritra, as Bellerophon is the bane of Belleros, and Argeiphontes is the bane or slayer of Argos with the myriad eyes.

Perseus and Herakles.

---

[1] Gr. φένω, φόνος, Eng. bane.

The conclusion is forced on us that the story of Perseus is only one of that large class of traditions in which one and the same person reappears under different names, and with some modification of his surroundings, and that the idea of this person has grown out of phrases which described originally the course of the sun in its daily or yearly round.

The myth of Theseus, the great hero of Athens, is even more transparent than that of Perseus, his counterpart at Argos. He is the son of Aigeus (Ægeus), the Athenian king (or, as some said, of Poseidon), and of Æthra, the pure air. But Aigeus himself is only Poseidon under a name denoting the dash of the waves on the shore. The tale which makes him the son of Poseidon goes on to say that during his childhood his father gave him the three wishes which appear again and again in Teutonic popular stories, and sometimes in a ludicrous form.[1] The favour of the sea deities to Theseus is also shown in the anecdote told by the geographer Pausanias, that when the Cretan king Minos cast doubts on his being a son of the sea-god, and bade him, if he were such, to bring up a ring thrown into the sea, Theseus dived, and reappeared not only with the ring, but with a golden crown which Aphroditê herself had placed upon his head. His youth was passed at Troizen, where he was to remain until he should be able to lift a great stone, under which his father had placed his sword and sandals. These have, of course, marvellous powers, and they are, in fact, the sandals of Hermes and the sword of Apollo Chrysaor. The very mode in which he has to win them is repeated in many stories, as in the tale of Herakles and Echidna, in the English legend of King Arthur,[2] and in the tradition which first took shape in the story of the Volsungs, and afterwards grew up into the Lay of the Nibelungs (or children of the mist). In this myth Odin, or Woden, driving to its

xxxiv. Theseus.

---

[1] *Myth. Ar. Nat.* ii. 62.
[2] *Popular Romances of the Middle Ages,* p 2.

hilt in an oak trunk the sword Gram, leaves it there for the man who should be able to draw it out. It is drawn out by Sigmund, and when afterwards broken it is forged afresh for Sigurd by Regin, the smith, who answers to the Hellenic Hephaistos.[1] Having recovered the sword and the sandals, Theseus goes to Athens. His journey is signalised by exploits which later mythographers, who assigned twelve labours to Herakles, regarded as six in number. Among them is the slaying of the giant Periphetes, of the robbers Sinis and Skeiron, of the sow of Krommyon,[2] and of the cruel Prokroustes (Procrustes), who tortured his victims by stretching out or cutting off their limbs to suit the length of the bed on which he laid them.[3]

Theseus now enters Athens, the dawn-city, with a long flowing robe, and with his golden hair tied gracefully behind his head. His soft beauty excites the mockery of some workmen, who pause in their task of building to jest upon the maiden who is unseemly enough to walk about alone. It is the story of Dionysos, Achilles, and Odysseus in woman's garb; but Theseus is mightier than they, and without saying a word he unspans the oxen of the builder's waggon, and hurls the vehicle as high above the temple pillars as these rose above the ground.[4] He is in the city which ought to be his home; but he may not rest there. In the war waged by Minos for the death of his son Androgeos, who had been slain on Attic soil, the Cretan king had been the conqueror. With the war had come famine and pestilence, and thus the men of Athens were driven to accept terms which bound them for nine years to send yearly a tribute of seven youths and seven maidens as victims to feed the Minotauros. Twice

Theseus and the tribute children.

---

[1] See p. 65, note 2. [2] *Myth. Ar. Nat.* ii. 63.
[3] This notion seems scarcely Greek. The story is told of the men of Sodom in the Arabian myth. (S. B. Gould, *Legends of Old Testament Characters*, i. 200.) But generally in stories in which Poseidon is prominent, the existence of Semitic influence is at least possible; and this possibility must be always taken into account in the examination of details, which seem to be non-Aryan in character. [4] Pausan. i. 19. 1.

had the black-sailed ship departed from the haven with its doomed freight, when Theseus offered himself, as one of the tribute children, to do battle with the monster. In this task he succeeds, but only through the aid of Ariadne, the daughter of Minos, as we shall find Iason in the Argonautic tradition performing the bidding of Aietes (Æetes) only because he has the help of his daughter Medeia. The thread which Ariadne places in his hand leads him through all the mazes of the murky labyrinth, the work of the cunning artist Daidalos; and when the monster who held his orgies within it is slain, she leaves her home with the man to whom she has given her love. But she herself must share the woes of all who love the bright sun-god. Beautiful as she is, she must be abandoned in Naxos, while Theseus goes upon his way, and in his stead comes the vine-crowned Dionysos, who places on her head a glittering diadem to shine among the everlasting stars. Theseus himself fulfils the doom which places him in the ranks of the Fatal Children. He forgets to hoist the white sails in token of victory, and Aigeus, seeing the black hue of the ship, throws himself into the sea, which after him is called the Egean.

In another adventure, Theseus is the enemy of the Amazons, mysterious beings who are slaughtered not only by Theseus, but by Herakles and Bellerophon. Of these Amazons, Antiope[1] becomes the wife of Theseus, and the mother of his son Hippolytos, who repulses the love of his stepmother Phaidra. Deceived by the lie of Phaidra, who plays the part of Potiphar's wife in the story of Joseph and of Anteia in that of Bellerophon, Theseus lays his curse on his son, and Hippolytos is slain by a bull which Poseidon sends up from the sea. But Hippolytos, like Adonis, is a being whom death cannot hold in his power, and Asklepios raises him to life, as in the Italian tradition Virbius, the darling of the goddess of the

Theseus and the Amazons.

[1] This name answers to Antigone.

groves, is brought back from the dead, and entrusted to the care of the nymph Egeria.

Theseus, indeed, like Herakles, is seen almost everywhere. He is one of the chiefs who sail in the divine Argo to recover the golden fleece. He joins the princes of Etolia in the hunt of the Kalydonian boar, and he takes part in the war of the Epigonoi before Thebes. But a more noteworthy myth is that which takes him, like Orpheus, into the nether world to bring back another Eurydike in the form of the maiden Persephone. His friend Peirithoös had already aided Theseus when he took Helen from Sparta and placed her in the hands of his mother Æthra, an act requited in the myth which takes Æthra to Ilion and makes her the bondmaid of Helen. The attempt of Peirithoös ends in disaster, and Theseus himself is shut up in Hades, until Herakles comes to his rescue. The presence of the Dioskoroi, the bright Asvins or horsemen of the Vedic hymns, complicates the story. These carry away Helen and Æthra; and when Theseus comes back from Hades he finds that Menestheus is king in Athens. He therefore sends his sons to Euboia, and hastens to Skyros, where the chief Lykomedes hurls him into the sea. But though his life thus closes in gloom, his children return at length with Æthra from Ilion, and are restored to their ancient inheritance.

Theseus and Peirithoös.

This is the Theseus who in the pages of the historian Thucydides consolidates the independent Attic Demoi, or boroughs, into one Athenian state, over which he rules as a constitutional sovereign, confining himself strictly to his constitutional functions.[1] The truth is that Thucydides could scarcely have framed such a picture, had not the Athenians, looking on Theseus as a real man, gradually made out his life to have been like that of real men, by leaving out of sight the marvellous tales which were told about him. Some even said that the

Theseus and the Athenian Commonwealth.

[1] Thuc. ii. 15. 3.

slayer of the Minotaur was not the same man as the founder of the Athenian commonwealth; but for this doubling of his person they had no more warrant than others had for stripping the story of Theseus, the son of Æthra, of all its wonderful incidents.

The story of Oidipous, a name with which we are more familiar in its Latin form, Œdipus, exhibited in the Bœotian Thebes, with sufficient differences of names and local colouring to insure belief in its complete originality, the legend of Perseus at Argos and of Theseus at Athens. His father Laios is said to have received from the oracle at Delphi the same warning which was given to Akrisios. The child, therefore, was exposed immediately after his birth on the side of the hill Kithairon (Cithæron); but some said that, like Dionysos and Perseus, he was placed in a chest which was cast into the sea. Like them he was rescued and taken to Corinth, where he passed as the son of Polybos and Merope. But the doom which was on Œdipus and his sire was not to be thus averted. As Œdipus was journeying from Corinth to Thebes, he met on the road an old man in a chariot, and was ordered to get out of the way. On his refusing to do so the old man struck him, and was instantly slain by Œdipus. Going on to Thebes, Œdipus found the city in great distress from drought and sickness, caused by the Sphinx, who, sitting on the brow of the hill over the town, uttered dark riddles, and who could not be overcome except by one who should expound them. Many had essayed the task, but all had failed, until Œdipus solved her enigmas. With a wild roar the Sphinx threw herself from the cliff, and the parched soil was refreshed with abundant rain. Œdipus must now receive the reward due to his prowess. It had been proclaimed that whoever should deliver the city from the Sphinx should marry the beautiful Iokastê, who had been the wife of Laios. Œdipus was thus wedded to his own mother, for he knew not who his parents were. Here probably, in

xxxv. Œdipus.

its earliest form, the myth ended; and thus far it resolves itself into simple phrases, which spoke of the thundercloud as looming over the city from day to day, while the waters remained imprisoned in its gloomy recesses; of the sun, as alone being able to understand her mysterious mutterings, and so to defeat her schemes; and of his union with the mother from whom he had been parted in his infancy. In Œdipus, therefore, there was the wisdom of Sisyphos, Tantalos, and Phœbus; in Iokastê the unfading youthfulness of Ushas.

But the Greek mind would dwell upon the moral aspects of the tale. There would be the fact of the parricide and the incest, and so a further narrative would say that Erinys, the revealer of secrets,[1] brought a plague on the city for the murder of Laios; that the Delphian oracle charged them to get rid of the guilty man; and that when, after long search, it turned out that Œdipus was the murderer, Iokastê slew herself in her bridal chamber, and Œdipus tore out his eyes that he might not see the misery which he had wrought. In other words, the sun has blinded and shrouded himself in vapour, clouds and darkness have closed in about him, and his gleaming orb is lost to sight. But if Iokastê, the tender mother who had watched over him at his birth, is gone, the evening of his life is not without its consolation. His sons fill the city with strife and bloodshed, his daughter Ismene wavers in her affection, but there yet remains one who will never forsake him, and whose voice shall cheer him to the last. Guided by Antigone, Œdipus draws nigh to the haven of rest. His feet tread the grass-grown pathway, over his head the branches sigh in the evening breeze; and when an Athenian in holy horror bids him begone from the sacred grove of the Eumenides, Œdipus replies that their sanctuary can never be violated by him. He is not merely their suppliant but their friend, and it is they who will guide him peace-

Œdipus and Theseus.

[1] See p. 59.

fully through the dark valley of the shadow of death. One prayer only he has to make, and this is that some one will bring Theseus, the Athenian king, to his side before he dies. The wish is realised, and we see before us perhaps the most striking of all mythical groups: the blinded Œdipus, sinking peacefully into his last sleep, as he listens to the voice of the man who rules in the city of the dawn-goddess Athênê, and feels the gentle touch of his daughter's hand, while over him wave the branches in the grove of the Eumenides, benignant always to him, and now reflecting more than ever the loveliness of the Eastern Saranyû. Then comes the signal of departure—the voice of the divine thunder, which now, as before when he encountered the Sphinx, Œdipus alone can understand. Without a murmur he makes ready to obey the summons, and with Theseus alone, the son of Sea and Air, by his side, calmly awaits the end. With wonderful—although, we can scarcely doubt, with unconscious—fidelity to the old mythical phrases, the poet tells us of the death of the hero who has passed away by no touch of disease, for sickness could not fasten on his glorious form, by no thunderstroke or sea-roused whirlwind, but guided by some heaven-sent messenger, or descending into the kindly earth where pain and grief can never affect him more.[1]

Such was the myth which the genius of Sophokles has embodied in, perhaps, the noblest of his tragedies. In the marriage of the mother with the child the poet discerned a gulf of infinite horror, the darkness of which might yet be lightened by the true human feeling, the genuine shrinking from impurity, which marks the unconscious and unwilling offenders in this awful drama. But this moral world was one into which the mythical phrases about the dawn and the sun never led the earlier poets who composed the hymns of the Rig Veda. Nor could they do so, for with them the myths had not reached

<small>Moral aspect of the myth of Œdipus and Iokastê.</small>

[1] Soph. *Œd. Col.* 1658-1663.

the secondary stage,[1] in which the meaning of the names employed has been wholly, or almost wholly, forgotten. They could speak of Indra in one hymn as the child of Dahanâ, in another as her husband. For them these beings had the feelings and affections of mankind; but they were not human. They were not clothed in definite human forms, and they might be regarded indifferently in one aspect or another without the intrusion of ethical considerations. But the marriage of Œdipus and Iokastê was significant to the Greek, not only as awakening a feeling of unspeakable horror, but as the result of a necessity against which it was impossible to struggle.[2] In utter unconsciousness of the misery in store for him, Œdipus is hurried on by a power which he cannot resist; and the notion of this strong compulsion was likewise the natural result of the old myth-making phrases. The sun cannot pause in his journey. He has no free action, and he must be greeted in the evening by the twilight from which he had been parted in the morning. The expressions used in speaking of this inevitable doom acquired, when applied to human action, a notion of moral necessity called by the Greeks Ananké, or of destiny, which they called Moira.

Of the names which occur in this myth, some explain themselves; of the meaning of others we must be content to express our ignorance. That Laios is a being who answers to Leto, the mother of Phœbus, and thus represents the darkness from which the sun springs, is manifest. The word itself reappears in that of the Vedic Dasyu, an enemy, a name frequently applied to Vritra, the enemy of Indra. It is seen again in the name Leophontes, applied to Hipponoos (known also as Bellerophon), the slayer of Leos, the foe, for with lion-slaying, with which some have connected it, it can have nothing to do, as in that case the word must have been Leontophontes. It reappears also in the word *despot*, which answers to the Sanskrit *dasapati*,

Œdipus and the Sphinx.

---

[1] See p. 9.   [2] See p. 61.

the lord or conqueror of the enemy.[1] The origin of the name Œdipus is far less clear. Of the Greeks, some thought that it denoted a man with swollen feet; others supposed that it meant the man who knew the riddle of the feet, this notion being perhaps suggested when in later times the Sphinx was imagined to have propounded one enigma, or puzzle, only, namely: 'What creature goes on four feet in the morning, on two during the day, and on three in the evening?' It must, however, be remembered that in the drama of Sophokles nothing is said of any riddle at all. The utterances of the Sphinx are there strictly dark sayings, or words uttered in a language which none can understand except Œdipus; and this riddle of the feet may have been suggested by the fancy that the termination of the name was really the word for foot.[2] Of the name Sphinx we can speak more positively. It means one who binds fast,[3] and who thus, as imprisoning the rain clouds, causes drought and sickness. The Sphinx, therefore, belongs to that class of beings of which the Vedic Ahi (Echidna), the throttling serpent of darkness, and Vritra, who hides the clouds in his secret caves, are the types. That the notion of the Sphinx came from Egypt, was the mistake of a later time. The Greeks had the idea and the name,[4] which is purely Aryan, for ages before Egypt was thrown open to Greek merchants or travellers. The Greek Sphinx has the head of a woman, with the body of a beast, the claws of a lion, the wings of a bird, and a serpent's tail, and might be represented in any attitude; but when Greeks came into Egypt, and found figures with a woman's head

---

[1] A cognate Greek form is λάσιος, rough, hairy. The name, therefore, had reference probably at first to the aboriginal inhabitants of countries brought under subjection by Aryan invaders. Compare Δαός, Davus, as a common name for slaves.

[2] If the word is related to the Greek οἶδα, the Latin *vidi*, the English *wit*, then the name Œdipus has exactly the same meaning with that of Sisyphos.

[3] Gr. σφίγγω, Lat. pango.

[4] This conclusion is strengthened by the existence of the cognate form Phix, answering to the Latin figo, fix-i, to fix.

joined to a lion's body, they called them naturally by the same name, and afterwards fancied that they had got the idea itself from the Egyptians. The notion of the riddles or mysterious utterances of the Sphinx was suggested, it can be scarcely necessary to say, by the mutterings and rumblings of the thunder, which men cannot understand. Œdipus alone knows the strange language, because he has the wisdom of Phœbus, the lord of light, and of the beings who, like Sisyphos, Tantalos, and Midas, share his nature or reflect his powers. The discomfiture of the Sphinx by Œdipus is, therefore, the victory of Indra, who smites his enemy Vritra, and immediately brings rain on the thirsting earth; and so we are told that the rain pours down on Thebes as soon as the Sphinx hurls herself from the cliff; and either the same or like effects follow the smiting of Python by Phœbus, and of Fafnir by Sigurd. In each case the imprisoned waters are let loose.

Œdipus dies in the sanctuary of the deities known as the Eumenides or gentle beings. It was commonly supposed that the name was given to them by way of Euphemism, or, in other words, for the purpose of averting their anger by ascribing to them qualities the very opposite to those which characterised them. We have, however, no reason for thinking that this was the case at the first. Indeed, it could not have been so when the forefathers of the Greeks departed from the common Aryan home in Central Asia. When the Greeks spoke of the Eumenides, they meant the beings whom they also called Erinyes; and there is no doubt that for the Greeks of the age of Æschylus and Sophokles the Erinys was an object of awful dread. But terrible though she be, she is still in the Iliad Eërophoitos, the being who wanders in the air, and thus reflects still the Vedic Saranyû,[1] the morning light, creeping or spreading with a flush over the sky. But, as we have seen, the old phrase, 'Saranyû will find you out,'

[1] See p. 59.

led naturally to the thought of a being who, as detecting wicked doers, was represented in gloomy and fearful colours. The Erinyes thus become Furies; but as being of a nature akin to that of Œdipus, they could not but welcome him to their home. The death of the Theban king is thus the death of the Sun in the Groves of the Dawn, which are otherwise called the Hyperborean gardens, and represent the fairy network of clouds which are the first to receive and the last to lose the light of the sun in the morning and the evening. Hence, although his last home is ushered in by peals of thunder, the Eumenides still are to him what their name proclaimed them to be, and his last moments full of a deep peace.

With the death of Œdipus the life of his devoted child Antigone draws towards its close. In this bright and beautiful being some have seen the light which sometimes flushes the eastern sky when the sun sinks to sleep in the west.[1] The name must undoubtedly be compared with such names as Anteia, Antiope, Antikleia; and the love of Antigone for Œdipus seems to answer to that of Selênê for Endymion or of Echo for the dying Narkissos (Narcissus). When in their unnatural strife the two sons of Œdipus slew each other, the body of Polyneikes, who had attacked the city with the aid of foreign foes, was cast forth unburied by the commands of Kreon, and in defiance of those commands, Antigone buried it. Kreon, therefore, ordered her to be buried alive; and when his son, Haimon, to whom she was betrothed, found her dead, he slew himself over her body. The motives and feelings which animated Antigone in her defiance of Kreon are elaborately analysed by Sophokles in the great drama which bears her name; but it is enough to say of them that they seem to belong rather to the Eastern than to the Western world. They may be a genuine portion of the Persian legend which Herodotos has clothed in a Greek

The children of Œdipus.

[1] Bréal, *Mythe d'Œdipe,* 21.

dress in the story of the Seven Conspirators.[1] But we cannot well avoid noticing the many instances in which those who mourn for mythical heroes and heroines taken away, put an end to their own lives by hanging. It is thus that Haimon ends his misery, when he finds that he has come too late to save Antigone ; it is thus that Iokastê hides her shame from the world ; it is thus that Althaia and Kleopatra follow Meleagros to the unseen land ; it is thus that Deianeira dies for the unwitting act which has brought about the death of Herakles. They are, in fact, choked or strangled ; and thus the death of these beings is strictly the victory of Ahi, the throttling or strangling snake ; and the tradition may have determined for the tragic poets the mode in which these luckless beings must die.

The main features of the myth of Œdipus are reproduced in that of the Arkadian Telephos. The former is the son of Laios, the darkness with its shaggy and re- pulsive garb, and of Iokastê, the dawn-light. The latter is the child of Aleos, the night in its blindness, and Augê, the brilliant morning. Œdipus is left to die on the slopes of Kithairon. Telephos is laid on the side of Mount Parthenion. There the babe is suckled by a doe (as Romulus and Remus are nourished by a wolf, and Cyrus in the Persian story by a dog), and brought up by the Arkadian king, Korythos. Like Œdipus, he goes to Delphi to learn who is his mother ; and at Delphi he is bidden to go to the Mysian king, Teuthras, in whose house he finds Augê, whom Teuthras promises to him as his wife. From Iokaste Augê differs only in this, that she will not wed Telephos, although she knows not who he is. Telephos thereon resolves to slay her, but Herakles reveals their relationship, and Telephos leads his mother back to her own land, as Perseus brought back Danaê. In another version of the myth he becomes the husband of Argiope, another of the goodly company of dawn maidens, and is

(Œdipus and Telephos.

[1] Herod. iii. 70 *et seq.*

himself king of Mysia when the Achaians come to Ilion to take vengeance for the misdeeds of Paris. In this war he is smitten by Achilles, and is told that only the man who inflicted the wound can heal it. The phrase Telepheia Traumata denotes wounds which cannot be cured; but Achilles was at length persuaded by Agamemnon to falsify the proverb by undoing his own work. He healed Telephos by applying the rust of the spear which had pierced him.[1]

It seems strange to find Paris amongst the ranks of the bright beings of the day or the dawn; and there is no doubt that as the seducer who takes away not merely Helen, but her treasures also, the treasures which play so prominent a part in the Volsunga Saga and the Nibelungenlied, Paris represents strictly the Vedic Pani, both in his name and in his acts. He is in this aspect the thief of the night, who brings destruction on his city and his kinsfolk; but the disintegration of myths produces strange results, and beings whose names and exploits point clearly to their solar origin, are found ranged by the side of others who are akin rather to the night and the darkness. There is no sort of doubt that Telephos, whose name, answering to Hekatos, Hekate, and Hekaergos, denotes the far-reaching action of the light, reflects the brightness which rests on the forms of Perseus, Kephalos, or Œdipus. It is even more transparently clear that Sarpedon, the king of Lykia (the realm of light), with the golden stream of Xanthos flowing through it, is the kinsman of Phœbus, Helios, and Surya. But Telephos and Sarpedon are both found among the allies of the Trojans in their struggle with the Achaians, the kinsfolk and the avengers of Helen. They are not indeed called allies of Paris, for after his crime at Sparta Paris has perhaps neither allies

Paris and his kinsfolk.

---

[1] The remedy is suggested by the equivocation of the homogeneous words *ios, ion*, denoting rust, poison, an arrow, and the violet colour, and the verb ἰάομαι, to heal.

nor friends; and thus the contrast is heightened between his career after his sojourn in the house of Menelaos and the brighter time which had preceded it. In Paris, therefore, it would seem that two conflicting notions are not so much combined as placed side by side. His exposure as an infant on Ida, his preservation, the splendid promise of his youth, his prowess and his gentleness, are features common to almost all the stories of popular heroes which we have thus far examined. The parallel might be pushed closer. In the later time he is sullen, capricious, and uncertain; but so also are Meleagros and Achilles, and the latter is not less indignant at the loss of Briseis than the former is at the demand for the surrender of Helen and her treasures. Either then we must make a distinction between Paris the Ilian hero and the subject of local Eastern myths, and Paris in his relations with the Western Achaians; or we must conclude that his beauty and brightness are those of the night and not of the day.[1] There is seemingly nothing beautiful or attractive in the Vedic Panis, the seducers of Saramâ, or perhaps in Laios or Aleos, the fathers of Œdipus and Telephos; but the moon-goddesses, who belong necessarily rather to the night than to the day, are all beautiful, whether it be Selênê, whose love is given to the Sun-god; or Asterodia, with her multitude of children, the countless stars; or Kalypso detaining Odysseus as a not-unwilling captive in her cave; or the queen of the Horselberg enticing Tanhaüser into her paradise; or the lady of Ercildoune drawing Thomas the Rimer away from the haunts of men; or Ursula moving placidly amongst her eleven thousand virgins. The solemn and sombre beauty of the night, lit up only by the stars, is embodied in the image of the mortal Gorgon Medusa; and

---

[1] The former is the view of Preller, *Griechische Mythologie*, ii. 413; the latter that of Professor Max Müller. Paris is also called γυναιμανής; but this feature marks the Vedic Indra as well as the gods of later Hindu mythology. The epithet Alexandros applied to Paris has an equivocal meaning; and it might be rash to lay much stress upon it.

we may, if we please, regard Paris as kinsman to any or all of these beings rather than of those who can belong only to the regions which lie between the morning dawn and the evening twilight.[1]

The story of the birth and infancy of Œdipus and Telephos is repeated substantially in that of Pelias and Neleus, whose mother, Tyro, becomes the wife of Poseidon. Her children are thus, like Aphroditê and Athênê, the children of the waters. They also, like the Dioskouroi or the Asvins, belong to the class of correlatives,[2] who sometimes appear as bound together in the closest friendship, and sometimes as fierce antagonists. Pelias and Neleus, like Œdipus and Telephos, are left to die; but a mare suckles the one, a dog the other, and they live to avenge the wrongs of their mother Tyro on the iron-hearted Sidêro, who had taken her place in the house of Salmoneus. The sequel of the tale, in which Pelias drives his brother from the throne of Iolkos, belongs to the legend of Iason and the Argonauts.

Pelias and Neleus.

A similar twin appear in the Latin Romulus and Remus, who, like Perseus and Dionysos, are exposed on the waters. A wolf,[3] drawn to their cries, suckles them till they are found by Acca Larentia, the wife of a shepherd named Faustulus. In his house they grow to be as stalwart and beautiful as any whose nature they share. But the friendship between the two is not life-long. Romulus delivers Remus from Amulius, into whose hands he had fallen, and slays the usurper; but in the building of the walls of Rome, Remus shows his contempt for the work, and is killed by his brother, who thus becomes sole king of the new city. After a reign the length of which is determined carefully by the thoroughly artificial chronology of the Roman kings,[4] Romulus is

Romulus and Remus.

---

[1] See further *Myth. of Ar. Nat.*, ii. 77 &c. *Tales of Ancient Greece*, Œnônê, p. 167.
[2] See p. 83.
[3] The Latin lupus is akin to the Greek λύκος. See note i. p. 106.
[4] See *History of Greece*, vol. i. p. 607.

taken away in a thunderstorm, wrapped in the clouds which are to bear him in a fiery chariot to the palace of Jupiter.[1]

From the legend of Romulus the myth of Cyrus differs only in the fact that it has gathered round an unquestionably historical person. But Charles the Great is as historical as Sir Walter Raleigh, while there is also a mythical Charles the Great, with whom the former has scarcely a feature in common. The difference is a matter of small importance, so long as we remember that we learn nothing of the history of Charles the Great from the traditions of his Paladins, and that the latter derive no sort of authority or credibility from the former.[2] So far as the myths are concerned, they teach us nothing either as to Cyrus or to Charles the Great; and when we come to analyse them, we find that they resolve themselves into the usual materials of all such narratives. As in the Theban story Laios is the enemy[3] of the devas or bright gods, so Astyages seems to be only a Grecised form of Asdahag, the Azidahaka or biting snake of Hindu legend, and the Zohak of the epic of Firdusi.[4] Like Akrisios in the Argive legend, he is told that if his daughter Mandane has a son, that child will live to be king in his stead. The babe is born; but the infant exposed is the dead offspring of the wife of the herdsman in whose hands Cyrus is placed with an order for his destruction. Under his roof the boy grows up with the true spirit of kingship. In the village games he plays the part of the despot so well that the father of a boy who has been scourged by his orders complains to Astyages of the insult. The inquiry which follows leads

<small>Cyrus.</small>

---

[1] It is quite possible that the twin Romulus and Remus are the creation of a late age. Remus and Romus are both an older form of Romulus; and the rivalry might be suggested, when the two forms of the same name were regarded as denoting two persons.
[2] See further *Myth. of Ar. Nat.* book i. ch. ix.
[3] Dasyu, Δήϊος. See p. 123.
[4] On this point Professor Max Müller and others express themselves without any doubt. I have qualified the statement, because it is now said that Assyrian cylinders exhibit the name in a form which can scarcely be reconciled with this interpretation. The point is not one of great moment.

to his detection, and Astyages takes an awful vengeance on Harpagos ; but his own fears are lulled by the Magi, who assure him that the election of Cyrus as king of the village boys fulfils the terms of the prophecy.[1] In due time Harpagos requites Astyages for his cruelty by inciting Cyrus to revolt. The sequel is merely an institutional legend, of much the same value as the legend of the establishment of the Median monarchy by Deiokes, in whom we have apparently the Dahak, or biter, of Hindu mythology.[2]

To the same class with Romulus, Cyrus, Œdipus, Cadmus and others, we may assign the Cretan king Minos.

Minos and Manu.

We have already seen that Cretan myths bring us very near to Semitic ground, and that therefore we have to move warily in the attempt to analyse legends belonging or supposed to belong to this island. But his name is unquestionably Aryan. He is pre-eminently and simply *man*, the measurer or thinker, the Indian Manu ; and if in the Hindu legend the lawgiver Manu enters the ark with the seven rishis or sages at the time of the great deluge, so is Minos the father of Deukalion, in whose days the floods are let loose in the West. Minos, therefore, as representing the whole family of man, becomes not merely like Manu a giver of earthly codes, but a judge of the nether world. In the Eastern story, Manu is the builder of the ark ; and this notion may perhaps have led

[1] In the *Œd. Tyr.* of Sophokles, 972, the prophecies about Œdipus are treated in a precisely similar fashion. We have already seen how closely the sentiments put into the mouth of Antigone in reference to the burial of her brother's body correspond with those which we find in Herodotos, iii. 70 *et seq.* in the story of the Seven Conspirators. It is not easy to withstand the inference that Sophokles may have received both stories from the historian.

[2] The story of Chandragupta agrees essentially with that of Cyrus. To save him from a chief who has slain his father, his mother places him in a vase and leaves him at the entrance of a cattle-pen. A bull, named Chando, guards the child, and a herdsman, noting the wonder, rears him as his own. Chandragupta, like Cyrus, takes to playing the part of king ; but instead of scourging his companions, he has their hands and feet struck off with axes made of goats' horns for blades, and with sticks for handles. The lopped limbs are restored whole at his word when the games are over. Max Müller. *Sanskr. Lit.* 290. See also *Myth. of Ar. Nat.* ii. 84.

to the idea of the naval greatness and power of Minos. But Minos in the Western tradition is the son either of Zeus and Europê, the heaven and the morning, or of Lykastos and Ida, the brilliant heaven-god and the earth his bride;[1] and as such, he boasted that whatever he desired, the gods would do. We are now brought to a series of incidents, which are seemingly of Phenician growth. At the wish of Minos, who promises to offer it in sacrifice, Poseidon sends up a bull from the sea. Minos offered one of his own cattle in its stead; and Poseidon not only made the bull mad, but filled Pasiphaê, the wife of Minos, with a strange love for the monster. From these springs the Minotauros, who in his den hidden far away within his labyrinth of stars devours the tribute children sent from the city of Athênê, until he falls by the sword of Theseus,[2] Minos, we are told, met his end in the distant evening land, where the sun goes down.[3] He is killed in Sicily by king Kokalos, the eyeless gloom of night.[4]

Pominent amongst the allies of the Trojans in their war with the Achaians, are the solar heroes of Lykia, the land of light, Sarpêdôn and Glaukos. The former is the creeping light of heaven, and he is doomed to die young. The charge of avenging him he leaves to his friend Glaukos, the sun-god in his brilliant strength. But although Sarpêdôn must fall, no decay must be allowed to mar his beauty. The tears of Zeus fall like drops of blood from the heaven in his grief for the death of his child, and Phœbus is charged to bathe the body in Simoeis, and wrap it in ambrosial robes; while Sleep and Death, Thanatos and

Sarpêdôn. Glaukos.

---

[1] See p. 41. [2] See p. 123.
[3] Preller, *Griechische Mythologie*, ii. 122.
[4] We can scarcely fail to connect this name with that of Horatius Cocles, and with the Latin adjective *cæcus*, blind, a word made up of *ka*, a particle denoting separation, and the root *oc*, which we find in the Latin *oculus*, the German *Auge*, and the English eye: *half, halt*, and probably the Latin *cælebs* being formed in the same way. (Bopp, *Comparative Grammar*, § 308.) The name may also be akin to Cacus, with which we shall have to deal in the Latin myth of Recaranus.

Hypnos, are bidden to bear it away to his Lykian home, which they reach just as Eos is spreading her rosy light through the sky. According to the poets of the Iliad, his cairn was raised high to keep his name alive amongst his people. But another version of the myth spoke of him as risen again; and this earlier stage of the story is seen in the legend of Memnon in the same poem. This Ethiopian chief is the son of Eos, the morning: and the phrase was so transparent that he must be made to rise again. On his death his mother weeps tears of dew, until her prayers constrain Zeus to bring him up from the nether world; and two flocks of birds meet in the air and fight over Memnon's funeral sacrifice, until some of them fall as victims on the altar. Of Memnon's head the story was told that it retained the prophetic power of the living Helios or of Surya. The story is found in the myth of the Teutonic Mimir, and it might have been related of Kephalos, the head of the sun.

Kephalos, as we have already seen,[1] is the hero of the legend of Prokris, the daughter of Hersê, the dew, and Erechtheus the mythical king of Athens. Her father, whose name occurs also in the form Erichthonios, is called a son of Hephaistos and Gê, the fire and the earth. Like Kekrops (Cecrops), he was born in the form of a serpent and was brought up by Athênê. The birthplace of Prokris is the city of the dawn; and while her mother is the dew, she herself is simply a dewdrop.[2] The jealousy of Eos prompted the temptation of Kephalos, who, going away from Prokris, whose love he had won, re-

Kephalos and Prokris.

[1] See p. 22.
[2] It is wonderful that such a man as Preller could regard the name Prokris as an abbreviated form of ἡ προκεκριμένη, on the ground that πρόκριν is used in the Hesiodic poems for πρόκρισιν. But Prokne, the other form of Prokris, cannot possibly be referred to ἡ προκεκριμένη. Preller (*Griechische Mythologie*, ii. 145) further adduces the phrase, τὴν περὶ πάντων Ζεὺς Κρονίδης τίμησε, as applied to Hekate, in support of his etymology, and of his belief that Prokris is the moon. But far from being honoured, Prokris is throughout neglected and despised, and at last killed: and the notion of her being the moon fails to explain any one of all the incidents of the myth.

turned in disguise (as Sigurd in the Volsung tale returns to Brynhild),[1] and having won her love, again in his altered form revealed himself to her as her husband. In an agony of grief and shame, Prokris fled away to Crete, and there dwelt in deep sorrow, until at length she was visited by Artemis, who gave her the spear which never missed its mark, and the dog who never failed to track his prey. So with the hound and the spear Prokris came back to Athens, and was there always the first in the chase. Filled with envy at her success, Kephalos begged for the spear and dog, but Prokris refused to give them except in return for his love. This Kephalos gave, and immediately discovered that it was his wife, Prokris, who stood before him. Fearing still the jealousy of Eos, Prokris kept near Kephalos, until his spear smote her as she lay hidden in the thicket. Bitterly grieving at her death, Kephalos left Athens, and aided Amphitryon in ridding his land of noxious beasts. Then journeying westwards, he reached the Leukadian cape, where his strength failed him and he fell into the sea. Such is the simple tale which relates the loves of the sun and the dew, loves marred by the rivalry of Eos, the ever youthful bride of the immortal but decrepit Tithonos, from whose couch, drawn by the gleaming steeds Lampos and Phaethon, she rises into heaven to announce to the gods and to mortal men the coming of the sun. We have seen that in the very phrase which speaks of the love of Eos for the sun we have the groundwork for her envy of Prokris; and so again, when we are told that though Prokris breaks her faith, yet her love is still given to the same Kephalos, and only given to him, we have a myth which could not fail to spring up from phrases telling how the dew seems to reflect many suns which are yet the same sun. That this myth might take a form which, interpreted by the conditions of human life, would state a mere impossibility, is strikingly shown by the legend, already noticed, of Krishna and the

[1] See p. 7.

dark giant Naraka. But the very extravagance of the tale exhibits only the more strikingly its marvellous truthfulness to the outward world of phenomena.

The great work of Grimm has placed beyond all doubt the close connexion of Greek, and indeed every other form of Aryan, tradition with that of the Teutonic and Scandinavian nations. None probably will be found to question now the close affinity of Teutonic or German with Norse mythology; but the tests which Grimm applied to the subject nearly fifty years ago are precisely those which have been applied by comparative mythologists with such wonderful results to the traditions of the Greeks and the Hindus. The first of these is the affinity of the dialects spoken by all Teutonic and Scandinavian tribes; the second is their joint possession of terms relating to religious worship; the third is found in the identity of mythical notions and nomenclature, which can be traced in a comparison of their popular traditions. But Grimm saw further the greater prominence of certain characteristics in one system as contrasted with another, and he drew the conclusion that where these characteristics had faded into the background, this had not been their condition from the first. Thus the gods of the whole Aryan world eat, drink, and sleep; but beings who eat, drink, and sleep must die. The Northern mythologies kept this notion before the people with startling clearness; the Southern disguised it, and practically put it out of sight, but it was there nevertheless. The Olympian gods feast on ambrosia, and are refreshed by nectar, the Soma of the Hindu;[1] but they can be wounded and suffer pain, they may hunger and thirst; and to the Norse mind the inference was oppressively plain. The beautiful Balder has his yearly death and resurrection; but the time will come when the great enemy of the gods will be let loose, and Asgard shall be desolate. This enemy is Loki, the fire-god, who, in punish-

[1] See p. 81.

ment of his misdeeds, is put in chains like Prometheus, and whose release just before the coming on of the twilight of the gods is in close agreement with the release of the chained Prometheus, by whom the empire of Zeus is to be brought to an end. It is true that the Northern Odin or Woden is the All-Father, from whom men may expect substantial justice; in the Promethean tradition Zeus is an arbitrary tyrant, with a special hatred for mankind. But it would, perhaps, be difficult to determine how far the purely spiritual colouring thrown over the myth is due to the mighty genius of Æschylus; nor is it a hard task to imagine a Prometheus in whom we should see simply a counterpart of the malignant and mischievous Northern fire-god. On the other hand, even in the case of Loki himself, there linger to this day among the common people many conceptions in which he is taken by turns for a beneficent and for a hurtful being—for sun, fire, giant, or devil.

In the myth of Balder he appears in his most malignant aspect. The golden-haired Balder is the most beautiful of all the dwellers in Valhalla; but, like Sarpêdôn and Memnon, he is doomed to an early death, a death which takes place yearly at the winter solstice. In the oldest English traditions Balder appears as Bäldäg, Beldeg, a form which would lead us to look for an old High German Paltac. Paltac is not found, but we have Paltar. It is possible, therefore, that the two parts of the word may be separated, and thus the name Balder may be connected with that of the Slavonic Bjelbog, Balbog, the pale or white shining god, the bringer of the days, the benignant Phoibos. This conclusion is strengthened by the fact that the old English Theogony gives him a son, Brond, the torch of day, and that Balder himself was also known as Phol. The being by whom he is slain is Hödr, a blind god of enormous strength, whose name may be traced in the forms Hadupracht, Hadufians, and many more, to the Chatumerus of Tacitus, and which may perhaps be connected with that

XXXVI. Balder.

of the Greek Hades.¹ He is simply the demon of darkness triumphing over the lord of light. As in the case of Sarpêdôn and Memnon, we have two forms of the myth. The one ends with his death; the other brings him back from the under-world.² The former agrees strictly with the primitive notion that the heavenly bodies were created afresh every day. The cause of his death is related in a poem of the older Edda, called Balder's Dream. In this poem Odin goes as Wegtam, or the Wanderer, to the house of the Völa, or wise woman, whose knowledge exceeds even his own: but his efforts to save Balder from his doom are vain. All created things are called upon to swear that they will do Balder no harm: but the mistletoe is forgotten, and of this plant Loki puts a twig into the hand of Balder's blind brother Hödr, who, using it as an arrow, unwittingly slays the bright hero, while the gods are practising archery with his body as a mark. Soon, however, another brother of Balder avenges his death by slaying his involuntary murderer.³

The shooting of arrows at beings pre-eminent for their brightness and their beauty is an incident common to a vast number of myths, and cannot in fact be considered as peculiar to the Aryan tribes. When Isandros and Hippolochos were disputing for the Lykian throne, it is determined that the kingdom shall belong to the man who could shoot a ring from the breast of a child without hurting him. Laodameia, the mother of Sarpêdôn, offers her son for the venture. This is the foundation of the story of William Tell, which is now on all hands acknowledged to have no historical basis whatever; and it is enough to say of it, that the hat set upon a pole before which all passers-by were to do obeisance is another form of the golden image set up to be worshipped on the plain

_{Cloudeslee and Tell.}

---

[1] Grimm (*Deutsche Mythologie*), *Teutonic Mythology*, i. 246. English translation by J. S. Stallybrass.
[2] See p. 72.
[3] Balder belongs to the class of murdered and risen gods. On these, see Bunsen, *God in History*, ii. 458. See also *Myth. of Ar. Nat.* ii. 96.

of Dura; and that, as in the story of the Three Children, so here the men who achieve the work of Swiss independence are three in number. The story was familiar to English hearers in the ballad of Clym of the Clough, in which William Cloudeslee, whose name attests his birth in the cloud-land, is compelled, under penalty of death, to hit an apple on the head of his son, a child of seven years old, at a distance of six paces. In the Swiss tale the tyrant who gives this sentence is slain: in the English story the king expresses his hope that he himself may not serve as a mark for Cloudeslee's arrows. But Cloudeslee with Adam Bell and Clym of the Clough form another group of three, answering to the Swiss trio.[1] We may thus look on Tell as the last reflexion in Europe of the sun-god, whether we call him Indra, or Apollo, or Ulysses.[2]

We have seen in the myth of Phœbus Apollo how the newly-born god reaches his full strength and majesty as soon as the golden sword, from which he has his title Chrysâôr, is girded to his side. This mighty bound from helplessness to power is exhibited, as we might expect, still more strikingly in the expressions applied to the Vedic Vishnu.[3] Regarded strictly, Vishnu is nothing but a name for the supreme and all-powerful god, and as such it is manifestly used in many passages of the Rig Veda. Thus he is both Indra and Agni. He is a son of Prajâpati, the lord of light; and he is also Prajâpati himself. So interchangeable, indeed, are the names of all the gods, that we are left in no doubt as to the real monotheism[4] of the Aryan conquerors of India. But this monotheistic conviction never interfered with the use of language

XXXVII.
Vishnu.—
The Dwarf
Incarnation.

[1] Grimm remarks that Cloudeslee's Christian name and Bell's surname together give us the two names of the Swiss hero. *Deutsche Mythologie*, 355. For other forms of the legend see *Myth. of Ar. Nat.* ii. 100.
[2] Max Müller, *Chips from a German Workshop*, ii. 233.
[3] Mr. Dowson, in his *Classical Dictionary of Hindu Mythology*, assigns the name to a root *ish*, to pervade. It may be compared with the Greek ἴς, βία, βίος, and the Lat. vis, vita.
[4] *Myth. of Ar. Nat.* vol. ii. p. 102.

which had no meaning except with reference to the phenomena of the outward world: and in this aspect Vishnu is pre-eminently the being who traverses the heaven in three strides—these strides being regarded by some as denoting his manifestation in the form of fire on the earth, of lightning in the atmosphere, and of the sun in the heaven —in other words, as showing his identity with the Trimurtti of Agni, Vayu, and Surya. It is far more likely, as other commentators asserted, that they refer to the rising, culmination, and setting of the sun; and this conclusion seems to be placed beyond doubt by the myth of the Dwarf Incarnation with which the name of Vishnu is most closely associated. This incarnation cannot fail to suggest a comparison with the myth of the maimed Hephaistos. The fire at its birth is weak, its flame puny; and it was an obvious thought that none could say how mighty a power lay behind this seeming helplessness. Thus when Bali, the great enemy of the gods, terrifies Indra, the latter beseeches Vishnu to take the form of a dwarf, and so to deceive the foe. Vishnu accordingly obtains from the Asuras as much ground as he can lie upon, or as much as he can cover in three strides. Having obtained this boon, he 'assumed a miraculous form, and with three paces took possession of the worlds.' With one step he occupied the whole earth, with a second the eternal atmosphere, with a third the sky. In later traditions, Bali has no sooner granted the seemingly moderate request of Hari, the dwarf, than the body of Vishnu expands until it fills the whole universe, and Bali is bound with the nooses of Varuna. In some, again, the dwarf appears as the child Kumâra, the son of Aushasî, the daughter of Ushas, the dawn, and thus we find ourselves dealing with phrases which the Hindu commentators knew to be mere phrases, no disparagement being done to Varuna or other deities by saying that it is their part to do the bidding of Vishnu.

'King Varuna and the Asvins wait on the decree of this

ruler, attended by the Maruts: Vishnu possesses excellent wisdom, which knows the proper day, and with his friend opens up the cloud.

'The divine Vishnu, who has chosen companionship with the beneficent Indra, himself more beneficent, the wise god has gratified the Arya.'[1]

So when Indra is about to smite Vritra, he beseeches the aid of Vishnu.

'Friend Vishnu, stride vastly: sky, give room for the thunderbolt to strike; let us slay Vritra and let loose the waters.' *Vishnu and Indra.*

But for all this Vishnu is described as making his three strides through the power of Indra.

'When, Indra, the gods placed thee in their front in the battle, then thy dear steeds grew.

'When, thunderer, thou didst by thy might slay Vritra, who stopped up thy streams, then thy dear steeds grew.

'When by thy force Vishnu strode three steps, then thy dear steeds grew.'[2]

To heighten the seeming inconsistency, we are told that mortal man cannot comprehend the majesty of the being who thus owes his greatness to another.

'No one who is being born, or has been born, has attained, O divine Vishnu, to the furthest limit of thy greatness.'

The nature of the mythical Vishnu is thus as clear as that of Helios or Selênê. He dwells in the aerial regions, where the many-horned and swiftly moving cows abide.

'Here that supreme abode of the wide-stepping vigorous god shines intensely forth.'

But the worship of Vishnu is noteworthy chiefly for the symbols employed in it—the upright and oval emblems denoting the active and passive powers in nature. This worship might easily assume the most gross *The worship of Vishnu.* and horrible forms; and there is no doubt that it became

---

[1] R. V. i. 156. Muir, *Sansk. Texts*, part iv. p. 66.
[2] R. V. viii. 12. Muir, *Sansk. Texts*, part iv. p. 77.

far more debasing and corrupting among the Semitic tribes than among the Hindus. In the Jewish temple itself under the idolatrous kings these emblems appeared as the Ashera on the circular altar of Baal-peor, the Priapos of the Jews. For this Ashera the women wove hangings, as the Athenian maidens embroidered the Peplos for the ship presented to Athênê at the great Dionysiac festival. Before this emblem at the winter solstice they wept for Tammuz, the fair Adonis, and rejoiced when he rose again. Hence in the Ashera we have the symbol under which the sun, invoked with a thousand names, has been worshipped throughout the world as the restorer of the powers of nature after its conquest by the deadly winter. As such, also, the symbol became a protecting power, like the Palladion, which guarded the city of Troy : the rod or staff of wealth placed in the hands of Hermes,[1] the budding Thyrsos of the worshippers of Dionysos, and the Seistron of the Egyptian priests. The rod thus grew into a tree of life, and in conjunction with the oval emblem became the stauros or cross of Osiris, the Egyptian symbol of immortality, the god himself being crucified to the tree which denoted his fructifying power.[2] In the form of a ring inclosing a four-spoked cross this emblem is found everywhere, and especially in the legends which turn on the rings of Freya, Hilda, Venus, or Aphroditê. In a late version of these traditions given by Matthew of Westminster, Roger Hoveden, and other chroniclers, a newly married youth places his wedding ring on the statue of Venus, and finds to his dismay not only that he cannot dislodge it from her stony finger, but that the goddess herself claims to stand to him in the relation of Aphroditê to Adonis. In its distinctively Christian form, the myth substituted the Virgin Mary for Aphroditê, and the knight whose ring she refuses to surrender looks on himself as betrothed to the mother

---

[1] *Hymn to Hermes*, 529.
[2] *Myth. of Ar. Nat.* ii. 115, and Appendix C.

of God, and dedicates himself to her by taking the monastic vows. When we add that from its physical characteristics the Ashera, which the Greeks called the Phallos, suggested the emblem of the serpent, we have the key to the tree and serpent worship, which has given rise to much not altogether profitable speculation. It is scarcely necessary to say that the tree thus worshipped was not the full-foliaged growth of the forest, but simply an upright stake or post, which sometimes sprouted, but never assumed the form of a freely growing tree, while the serpent in this aspect was certainly not the deadly creature which is commonly supposed to be denoted in this cultus. The Phallic serpent was never regarded with dread, or looked upon as having any but a beneficent and life-giving power ; and the tree never had any more branches or foliage than a Maypole, with which it is in fact identical. The emblems employed in the worship of Vishnu represent, therefore, the sun and the earth, the Linga denoting the former in its active life-giving power, the Yoni typifying the earth as the recipient of his fertilising heat. The latter thus becomes an ark, containing all the generations of all living things, and this ark reappears in the Argo which shelters all the Achaian chieftains in their search for the Golden Fleece. This mystic vessel, which is endowed with the powers of reason and speech, is seen again in the shell of Aphroditê, and in the ship borne to the Parthenon at Athens in the solemn procession of the Panathenaic festival. It is also the vessel of which Tacitus speaks as the ship of Isis in the worship of the Teutonic Suevi; and this ship is also the vehicle of the earth-goddess Herth or Aerth, which was covered with a robe not to be touched with profane hands.[1] In Hindu and Egyptian mythology it takes the form of the Lotus, the symbol of the earth and its fecundation. We are thus brought to the multitude of myths which speak of cups and drinking vessels inexhaustible in their supplies. Among

[1] See further *Myth. of Ar. Nat.* ii. 109.

these is the horn of Amaltheia, the nurse of Zeus in the cave of Diktê, of Bran, and Ceridwen, and Huon of Bordeaux; the table of the Ethiopians;[1] the wishing quern of Frodi;[2] the lamp of Allah-ud-deen; and the well of Apollon Thyrsis in Lykia.[3] To these must be added the goblet of the sun bestowed in the Persian legend on Jemshid, and the Sangreal brought into Europe, it is said, by Joseph of Arimathæa.[4]

In most of the shapes assumed by the myths connected with the symbols employed in the worship of Vishnu, no idea is more prominent than that of a mysterious knowledge; and the possession of a knowledge hidden from the profane was supposed to be imparted to the initiated in the great mysteries of the ancient world. The nature and extent of this knowledge have been long and earnestly debated; but of the general character of the Eastern mysteries we can be under no doubt. The wailing of the Hebrew women at the death of Tammuz, the crucifixion and resurrection of Osiris, the adoration of the Babylonian Mylitta, the Sacti ministers of Hindu temples, the cross and crescent of Isis, the rites of Baal-Peor, are features which speak for themselves, when we consider the great festivals or mysteries of Phenicians, Assyrians, Egyptians, and Hindus. We have no reason for supposing that those of the Hellenic tribes were essentially different in their character; and it is clear that in these mysteries the effects of foreign influence would be far more deeply felt than in myths which did not so immediately touch the religious instincts of mankind. There is no doubt that the Hellenic mysteries were not less dramatic than those of the East. Every act of the great Eleusinian festival reproduced incidents in the legend of Demeter. The processions of Athênê and Dionysos exhibited the same symbols which were seen in the worship of Vishnu, Isis, and Hertha; and from the

Eastern and Western Mysteries.

---

[1] Herod. iii. 18. [2] Thorpe, *Translation of Sæmund's Edda,* ii. 150.
[3] Paus. vii. 21. 6. [4] *Myth. of Ar. Nat.* ii. 122.

substantial agreement of rites we may infer the substantial identity of doctrines.

When from Vishnu we are led naturally to the sun-gods of the later Hindu mythology, we find the same flexibility of attributes which marks the deities of the Rig Veda. In the Mahâbhârata, Krishna, the most prominent perhaps of the later gods, is himself Vishnu, and, as such, performs his special feats.

<small>xxxviii. Krishna.</small>

'Thou, Krishna, of the Yadava race, having become the son of Aditi, and being called Vishnu, the younger brother of Indra, the all-pervading, becoming a child, and vexer of thy foes, hast by thy energy traversed the sky, the atmosphere, and the earth in three strides.'[1]

Krishna is thus Hari, the Dwarf. He is also Govinda, the son of the bull, and the protector of cattle; and, again, he is the son of Hari, from whose black hair he is said to spring. At the same time he is called 'the soul of all, the omniscient, the all, the all-knowing, the producer of all,' and he is made to speak of himself as the maker of the Rudras and the Vasus, as having Dharma (righteousness) as his 'beloved first-born mental son, whose nature is to have compassion upon all creatures.' 'In his character,' he says, 'I exist among men, both past and present, passing through many varieties of mundane existence. I am Vishnu, Brahma, Indra, and the source as well as the destruction of things. While all men live in unrighteousness, I, the unfailing, build up the bulwark of righteousness, as the ages pass away.' So, clearly, may even Krishna be simply a name for the One Ever-living God.

Like the Hellenic and Teutonic solar heroes generally, Krishna is one of the fatal children. Kamsa, the tyrant of Madura, warned that his sister's son shall deprive him of his throne and his life, seeks to slay her, but is pacified by her husband's promise to deliver all her children into his hands. Six children are thus sur-

<small>The birth and infancy of Krishna.</small>

[1] Muir, *Sansk. Texts*, part iv. p. 118.

rendered and killed; but the tyrant nevertheless shuts up Devaki and her husband in prison. When the seventh child was about to be born, Devaki prays that this one at least may be spared; and it is rescued by Bhavani, the Eileithyia of the Hindu.[1] But the suspicions of Kamsa are still active; and when Devaki was to become a mother for the eighth time, he is eager to destroy her offspring. As the hour drew near, her form became more beautiful and brilliant. The dungeon was filled with a heavenly light, like that of the golden shower which visited Danae in her prison house,[2] and the air rang with the music of the heavenly choir, as the gods with Brahma and Siva at their head poured forth their gladness in song. The report of these marvels strains the fears of Kamsa to the highest pitch; but while he is dreading the future, Krishna is born, like Vishnu, with four arms,[3] and with all the attributes of that god. In the words of the Vishnu Purana—

'On the day of his birth the quarters of the horizon were irradiate with joy, as if more light were diffused over the whole earth. The virtuous experienced more delight; the strong winds were hushed, and the rivers glided tranquilly when Janárddana was about to be born. The seas with their melodious murmurings made the music, while the spirits and the nymphs of heaven danced and sang.'[4]

For a moment the veil is lifted from the eyes of his parents, who behold the deity in all his majesty; but when it falls on them again, they see only the helpless babe in the cradle. The father then hears the voice of an angel, bidding him take the child to Gokala, the land of cows, where in the house of Nanda he would find a new-born maiden, and charging him to bring back this child, and to leave Krishna in her place. To enable him to do this, the fetters fall off from his limbs,

---

[1] Slightly modified, Bhavani is the more modern name Bhowonee. It is akin to the Greek φύω, φύ-σις, the Latin fu-i, &c.
[2] See p. 111.
[3] These four arms may be compared with the four-spoked wheel of Ixion.
[4] *Myth. of Ar. Nat.* ii. 134, note 1.

and the prison doors open of their own accord. Having done as the angel told him, he returns to the dungeon, when the doors close again, and the chains fasten themselves on his wrists. The cry of the infant thus brought back instead of Krishna rouses the warders, who carry the tidings of its supposed birth in the dungeon to the king. At midnight Kamsa enters the prison, and Devaki vainly beseeches mercy for the babe. But before Kamsa can slay it, the child slips from his grasp, and he hears the voice of Bhavani, who tells him that his destroyer has been born, and placed already beyond his reach. In a fever of rage and fear, the tyrant summons his council, who advise him to order the death of all the children under two years old throughout his dominions. The order is issued, but it is ineffectual. Meanwhile, Krishna is exposed to other dangers. The demon Putana, taking up the child, offered him her breast to suck, the doom of all who are so suckled being instant death; but Krishna draws it with such force as to drain Putana of all life. As the child grew up, he became the darling of the milk-maidens. In these some have seen the stars of the morning sky; and it may be noted that Krishna is described as stealing their milk, a phrase which may perhaps point to the putting out of the light of the stars by the sun, and which seems to be illustrated by the Greek myth which connected the formation of the Milky Way with the nursing of Herakles by Hêrê. The maidens resented the wrong done to them; but Krishna opened his mouth, and revealed his full splendour, so that they saw him receiving the adoration of all created things.

The myth goes on to tell us that in the harvest feast of Bhavani, the Greek Dêmêtêr, the Gopias, or milk-maidens, pray that they may become the brides of Krishna;[1] Krishna and and as playing on his lute in their company, he the Gopias. becomes Apollon Nomios, while each maiden supposes that she alone is his partner in the dance—a fancy which

[1] *Myth. of Ar. Nat.* ii. 135, note 2.

we have already seen in the story of the giant Naraka. In the Bhagavata Purana, we are told that Brahma, wishing to test the reality of the incarnation of Vishnu in Krishna, came upon him as he and Balarama were sleeping among the shepherd youths and maidens, and took away all, leaving Krishna and Balarama alone. Krishna, however, created a like number of maids and maidens so precisely resembling those which had been stolen away, that when Brahma returned at the end of the year, he was astounded to see before him the troop which he thought that he had broken up. When he went to the prison, he found that all his captives were still there; and the power of Krishna was thus placed beyond question.

Krishna after this slew the Dragon, or Black Snake, Kalinak, the old serpent with the thousand heads, who, like the dragons at Thebes and Pytho, or like Vitra and the Sphinx, poisons or shuts up the waters. In the fight Krishna frees himself from its coils, and stamps upon its heads until he has crushed them all. His death, we are told, was brought about by a huntsman, who shot him in the foot with an arrow, thinking that he was aiming at a gazelle. The god had placed himself among the bushes, so that his heel, in which alone, like Achilles, he was vulnerable, was exposed, and he thus incurs the doom of Balder, Adonis, and Osiris.

Krishna and Kalinak.

Osiris is the same god as Ra, the Sun, and the greatest of the Egyptian deities.[1] Egyptian mythology lies strictly beyond the limits of our present subject; but although we are not committed to theories which rest on evidence obtained from the land of the Nile valley, it is yet worth noting, that while some of the Egyptian myths seem to have a more direct reference to

Osiris.

---

[1] The Egyptian Amen-ra, or Kneph, the ram-headed and horned god, who reappears in the horned Zagreos, is the deity known to the Greeks as Zeus Ammon, whose name they erroneously connected with the sand, *ammos*, with which his temple in the oasis was surrounded. Of this Ammon or Amoun, Alexander the Great proclaimed himself the son; and as such, placed the ram-horns on his head upon his coins.

facts of astronomy than may be found generally in Greek tradition, they had their foundation, as a whole, in phrases which described the phenomena of the outward world in all its parts. The origin of the Egyptian people and of their civilisation is a question into which we cannot enter; but probably none will be found to assert that the Egyptian people come from the stock which has produced the Aryan nations of Europe and Asia. The character of this wonderful valley would go far towards accounting for the forms assumed by the religion, laws, and customs, which grew up within it; and it is enough for us to mark that their growth betrays no working of Aryan influences, while in their turn the institutions and traditions of the Aryan tribes were but little affected by those of Egypt. That there was some interchange of thought as well as of commerce in prehistoric ages between Greeks and Egyptians, is proved by the presence of Egyptian words in a dress which seems altogether Hellenic and Aryan; and such words as Harpokrates and Rhadamanthys justify a like inquiry to that which names like Melikertes, Athamas, and Kadmos, warrant, when we deal with the myths and legends of Bœotia. Speaking generally, however, we may safely say that between the main body of Greek and Egyptian myths there was no direct connexion, and no points of likeness which cannot be explained by the working of independent minds on the same facts or the same materials. Io, for instance, was the horned maiden of the Greeks, and her calf-child was Epaphos; but the Egyptians worshipped the calf-god Apis, and had Isis as their horned maiden. There was nothing here which might not have grown up independently in Egypt and in Greece; nor is any notion of borrowing needed to account for the likeness of myths suggested by the horns of the new moon. But after Egypt had been thrown open to Greek commerce, the Greeks were so impressed with the grandeur of the country and the elaborate mystical systems of the priesthood, that they were tempted not only to identify their own deities with those of Egypt, but to fancy that their names as well as the actions ascribed to them were derived from that country. When for this fact no evidence was asked or furnished beyond the mere assertions of Egyptian priests, there was clearly no difficulty in making any one Greek god the counterpart of a deity in the mythology of Egypt, and Herodotus could quietly carry away with him the conviction that the name of the Greek and Aryan Athênê was only that of the Egyptian Neith read backwards. Nor need we hesitate to say that the mystical system of the Egyptian priests, which made so profound an impression on the mind of Herodotus, was grafted in the process of ages on simpler myths, which corresponded essentially with the phrases which lie at the root of Hindu, Greek, and Teutonic mythology. Thus the sleep of Uasar (Osiris) during the winter, before his reappearance in the spring, is the sleep of the fair maiden who is waked up by Sigurd, and answers to the sojourn of Balder in the unseen world, and to the imprisonment of Korê or Persephone in Hades. It is of this Osiris that the horned maiden Isis is both the mother and the wife, and the dog-headed Anubis, Anupu, is their companion. Osiris is killed by his brother Set or Sethi, as Balder is killed by Hödr; but after his imprisonment beneath the earth he rises to a new life, and becomes the judge of the dead. This office is denoted by his title Rhot-amenti, king of the under-world, and this name was manifestly borrowed by the Greeks, who made Rhadamanthys, Minos, and Aiakos the judges before whom all must appear after death. The son of Isis and Osiris was Horos, who is represented as a boy sitting on a lotus flower with a finger in his mouth. His name, Har-pi-chruti, Horus the child, was thrown by the Greeks into the form of Harpokrates. The calf-god Apis, with whom the Greeks naturally identified their own Epaphos, was supposed to manifest himself from time to time in a bull, which was recognised by certain signs. This bull was then consecrated, and received high worship. It was not suffered to live more than twenty-five years, and his burial was followed by a general mourning, until a new calf with the proper marks was discovered. Apis deified after death becomes Serapis.

The Egyptian Neith, whose name, in the belief of Herodotus, when read backwards became that of Athênê, was a veiled deity, often associated with Phthah, the pigmy god, answering, perhaps, to the Hari of the Hindu. Of the Phenix the historian speaks as a bird in which the Egyptians saw the emblem of immortality; but he says nothing of the resurrection of the Phenix from its own ashes, while others, instead of saying that a new Phenix sprang full-grown from the funeral pile of the old one, spoke of a worm which came out from the dead body, and gradually grew up into another Phenix. *(Neith and the Phenix.)*

Although, in the mighty harvest of myths which described the impressions made on primitive man by the heavens and the light and the objects seen in them, those which relate to the sun and the great company of solar heroes are much the most prominent and important, the moon and the stars were nevertheless not forgotten. We have seen the moon already in the primary myth of Endymion and Selênê; and whatever else is told us of her, harmonises exactly with the appearances of nature. She moves across the heaven in a chariot drawn by white horses, answering to the golden-coloured steeds of the flaming sun-god. She is said to love the crags, the streams, and the hills, and she herself is loved by Pan, who entices her into the dark woods under the guise of a snow-white ram. Lastly, she is Asterodia, the queen of the starlit heavens. *(The moon and stars.)*

A more distinctively lunar myth is brought before us in the legend of the Argive Io. Io, who is said to be the daughter of Inachos, is pre-eminently the horned *(Io and Argos.)*

maiden, whose existence is one of many changes and wanderings, and of much suffering. In fact, her life is that of the moon in its several phases, from the new to the full, and from the full to the new again. She is the pure priestess of heaven, on whom Zeus looks with love. But this love wakens the jealousy of Hêrê, and, to save Io from her hands, Zeus vainly changes the maiden into a heifer, the symbol of the young or horned moon. Hêrê gains possession of the heifer, and places her in the charge of Argos Panoptes, who has a thousand eyes, some of which he opens when the stars arise, while he closes others when their orbs go down. These phrases, it is obvious, point simply to the revolution of the starry heavens. Whether the eyes of Argos are placed on his brow and on the back of his head, or whether, as in some versions, they are scattered all over his body, he represents the star-lit sky watching over the moon, which seems to belong to a different order of beings.[1] He is thus Asterion, the guardian of the Daidalean maze, or labyrinth of stars. From this bondage she is rescued at the bidding of Zeus by Hermes, who appears here as the god of the morning-tide. By the power of his magic rod, and by the music of his lyre (the soft whisper of the morning breeze), he lulls even the sleepless Argos into slumber, and then his sword falls, and the hundred eyes are closed in death, as the stars go out when the morning comes, and leave the moon alone in the heaven. In revenge for the slaughter of Argos, Hêrê sent a gadfly, which stung the heifer Io, and drove her in agony from land to land, through Thebes into Thrace, and onwards until she reached the desolate crags of Caucasus, where the Titan Prometheus hung chained to the rock while the vulture gnawed his liver.[2]

From Prometheus, Io learnt that her wanderings were

---

[1] Whether Shelley was thinking of the story of Io and Argos, or not, the antagonism between the moon and the stars is clearly expressed in his lines which speak of the former as wandering companionless among the stars that have a different birth. See further *Myth. of Ar. Nat.* ii. 139.

[2] See p. 137.

little more than begun. She must cross the heifer's ford, or Bosporos, which was said to bear her name. She must journey through the country of the Chalybes; she must trust herself to the guidance of the Amazons, who will lead her to the rocks of Salmydessos; she must encounter the Graiai and the Gorgons in the land of the gloaming and the night; and finally, she is to see the end of her sorrows when she reaches the wells or fountains of the sun. There in the Ethiopian land will be born her child Epaphos, and the series of generations will roll on, which are to end in the glorious victories of her descendant Herakles.

The wanderings of Io.

The mention of Ethiopia was regarded by the Greeks as pointing to a connexion between Greece and Egypt, Io being identified with Isis, and Epaphos with the calf-god Apis. No objection need be raised against this identification so long as it is not maintained that the Hellenic names and conceptions of the gods were borrowed from those of Egypt. The great Athenian poet would naturally introduce among the regions visited by Io places which excited his curiosity, his wonder, or his veneration.[1] Of the strange results produced by the method

Io, Epaphos, and Apis.

---

[1] Mr. Bunbury, in his *History of Ancient Geography*, has conclusively shown the uselessness of looking for any definite geographical system in this or in other mythical voyages or wanderings mentioned by the Greek epic, lyric, or tragic poets, and that indeed great mischief has been done by ascribing even to professed geographers and historians a knowledge greater than they possessed or could possess. The ancient writers erred purely from ignorance; we fall into no less serious errors from supposing that they had before them accurate delineations of the form of the earth, such as only exact scientific determination of latitude and longitude has rendered possible. The bearing of these remarks on a multitude of speculations relating to the geography of the ancient world is obvious; and unless the objections thus raised can be refuted, no room is left for the decision of any geographical question on the mere weight of statements made by any ancient authorities. The blow falls not merely on the poems which we now receive as Homeric, nor merely on the assertions of Herodotus or Thucydides or Xenophon, but even on scientific astronomers like Hipparchos, and systematic geographers like Strabo. Not any one of these had any adequate guarantee against mistakes and blunders of the most serious kind; and in some respects the men of science were rather worse off than those who made little or no pretension to it. In the words of Mr. Bunbury, 'Instead of at once drawing the line, as would be done without hesitation in the case of a mediæval writer, between what was accurate and

which Herodotus has applied to the legends of Io with those of Europa and Medeia in the opening chapters of his Histories, it is scarcely necessary to say much. His story is, that when a Phenician merchant ship chanced to come to Argos, Io went on board to make choice of things to be purchased; that the captain of the vessel carried her away either with or against her will; and that this offence led the Greeks to make reprisals by carrying off Medeia from Kolchis. Between this tale and the genuine tradition there is no likeness whatever; and we might not have known that he was even speaking of the same Io had he not called her the daughter of Inachos. This meagre *caput mortuum*, or dead head, was the natural result of stripping the old stories of all their marvellous and extraordinary incidents, and then regarding the skeleton which remained as a framework for a real history. It must be remembered, however, that Herodotus was not the only offender after this sort. Adopting the same fashion, the historian Thucydides makes a very plausible narrative of the Trojan war by leaving out all that is said about Hektor and Helen

trustworthy, and what was vague and inaccurate, the most fanciful suggestions have been made, and ingenious theories invented, to account for what was simply erroneous. Even the supposition of vast physical changes has been introduced or adopted, rather than acknowledge that Herodotus or Strabo can have made a mistake.' The absurdity of looking for clear geographical statements in epics like the *Iliad* and *Odyssey* is shown by the fact that the poets had no words for the points of the compass; but the vagueness with which even such terms as they had are used has led to controversies which are as unprofitable as they are wearisome. A larger amount of geographical information seems to be blended with the traditions of the Argonautic expedition; but these details are the additions or inventions of comparatively late ages, while the Orphic Argonautica must be assigned to a time subsequent to the first century of the Christian era. The later versions placed the voyage in the Black Sea. In the *Odyssey* the story is connected chiefly with the dangers of the rocks called Planctæ; and the poet places these rocks between the shoals of the Seirens and the whirlpools of Skylla and Charybdis, which were generally connected with the western parts of the Mediterranean. It may of course be said that Planctæ and Symplegades were two names for the same thing; but this was not the idea of the Homeric poet, and, as Mr. Bunbury insists, nothing is gained by the attempt 'to combine into one narrative stories originally quite unconnected with one another, and to give a definite form to what the earliest poets and their hearers were contented to leave wholly vague and unsubstantial.' This remark applies with special force to the utterly indefinite wanderings of Io.

and Achilles, and almost all the other actors in the tale. We have already seen the effect of this treatment in the case of the story of Theseus.[1] The method and the results are alike worthless.

In one version of the myth of Io, Argos Panoptes is slain by Bellerophon, the slayer or bane of Belleros. But this hero, whose name is said to be Hipponoös, and who is called a son of Glaukos, is also called Deophontes, or Leophontes, that is, the slayer of the being or beings whose name reappears in that of the Theban Laios. His father Glaukos is called a son of Sisyphos; and the nature of Sisyphos, like that of Tantalos, has been explained already.[2] But we must not forget that in Sisyphos the idea of unrighteous craft has displaced the notion of the exalted wisdom which belongs to Phœbus; and the taint of his subtlety, descending to his posterity, especially affects the character of Odysseus as drawn in the Aias (Ajax) of Sophokles. Hipponoös is pre-eminently a slayer of monsters; and in Belleros we have a being whose name is akin to that of Vritra, the great enemy of Indra. Both contain the same root *var*, to cover and so to hide. But the same source furnished also a name for wool, the Greek *eiros* and *erion*, the Sanskrit *urna*, and through these for the goat, *urnaya*, and the spider, *ar-achne*, the one as supplying wool, the other as serving to weave it. Then we have *aurnavabha*, the wool-weaver, one of the enemies slain by Indra, and so we come through the Russian *volna*, the Gothic *vulla*, and the Latin *villus* and *vellus*, to the English *wool* and *fleece*. From the notion of hairiness and woolliness we pass easily to that of mere roughness; and so we find that the term *varvara* was applied by the Aryan invaders of Europe to the negro-like aboriginal tribes, and *varvara* is the *barbarian* as known to the Greeks and Romans. But the Sanskrit Varvara transliterated into Greek would also yield the word Belleros, and thus we can form some idea

[margin: Hipponoös, Bellerophontes.]

---

[1] See p. 119. [2] See pp. 8, 98.

of a being of whom the Greek myth gives otherwise no account whatever. The mythographers invented a noble Corinthian of this name to serve as the victim of Hipponoös; but the explanation is worth no more than the derivations given by the Greek poets for such names as Œdipus and Odysseus. Belleros, then, is some shaggy and hairy monster; and as Indra is Vritrahan, and the Teutonic Sigurd is Fafnirbana, so is Bellerophon the bane or slayer of Belleros. But among the chief enemies of Indra is the black cloud which is sometimes called the black skin, while the demon of the cloud appears as a ram, or a shaggy and hairy creature, with ninety-nine arms. This wool-covered animal is, therefore, reproduced not only in the monster Belleros, but in the Chimaira (Chimera),[1] another monstrous being slain by Hipponoös, which has, like Kerberos and Orthros, a triple body. His victory over this foe is won by means of the winged horse Pegasos, from whose back he pours down his deadly arrows on his enemy.

After the slaughter of Belleros, Hipponoös, the myth goes on to tell us, fled to the court of Prœtos, whose wife, Anteia, fell in love with him. When Bellerophon shut his ears to her persuasions, Anteia accused him to Prœtos of an attempt to corrupt her, and Prœtos sent him to Iobates, king of Lykia, with letters charging him to put the bearer to death. This Iobates would not do; but he imposed on him some tasks which he thought impossible. The most formidable of these were, perhaps, the slaying of the Chimera, already mentioned, and the conquest of the Solymoi and the Amazons. After this he married the daughter of Iobates, and then tried to rise to heaven on Pegasos; but Zeus sent a gad-fly, which stung

Bellerophon and Anteia.

---

[1] This name may be the result of a confusion like that between Arkshas and Rikshas, Leukos and Lukos : see p. 42. The word Chimaira denotes properly not goats of any age, but only those which are a year old. A Chimaira is thus, strictly, a winterling, that is, a yearling, just as the Latin words bimus and trimus (bi-himus, hiems) denote things of two or three winters old. But the sun slays the winter, and his enemy is therefore necessarily a chimera.

the horse and made him throw his rider. Bellerophon was not killed, but his strength was broken, and after wandering for some time alone on the Aleian plain he died. The chief features of this myth have already been seen in many others. The tasks imposed on him answer to the labours of Herakles, Perseus, Theseus, and other heroes. Like them, he wins his bride after fights with deadly and monstrous enemies. His attempt to rise to heaven is the attempt of Phaethon to drive the chariot of Helios, or of Ixion to gain possession of Hêrê. The gad-fly which stings Pegasos reappears in the story of Io. The fall of Hipponoös is the rapid descent of the sun towards evening, and the Aleian plain is that broad expanse of sombre light through which his orb is sometimes seen to travel sullenly and alone to his setting.

A moon-goddess of greater majesty and power than Io is seen in Hekate, who stands to Phœbus Apollo, as Hekatos, in the relation of Diana to Dianus or Janus. As such she falls into the rank of correlative deities, like the Asvins and the Dioskouroi.[1] She is the queen of night, and as such is described as springing either from Zeus and Hêrê, or from Leto, or from Tartaros, or again from Asteria.[2] According to the Hesiodic poet, she is the benignant being, always ready to hear those who pay her honour. She is the giver of victory in war, the helper of kings in doing justice, the guardian of flocks and vineyards. These were powers which could scarcely fail to throw over her an air of mystery and awe. At times when her orb is dark she would be described as the inhabitant of a dismal region, caring nothing for anyone; and the flaming torch which she gives to the sorrowing Dêmêtêr would make her a goddess of the dark nether world. Like Artemis, she is accompanied by hounds, akin to Kerberos (Cerberus), and the awful dogs of Yama. In one more step we reach the notion of witchcraft. It is from a cave

xxxix. Hecate.

[1] See p. 59.   [2] Hesiod. *Theog.* 411.

that she marks the stealing away of Persephone; and her form is only dimly seen as she moves among the murky mists. She thus becomes the spectral queen who sends vain dreams from her gloomy realm; and as imparting to others the evil knowledge of which she has become possessed herself, she assumes a fearful aspect with three heads or faces, which denote the monthly phases of the moon.

As a sister of Phœbus, and so belonging, like Hekate, to the class of correlative deities, Artemis was in the estimation of the Greeks a moon-goddess. But her attributes are indistinct, and the Asiatic Artemis must be regarded, like Poseidon, as scarcely a genuine Hellenic deity. Like Phœbus, his sister is a child of Leto, born like himself in Ortygia or Delos; and with Athênê and Hestia she forms the group of three deities over whom Aphrodite has no influence. Like her brother, she has the power of life and death, and those who honour her are wealthy, and reach a happy old age. Like him, she takes delight in song; and as he destroys the Python, so she is the slayer of Tityos. Between the Delian and Arkadian Artemis there are but few points of difference. The latter is attended by fifty ocean and twenty river nymphs, with whom she chases her prey on the heights of Erymanthos, Mainalos, and Taygetos. Her chariot is the workmanship of Hephaistos, and her dogs are provided by the wind-god, Pan.

<small>XL. Artemis.</small>

But this Hellenic Artemis is very different from the cosmical deity worshipped under this name in Asia Minor and elsewhere. The Artemis, called Taurian or Tauropola, is a demon glutted with human sacrifices, and is, in fact, the Semitic Moloch in a female form. The ideas associated with her were ideas essentially Semitic, the result of processes of thought which had reached to certain definite notions of forces at work in nature. The Ephesian Artemis was thus no fair maiden radiant with the purity of Hebe or Athênê,

<small>Artemis Tauropola, Iphigeneia, Britomartis, and Diktynna.</small>

but a mummied figure, covered with breasts, to denote the reproductive powers of the Kosmos, holding a trident in one hand and a club in the other; and her worship, as we might expect, corresponded with the ideal which it was designed to exhibit.[1] This ideal was embodied in the cultus of Adonis, the god slain by the boar's tusk, and rising again in his ancient splendour and majesty. Whatever may have been the origin of this idea, it exercised a powerful influence both in the West and in the East, and carried with it especial force in the latter. Adonis cannot rise to the life of the gods till he has been slain. Eos, who closes as she had begun the day, must disappear, in other words must die, if the morning light is to be seen again, and the same thing must be said of Endymion and Narkissos, of Sarpedon and Memnon. But these are all children of the heaven or the sun; and thus the parents may be said to sacrifice their children, like Tantalos or Lykaon. It is for this reason that Iphigenia must die, in order that Helen may be brought back from Ilion; but Helen is herself known as Iphigeneia, and thus her return is nothing more than the resurrection of the victim doomed to death by the words of Kalchas, and Iphigeneia thus becomes the priestess of Artemis, whose wrath her slaughter was to appease. With an unconscious adherence to the meaning of the old phrases, the myth went on to identify Iphigeneia with Artemis; in short, to tell us that the evening and the morning are the same, but that the evening light must die at night before she can spring into life again at dawn. Lastly, Britomartis, whatever be the origin of her name, is manifestly another form of Artemis. She, too, is a daughter of Leto, or of Zeus and Karmê, and she flies from the pursuit of Minos, as Artemis flies from that of Alpheios. To escape from him she throws herself into the sea, and being rescued by the nets of fishermen, is carried to Ægina, and worshipped there under the name Aphaia. But the word for nets, Diktya, which is supposed

---

[1] Farrar, *St. Paul*, ii. 14 *et seq.*

to explain the title of Artemis Diktynna, carries us to the Diktaian cave in which Zeus is born and nursed, and to the kindly Diktys of Seriphos,[1] and we are left in little doubt that Artemis Diktynna is simply Artemis the light-giving, and that the conversion of light into nets is merely the result of an equivocation like that which changed the seven stars into Seven Rishis or sages.[2]

It is perhaps not more doubtful that in the queens of fairyland, from Kalypso and Kirke downwards, we see the fair, yet weird, beauty of the moon, a beauty associated necessarily with the ideas of secrecy and languor, and so connected easily with the notions of sloth, sensuality, and treachery. We may trace the blending of these notions in the picture of Kalypso, and still more in that of Kirke. Their abode is the enervating home in which the bright heroes are tempted to pass luxurious days, taking no count of months and years as they roll along. Here they are withdrawn from all intercourse with the world of men; and if they reappear, they are regarded with suspicion, dislike, or dread. In short, the fairy realm is the land of slumber, and the palace of the queen is a very castle of indolence, in which Kirke may be more sensual and more treacherous than Kalypso, but in which both make use of spells and charms not easily to be resisted. This is the home of Tara Bai, the Star-maiden,[3] of Hindu folklore, the being who can neither grow old nor die, and the witchery of whose lulling songs no mortal may withstand. It is the Horselberg to which the Venus of mediæval tradition entices the ill-fated Tanhaüser, the Ercildoune where the fairy queen keeps Thomas the Rimer a not unwilling prisoner.[4]

Kirke (Circe) and Kalypso.

---

[1] See p. 111.   [2] See p. 42.

[3] Transliterated into Greek, Tara Bai is the Asteropaios of the *Iliad*, 12. 102. Frere, *Deccan Tales*, p. 44.

[4] No one probably will attribute the agreement of the names Horselberg and Ercildoune to accident. In each case we have the berg, hill, or down of the moon-goddess Ursel, or Ursula, a name which through the forms Ursa, Arktos, and Arksha, takes us back to the original word denoting splendour or bright-

These beautiful beings may not have the malignant cunning by which Kirke seeks deliberately to bring men below the level of brutes; but the atmosphere of the palace of Kirke is the air in which each dwells. <small>Tanhaüser and Thomas the Rimer.</small> Their abodes are not penetrated by the wholesome sunshine of the daytime, they know nothing of the pure pleasures of the open air. The men who tarry in their chambers must be therefore under a spell; and thus we reach the fully developed notion of imprisonment in the land of Faery. Here knowledge may be obtained, but it can be obtained only under a penalty. At the end of seven years Thomas the Rimer is suffered to return to the earth with an accumulation of superhuman wisdom; but he returns under an oath to go back to Elfland whenever the summons should come. It came, the story went, when he was making merry with some friends. A hart and a hind were seen moving slowly up the street of the village: Thomas knew the sign, and following the animals to the wood, was never seen again.[1] In the case of Tanhaüser the myth betrays the working of more marked Christian feeling. Like Thomas the Rimer, he longs after a time to exchange the sensuous enjoyments of his fairy paradise for the more healthy occupations of the upper earth, and he makes his escape with an overwhelming sense of sin on his soul, for which he vainly seeks absolution. He goes to the pope, whom the story calls Urban IV. The pope tells him that there is as much chance of his salvation as there is of his pastoral staff bursting into leaf and blossom. Tanhaüser departs in despair, and re-entering the Horselberg, disappears for ever. Soon afterwards the pope's staff begins to bud. Messengers are sent to summon the penitent back to the papal presence; but it is too late. The minne-

---

ness which gives us the Hindu raja, and the Latin rex, reg-is, on the one side, and the Hindu Rishi with the Teutonic Bragi on the other.

[1] For the parallel with Chaucer's 'Rime of Sir Thopas,' see *Myth. of Ar. Nat.* i. 411.

singer cannot be found. He has re-entered the fairy land, like Olger the Dane, never to leave it again.

Here, then, we have the idea of an unbroken or death-like slumber, such as that of the Cretan Epimenides, who, tending his sheep, fell asleep in a cave, and did not wake for half a century. But Epimenides was one of the Seven Sages of Hellas, and these reappear in the seven Manes of Leinster, and the Seven Champions of Christendom. These again are the Seven Sleepers of Ephesus, where the tradition went that St. John was not dead, but only slumbering till the great consummation of the world should come.[1] This mystic group of seven is seen, lastly, in the Seven Rishis of ancient Hindu story. These wise men were said to be the instruments through whom the Veda was imparted to man. They are mortal, but they are united with the immortals. With their hymns they caused, it is said, the dawn to arise and the sun to shine. With Manu, we are told, they entered the ark,[2] and there remained until the vessel rested on the peak Naubandhana. The story ran that these Rishis had each his abode in one of the seven stars of the Great Bear. The homonym, as we have seen, is easily traced. Round the same root or base sprang up words denoting brightness and wisdom, and the words so produced might be easily interchanged. In the West a name for bears was obtained from the same source; and thus we have the parallel of seven shiners, seven sages, and seven bears.[3]

The story of the giant-hunter, Orion, is a myth relating to the daily round of the sun; but the name, like that of Athamas, Melikertes, and Kadmos, may come from a Semitic source.[4] It is significant that he

---

[1] For other instances, see *Myth. of Ar. Nat.* i. 413.

[2] See p. 132. Manu is, of course, *man*, the measurer or thinker. As such, he is the child of Svayambhu, the self-existent, just as the Germans spoke of their ancestor Manu as the son of Tiu or Tuisco.

[3] See note, p. 42.

[4] The older form of the name is Oarion. According to Pindar, as cited by Strabo, he was born at Hyria; and he is also called a son of Hyrieus, who is, of course, the eponymos of Hyria. He is also said to be a son of Oinopion,

should be called a son of Poseidon, and that, although they represent the same powers, there is a strong antagonism between him and Apollo with his sister Artemis. At Chios, we are told, Orion sees the beautiful Aero; but when he seeks to make her his bride he is blinded by her father, who, by the advice of Dionysos, comes upon him in his sleep. Orion is now told that he may yet recover his sight, if he would go to the east and look toward the rising sun. Thither he is led by Kedalion, whom Hephaistos sends to him as his guide. On his return he vainly tries to seize and punish the man who had blinded him, and then wandering onwards meets and is loved by Artemis. Of his death many stories were told. In the Odyssey he is slain in Ortygia by Artemis, who is jealous of her rival Eos. In another version Artemis slays him unwittingly, having aimed at a mark on the sea, which Phœbus had declared that she could not hit. This mark was the head of Orion, who had been swimming in the waters. Asklepios, we are further told, seeks to raise him from the dead, and thus brings on his own doom from the thunderbolts of Zeus.

In Aktaion, the son of the Kadmeian Autonoë, we have another hunter, who is a pupil of the Centaur Cheiron, and who is torn to pieces by his own dogs, in punish- Aktaion.
ment, we are told, for his rashly looking on Artemis when she was bathing in the fountain of Gargaphia. With the myths of these hunters, who probably embody ideas which were much more Semitic than Hellenic, we may compare those which tell us of other mysterious hunters and dancers of the heavens, the Telchines and Kouretes, who with the kindred Kabeiroi and many more seem to be importations from Semitic lands.

and Oinopion is called a son of Dionysos. He is thus directly connected with a deity whose ritual was brought into Western Hellas from Asia; and in him as well as in Dionysos we have an embodiment of the cosmical ideas by which Semitic theology is pointedly distinguished from the simpler mythology of the Aryan tribes. Brown, *Great Dionysiak Myth.* i. ch. x. sect. 5. The hound of Orion became, it is said, the dog-star Seirios, who marks the time of yearly drought. For the significance of the name see *Myth. of Ar. Nat.* ii. 290, note 1.

CHAPTER III.

THE FIRE.

THE idea of the fire which burns upon the earth is closely connected with, and is perhaps inseparable from, the thought of the fire which, having its seat in the sun, imparts life and heat to the whole visible universe. For these fires, between which at first the Aryan conquerors of India did not much care to draw any sharp line of distinction, the Hindu name was Agni. Sometimes they spoke of two heats one in the other, which are ever shining and filling the world with their splendour. Hence Agni is spoken of sometimes as the great god who fills all things, sometimes as the light which illumines the heavens, sometimes as the lightning, and sometimes as earthly fire. The flexible and interchangeable characteristics of the old Vedic gods allow them to pass without an effort from one name or thought to another. There is no rivalry between them, and no antagonism. Agni, Varuna, Indra, each is greatest; and when each is so named, the others are for the moment unnoticed or forgotten. Or else Indra is called Agni, and Agni Indra, each being Skambha, the supporter of the universe.

<small>I. Agni.</small>

Agni, however, can scarcely be said to have acquired any purely spiritual character. He is rarely besought, as Varuna is, to forgive sin. In the earlier hymns he is the fire which men prize as an indispensable boon. He bears up the offerings of men to the gods on the flames which soar heavenward, and he is therefore,

<small>The parentage and birth of Agni.</small>

like Hermes, the messenger of the deities.[1] He has the wisdom of Phœbus and Indra. He is the originator of all things, but he is also created or kindled by Manu, who thus answers to the Greek fire-givers Hermes, Prometheus, and Phoroneus, the two latter representing the Vedic Pramantha and Bhuranyu. So thoroughly were the Vedic poets aware of the nature of the materials with which they were dealing, that they speak of the sticks which Manu rubbed together to bring forth the sparks as the parents of Agni, who, of course, is said to devour or destroy them, as do all the fatal children. The language of the hymns in reference to Agni is singularly transparent. The phrases employed describe exactly the phenomena of fire.

'O Agni, thou from whom undying flames proceed, the brilliant smoke-god goes towards the sky, for as messenger thou art sent to the gods.

'Thou, whose power spreads over the earth in a moment when thou hast grasped food with thy jaws, like a dashing army, thy blast goes forth: with thy lambent flame thou seemest to tear up the grass.

'Thy appearance is fair to behold, thou bright-faced Agni, when like gold thou shinest at hand.'

But he is also 'black-backed' and 'many-limbed.' He is 'laid hold of with difficulty, like the young of tortuously twining snakes.' He is the consumer of many forests as a beast is of fodder; but he is puny at his birth, and his limbs are twisted like those of Hephaistos. He is kept

---

[1] Hermes, as we shall see, is not the fire. But one method of producing fire was by rubbing pieces of wood together until they are kindled. For this the Hindu name was Pramantha, which in Greek became Prometheus, and to which the Greek, interpreting the word with reference only to his own language, gave a wholly wrong explanation. But this process may be performed by the wind as well as by man. The storm may dash the branches of a forest together till they burst into flame; and therefore the poet of the Hymn to Hermes says that men praise him as the giver of the great boon of fire to mortals. This coincidence between Hindu and Hellenic tradition with regard to gods so widely differing from each other as those of the fire and the wind is very remarkable, and should be carefully noted.

alive at first by clarified butter, and, like Hermes, he soon reaches his full strength. After a little while his flames roar like the waves of the sea. But Hermes, the raging wind, must leave untasted the food roasted by the flames which he has kindled, while Agni devours all on which he lays his hands, 'shaving off the hair of the earth as with a razor.'

He is pre-eminently the regulator of sacrifices, and, as such, answers to the Greek Hestia and the Latin Vesta, the deities of the household hearth and sanctuary. Of every one of the worshippers he is called at once the father, mother, brother, and son. He is Vasu,[1] the lord of light. He shields men from harm during life, and after death is the Psychopompos, or guide of souls, in the unseen world. In short, Agni is but a name for the One God.

Agni and Hestia.

'They call (him) Indra, Mitra, Varuna, Agni, that which is one; the wise call it many ways, they call it Agni, Yama, Mâtarísvan.' But there was, at the same time, in India as elsewhere, the tendency to discern in each name the mark of a distinct personality, and to invent for each a distinct mythical history. This tendency specially affected the popular belief and the popular practice, and the monotheistic convictions of the sacerdotal caste were not allowed to interfere with either. Thus, because two of the flickering tongues of the black-pathed Agni were called Kali, the black, and Karali, the terrific, these became names of Durga, the wife of Siva; and a bloody sacrificial worship was the necessary consequence.

Not only is Agni, like Ushas and Eos, a being who can never grow old. He is peculiarly Yavishtha, the youngest of the gods—a name which is never applied to any other Vedic deity, but which reappears in the Hellenic Hephaistos.[2] In the West no word corresponding to Agni

---

[1] On this word, see *Myth. of Ar. Nat.* ii. 193, note 1.

[2] This identification Professor Max Müller regards as scarcely open to doubt. For the evidence, see *Myth. of Ar. Nat.* ii. 194, note 1.

is found as the name of any deity. The Greek dialects seem to have lost the word, which in the form of the Latin *ignis* and the Lithuanian *agni* denotes only the physical fire.

In marked contrast with Hermes, who longs to eat of the food which the flames devour, we have in the Vedic Bhuranyu another deity who is the actual fire, and who is represented by the Argive Phoroneus.[1] The latter is described as the first of men and the father of all mortals. The names of his wives, Kerdo and Telodike, point to the influence of fire on the comforts of life, and to the judicial powers of the Greek Hestia.

Agni, Bhuranyu, Phoroneus.

But neither in the case of Phoroneus nor in that of Hestia was the growth of a secondary mythology possible. The phrases applied to them interpret themselves. Hestia, the eldest child, it is said, of Kronos and Rhea, is the goddess of the household sanctuary, or rather of the fire burning on the hearth. As, according to the law and morality of the old world, all men would be regarded as enemies unless by a special compact they had been made friends, so Hestia presided over all true and faithful dealing; and as the household was the centre of all kindly affections, she was described as always pure and undefiled. Poseidon and Phœbus, we are told, sought each in vain to have her as his wife, and this is practically all that is related about her. Nor can we be surprised that we hear no more. Hestia remained to the end, as she had been from the first, the household altar the sanctuary of peace and equity, the source of all happiness and wealth. From this point of view her influence was more deeply felt, and wrought more good, than that of any other Olympian deity. Her worship involved direct and practical duties. She could not be

II.
Hestia, Vesta.

---

[1] The name belongs to the same group of words with the Gr. πῦρ, πίπρημι, the Teutonic *feuer*, fire, *brennen*, burn.

fitly served by men who broke their plighted word, or dealt treacherously with those whom they had received at their hearths; and thus her worship was almost an unmixed good, both for households and for the State. As the State or city, the Polis, was only a collection of tribes, the tribes a collection of clans, and these again of families, so the city, the tribe, and the clan had each its own altar or hearth, where alone the common worship of each might be held. In the Prytaneion of each town, where the Prytanes or elders held their meetings, the sacred fire, burning on the public hearth, was never suffered to go out. If, however, at any time it went out, either from neglect or by accident, it was restored by fire obtained by rubbing together pieces of wood, which are called in the Vedic hymns, as we have seen, the parents of Agni, or by kindling them with a burning-glass, but never by ordinary fire. Through Hestia alone the bond of union was kept up with the parent State, when a portion of the citizens were sent out to form a colony, fire from the public hearth being carried with them to serve as the link which was to bind together the new home with the old. The application of the same idea to the Kosmos, or order of the outward world generally, led to the notion that in the centre of the earth (regarded as a flat surface) there was a hearth which answered to the hearth placed in the centre of the whole universe. In all this, however, we have imagery rather than mythology; and the Hestia of the Greeks remains as strictly an embodied idea as does the Roman or Latin Vesta.[1] In the latter we have a deity which is, of necessity, as much Latin as she was Greek, having been brought by Greeks and Latins from the common home of the Aryan tribes. Her purity demanded a like purity in those who

---

[1] By Preller the names Astu and Hestia are referred to the Sanskrit *vas*, to dwell, and are thus regarded as akin to the Gr. ἕζω and ἵζω, the name Vesta being thus connected with the Latin *Sedes*. But probably Hestia may be referred with more reason to Vasu, as a name denoting the splendour of Agni. See note 1, p. 166.

were dedicated to her special services; and, like the Gerairai at Athens, the Vestal virgins only could handle the sacred fire which was the symbol of her presence.

With the Latin Vesta, as the guardian of the hearth. we may fairly compare the other Latin deities who are concerned especially with the interests and welfare of the household, even though the conception of these gods may not be connected immediately with the idea of fire. Among the most important of these are the Lares, the true protectors of the home, being, in fact, the spirits of the ancestors who had founded and successively borne rule in it. They all belong to the class known as Penates, or household gods, whose name seems to be derived from *penus*, a store of food. Hence there were public as well as private Penates, as there was also a Hestia or Vesta of the city, or tribe, or clan, as well as of separate households, to which the altar in the Prytaneion of the Polis or State corresponded. The Lares were commonly addressed as the Manes, a general name for the spirits of the dead, denoting their goodness or kindness, and answering, therefore, to that of the Greek Eumenides. It recurs in the name of the Italian goddess Mana, and in the word *immanis*, cruel. The spectres of the dead were termed Larvæ, those of them which were supposed to be capable of injuring the living being called Lemures. *The Latin Lares and Penates.*

The term Yavishtha, applied only to Agni, sufficiently explains the name of the Greek Hephaistos as the youngest of the gods, the fire being regarded as newly springing into life whenever it is kindled. Agni, too, like Hephaistos, is at times puny and distorted; but his existence as the fire was never so lost sight of as to convert his personality into that of a lame and ugly dwarf. This was reserved for the Hellenic fire-god, who must have a human shape; and thus Hephaistos becomes a being like Regin, the stalwart but stunted smith of the Volsung legend. He is called the son of Zeus and Hêrê, but some- III. *Hephaistos.*

times of Hêrê only, as Athênê in the ordinary tale is the daughter of Zeus alone. His ugliness, it is said, so displeased his mother that she wished to cast him out of Olympos; and when afterwards he took her part in a quarrel, Zeus hurled him from heaven, and he fell maimed and wounded in Lemnos. Another tale spoke of him as not knowing his parentage, and perplexed by its mystery. The stratagem by which he discovered it reappears in the Norse story of the Master-smith who, like Hephaistos, possesses a chair, from which none who sit in it can rise against the owner's will. Entrapped in this seat, Hêrê is obliged to own him as her son.

The Olympian dwelling of Hephaistos is a palace gleaming with the splendour of a thousand stars. At his huge anvils mighty bellows keep up a stream of air of their own accord, and the giants Brontes, Steropes, and Pyrakmon (the thunder, lightning, and flames) aid him in his labours. With him dwells his wife, who in the Iliad is Charis, and in the Odyssey Aphroditê;[1] but these poems make no mention of his children. In Apollodoros we have a story which makes him and Athênê the parents of Erichthonios, and a legend which represents him as the father of the robber Periphetes.

The home of Hephaistos.

When in the Iliad the armour of Achilles is lost with the dead body of Patroklos, it is Hephaistos who, at the prayer of Thetis, forges the impenetrable mail in which Achilles is to avenge the death of his friend. The story reappears in the traditions of Northern Europe, which speak of Regin, the son of Hialprek, king of Denmark, as fashioning a new sword for Sigurd at the prayer of his mother Hjordis. In English folklore their place is taken by the limping Wayland Smith.

Hephaistos and Thetis.

In the Odyssey the lay of Demodokos tells us that the chains wrought by Hephaistos to entrap Ares and Aphroditê are so fine that they catch the eye scarcely

---

[1] The two are substantially the same. See p. 75.

more than spiders' webs. We thus see the close affinity of his work to the marvellous artistic skill of Daidalos (Dædalus). This name at first was a general term, denoting qualities similar to those which obtained for Odysseus the epithet Polymetis. As we might expect, there is little consistency in the myths which have grown up around it. The commonly received story calls him a son or descendant of the Athenian king, Erechtheus, the father of Prokris, and says that he was banished for murdering Kalos, because the latter surpassed him in his craft. Daidalos then went to Crete, where he made the wooden cow for Pasiphaê, and also constructed the labyrinth for the Minotaur. For doing this he was shut up by Minos ; and as no ships were left on the coast, Daidalos fashioned a pair of wings for himself, and another for his son Ikaros, and fastened them on with wax. Daidalos thus made his escape to Sicily ; but Ikaros mounted too near the sun, which melted the wax of his wings, and falling into the sea which bears his name, he was drowned. Nothing more is recorded of Daidalos, except that he executed many great works of art in the West. Of Ikaros we need only say that he belongs to the class of secondaries, and thus stands to Daidalos in the relation of Phaethon to Helios, or of Patroklos to Achilles.

Hephaistos and D. idalos (Dædalus).

Of the Latin Vulcan it is enough to say that he is a god of fire, whose name, like that of Agni, clearly denotes his office, for it points to the Sanskrit *ulka*, a firebrand, a meteor, and to the Latin words *fulgere*, to blaze, and *fulgur* and *fulmen*, names for the flashing lightning. When the Latin poets identified him with the Greek Hephaistos, they gave him Venus as his wife. He is sometimes called Mulciber, as softening the heated iron.[1]

IV. Vulcan.

Of the Teutonic fire-god, Loki, something has been already said in reference to the vitality of the Aryan gods.[2]

---

[1] Mulciber is one of the many names belonging to the group mentioned in p. 28, note 1.   [2] See p. 137.

The name, we may now note, was originally Logi, a word akin to the old verb *liukan*, the Latin lucere, to shine, the modern German *lohe*, glow. The form Loki was substituted from a supposed connexion of the name with the verb *lukan*, to shut or lock; and the character of the god was modified accordingly. He now becomes, like Poseidon Pylaochos, the being who has the keys of the prison-house, and may be compared with the malignant Grendel in Beowulf, or the fire-demon Grant— names connected with the old Norse *grind*, a grating, and the modern German *grenz*, a boundary. But Loki never assumed the character of the Semitic devil or the Persian Ahriman. As in the case of Hephaistos, his limping gait and misshapen figure provoke the laughter of the gods. He is not, like Hephaistos, cast forth out of heaven; but he is bound for his evil deeds, not to be set free until the twilight of the gods has come.[1] He will then, in the form of the wolf Fenris, hurry to swallow the moon, and will war against and overcome the gods.[2]

V. Loki.— Fenris.

The traditions relating to Prometheus are closely connected with the mythology of Zeus.[3] But the former are perhaps remarkable chiefly as standing out in strong contrast with the idea of the Hesiodic Ages. In the latter, the existence of man on the earth begins with a golden age, during which sicknesses were unknown and the earth yielded her fruits without tillage or toil. To the men of this happy time death came as a gentle sleep, and they themselves passed into a state in which they became the guardians of the good and the punishers of evil doers. The second age was that of silver, in which men incurred the wrath of Zeus for withholding honours due to the gods; but these also at their

VI. Prometheus.— The Hesiodic Ages.

---

[1] Grimm, *Teutonic Mythology* (Stallybrass), vol. i. ch. xii. sect. 5.
[2] Grimm believes that the last day of the week, now known as Saturday, was originally called after this god. Instead of Saturday, the old Norse has laugardagr, the Swedish lögardag, the Danish löverdag. See further *Myth. of Ar. Nat.* ii. 200.
[3] See p. 37.

death were reckoned among the blessed. The age next following was the brazen, the age of men who ate no corn, and had hearts of adamant. These fought with and slew each other, like the men who sprang from the dragon's teeth in the legend of the Theban Kadmos (Cadmus), and went down unnamed to the under world. Between these ages there are no periods of transition. One race is swept away and another succeeds. The last age was the age of iron, in which the poets supposed themselves to be living, and which was to be commensurate with the duration of man on the earth. But the vast body of epical tradition related to men who could not be classed with those of either the gold, the silver, or the brazen ages, and who in bravery, power, and strength of will, immeasurably surpassed the degenerate creatures of the age of iron. It thus became necessary to find a place for them, and so the Heroic age was interposed immediately before that of iron. The heroes themselves were faulty enough, and many of them brought on themselves a dark doom; but their better qualities break the ethical order of primæval ages which otherwise runs steadily from the better to the worse. In the Promethean story, as related by Æschylus, this order is completely reversed. The Æschylean legend insists that men had not lost high powers, but that they had never been awakened to the consciousness of the powers with which they were endowed. For them sight and hearing were useless, and life presented only the confused images of a dream. They were utterly unable to distinguish the seasons, or the rising and setting of the stars. From this depth of misery they could be rescued only by bestowing on them the blessing of fire: but the very idea of this gift implies that till then fire was a thing unknown to men on the earth. They might see the lightning flash across the sky, or the fiery lava stream hurrying down the slopes of a volcano; but fire, nevertheless, was a thing which they had never thought of mastering and turning to their own use. Some wiser being, therefore, than man must bring it to them in a form which should deprive it of its terrors. This being is Prometheus, who, ascending to the palace of Zeus, fills a ferule with fire, and by bringing to them this boon, opens a door of hope for the woe-begone race of men. With this story the Hesiodic idea cannot possibly be reconciled. In the Theogony men are deprived of the boon of fire by Zeus, in revenge for the trick which left the fat and bones of victims as the portion of the gods in the sacrifices;[1] but they are not deprived of the wisdom and the craft imparted to them by Prometheus. Their condition, in short, has nothing in common with that state of unawakened powers which is the very foundation of the Æschylean legend; and this fact becomes clearer the more that we may examine the myth. Prometheus, as we have seen, had been an ally of Zeus, for whom he had hurled Kronos and his adherents into the abyss of Tartaros; and for this great benefit he might have remained always in Olympos, had not his anger been roused by the gross injustice of which Zeus became guilty when he found himself securely seated on his throne. To each of the gods he assigned his place and function; of men he took no count. His desire was to sweep them altogether from the face of the earth; but it is clear that he wished this, not because (as the Hesiodic Theogony had it) man was becoming too wise or powerful, but because he was too mean and helpless to be suffered to

---

[1] In the contest between gods and men in Mekônê, Prometheus, it is said, divided an ox, and placing the meat under the stomach, and the bones under the more inviting fat, called on Zeus to make his choice between them. Zeus eagerly placed both hands on the heap of fat, and was enraged on finding that only a heap of bones lay beneath it. In relating this story the Hesiodic poet says, strangely enough, that Zeus saw through the trick from the first, and that it was therefore no trick at all. But this is inconsistent with the feverish eagerness of Zeus to lay his hands on the fat. The god is really outwitted. Æschylus, however, is not less inconsistent in giving his own version. Miserable as men were before they received the boon of fire, they yet had a knowledge of things to come, and could see clearly the course and close of their lives. This power Prometheus takes from them, giving them blind hopes and dreams in its place, while he also instructs them in divination, thus restoring to them in some measure the very power of which he had deprived them.

cumber the earth. He expresses no fear, and Prometheus opposes him not for his severity to enemies whom he dreads, but because he feels no pity for beings whose misery calls only for compassion. The gift of fire now bestowed on man by Prometheus rouses Zeus to fury, and Prometheus is sentenced to a punishment far surpassing the worst agonies of mankind.

The name Prometheus represents, as we have seen, the Vedic Pramantha.[1] To the Greeks it suggested a connexion with words springing from the root con- tained in the names Metis and Medeia. It came, in short, to mean Forethought or Providence; and the idea of Epimetheus, or Afterthought, was at once suggested. But to be wise after an event is often to be wise too late; and thus the rashness of Epimetheus brings on him a terrible punishment for the offence which had already brought down the wrath of Zeus on his mightier brother. He had been warned to receive no gifts from the gods; but the advice of Prometheus was thrown away. The temptation came in a form which it was impossible to resist. By the bidding of Zeus, Hephaistos took earth and moulded it into the shape of a woman. This image Athênê dressed out in a beautiful robe, while Hermes gave her the power of words and a greedy mind, to cheat and deceive mankind. Zeus then led Pandora (for so she was named, as being, it was supposed, the gift of all the gods) to Epimetheus, who received her into his house. Thus far men had been plagued, it is said, with no diseases; but in the house of Epimetheus was a great jar or cask, whose cover could not be lifted without grievous consequences to mankind. Pandora, of course, raised the lid, and a thousand evils, strife and war, plague and sickness, were let loose. The air was filled with the seeds of diseases, which took root wherever they fell; and the only possible alleviation of their woe was rendered impossible by the

Prometheus and Epimetheus.

[1] See p. 165.

shutting up of Hope, which alone remained a prisoner within the cask, when Pandora in her terror hastily replaced the cover.[1]

But in truth these tales are in great part the result of a mistaken etymology. The name Prometheus has no necessary connexion with forethought, and Epimetheus was called into being only by the exigencies of this error. Prometheus, so far as his name will carry us, is simply a giver or bringer of fire. The various functions ascribed to him by Æschylus make him virtually the creator as well as the preserver of men; and we are thus brought back to the language in which the poets of the Vedic hymns address Agni. This creative power reappears especially in his son Deukalion, in whose days the flood overwhelmed all Hellas. The wickedness of man, we are told, had reached its height in the iniquity of Lykaon and his sons, and Zeus resolved to punish them. The waters began to rise; and Deukalion bade his wife, Pyrrha, make ready the ark which he had built on the warning of his father Prometheus. Then getting into it, he and his wife were borne for eight days on the waters; and on the ninth the ark rested on the heights of Parnassos. There, having left the ark, they offered sacrifice to Zeus,

Prometheus and Deukalion.

---

[1] Some have thought that Hope was shut up in the cask out of mercy to men, and not to heighten their misery. But this is clearly not the meaning of the story in Hesiod, for Pandora does not bring the cask with her. She finds it in the house of Epimetheus, and the diseases and evils can do no hurt till they are let loose. Hence the shutting up of Hope makes matters worse instead of better. Nor is this the only difficulty connected with the tale. In the version given by Æschylus, Prometheus mentions, as one of his reasons for wishing to bestow on men the gift of fire, the crowd of diseases and plagues which without it they were unable either to avoid, to mitigate, or to cure. But the Hesiodic legend is, indeed, inconsistent throughout. The mere comparison between the forethinker and the afterthinker implies that there must be some advantage in the one, some loss in the other. But in the Theogony, and in the Works and Days, there is no more to be said in behalf of one than of the other. The provident and the improvident are alike outwitted and punished; and the gain, if any there be, is to the man who does not see the coming evils as they cast their shadows before them. In the story of the gift of fire by Prometheus and in that of the letting loose of the evils by Pandora we have two contradictory legends. We can but take them as they are, for the task of reconciling them is hopeless.

who sent Hermes to grant any prayer that Deukalion might offer. Deukalion prayed for the restoration of the human race, and Hermes said that he and his wife should cover their faces with their mantles, and cast the bones of their mother behind them as they went upon their way. The wisdom which came to him from his father Prometheus taught him that his mother was the earth, and that they were to cast the stones behind them as they went down from Parnassos. The stones thus thrown became men and women, who at once began the life of hard toil which ever since that day has been the lot of mankind. By some this flood was assigned to the reign of Ogyges,[1] a mythical king of Athens; but there are many variations in the tale. Some said that all men then perished; others held that the men of Delphi escaped. So in the Babylonish story of Xisuthros the flood spares all the pious. In some versions of the Indian tale, Manu, as we have seen, enters the ark with the seven sages or Rishis, who remain with him till they land on the peaks of Naubandhana.

The name Deukalion comes from the same source with that of Polydeukes (Pollux), the brilliant son of Leda. But one of the most noteworthy features of this myth lies in its ramifications into others. The legend of his father Prometheus is bound up with the legend of Zeus, Io, and Herakles, of Epimetheus, Pandora, Athênê, and others. Deukalion, again, is the father of Minos, and Minos is the Indian Manu (the thinker or man), who enters the ark in the east. Minos in his turn is the father of Ariadne, whom Theseus led to Naxos after slaying the Minotaur with her help, and he is further connected with Argive tradition through the tale of Nisos and Skylla. Deukalion is further called the father of Hellen, the eponymous ancestor of the Hellenes, and of Protogeneia, the early morning. The latter becomes the mother of Aëthlios, the toiling and striving sun, who like

Ramificatio of the myths of Prometheus.

---

[1] See p. 49.

Herakles and Achilles labours for others, not for himself, and Aëthlios, as we have seen, is the father of Endymion, who sleeps in the cave of Latmos, and from whom spring the fifty children of Asterodia. The mode adopted by Deukalion in repeopling the earth reappears in the traditions of some savage tribes, who would seem to have nothing in common with any of the Aryan nations. The Macusi Indians of South America relate that the last man who survived the flood re-peopled the world by changing stones into men. According to the Tamanaks of Orinoko, it was a pair of human beings who cast behind them the fruit of a certain palm, and out of the kernels sprang men and women.

The myths of the fire-gods already noticed have shown us that men may see the fire not only as it burns ordinarily on the earth, but as it flashes in the lightning across the heavens, or issues in blood-red streams from the bowels of the volcano. The lightnings are the mighty flames in which irresistible weapons are forged for the hands of the gods, or they are the weapons themselves. The rivers of fire which hurry down the sides of burning mountains are the floods sent forth by rebellious giants chained to scorching couches in their depths. We have here the simple framework of myths which tell us of the gigantic moulders of the thunderbolts, or of rebels to the power and the majesty of the gods. For the most part the stories do not go far beyond these simple ideas, which are exhibited with an iteration which is apt to become tedious. It is happily unnecessary to go through the cumbrous genealogies with which the Theogonies are overloaded; but we can be under no doubt that, when Arges, Steropes, and Brontes are spoken of as Kyklopes, these are the lightning flashes which plough up the stormy heaven. The affinity of these gigantic beings with the Kyklopes, or Cyclopes, of the Odyssey is distant, although it may be traced. The atter have seemingly nothing to do with fire. The Kyklops whom Odysseus blinds is the son of Poseidon

VII. The Titans.

and the nymph Thoôsa; in other words, he is the child of the waters, and instead of forging armour, he feed his flocks on the hill side.[1] We are tempted to discern in these shaggy troops of goats the rough vapours which cling to the mountains, and in the Kyklops himself the blackening cloud through which, like a solitary eye, glares the ghastly and shrouded sun. There seems to be every reason to carry us to this conclusion, and none to stand in the way of it. Odysseus, it is true, is a solar hero, and he may therefore be said to be putting out his own eye and extinguishing himself when he blinds Polyphemos. But we have already seen that this distinction between the agent and the patient, when both are identical, is common to a large number of myths;[2] and it is exhibited most conspicuously in the stories of Ixion and Sisyphos, where the former is the wheel on which he is stretched, while the latter is the sphere which he is compelled to roll up to the mountain summit.

The distant kinsmen of these Kyklopes are seen in the ministers of the fire-god Hephaistos. These, with the hundred-handed monsters, called Hekatoncheires, are the true Gigantes, the earth-born children of Ouranos, who thrusts them down into Tartaros. The Titans, however, remain free; and between these and their father another war is waged, which ends in the mutilation of Ouranos and the birth of Aphroditê and the Erinyes. The Kyklopes are now brought up from their dungeons, and Kronos, who swallows the things which he has made and vomits them forth again, becomes the lord of heaven. A second imprisonment of the Kyklopes soon follows, and lasts until the Titans, led on by Zeus, hurl Kronos from

The Kyklopes (Cyclopes).

---

[1] Mr. Brown regards the Kyklopes as belonging properly to Semitic mythology, and thinks that their name describes them as circle builders. *Great Dionysiak Myth.* i. 111. It seems strange, to say the least, that if the poet wished to say that they raised circular structures, he should say instead that they had round faces. But it does not, therefore, follow that Semitic ideas may not underlie the traditions of these uncouth creatures.

[2] See p. 107.

his throne, and put the Diktaian, or light-born, king in his place. Zeus now makes use of the Kyklopes for the purpose of crushing the Titans, who are avenged when Phœbus Apollo smites the Kyklopes for slaying his son the healer Asklepios. The myth is, in truth, running round in circles, with little variation beyond that of names.

But in its several versions the two images of the cloud and the lightning are closely connected; and this con-nexion may be traced through a vast number of popular stories, in which the lightning becomes an arrow capable of piercing and laying open the side of a mountain and displaying for an instant marvellous treasures of gems and gold. These mountains are the cloud-masses which in many stories are converted into birds, and especially swans and eagles. As the clouds carry the lightnings within them until the time comes for using these awful weapons, so these birds carry each a stone capable of splitting the hardest substance. In the end the stone becomes a worm, especially in traditions derived by the Jews from their contact with the Iranian tribes. The wonder-working pebble Schamir is thus discovered by Benaiah, the son of Jehoiada, who watches a moor-hen bringing a worm which, when placed on a piece of glass laid over her nest, splits it to pieces. In stories told by Ælian and Pliny, woodpeckers and hoopoes get at their young by means of a grass which has the power of splitting rocks; and thus we reach the class of plants known as Saxifrage or Sassafras. These grasses either reveal treasures or restore life, as in the legends of Glaukos and Polyidos, the Snake-Leaves, and many more.[1] Of the same sort is the German Luck-flower, which enables the possessor to go down into the rocks which gape to receive him, and to fill his pockets with treasures, while the beautiful queen of the palace bids him take what he pleases, warning him only not to forget the best. This warning the peasant supposes to

[1] See p. 6.

Myths of the lightning, Schamir, Sassafras, Sesame.

apply to the stones, and leaving the Luck-flower behind, he finds, when the rocks close with a crash, that the mountain is closed to him for ever.[1] In the Arabian Nights story of Ali Baba and the Forty Thieves the flower has disappeared; but the spell lies in its name, and the forgetting of the word involves the same penalty which the German peasant incurs by leaving the flower itself in the cave. In the story of Allah-ud-deen the utterance of the charmed word by the African magician, amidst the smoke and vapour of the fire which he has kindled, causes a shock which reveals a way into the depths of the earth and lays bare its hidden treasures. In the story of Ahmed and the Peri Banou the Sassafras is an arrow whose flight the prince follows, until he finds it just where an opening in the rocks shows him a door, by which he enters a splendid subterranean palace. Here he dwells with the fairy queen, until he again longs for his old life on the earth, and is suffered, like Thomas of Ercildoune,[2] to depart under a promise that he will soon come back. But if the name of the flower can be found as effectual as the flower itself, it is obvious that any magical formula could be substituted for the name, the lightning flash being represented by the lighting of a miraculous taper, the extinguishing of which is followed by a loud crashing noise. This is the form assumed by the myth in the Spanish legend of the Moor's Legacy, as related by Washington Irving;[3] and although, when they are reduced to their primitive elements, these tales may seem poor and monotonous, the astonishing variety of incident which may be evolved from these magic materials is matched only by the wonderful richness of colouring which marks the folklore connected with the phenomena of thunder and lightning.

[1] For other versions of this myth, see *Myth. of Ar. Nat.* ii. 217.
[2] See p. 160.
[3] *Tales of the Alhambra.* See further *Myth. of Ar. Nat.* ii. 219

CHAPTER IV.

THE WINDS.

<small>1.
Vayu, the Maruts, and Rudra.</small>

AMONG the names given to the god known in the Rig Veda as Dyu, Indra, and Agni, is Vayu, a word denoting the gentler movements of the air, and answering to the pipings of the Greek Pan, and the soft breath of the Latin Favonius. With Agni and Surya he forms the earlier Hindu Trimurtti; but the phrases addressed to him never leave us in doubt as to his character. He comes early in the morning to chase away the demons, and the Dawns weave for him golden raiment, while Indra himself is his charioteer. But the more violent forces of the wind, which find expression in the Hellenic myths of Boreas and Hermes, are in the Veda represented by the Maruts who aid Indra in his war with Vritra. The language in the one case is as transparent as in the other. The Maruts, like Hermes, overturn trees, and root up forests; they roar like lions and are swift as thought; they shake the mountains, and are clothed with rain. In their hands are spears and daggers, the fiery lightnings; and the worshipper may hear the cracking of their whips as they go upon their way. After their mightiest exploits, they resume, 'according to their wont, the form of new-born babes;' and in this phrase we have very much more than the germ of the Hellenic myth of Hermes. It is impossible to suppose that the poet knew not whom he was addressing, when he said:

'On what errand are you going, in heaven, not on

earth? From the shout of the Maruts over the whole space of the earth men reeled forward.

'Lances gleam, Maruts, upon your shoulders, anklets on your feet, golden cuirasses on your breasts, and pure waters shine on your chariots; lightnings blazing with fire glow in your hands, and golden tiaras are towering on your heads.'

But more especially, as their name denotes, they are the crushers or grinders.[1] They are the children of Rudra, the Father of the Winds, who, like the Asvins and Agni, like Proteus and Phœbus, can change their form at will. But Rudra, it must be remembered, is worshipped also as the robber, the deceiver, the master-thief; and thus another point of the closest connexion is furnished between the Eastern and the Western myths. The Hellenic story ran that Hermes, the son of Zeus and Maia, was born early in the morning in a cave of the Kyllenian hill, and having slumbered peacefully in his cradle for two or three hours, stepped forth from the cave. Finding a tortoise, he killed it, and with its shell made a lyre by fastening sheep-gut cords across it. Then, as the sun was going down, he came to the Pierian hills, where the cattle of Phœbus were feeding, and made ready to drive them to Kyllene. Fearing that the track of beasts on the sand might betray his theft, he drove them round about by crooked paths, so as to make it appear that they were going to the place from which they had been stolen; and his own feet he covered with tamarisk and myrtle leaves. As he passed he saw an old man at work in a vineyard near Onchestos, and whispered into his ear a warning that he should take care not to remember too much of what he had seen. When the next morning dawned he had reached the stream of Alpheios, and there gathering logs of wood he rubbed the pieces together till they burst into flame. This was the first fire kindled on the earth, and so Hermes

II. Hermes. The story of the Hymn.

[1] See note p. 28.

is called the giver of fire to mortal men. Then taking two of the herd, he cut up their flesh into twelve portions; but he did not eat of the roasted meat, although he was sorely pressed by hunger. Having quenched the fire, he trampled down the ashes with all his might, and hastening on to Kyllene, darted into the cave through the bolt-hole of the door as softly as a summer breeze, and there lay like a babe, playing among the cradle-clothes with one hand, while with the other he held the tortoise lyre hidden beneath them. When the morning dawned, Phœbus, coming to Onchestos, saw that his herds had been stolen. Meeting the old man at work in the vineyard, he asked if he knew who had taken them; but the man bethought himself of the warning of Hermes, and he could remember only that he had seen cattle moving and a babe walking near them, wrapped in purple mist. Going on to Pylos, Phœbus came on the confused cattle tracks, which he followed till they brought him to the cave of Maia. Entering it he found the babe Hermes asleep, and roughly waking him, demanded his cattle. The child pleaded his infancy. A babe of a day old cannot steal cattle, or even know what sort of things cows are. As Hermes gave this answer, his eyes winked slily, and he made a long, soft whistling sound, as if the words of Phœbus had mightily amused him. Refusing to take this excuse, Phœbus caught up the child in his arms; but Hermes made so loud a noise that he quickly let him fall. Taking this as a sign that he should find his cows, Phœbus told Hermes to lead the way. Then Hermes, starting up in fear, pulled his cradle-clothes over his ears and reproached Apollo for his cruelty. 'I know nothing of cows,' he said, 'but the name. Zeus must decide the quarrel between us.' So the strife was carried to the tribunal of Zeus, who first heard the complaint of Apollo and then listened to Hermes. Winking his eyes, and holding the clothes to his shoulders, the babe protested that he knew not how to tell a lie, and that he could but play like other children in his cradle. With a laugh Zeus bade them both be friends, and then bowed his head as the Olympian king. At that awful sign Hermes dared not disobey, and hastening to the banks of Alpheios, he brought out the cattle from the folds where he had penned them. Just at this moment Phœbus saw the spot where the fire had been kindled, and the hides and bones of the slaughtered cattle, and wondering how a babe could flay whole cows, he seized him again, and bound him with withy bands, which the child tore from his body like flax. In his terror Hermes thought upon his tortoise lyre, and called forth from it music so soft and soothing that Apollo, forgetting his anger, besought Hermes to teach him his wonderful art. At once Hermes granted his prayer. 'Take my lyre,' he said, 'which to those who can use it deftly will discourse of all sweet things; but to those who touch it, not knowing how to draw forth its speech, it will babble strange nonsense, and rave with uncertain moanings.' Apollo took the lyre in his hand and filled the air with its music; and Hermes, taking courage, prayed that to him also might be granted the secret wisdom of Phœbus. This, however, he was told, might not be. None but the sun-god could know the hidden counsels of Zeus. Still there were other things which mortal men might never learn, and these he might be taught by the Thriai,[1] the three hoary-headed sisters who dwell in the clifts of Parnassos.

To explain this strange tale, which after all is as self-luminous as it is strange, we have first to account for the name. Transliterated into the old language of India, Hermes, through its cognate form Hermeias, would become Sarameyas, and Sarameyas would denote the son of Saramâ. But we have already seen that

<small>Hermes and Saramâ.</small>

---

[1] In the name Thriai we have the softened sound which appears in our three. We may compare the names Thrinakia and Trinakria, and the Treiskephalai, which Herodotus (ix. 39) mentions as another name for Dryoskephalai, thus showing that the cognate forms Drus and Tree had both found their way into Hellas.

Saramâ is Ushas or the dawn as creeping along the sky.[1] Sarameyas might thus at first have been strictly the breeze which comes with the dawn, and may be regarded as its child; but with the westward migration of the Greeks the word became more and more associated with the idea of air in motion, and of sound as connected with it. The idea of the breeze gradually shut out the idea of the morning, and so the name Hermes came to represent the wind, but the wind in all its moods and measures, and not merely as the storm or the hurricane. Examined from this point of view, the story becomes transparent. Like the fire which steps out with a puny flame from its dark prison-house, the wind may freshen to a gale before it be an hour old, and sweep before it the mighty clouds filled with the rain that is to refresh the earth. Where it cannot throw down, it can penetrate. It pries unseen into holes and crannies, it sweeps round dark corners, it plunges into glens and caves; and when the folk come out to see the mischief that it has done, they hear its mocking laughter as it hastens on its way. These few phrases lay bare the whole framework of the tale, and account for the slyness and love of practical jokes which stamp the character of Hermes. The babe leaves the cradle when he is scarcely more than an hour old. The breath of the breeze is at first soft and harmonious as the sounds which he summons from his tortoise lyre. But his strength grows rapidly, and he lays aside his harp to set out on a plundering expedition. With mighty strides he drives from the pastures the cattle, or clouds of Apollo, the god of the light and the heaven. All the night long Hermes toiled, the poet tells us, or, as we should say, the wind roared, till the branches of the trees, rubbing against each other, burst into flame; and so men praise Hermes, like Prometheus, as the giver of the kindliest boon, fire. The flames, fanned by the wind, consume the sacrifice. But the wind, though hungry, cannot eat of it,

[1] See p. 58.

and when the morning has come, he returns to his mother's cave, passing through the opening of the bolt like the sigh of a summer breeze, or mist on a hill side. The wind is tired of blowing, or, in the words of the Hymn, the feet of Hermes patter almost noiselessly over the stony floor, till he lies down to sleep in the cradle which he had left but a few hours ago. So with every other feature of the story. When Apollo charges the child with the theft of the cattle, the defence is grounded on his tender age. Can the breeze of a day old, breathing as softly as a babe new-born, be guilty of so much mischief? Its proper home is the summer-land; why should it stride wantonly over bleak hills and bare heaths? Nor is the meaning of the compact between Hermes and Apollo less obvious. The wind grudges not his music to the sun; but it is impossible for him to reach the depths to which the sun's light penetrates. Still there are other things to which it may attain. He can be the guardian of the bright clouds. His song shall cheer the sons of men; his breath shall waft the dead to the world unseen; and when he wills, he may get wisdom by holding converse with the hoary sisters far down in the clifts of the mountains, as the wind may be heard mysteriously whispering in hidden glens and unfathomable caverns. Faithful to the spirit of the myth, the poet adds that his friendship for men is not equal to his love for the sun. The wind has a way of doing men mischief while they sleep.

We are thus able to account for all the functions of Hermes and all the shades of his character. The soft music of the breeze would naturally associate the idea of him with that of the harp or lyre. As driving the clouds before him, he would be the messenger of Apollo, and this office would soon be merged in that of the herald of Zeus and all the gods. As the god of the vocal wind, he would be skilled in the use of words, and he would be employed in tasks wherein eloquence was needed. Thus in the Iliad he appears before Priam in the time of his anguish, not in

The Hermes of the Iliad.

his divine character, but as a servant of Achilles, and by the force of his words alone persuades the old man to go and beg the body of Hektor. So, too, he wins the assent of Hades to the return of Persephone from the under-world. He thus becomes connected with all that calls for wisdom, tact, and skill, in the intercourse between man and man, and hence he is exhibited at once as a common robber, and as the presiding god of wealth.

The story of Hermes is found in a thousand forms in all Aryan lands. It is the story of the master-thief, em-
<small>Hermes the Master-Thief.</small> bodied in the strange Egyptian tale of Rhampsinitos as related by Herodotus. In all the versions of this myth the thief is a young and slender youth, despised sometimes for his seeming weakness, never credited with his full craft and strength. No power can withhold him from doing aught on which he has set his mind ; no human eye can trace the path by which he conveys away his booty. So against Hermes bolts and bars are of no avail ; and the babe whom Phœbus can seize and shake in his arms is the mighty marauder who has driven off his cattle from Pieria. When his work is done, he looks not much like one who needs to be dreaded ; and the soft whistling sound which closes his defence wakes a smile on the face of Phœbus, as the English or Scottish squire laughs on finding himself tricked in the Northern story.[1] In each case the robber is exalted to the same high dignity. 'Well, friend,' said Apollo to Hermes, 'thou wilt break into many a house, I see, and thy followers after thee ; and thy fancy for beef will set many a herdsman grieving. But come down from thy cradle, or this sleep will be thy last. Only this honour can I promise thee, that thou shalt be called the Master-Thief for ever.'[2]

But there are sides to the character of Hermes which also describe with singular fidelity the action and power of

---

[1] Precisely the same incident is given by Horace, *Od.* i. 10.
[2] *Hymn to Hermes*, 292. See also p. 18, and Appendix I.

air in motion. As nothing can withstand the fury of his rage, so no living thing can resist the witchery of his harping. As he draws nigh, life is wakened, where before there had only been the stillness of the dead. His lyre is the harp of Orpheus, or of the Finnic Wäinämöinen,[1] the son of Ilmatar, the daughter of the air whose singing draws the sun and moon from heaven. He is the Erlking whose mysterious harmony is heard by the child nestled in his father's arms. He is the piper of Hameln, who drives away the noisome rats, but who also draws the children of the town, happy and joyous, to the blue river, where they leave all their griefs behind them, as gently as the Homeric Psychopompos leads the dead across the waters of Lethe.

The staff or rod, which Hermes received from Phœbus as the sign of his dominion over the cattle of the sun-god, was regarded as denoting his heraldic office. It is the emblem which especially marks the worship of the Eastern Vishnu;[2] and it was necessarily endowed with magic properties, and had the power even of raising the dead. The fillets of this staff were sometimes displaced by serpents; and the golden sandals, which in the Iliad and Odyssey bear him of themselves through the air more swiftly than the wind, were at length fitted with wings, and the Orphic hymn-writer salutes him accordingly as the god of the winged sandals. In the legend of Medusa these sandals bear Perseus away from the pursuit of the angry Gorgons into the Hyperborean gardens, and thence to the shores of Libya.[3]

Hermes and Perseus.

In the literature of Rome, Hermes was identified with, and all the deeds related of him were ascribed to, the Latin Mercurius (Mercury), with whom he has scarcely a feature in common. Mercurius was a genuine Latin deity of traffic and gain.[4] But it is especially noteworthy that the Roman Fetiales, or heralds,

Hermes and the Latin Mercurius.

---

[1] *Myth. of Ar. Nat.* ii. 245.   [2] See p. 139.   [3] See p. 113.
[4] The name is connected immediately with *merx*, commerce.

refused to admit the identification. A deity better answering from this point of view to the Greek Hermes is found in the Latin Laverna, the guardian and patron of thieves. The two names exhibit, after the usual Latin fashion, nothing more than the abstract conceptions of traffic and thievery.

In Orpheus, who is generally called a son of the river Oiagros and the muse Kalliope,[1] we have a being who in some points resembles Hermes. The latter has a lyre, the music of which charms those who have ears to hear and hearts to feel it. The influence of the harp of Orpheus is extended beyond living things, to stocks, stones, and trees. What, then, is Orpheus? Is he the breeze of the dawn, the moving air which may freshen to a gale, dragging everything thing away in its impetuous haste? Or is he the sun-god himself, joined for a little while with a beautiful bride whom he is to recover only to lose her again? There can be but little doubt that the colouring of a solar myth has been laid over the framework of a tale which originally turned, like that of Hermes, upon the effects of air in motion. The name of his wife Eurydike is one of the many names which denote the wide-spreading flush of the dawn.[2] This fair being is stung by the serpent of night. Wretched at her loss, Orpheus has no longer the heart to wake from his golden lyre the music which made men, beasts, and trees, follow him in his course. He determines, therefore, to seek Eurydike in the land of the dead, and having soothed the dog of Hades, Kerberos (Cerberus), with his song, he is brought before Polydegmon and Persephone, who suffer him to lead his wife away, on condition that he shall not look on her face till she has reached the earth. It is almost needless to say that Orpheus, forgetting his promise, looks round too soon, and Eurydike vanishes away, like mist at the rising of the sun. The grief of

III. *Orpheus.*

[1] The beautiful-voiced. [2] See p. 14.

Orpheus again silences his music, until he dies on the banks of the Hebrus.

Although there can be little doubt that the name Orpheus is the Greek form of the Vedic Ribhu or Arbhu, a name which seems at a very early period to have been applied to the sun, the story is essentially connected with the idea of sound rather than with that of light. The notion of the tale is more simple than that of the myth of Hermes. Orpheus is a harper only, although his harp is one which can set even things inanimate in motion; but Hermes is also the marauding thief, and on his plundering expeditions he lays aside his lyre, to resume it only when he comes back to lie down like a child in his cradle. As time went on the power of Orpheus as a musician put out of sight all other features of his character. Thus he is sent to the gathering of the Argonauts, and no sooner does he call on the divine ship Argo,[1] which the heroes had vainly tried to move, than the vessel, charmed by his tones, glides gently into the sea. The same tones wake the voyagers in Lemnos from the spell which makes Odysseus dread the land of the Lotos-eaters. At the magic sound the Kyanean rocks parted asunder to make room for the speaking ship, and the Symplegades which had been dashed together in the fury of ages remained steadfast for evermore.

Orpheus and the Argonauts.

The same spell belongs to the music of the Seirens, who by their sweet singing lure unwary mariners to the shoals and rocks amidst which they dwell. These beings meet their doom, in one version of the myth, at the hands of Orpheus; in another, by the means of Orpheus. They may perhaps represent, as some have supposed, the Seirai or belts of calms which are so treacherous and fatal to seamen; or their name may be connected with the Syrinx or pipe of Pan, and with the

Orpheus and the Seirens.

[1] See p. 119.

Latin *susurrus*, a whispering sound, or perhaps with the Italian *Silanus*, a word for gushing or bubbling water. But this is a point of minor importance, so long as we mark the fact that none who heard their song could be withheld from rushing on their own destruction. In the story of Odysseus, the wanderer breaks the spell by filling the ears of his mariners with wax, while he has himself lashed to the mast of his ship. In the Orphic legend the harper proves himself more than a match in their own art, and the Seirens, throwing themselves into the sea, are changed into rocks, according to the doom laid on them when they should meet with a rival more skilled in music than themselves.

The notion of shrubs and trees as moved by the harping of Orpheus has run out into some strange fancies. We Teutonic and other versions of the myth. have seen the children following the piper of Hameln into the depths of the blue river.[1] In some popular stories the musician who can make everything dance at his will is versed in the thievish tricks of Hermes. In the German story of the Jew among the Thorns the myth is blended with the common tradition of the Three Wishes, one of these wishes being for a fiddle, which shall make everyone dance, and which in the issue rescues the servant at the gallows.[2] We find this fancy in a less developed form in the story told by Herodotus of Arion, whom he calls a son of Poseidon. The harp here, although it gives them wonderful delight, fails to win mercy for Arion from the seamen who are resolved to have his wealth at the cost of his life. The minstrel leaps into the sea, and a dolphin carries him to Corinth; and Arion recovers his harp from the sailors, whose iniquities are laid bare and punished. In the Icelandic story the harp of Sigurd in Bori's hand makes chairs and tables dance, and kings and courtiers reel, till they fall from sheer weariness, while Bori makes off with his bride, who was about to be given to some one

---

[1] See p. 189.   [2] See further *Myth. of Ar. Nat.* ii. 244.

else; and at length, in the Irish tale of Maurice Connor, it has the power of waking the dead as well as of stirring the living. In the Eastern story of Gunâdhya this harp is connected with the legend of the Sibylline books[1] and king Tarquin, who is here represented by Sâtavâhana, to whom Gunâdhya sends a poem of seven hundred thousand slokas written in his own blood. The king rejects the poem, objecting to the dialect in which it is written. Gunâdhya thereon burns a part of the poem; but while it is being consumed, his song brings together all the beasts of the forest, who weep at the beauty of his tale. Sâtavâhana falls ill, and is told that he must eat game; but none is to be had. The beasts were all listening to Gunâdhya. Hearing this, the king hurries to the spot, and buys the seventh portion, which was all that now remained of the poem. In these traditions of the Latin Sibyl and the Hindu poet we have two versions of a story, the framework of which must have been in existence before the dispersion of the Aryan tribes from their common home.

In contrast with Orpheus and Hermes, we have the gentle or intermittent breeze in Pan, whose name answers, as we have seen, to that of the Vedic Pavana.[2] The reed pipe of this god is only another form of the harp and lyre belonging to the deities of the winds; but when in the (so-called) Homeric Hymn he is said to have received his name because all the gods were cheered by his music, we have a mistake of precisely the same kind as that which gave birth to the name and the character of Epimetheus,[3] the mistake of attempting to explain a name without making an effort to discover the forms which it may have assumed in cognate dialects. We have already seen that such pitfalls could not possibly be avoided by etymologists who know only one language, and who regard all other languages as unworthy of either study or thought. Some of the details of the myth are grotesque and uncouth

IV. Pan.

[1] Ihne, *History of Rome*, i. 79.   [2] See p. 44, note 4.   [3] See p. 175.

enough; but whether these are to be traced to non-Hellenic or non-Aryan, and so possibly to Semitic sources, it might be rash to affirm. In all of them, nevertheless, the idea of wind stands out prominently. It is the notion, not so much of the soft and lulling strains of Hermes in his gentler mood, or of the irresistible power of the harp of Orpheus, as of the purifying breezes, which blow gently or strong, for a long or a little while, waking the echoes now here now there, in defiance of all plan or system, and with a wantonness which baffles all human power of calculation. To this idea the Hymn to Pan adheres with a singular fidelity, as it tells us how the god wanders sometimes on the mountain summits, sometimes plunging into the thickets of the glen, sometimes by the stream side or up the towering crags, or singing among the reeds at eventide. So swift is his pace that the birds of the air cannot pass him by. With him play the nymphs, the water-maidens; and the patter of their feet is heard as they join in his song by the side of the dark fountain. Like Hermes, again, and Sarameya, Pan is the child of the dawn and the morning, under whatever names they may be spoken of; and it is his wont to lie down at noontide in a slumber from which he takes it ill if he be rudely roused. Sometimes, as in the Hymn, he is the son of Hermes and of the nymyh Dryope, sometimes of Hermes and Penelope, sometimes of Penelope and Odysseus. But Penelope is the bride of the toiling and wandering sun, who is parted from her at eventide; and to be her son is to be the child of Saramâ, and so of Hermes. Nor is the idea changed, if he be spoken of as the son of heaven and earth, Ouranos and Gaia, or of air and water, Æther and a Nereid.

As the soft and benignant breeze, Pan is the lover of Pitys, the pine tree or nymph of the pine tree. As such, he Pan and Boreas. roused, it is said, the jealousy of Boreas, the rude north wind, who hurled the maiden from a rock and changed her into the tree which bears her name. Of Boreas himself there is little to be said. He is called a son of Astraios and Eôs, the starry night and the dawn, and the husband of Oreithyia, the daughter of Erechtheus, the king of the dawn-city. His true character was as little forgotten as that of Selênê in the myth of Endymion, and thus as a germ in mythology his name remained comparatively barren. The Athenian was scarcely speaking in mythical language, when he said that Boreas had aided his countrymen in scattering the fleets of Xerxes,[1] or when he described him as striking down the loving and tender Pitys, because she was wooed by the gentle breeze of summer. In another tale Pan is the lover of the nymph Syrinx; but this phrase simply speaks of the wind playing on its pipe of reeds by the river's bank. The story runs that Syrinx, flying from Pan, as Daphne fled from Phœbus, was changed into a reed; but this is only another form of the myth which made him the lover of the nymph Echo, whose unrequited love for Narkissos (Narcissus) is merely the complement, as we have seen, of the unrequited love of Selênê for Endymion.[2]

The power of Hermes and of Orpheus is exhibited again in the myth of the Theban Amphion. This hero is the twin brother of Zethos, and the two are, in the words of Euripides, the Dioskouroi riding on white horses. In short they are the Asvins, and so fall into the ranks of the correlative deities. Their mother is Antiope; and her fortunes differ but little from those of the mother of Pelias and Neleus,[3] or of Romulus and Remus. In one version of the tale she is a daughter of Nykteus, the brother of Lykos; in another she is the wife of Lykos. In fact she is both, for the dawn-goddesses are at once the children of darkness and the brides of the light. Her offspring, like the other Fatal Children, are exposed at their birth, and like them are rescued by shepherds. Zethos grows up a tender of flocks, while Amphion receives from

v. Amphion. Zethos.

[1] Herod. vii. 189.   [2] See p. 151.   [3] See p. 130.

Hermes a harp which makes the stones not merely move, but fix themselves in their proper places as he builds the walls of Thebes. In one version of the myth Zethos becomes the husband of Prokne, the daughter of the Athenian Pandion; and according to this story Prokne killed her own child by mistake, when she intended to slay the eldest son of Niobe, who was wedded to Amphion. In another version Prokne is the wife of Tereus, who cuts out her tongue when her son Itys is born, and hides her away with her babe. Tereus then marries Philomela, telling her that her sister Prokne was dead. The sisters discovered his guilt, and Prokne killed Itys, whose flesh she served up as a meal for Tereus. In the sequel Tereus is changed into a hoopoe, while Prokne becomes a swallow, and Philomela a nightingale. Like Niobe, Prokne weeps herself to death. In order to explain the story, we have only to remember that the swallow is closely associated with the nightingale as a bird of spring; and it is quite possible that the myth in earlier forms may have spoken of the wife of Tereus as either Prokne or Philomela, without drawing any distinction between them. Of these two names Prokne is only another form of Prokris, and Prokris, as we have seen, is the dew,[1] which is here represented as offering the limbs of the murdered child to her husband, the sun, as he dries up the dew drops. Philomela, again, is one who loves the flocks, or the one who loves apples;[2] but the sheep or flocks of Helios become the apples of the Hesperides, and thus Philomela is strictly the lover of the golden-tinted clouds which greet the rising sun.

The dirge-like sound of the wind is signified in the Bœotian story of Linos, who is torn to pieces by dogs, and for whom matrons and maidens mourned at the feast called Arnis, because, as it was said, Linos had grown up among the lambs. The more vigorous wind from the west or the evening land was known as Zephyros, the son of Astraios, the starry heaven, and of Eôs, who both

Linos; Zephyros; and the Harpies.

[1] See p. 22.   [2] Both apples and sheep are μῆλα.

closes and begins the day. His wife is the Harpyia Podarge, the white-footed wind, who, as Notos Argestes, drives before her the snow-white vapours, and who is the mother of Xanthos and Balios, the immortal horses of Achilles. Harpyia is itself only a name for the strong fresh breeze, as the force which catches up and sweeps away that with which it may come into contact. In Hesiod the Harpyiai, or Harpies, are described as the beautiful daughters of Thaumas and Elektra; by Virgil they are represented as loathsome beings, the change being brought about by the process which converted the lovely Saranyû of the eastern land into the vengeful fury of the west.[1]

In the Odyssey all the winds are placed by Zeus under the charge of Aiolos (Æolus), who is called a son of Hippotes, and who is entrusted with the power of rousing or stilling them at his will. Beyond this statement the poem has nothing more to say of him than that he was the father of six sons and six daughters, and that he lived in an island called after his name. The word may be, and probably is, connected with the names Aia and Aietes, and may denote the changeful and restless sky from which the winds are born.

VI. Aiolos (Æolus).

But Aiolos, Linos, Zephyros, Pan, and all the other wind-gods already mentioned, are not the only conceptions of the effects of air in motion to be found in Greek tradition. The Vedic Maruts are the winds, not as harpers or singers, but simply as the grinders or crushers of everything that comes in their way. These crushers or pounders reappear in Greek myths under more than one form. They are the Moliones, or mill-men, and the Aktoridai, or bruisers of grain, who have one body with two heads, four hands, and four feet. These beings aid Herakles in his struggle with Augeias, but turning against him are slain by him near Kleonai. They are also the Aloadai, the sons of Iphimedousa, whose love for Poseidon led her, it is said, to roam along the sea-shore, pouring the salt water over her body. These

[1] See p. 59.

Aloadai,[1] or giants of the threshing-floor, are said to be nine cubits in breadth, and twenty-nine in height, when they are nine years old. They are called Otos and Ephialtes, the pusher and leaper, and thus are the wind and the hurricane. These brothers seek to lay hands, the one on Hêrê, the other on Artemis; but the latter goddess so runs between the brothers that they, aiming at her at the same time, kill each other; a clear image, it would seem, of the thunder clouds which destroy each other with their own discharges.

The fury of the storm winds furnished the conception of the Hellenic god of war. Arês, the god imprisoned by the Aloadai, with whose name his own is closely akin, represents the storm-clad heaven, which serves as the battle-field of the raging tempests. Athênê, as the goddess of the pure unclouded air, is thus his natural enemy.[2] He is, in short, a deity of mere tumult and confusion, and in no sense a god of war, unless war is taken as mere quarrelling and slaughtering for its own sake. He is, indeed, a son of Zeus and Hêrê; but the men of the mythopœic age could only speak of him in accordance with their ideas of the phenomena which were signified in his person. The battles of the atmosphere seem to be entirely arbitrary, without motive, and without purpose. Hence of the merits of contending parties Arês has no knowledge and no care. He changes capriciously from one side to another, and even takes pleasure in plaguing men with sickness and epidemics. He thus becomes the object of hatred and disgust to all the gods. Where the carcases are likely to lie thickest, thither like a vulture he will go; but

VII.
Arês.
Mars; Enyo.

---

[1] The etymological identity of the Aloadai and the Molionids is established if the Greek Alôê, a threshing-floor, belongs to the group of words containing the root *mal*, which has yielded beyond doubt the Greek Mylê, the Latin mola, our *mill* and *meal*. There is no proof that words in Greek assume an initial *m* which is merely euphonic, but there is abundant evidence that Greek words which originally began with this consonant occasionally drop it. Thus we have *moschos*, and *oschos*, for a tender shoot or branch, *ia* for *mia* in the *Iliad* and *Odyssey*, the Greek οὐλαί for the Latin mola, while the form Maleuron is mentioned as an equivalent for Aleuron, ground corn. See note p. 28.

[2] *Myth. of Ar. Nat.* ii. 254.

he is frequently overcome, and when he is wounded his roar is as loud as that of nine or ten thousand warriors. He has, in short, neither majesty nor dignity. His chief characteristics are his huge size and his bodily strength; and when prostrate on the battle-field, his body was said to cover many roods of ground. In this fact we have conclusive proof that the idea of Arês has reference to the huge storm clouds, charged with lightning and loaded with thunder, which fill the heavens in time of tempest. In other words, the story of Arês has not advanced much beyond the stage of primary myths. The idea of ascribing this enormous bulk and stature to Phœbus Apollo would be preposterous. The conception of the Delphian god had left far behind it the notion of the god who was inseparable from the local habitation of the sun. But the life of Arês is little more than a series of disasters, for the force of the storm winds is after all uncertain and transitory. Hence he is defeated by Herakles, when he seeks to defend his son Kyknos (Cycnus) against that hero, and wounded by Diomedes, who fights under the protection of Athênê. In the Odyssey his name is connected with Aphroditê, whose love he is said to have obtained; but other traditions tell us that, when she seemed to favour Adonis, Arês changed himself into the boar which slew the youth of whom he was jealous. At Athens the court of the Areiopagos stood on the hill which bears his name. It was said that Arês, having slain Halirrhothios, the son of Poseidon, was here accused by the sea-god before the tribunal of the Olympian deities, that he was acquitted, and that the court was therefore called after him.[1] In

[1] Something has been already said of the large group or groups of words clustering round the roots which may be called *mar* and *mal*. The meagre mythology which has attached itself to the name of Arês may at least serve to show that to the former root we owe words denoting violent destruction; to the latter, words significant of slow decay by processes which may even impart much transient beauty. The idea common to both forms, we may now safely affirm, is that of crushing, grinding, or pounding; and thus we have in the Greek Mylê, the Latin mola, answering to our English

some traditions he is said to have been accompanied by a goddess named Enyo, who, like himself, delights in havoc and bloodshed. In the Hesiodic Theogony she is one of the Graiai; and the darkness was from the first the mother of fraud, deceit, and strife. But Arês himself is commonly known as Enyalios, as with the same meaning Poseidon is called Enosichthon, or the earth shaker.

The name of the Latin Mars is closely akin to that of the Greek Arês. But although their names thus correspond, the idea of the Roman Mars, who, as the strider, is called Gradivus and has his feminine counterpart in the war-goddess Bellona, is more dignified than that of the Homeric Arês. Among the Oscans we find the older reduplicated form Mamers, among the Romans Mavers or Mavors. The latter learnt to speak of him as the father of Romulus and Remus; but the names of these twin sons of the Vestal Ilia or Rhea Silvia are only different forms of the same word, and the twin belong to the ranks of the correlative deities,

<small>Mars and Romulus.</small>

---

mill and meal; but it may be traced through a vast number of words between the meaning of which there is no obvious connexion. In the Greek verb *marnamai* the word has acquired the sense of fighting, as Shakespeare speaks of the toil and *moil* of war. In the Latin *marcere*, it passes into the notion of slow withering decay; and so the term *mortal* denotes everything subject to disease and death, the *morbus* and *mors* of the Latins, which grind, and so dissolve them. So, too, as men were to the Greeks Brotoi, mortals, the gods were Ambrotoi, immortal, and were fed on Ambrosia, the Hindu Amrita, the food which cannot decay. The grinding power of time was expressed in the Latin *mora*, delay, and in the French *demeurer*. The root became necessarily fruitful in proper names, as of the Maruts, the Aloadai, the Moliones, the Aktoridai, of Arês, and of Thor Miölnir. It is seen also in the Greek Arete, virtue, which is supposed to have the battle-field for its birthplace. Except for a stray epithet here and there, it is scarcely necessary to trace the root into the second channel denoting ideas of softness, tenderness, and sweetness; but as we find the Latin fire-god, Vulcan, spoken of as Mulciber, it may be well to note that under the form *marj* or *mraj* it gave birth to the Greek *melgo*, the Latin mulgeo and mulceo, the English *milk*, all meaning originally to *stroke*, which only conveys in a modified form the idea conveyed by the word *strike*. In these words, as well as in the Greek Blax, Malakos, Malthasso, Meilichios, the Latin *marcidus*, and *mollis*, soft, the Greek *meli*, and the Latin *mel*, honey, it came to denote especially the notions of sweetness and gentleness. From the notion of melting the transition was easy to that of desiring or yearning; and we find it accordingly in this sense in the Greek Meledônê and Eldomai, which may be traced to the older Meldomai, and finally in Elpis, hope.

among which the Asvins and the Dioskouroi are pre-eminent. But the personality of the subjects of Roman mythical tradition is always more or less vague; and the name of the eponymous heroes of Rome seems as clearly invented to account for the name of the city as were those of Sparta, Orchomenos, and a host of others among the Greeks. How far the incidents in the story of Romulus were derived directly from Greek tales, we can scarcely venture to determine. We are told little more than that he vanishes away in a storm, and thenceforth is said to have been worshipped under the name Quirinus.

CHAPTER V.

THE WATERS.

<small>I.
Poseidon.
Proteus and
Nereus.</small>

AMONG the deities or beings connected with the waters we have the same distinction which we have already traced in those which belong to the upper air or the heavens. We have had sun-gods of two classes: those who have their local habitation in the orb of the sun or moon, from which they are never dissociated, as Helios, Selênê, Hekatê, Surya; and those who in their perfectly human personality exhibit, like Phœbus, the majesty and the beauty of the lord of day without any necessary dependence on the body of the sun. It is thus accordingly that we find Proteus and Nereus standing to Poseidon in the precise relation of Helios to Phœbus, or of Surya to Indra. There is only this difference in the two cases. The other names are all beyond doubt Aryan; but we cannot affirm this with any confidence about Poseidon, which may therefore be Semitic. That it is of non-Hellenic origin may perhaps be inferred from the fact that it has passed away altogether from the language of the modern Greeks, while the name of Nereus has furnished them with a word for water. Between Proteus and Nereus there is this distinction, that the former alone possesses the power of changing his shape at will. At the least the Hesiodic Theogony pointedly denies to Nereus the capricious fickleness of the kindred god. It speaks of him as the old man, because he is truthful, trustworthy, and kindly, because he remembers law, and knows good counsels and just words, whereas Proteus yields only to force. Like Proteus, Nereus is gifted with mysterious wisdom, and

Herakles follows his counsel in the search for the apples of the Hesperides.[1] His wife Doris is, like Asterodia, the mother of fifty daughters, who are also dwellers in the waters; and the ingenuity of later mythographers was vainly exercised in providing them with names. Pontos, the father of Nereus, is in the Iliad and elsewhere simply a name for the sea as a pathway from one land to another, thus showing that till the people who gave this name had seen the great water they had used it of roadways on land. Elsewhere he is described as a son of Gaia alone, and his son Thaumas becomes the father of Iris and the Harpyiai. In the Odyssey, Proteus is an old man who tends the seals of Poseidon, of whom he is said to be a subject or a son. He lives not far from the river Aigyptos, which may or not mean Egypt; and each day, when the heat is greatest, he raises himself from the deeps, and takes his rest on the seashore. It is at this time that Virgil[2] represents Aristaios as fettering the old man by the advice of his mother Arethusa. The attempt to bind him is followed by many changes of form. Proteus becomes first a fire, then a snake, and then assumes other aspects before he is compelled to return to his own proper shape. He is, in short, the Farmer Weathersky of the Norse Tales; nor must we forget that this power of transformation is possessed also by Thetis, and by the fairy who, in the ballad of Tamlane, can say:

> I quit my body when I please,
>   Or unto it repair :
> We can inhabit at our ease
>   In either earth or air.
> Our shape and size we can convert
>   To either large or small ;
> An old nutshell's the same to us
>   As is the lofty hall.

The daughters of Nereus are Nereids, and the Nereids are, etymologically, Naiads, the two forms of the word de-

---

[1] See p. 107. [2] Georg. iv. 439.

noting simply dwellers in the waters.¹ But the tendency was to multiply classes, and the former were assigned to the sea and the latter to fresh-water streams.

<small>Nereids and Apsaras.</small> With us the nymphs are generally supposed to be beautiful beings who may belong to any portions of the visible world. But the name denotes strictly water, the Greek Nymphê answering to the Latin Lympha; and thus the Latin Lymphaticus corresponds to the Greek Nympholeptos, the man enchanted or smitten by the nymphs, just as the Greek Seleniazomenos is parallel to the Latin Lunaticus, the lunatic or moon-struck man. The classification of nymphs as Oreads, Dryads, and others is therefore in strictness an impossible one. These beautiful creatures remain for the most part mere names; but their collective action is seen in the myths of Prometheus, whom they comfort in his agony,² and of Achilles, whom they cheer when his heart is riven with grief for his friend Patroklos. They are, in fact, the Vedic Apsaras,³ the movers in the waters, and endowed as such with the wisdom of the sea-gods Nereus and Proteus.⁴

These nymphs must, however, be distinguished from the Swan-maidens, and other creatures of Aryan mytho-

<small>Thetis.</small> logy and folklore, whose nature is more akin to the clouds and vapours. The lakes on which these maidens are seen to swim are the blue seas of heaven, navigated by the self-guided barks of the Phaiakians. Thetis herself, although called a Nereid, is rather akin to Proteus, for she can change her form at will; and Peleus gains her as his bride only by binding her as Aristæus bound Proteus. She belongs thus as much to the upper air as to the waters. When Hephaistos is hurled from Olympos, it is Thetis who

---

[1] The root *sna* in Sanskrit denotes washing. Round it are grouped such words as the Greek ναῦς, Latin navis, a ship, Greek νέειν, Latin nare, to swim, nix, niv-is, snow, Niobê, and many more.

[2] Æsch. *Pr.* V. 160 *et seq.*

[3] The Sanskrit *apa* and the Latin *aqua* are closely cognate forms.

[4] On the effect produced by Christian teaching on the relation of men to the nymphs, see *Myth. of Ar. Nat.* ii. 258.

gives him a place of refuge; and if she is married to a mortal, it is because she will not be the bride of Zeus, or, as in another version, because her child was to be mightier than his father; in other words, to belong to the class of Fatal Children. In a third version she wins Peleus as a husband, by promising that his son shall be the most renowned of all heroes, and she acts rather as a dawn-goddess than as a Nereid, when in the Iliad she preserves the body of Patroklos from decay.

It is, in truth, difficult to draw any sharp line of distinction between the dwellers in the water and the inhabitants of the air. The sun each day rises from the ocean, and sinks into it again. Aphroditê is born from the sea foam; Athênê at her birth is Tritogeneia;[1] and Daphne in like manner is the child of the Peneian stream. From this point of view they may all be regarded as children of Tritos, Triton, the lord of the waters, and the kinsfolk of Amphitrite. The latter in some traditions is the wife of Poseidon; in the Odyssey she is simply the purple-faced, loud-sounding sea.[2] To the waste of waters belong also the Seirens, whose doom was that they should live only until some one should escape their toils; and they are thus brought to their end, in one version of the myth, by Odysseus, in another by Orpheus.[3] But apart from the one characteristic of their beautiful and witching song, the mythology of these beings, if so it may be called, is thoroughly artificial. In form half fishes and half women, they are akin to Echidna, Melusina, and other like beings of ancient and modern story.

The kinsfolk of Triton.

The Seirens are the witches of the shoals. The demons of the whirlpools are Skylla and Charybdis, who, in the Odyssey, are placed on the rocks, distant about an arrow's flight from each other, between which the ship of the wanderer must pass. If he goes near the one he will lose six of his men as a prey to the six mouths

Skylla and Charybdis.

[1] See p. 71. [2] *Od.* xii. 97. [3] See p. 191.

which Skylla will open to devour them; but this will be a less evil than to have his ships knocked to pieces in the whirlpool of Charybdis, which thrice in the day drinks in the waters of the sea, and thrice spouts them forth again. Skylla, in short, as her name denotes, is one who tears her prey; while Charybdis[1] swallows them.[2] We find in Megarian tradition another Skylla, who gives her love to the Cretan Minos, and betrays the city to him by stealing from the head of her father Nisos the purple lock on which the safety of the place depends. Her treachery brings her no good. According to one tradition she is drowned in the Saronic gulf; in another she throws herself into the water, and is turned into a bird, after which her father, in the form of an eagle, swoops down into the sea.

Over all these inhabitants of the world of waters Poseidon is, in the later mythology, the supreme king. But there are grave reasons for thinking that neither the conception nor the name of this deity is Hellenic or even Aryan. Although the Greeks, like other Aryan tribes, have a character which markedly distinguishes them from tribes or nations belonging to other races of mankind, they were, nevertheless, brought into contact with many non-Aryan tribes or nations. The Greek lived almost more on the sea than on land, and his commerce took him especially to Egypt and the coasts of Palestine and Lesser Asia. But the natives of some of the countries thus visited were as completely children of the sea as the Greeks; and the greatness of the Phenicians as mariners, navigators, and colonists, dates from an earlier time than that of the Greeks. It would, therefore, be wonderful indeed if the intercourse between them had effects upon one side only, and if not a trace were found in Hellenic lands of Syrian or Egyptian or Phenician influence. Such traces, however,

The name Poseidon.

---

[1] The word belongs to the same group with Charon, Χάσμα; Eng. *gape, yawn,* &c.

[2] For the stories relating to the death of these beings, see *Myth. of Ar. Nat.* ii. 261.

are manifest, and they are not now disputed by anyone. The Greek alphabet is unquestionably Semitic, and Semitic words and names are found in Greek dialects and Greek mythology. The Bœotian Kadmos (Cadmus) is the man who comes from Kedem, the East; and it is in the land in which he is said to have made his abode that the Phenician influence is most clearly seen. It is here that we find in the mythical Athamas and Melikertes a reproduction of the Semitic Tammuz and Melkarth. When, then, we have a name which we cannot explain by a comparison with any Greek words, and for which we find no equivalent in the language or the traditions of cognate tribes—when the character of the person named is not self-consistent—when the stories told of him point to disputes and struggles for the establishment of his power, and when, lastly, these traditions seem to indicate the East as the birthplace of his worship, then we are at the least free to see what may be said for and against the notion that the god in question is not a Greek or an Aryan, but a Semitic deity. Such a name is that of the so-called sea-god Poseidon. It cannot be explained by referring it to any Greek words; and the attempts to connect it with Potamos and Posis are failures, because, beyond doubt, Poseidon was not, as this would show him to be, a god of fresh-water streams and rivers.[1] Nor can it with sufficient reason be connected with the root which gives us such words as Potis, Potnia, Potent, and others denoting power.

According to the Greek story, he was a son of Kronos and Rhea, and therefore a brother of Zeus and Hades; and we have already seen that when the three brothers cast lots for the sovereignty of the heavens, the sea, and the regions beneath the earth, that of the sea fell to the share of Poseidon, who received a trident as the emblem of his power. But Poseidon never became the

Poseidon, Here, and Athene.

---

[1] Preller, *Griechische Mythologie*, i. 443, tries to establish this connexion by means of the dialectical varieties Ποτῖδας, Ποτείδας.

god of the sea in the sense in which Helios is the sun, and Selênê is the moon. It is true that he has under his control the forces which affect its movements; but his abode is not within its waters. The true sea-god, as we have seen, is Nereus. With Poseidon it looks much as though his relation to the sea was an after-thought, or as though it was suggested by the fact that his worship had been introduced from a foreign land. He belongs, indeed, much more to the earth than to the waters. Thus he is Gaieochos, the keeper or guardian of the world, and Enosichthon, the earth-shaker. He also disputes with Hêrê, Helios, and Athênê the sovereignty of certain Greek cities, not all of which are on the sea-coast, while some are not even near it. The most signal of these contests was for the naming of Athens, which he wished, it is said, to call Poseidonia. In the council of the gods, who were summoned to settle the quarrel, Zeus decided that it should be named after the deity who should confer the best gift on mankind. Upon this Athênê produced the olive tree, and Poseidon the horse; and the victory was adjudged to the former, the olive being an emblem of peace and prosperity, and the horse a sign of war and wretchedness.

Poseidon is thus immediately connected with the horse; and the reasons for this connexion are certainly not apparent at the first glance. But even of this fact there are different accounts; for others maintained that Poseidon created the horse in Thessaly, while others again affirmed that the gift which he produced in his strife with Athênê was not a horse, but a fountain which he opened by a stroke of his trident on the hill of the Akropolis. Throughout Greece, indeed, it would seem that the efforts to establish his supremacy were met with a very strong resistance. He is said to have dried up the rivers when Hêrê refused to let him be king in Argos. In Corinth there was a compromise, by which Helios remained master of the

Introduction of the worship of Poseidon into Hellas.

Akropolis, while Poseidon was acknowledged as lord of the isthmus. In Delos and at Delphi he failed to carry his point, and he was content to give up his rights over the former in exchange for a temple on the island of Kalaureia, and over the latter for a sanctuary on the Cape of Tainaron. At Naxos he was defeated by Dionysos; but in Aigina (Egina) he was victorious over Zeus himself. In the Iliad we have further a very singular story, which tells us that he plotted with Hêrê and Athênê to put Zeus in chains, and that he was outwitted by Thetis, at whose warning the king of Olympos placed the hundred-handed Briareos by his throne to scare the conspirators. At last these quarrels were ended, and Poseidon took his place among the Hellenic gods as one of the three Kronid brothers. Henceforth his dwelling was especially at Aigai (Ægæ), where in his splendid palace he kept the gold-maned horses which bore his chariot over the waters. But the difference between himself and Zeus was sufficiently marked. Although he tells Hêrê that his power united with hers could match that of the father of gods and men, he is unable to withstand him alone. He is also compelled, as are Apollo and Herakles, to do the work of a bondman. With Phœbus he is made to build the walls of Ilion for Laomedon. When the task is done, Laomedon refuses to give him the covenanted recompense; and hence Poseidon, we are told, took the side of Agamemnon and Menelaos, when they came to Troy to avenge themselves on Paris.

Poseidon thus seems, to be pre-eminently a builder, who, it would seem is therefore called Asphaliaios, and who is, for whatever reason, especially connected not with ships only, but with the horse and the bull.[1] The same Phenician word, it is said, signifies both bull and ship; and so the fact that his worship was brought into Hellas by men who came in ships might lead to the

Poseidon, the horse and the bull.

---

[1] See the story of the bull in the form of the Minotaur, p. 105, and of the monster which ravages the fields of Marathon.

association of his name with the bull, although the connexion of the bull with the sanguinary Moloch of Semitic theology would seem to explain it sufficiently. But more particularly we may mark that the gods with whom he has disputes in Greece are the genuine Aryan deities, who seem to resent the intrusion of a stranger. Even after he had made good his footing in the halls of Olympos, he is still carefully distinguished from the gods who possess the wide heaven, and whose abode the gigantic Aloadai, the children of Poseidon, vainly attempt to storm. There can be little doubt, then, that his name is not Greek or even Aryan; and it may, therefore, be found possibly in tnat of the Phenician Sidon, Sid-on, the ship of Aun, or On, the fish-god, who is seen again in the name Dag-on, and who is the great enlightener and teacher. This On was better known to the Greeks as Oannes; but the name is found in Egypt, where Potiphera is his priest, and in the Jewish Bethaven, the house of Aven.[1] In the Syrian mythology this mysterious being is the husband of the fish-goddess Derketo, whom the Greeks called Atergatis, the mother of Sammuramit or Semiramis. But when the worship of Poseidon was introduced into Hellas, he was separated from his Syrian or Semitic mate, and wedded to Amphitrite, whose name carries us, as we have seen, to the Vedic god Trita, who reigns over the water and the air. We are thus brought back to the Greek Tritopator, to Tritogeneia as an epithet of Athênê, and to Triton, the son of Poseidon. We find it also on Persian soil, where the Trita or Traitana of India reappears as Thraetana, the slayer of the serpent Zohak, or Azi-dahaka, the biting Ahi, of Vedic tradition, which is seen in the Greek Echi-dna.

Among other inhabitants of the sea are Ino, the daughter of Kadmos and Harmonia, and her child Melikertes. In the Argonautic myth she plunges into the sea when she

---

[1] This is the general argument and conclusion of Mr. Brown, in his *Great Dionysiak Myth*.

fails to bring about the death of Phrixos. In the Odyssey she is the pitying nymph who hastens to the help of Odysseus as he is tossed on the stormy waters after the breaking up of his raft. Melikertes was also known to the Greeks as Palaimon the wrestler, or, as some would have it, Glaukos. The stories told of him scarcely call for notice; but his name is clearly that of the Semitic Melkarth; and thus the sacrifices of children in his honour, and the horrid nature of his worship generally, are at once and fully explained. Without going further, we have a sufficient warrant for the assertion that the influence of the Assyrian or Semitic religion and mythology on that of the Greek world was far more direct and important than any that came from Egypt. In the traditions associated with the names of Dionysos and Poseidon we have clear evidence of a determined but unsuccessful resistance made to the introduction of a Semitic ritual, which seemed to the Greek mind both unseemly and extravagant; and the whole of this evidence tends to prove that the stream of Assyrian or Phenician trade or enterprise set steadily in the direction of Bœotia. Of the general character of Assyrian religion we have a terribly vivid picture in the Old Testament. It was a systematic sun-worship, which would assume the most lascivious and the most cruel aspects. The sun had been worshipped at first under a multitude of names; and as in the Aryan world, so here, each name in process of time became the title of a different god. Thus Bel or Baal, and Moloch, the Ammonite Milcom, and the Sepharvaite Adrammelech and Anammelech, the Moabite Chemosh, and the kindred Shemesh and Shâmas, all (like Nebo and Tammuz) titles of the sun, became separate deities by the same process which assigned to Apollo and Helios, Perseus and Endymion, a distinct personality. That this sensual and loathsome worship had a terrible attraction for the Jews is proved by the ceaseless protests and complaints of the

Ino and Melikertes.

Prophets. In a less degree the same hurtful influence extended to the Greeks. The system of human sacrifices, for which the Semitic sun-god had an insatiable greed, never took deep root among them; but the spirit of Semitic worship is seen in the rites by which Artemis Orthia was honoured at Sparta, in the orgies of the Dionysiac devotees at Thebes, and of the worshippers who at Ephesus and elsewhere shared the grief of Aphroditê or Astarte (the Ashtaroth of the Old Testament, the Ishtar of Babylon) for the loss of her darling Adonis and her exultation on his return.

But even if Poseidon be regarded as an Hellenic god of the sea, he is still the lord only of the Thalassa or troubled waters; and there remains a being far more ancient and majestic, the tranquil Okeanos,[1] whose slow-moving stream no storm can ruffle. He dwells in the far west, where are the sources of all things. From him flow all rivers and all the tossing floods, all fountains and all wells.[2] He is, in short, himself the spring of all existence, whether to the gods or to men;[3] and with his wife Tethys he is the guardian of Hêrê, while Zeus is absent during his war with the Titans. The Hesiodic Theogony, which calls him a son of Ouranos and Gaia (heaven and earth), gives him three thousand daughters, who dwell in the lakes and fountains, and the same number of sons, who inhabit the murmuring streams.[4]

II. Okeanos, the Ocean Stream.

The Latin Neptunus is manifestly from his name,[5] the god of the cloud as the source of moisture and water, and therefore, in strictness of speech, not a god of the sea at all. But following the fashion of his time, Virgil gathered round him all the myths which in Greek poetry we find attached to the Hellenised Poseidon.

III. Neptunus.

In dealing with the myth of Osiris we have seen how

---

[1] See p. 49.
[2] *Il.* xxi. 195.
[3] *Il.* xiv. 246, 301.
[4] Hes. *Theog.* 365.
[5] It is closely akin to the Greek νίπτω, νίφος, νιφέλη, Lat. nebula, &c.

strongly the Greeks were tempted, after the opening of
Egypt to Hellenic commerce, to refer their own Danaos and
mythology to that of the mysterious people of the Egyptos.
Nile valley. We need not, therefore, be surprised if in
the Argive myths of the fifty sons of Aigyptos (Egypts),
and of the fifty daughters of Danaos, we find some foreign
names, Egyptus pointing to Egypt, and Belos to Phenicia.
It would be quite natural if details may have been invented
for their voyages or journeys to harmonise with them.
It is also possible that these voyages may have rested on
traditions of some historical journeys, and to some relations
between Egyptians and Greeks, for which we have no con-
temporary records. These, however, are mere speculations,
from which perhaps little profit can be derived. What is
beyond doubt is, that, if we put aside these two or three
words, there remains in the whole list on either side not a
single name which is not purely Greek or Aryan; and the
story of these two contending multitudes of sons and
daughters can find its explanation, it would seem, only by
a reference to the physical conditions of the Argive land.
The story ran that Danaos and Egyptus were twin sons of
Belos, brother of Agênôr, who was father of Kadmos and
Europa. The offspring of Danaos are fifty daughters,
those of Egyptus fifty sons, who may be compared with
the fifty children of Nereus, or of Asterodia and Endymion.
Aided by Athênê, Danaos builds a fifty-oared vessel, which
his daughters row to the Rhodian Lindos, and thence to
Argos, where they disembarked near Lerna during a great
drought caused by the wrath of Poseidon. He is soon
followed by Egyptus and his sons, who propose to marry,
each, one of the fifty daughters of Danaos. The offer is
accepted; but on the marriage day Danaos places a dagger
in the hands of each of his daughters, charging them
to slay their husbands. His command is obeyed by
all except Hypermnestra, who was wedded to Lynkeus.
The others bury the heads of the slaughtered men in

the marshland of Lerna, and place their bodies at the gates of the city. The punishment of the Danaides in the unseen world was the filling of sieves with water.[1] This myth is probably strictly geographical. The Argive soil is rich in wells or fountains, which in the myth are ascribed to Danaos, and these many wells are represented by his daughters. In the heats of summer these springs may fail, and even the beds of the larger streams, as the Inachos or the Kephisos, may be left dry, while during the rainy season these Charadrai or Cheimarrhoi, the *winter-flowing* streams, come down with great force and flood their banks. The wild pursuit of the sons of Egypt may thus be the rush of the winter torrents which threaten to overwhelm the Danaides or nymphs of the fountains; but as their strength begins to fail, they offer themselves as their husbands and are taken at their word. At length the waters of the torrents become even more scanty than those of the springs; in other words, they are slain by their wives, who may be said to draw or cut off the waters from their sources. The sources are the heads of the rivers, and thus the Danaides are described as beheading their husbands. The heads they are said to throw into the marsh-grounds of Lerna, according to the promise of Poseidon that that source should never fail, while the bodies, in other words, the dry beds of the rivers, are exposed in the sight of all the people. Lastly, we have to note that one of the Danaides refused to slay her husband, who is called Lynkeus. Of this name Pausanias gives the other form Lyrkeios. But Lyrkeios was the name by which the Inachos was known in the earlier portion of its course; and this part of the story would mean simply that while the other streams were dried up, the Lyrkeios still continued to flow.[2] The references

---

[1] For further details, see *Myth. of Ar. Nat.* ii. 266 *et seq.*

[2] This is the explanation of Preller, *Griechische Mythologie*, ii. 47. It is extremely ingenious, and probably not less correct than ingenious. The myth seems certainly to stand by itself, with few features in common with other Aryan traditions.

to Egypt seem uncalled for and superfluous. It is certainly possible, though it may not be likely, that the name Egyptus, or Aigyptos, as given in this legend, may be connected with Aigai, Aigaion, Aigialos, Aigina, words associated with Poseidon, who seems to have found his way into Hellas from Semitic lands. Hence it has been thought[1] that, when a foreign origin for the story was once suggested, the yearly inundations and shrinkings of the Nile presented a point of comparison with the winter torrents of the Peloponnesos. But the Nile is one stream only, while in the Argive legend we are dealing with a multitude of torrents and fountains.

[1] Preller, *Griechische Mythologie*, ii. 47.

CHAPTER VI.

THE CLOUDS.

The children of Nephele. THE Greek name for the cloud is Nephele, and Nephele is the first wife of Athamas, whose name reproduces that of the Semitic sun-god Tammuz. She is the mother of Phrixos and Hellê, whose story belongs to the great legend of the Argonauts; and the tradition that her husband Athamas was brother of Sisyphos shows that the early Greeks were well aware of his real character and functions. Without going here into the Argonautic story, we may yet mark that the fate of Phrixos and Hellê is precisely what their names would lead us to expect. The name of Phrixos was, indeed, connected with the roasting of the corn in order to kill the seed;[1] but although the explanation was etymologically wrong, it agreed with the true meaning of the myth. The stealing of the golden fleece is the carrying away of the sunlit clouds of evening from the regions of the gloaming to those of the dawn. Before their radiant forms can be seen again, the light in which they basked when the sun went down must die out utterly, and Hellê is this light. Phrixos is the cold air which cannot be destroyed. Hellê, therefore, falls off from the ram's back and is drowned in the Hellespont, while Phrixos survives to recover the lost treasure. We are dealing with a myth which has evidently been subjected

---

[1] The name was thus supposed to be connected with the verb φρύγω. The mistake may be compared with the explanations given of the names Oidipous, Odysseus, and many more. It belongs more probably to the group of words related to the verb φρίσσω, Phrixos being the cold, clear air, while Hellê is the air as warmed by the fostering heat of the sun.

PHRIXOS AND HELLÈ.

to Semitic influence; but we can be in no doubt as to the meaning which it conveyed to the Greek mind, when we are told that Nephele, finding that her husband's love was given to another, vanished away, and that her place was taken by Ino Leukothea, whose name proclaims her as the open and glaring day. This goddess of the blazing sunshine is naturally an enemy of the children of Nephele or the mist; and her enmity is shown in the drought which she brings upon the land. The Delphian oracle, being consulted on the plague, declares that the children of Athamas must be sacrificed. Ino seeks to bring the doom on Phrixos and Hellê, but the ram sent by their mother Nephele bears them away, and Athamas in his madness fulfils the prophecy of the Pythian priestess by slaying his son Learchos. He is now told that he may find a home in a spot where wild beasts receive him hospitably. Coming to the Aleian plain he sees the bodies of some sheep which the wolves have left untasted, and he thus closes his days in the region which witnessed the last wanderings of Hipponoös Bellerophontes.

As the story of Phrixos and Hellê belongs to the Argonautic tradition, so the Phaiakian myth cannot well be separated from the narrative of the Odyssey. The Phaiakians and Odysseus. The Phaiakian land is the abode of men who, we are told, are not good boxers or wrestlers, but whom none can surpass in running or in the management of ships. What their ships are we have already seen;[1] and we need only note here that the Kyklôpes[2] are the mortal enemies of these wonderful mariners, who love to sail across the blue seas of the sunlit heavens. The same mythical necessity at once kindles their warmest affections when they look upon Odysseus. No sooner has the wanderer cleansed his face, after reaching the palace of Alkinoös, than his form gleams like a golden statue, and the same air of kingly majesty is thrown over him when he stands in

[1] See p. 3.   [2] See pp. 36, 179.

the assembly of the Phaiakians, who, we are told, cannot help loving him when they see his glory.[1]

The snowcloud, which displays forms of wonderful and chilling beauty in the light of the winter sun, and vanishes when the sun regains its summer power, finds an embodiment in Niobê; but almost every incident in the story of this ill-fated being is told in many ways. By some she is called the mother of Phoroneus and the wife of Inachos; but the more popular version makes her a daughter of Tantalos, and the wife of the Theban Amphion. Her name may with many others be traced back to a root *snu*, to flow, to which belongs the Sanskrit Nyava, as from Dyu we have Dyava, the Greek Deo, which we find in the compound Dyava-matar, the Hellenic Dêmêtêr. We can, therefore, understand why she should be the mother of many children, whose number and beauty make her presumptuous. Contrasting her six sons and six daughters with the two children of whom alone Leto was the mother, she rouses the wrath of that goddess, who bids Phœbus and Artemis to avenge the affront. These accordingly slay all the children of Niobê with the arrows which never miss their mark, and Niobê on the summit of Mount Sipylos weeps herself into stone. She is, in short, the representative of winter, whose children are smitten by the arrows of Phœbus and Artemis, as the winter gives place to summer. Thus the myth that there were none to bury them, because all who might have done so had been turned into stone, indicates the petrifying power of frost; and thus also the tears of Niobê, as she sits on her stony seat, point to the weeping or melting of the frozen winter earth. With this myth we may compare that of Chionê, who is slain by Artemis for presumption much like that of Niobê, and whose name strictly denotes the snow of winter, for which

Niobê and Chionê.

---

[1] *Od.* vi. 225, viii. 21. The name of the Phaiakians must be compared with the large group of words containing the root *pha*, which denotes light of all degrees as well as the voice, which reveals the thoughts of the mind. Among these are the Greek φαίνω, φαιός, φῆμι, and the Latin fari, fatum, &c.

the Greek word is Chiôn, the Latin Hiems, which reappears in the Indian Himalaya, the region of eternal ice.[1]

As the bringers of rain to the dry and thirsting earth, the clouds are the cattle of the sun-god, who by their means refreshes and sustains the sons of men. But there are clouds of darkness and of drought as well as clouds which yield the milk or nourishment of rain. The former are represented by the Theban Sphinx,[2] the Hindu Vritra or Ahi or the Panis, or the Latin Cacus. Of the latter in the Rig Veda the guardian is Saramâ, the goddess of the dawn, while in the Odyssey they are tended by Phaethousa and Lampetiê, the bright and gleaming children whom Neaira, the early morning, bore to Helios Hyperion, the climbing sun.[3] But the children of the waters are closely akin to the inhabitants of the cloudland. The mists rise from the streams, lakes, and seas, and these mists may be beautiful, or gloomy, or even repulsive. Their most appalling form is perhaps that of the Cyclops Polyphemos, with whom we may compare the three daughters of Phorkos, who have but one tooth each and possess one eye only in common. These beings are called by Æschylus swan-shaped; and in all Aryan legends the clouds appear in the form of swans, eagles, or other birds, or of maidens who have wings to carry them through the air. The Sphinx is the winged hound in the dramas of Æschylus, and the black ravens who roam across the sky are the messengers of Wuotan or Odin. But the distinction between these two classes of vapours is clearly drawn. The one brings famine and sickness; the other restores the dead earth to life. To the latter class belong the nymphs who in the Delian Hymn wrap round the new-born Apollon his garment of morning mist, the Charites,[4] who in the Odyssey attend on the dawn-goddess Aphroditê, and the singing swans who fly seven times round Delos at the birth

Sidenote: The nymphs and the cattle of the sun.

---
[1] See further *Myth. of Ar. Nat.* ii. 279.　　[2] See p. 36.
[3] For the special aspect which the cattle of the sun assume in this legend, see *Myth. of Ar. Nat.* ii. 280.　　[4] See p. 63.

of Phœbus. Winged birds may easily in mythical language become winged maidens, who could show themselves in their human forms either at their will or on the ending of the enchantment under which they were held. Nay, Zeus himself, we are told, comes to Leda in the guise of a swan; and hence from the two eggs severally sprang Kastor and Helen, Polydeukes and Klytaimnestra (Clytemnestra). If in another version the brothers are said to be the sons of Zeus, while Helen is the child of Tyndareos, we must not forget that Tyndareos is only a name for Zeus the thunderer. We are thus introduced into a world of transformations and enchantments, in which the ship and the swan are prominent forms. These images come before us in a large number of mediæval traditions, of which the story of Beatrice, Matabrune, and Helias[1] may be taken as a type.

Under another name the rain clouds appear as the Hyades, who are said to be the daughters of Atlas and Æthra, the heaven and the pure air, or of Okeanos, the water, or of Erechtheus, the earth. As the nymphs of Nysa or Dodona, they are the guardians of the infant Dionysos, or the nurses of Zeus himself; and to requite them for their kindness, Dionysos makes Medeia, the wise daughter of the sun, restore them to youth when they had grown old, like the young clouds of morning which recall the vanished forms whose beauty glorified the sunset of the previous days. Their sisters are the Pleiades, whose name, indicating their kinship with vapour and water, was confused with that of the ringdove, Peleias; and so the story ran that they were changed into doves and placed among the stars. The Pleiades are generally said to be seven in number, six being visible and one invisible.

There remain in the popular traditions of the old Greeks a large number of mythical beings, whose origin it would be rash to attempt to define too sharply. Of their characteristics, some may be derived from mythical phrases

[1] *Myth. of Ar. Nat.* ii. 284.

relating to the forms, colours, and shades of clouds and mist; others clearly must come from a different source. But the names of many of these beings are mani- *The Graiai and the Gorgons. The Muses and the Pierides.* festly not Greek, and almost as clearly not Aryan, while some seem to be merely Greek translitera- tions of Semitic words. The Graiai and the Gorgons may represent only the gloaming and the night; but we have still to account for the fact, that of the three Gorgon sisters one is mortal, and that she is described as having been once beautiful, but as having become an object of horror under the ban of Athênê, who resented her rivalry. Poseidon, we are told, loved Medusa in the fair spring-time, and Medusa became the mother of Chrysaor,[1] and of the winged horse Pegasos, who rose through the heavens to the house of Zeus, where he bears the thunders and lightnings for the sovereign of Olympos. Here Medusa is simply another Leto, and may naturally be spoken of as mortal, since the birth of the sun must be fatal to the darkness out of which it springs. Her beauty, therefore, is that of the peaceful and moonlit night, vexed by no tempest; and it is not easy to explain the change which comes over her countenance, except by taking it as a picture of a storm. The fair face of the nightly heaven is now marred by the ghastly vapours which stream like dark serpents across it; and the horrible aspect thus imparted might well be regarded as a punishment for the presumption which dared to put her beauty into comparison with that of Athênê. That her offspring, Pegasos, was akin to cloud and vapour, is manifest not only from the name, which points to a source of waters, but from the myth that on the spot dinted by his hoof sprang the fountain Hippokrênê. He springs from the waters, as Poseidon may be taken as a god of the sea; and he is brought, as one legend went, ready saddled and bridled to Bellerophon, whom he bears in the battle with the Chimera. When the monster was killed, Bellerophon,

[1] See p. 85.

it is said, sought to rise to heaven on his back, but was either thrown or fell off from giddiness, while the horse continued to soar upwards. That Bellerophon is a purely solar hero, we shall see when we come to deal with the myths of the darkness; and hence in his relations with Pegasos, it is difficult to avoid the conclusion that we have a series of pictures representing the action of the thunder-cloud in reference to the sun. But Pegasos is also the horse of the Muses; and the Muses, like the clouds in many an Aryan myth, appear in the form of swans.[1] Of the rivalry between the Muses and the Pierides, we are told, that when the former sang, everything became dark and gloomy, while the song of the Muses brought back light and gladness, and Helikon leaped up in its joy and rose heavenwards, until a blow from the hoof of Pegasos smote it down. If, as it would seem, the myth exhibits the contrast between the sound of the winds in fine and in stormy weather, the rivalry of the Muses and the Pierides is a myth which must be compared with the stories of Hermes, Orpheus, and Amphion.

[1] Kallimachos, *Hymn to Delos*, 255.

CHAPTER VII.

THE EARTH.

IN all mythology the earth is treated as the mother or parent of all living things. Like Kronos, it may devour its children; but its powers of reproduction far exceed the sum of life which it takes away by the death of those who have done their work. Difference of Aryan from Semitic mythology.
In the Vedic hymns the earth is the bride of Dyaus; in the Hesiodic Theogony she is wedded to Ouranos, the Varuna of the Rig Veda, and from them proceeds the whole order of the visible and sensible Kosnos. It may seem almost a paradox to say that the thought of the earth as a producer and restorer would be more likely to lead men on to the thought of a power transcending nature, or the forces which we see at work in the outward world, than the impressions made on the human mind by the phenomena of the daily or nightly heavens; but on further thought, we can scarcely fail to see that the continuance of life on the earth, the unceasing restlessness, the perpetual change which is going on upon its surface, the sensitiveness of all vegetable and animal substances to the influences which act upon them from without, must inevitably lead men on to something more like a scheme of philosophy than any which could be furnished by mere phrases describing the phenomena of the day or the year. It does not follow that the condition of those who were thus led on should be happier than that of those who, from whatever cause, remained content with recording the impressions made upon them daily by the sights and sounds of the outward world. The

history of the Semitic nations seems to give no countenance to any such notion. The Aryan was satisfied with noting the birth of the sun from the darkness, his love for the dawn, his early separation from the bright being who had cheered him at the beginning of his career, his long toil, his fruitless labour, his battle with countless enemies, his final victory and reunion with the bright being from whom he had been parted long ago, his last sleep in the land of forgetfulness and his rising again to life and strength in the joyous regions of the dawn. The Phenician and the Canaanite could not rest here. They were themselves part of a mysterious system which whirled them through the realms of infinite space, a system characterised by an exuberance of power, by a majestic and rhythmical movement, by a force consciously exulting in the joyousness of its strength. In such notions as these we have the surest foundations of an orgiastic worship; and the worship of all the Semitic tribes was orgiastic to the core. The spirit of such a worship or ritual is beyond doubt aggressive and contagious. The enthusiasm with which it fills the worshipper will never allow him to rest in patient inactivity; and it moves him, unhappily, only in the direction of evil. It is better to praise Ushas, or Eôs, or Athênê, or the dawn, under any other name which we may assign to it, for the light, the food, and all the other blessings which it brings to us, than to lose ourselves in the labyrinth of cosmical movements, and in the idea of mystic revolutions, which may be typified by the frenzied dances of the worshippers. We may say therefore, broadly, that the Semitic deities are cosmical, while those of the Aryan nations are phenomenal; but the Semitic and Aryan tribes acted and reacted on each other, and, as we might suppose, the stronger influence was exercised by the former. Nor can we say that it was exercised without strenuous opposition. It is impossible to extract history from mythology, except in so far as the myths themselves may point to definite schemes for upsetting

DIONYSOS.

or changing the religious belief and worship of a people; and if the Bœotian and other myths are to go for anything, we can accept as undoubtedly historical the fact that the effort to introduce the wild orgiastic worship of the East into Hellas was received at first with a fierce antagonism, although in the end the resistance was overcome, and the foreign theology and ritual were accepted and maintained with a zeal which portended no good to the Aryan tribes which adopted it, and which in the end was fraught with mischief and disaster. This antagonism is brought before us most prominently in the legends relating to the god Dionysos, who is anything but the mere deity of the wine-cup and the revel, as some Western myths would represent him to be.

As in the case of Hermes, our chief Hellenic source for the myths relating to Dionysos is found in the Hymn addressed to the god. But there are, as we might expect from what has been already said, few beings in the wide range of Greek mythology more variously or, as we might imagine, more inconsistently described. For almost every incident in his history we have an almost endless number of variations. Some call him a son of Zeus and Dêmêtêr, or Io, or Diônê. Others make him a son of Ammon and Amaltheia the nurse of Zeus in the cave of Diktê. But the most popular tale was that which described him as a son of Zeus and Semelê, the daughter of the Theban Kadmos (Cadmus). We have seen that this name, like those of Athamas, Melikertes, and others occurring in the mythology of Bœotia, furnishes evidence that this part of Greece was largely affected by Eastern thought and Eastern worship. If, as it would seem, these names are unquestionably Semitic, it is possible and even likely that the other names which cannot be explained by words in Greek or other Aryan languages may be Semitic also. Among such names is that of Poseidon; and in his case we have seen that his worship was not only brought from Asia to

I.
Dionysos.

Greece, but that at first it encountered strong and general opposition. We shall see that precisely similar stories were related of Dionysos; and when we are obliged to admit that his name is not more Hellenic than that of Poseidon, the presumption is raised that here, too, we may be dealing with a deity originally Semitic.

The stories of his birth differed as widely as those of his parentage. One tale related that Kadmos, on learning that his daughter had become the mother of Dionysos, put her and her child in a chest, which the sea cast up on the shore of Brasiai; that Semelê was taken up dead; but that the babe was rescued and nourished by Ino.[1] This incident is repeated in the story of Perseus and Danaê, and in many more. Another version asserted that Hêrê, being jealous of Semelê, tempted her to her ruin. Semelê, thus urged, asked Zeus to visit her in his Olympian splendour, and was scorched by the lightnings as he approached her. Like that of Asklepios in the story of Koronis, the birth of Dionysos took place in the midst of the blazing thunderbolts, and Semelê departed for a long sojourn in the land of Hades. Dionysos was born, some said, in Naxos; according to others on Mount Nysa; but mountains of this name were found in many lands. In the general character of his life he belongs to the large class of gods and heroes who had to pass through a time of grievous toil and danger before they attained to fame and glory.

Dionysos and Semelê.

Having resolved, it is said, to leave Orchomenos, where he had spent his youth, he stood on a jutting rock, where his dark[2] locks streamed over his shoulders, and his purple robe rustled in the breeze. The splendour of his form caught the eyes of some Tyrrhenians who were sailing by. Leaving their vessel, they came to the rock,

Dionysos and the Tyrrhenian sailors.

---

[1] See p. 217.
[2] They are called κυάνεαι Whatever the shade may be, it differed greatly from the golden locks (ξανθαὶ κόμαι) of Phœbus and the solar heroes.

and seizing Dionysos, bound him with strong withy bands, which fell from him like leaves from a tree in autumn. In vain the helmsman warned them to have nothing to do with one who manifestly belonged to the race of the undying gods; but as they sailed away with Dionysos, suddenly there ran on the deck a stream of purple wine, and a fragrance of a heavenly banquet filled the air. Over the masts and sailyards a vine clambered; round the tackling tangled masses of ivy were mingled with bunches of glistening grapes, and bright garlands shone like jewels on every oar-pin. Smitten with fear, the sailors crowded round the helmsman, when suddenly a loud roar was heard, and a tawny lion with a grizzly bear stood fronting them. The men leaped over the ship's side, and were changed into dolphins; and Dionysos, once more taking his human form, rewarded the helmsman for his kindness, and brought a north wind, which carried the vessel to the land of Egypt, where Proteus was king. After sojourning a while in Egypt, he journeyed on through many lands, through Ethiopia and India and other countries, followed everywhere by crowds of women, who worshipped him with wild cries and songs. At last he returned to the Bœotian Thebes, where Kadmos had made his son Pentheus king. The latter received Dionysos with great suspicion. He could look only with disgust and dread on the strange rites which Dionysos taught to the women, and the frenzy with which he inspired them. But resistance was vain. Pentheus himself was smitten by a mad longing to witness the orgies of the women, as they congregated by themselves, allowing no man to be near them. For this purpose he climbed into a tree; but he was discovered in his lurking place by the women, who tore him to pieces, his own mother Agavê being the first to lay hands upon him.

Such a story as this, it is clear, could never have sprung up except in a country where at some time or other the introduction of a foreign ritual had been strongly resisted, and had been established by violence. The fact is rendered certain when we find a vast number of traditions all pointing to a change of this kind in the religion of the Hellenic tribes. But the story as given in the Homeric Hymn is of itself enough to show that, although Dionysos was undoubtedly a god of the vine, this was only one of many attributes assigned to him, and by no means his most important attribute. As Orion and Phœbus, Alpheios and Odin are hunters, so Dionysos is especially a wanderer, like Odysseus, Herakles, and Apollo, journeying round the world with the revolving seasons; and on him depends, or with him is closely connected, the power of growth which calls forth all the fruits of the teeming earth. His special characteristics seem again to be non-Aryan; and we are, therefore, justified in inferring that they may perhaps be Semitic. In Apollo, for instance, we have none of the violent passion, the vehement frenzy, the wild motion of Dionysos; and as time went on the conception of the latter seems to have been more and more shaped by Semitic ideas and forms of thought. The Dionysos of the Greek tragic poets may be described as a horned stranger from Nysa, a thyrsos-bearing, serpent-crowned god, called Chrysomitres, as a solar deity, but in his savage aspect Omestes, the eater of raw flesh. As in the case of Poseidon, the opposition to the foreign worship thus introduced ended in a compromise. He became the associate and rival of Dêmêtêr and Phœbus; and the joint ritual of Delphi, where Dionysos had as great a share in the Delphic oracle as Apollo, corresponded with the joint ritual of Dionysos and Dêmêtêr at Eleusis.[1]

If it be said that the name Dionysos has rather a Greek or an Aryan than a Semitic look, we have to remember that the argument is not one which may be trusted. To the Greeks generally the name of Prometheus denoted forethought. Their belief, as we have

[1] Brown, *Great Dionysiak Myth*, ch. vi. sect. 2.

seen, was wrong; but so thoroughly were they convinced of its truth, that they invented an Epimetheus, or embodiment of afterthought, whose heedlessness plunges mankind into a misery almost worse than that from which his brother had delivered them. Yet the name Prometheus was simply a Greek form of the Sanskrit Pramantha, or churn for producing fire. We have also seen that Phoroneus reproduces the Vedic Bhuranyu, as Hermes answers to Sarameyas, and Erinys to Saranyû, although the Greek was profoundly ignorant of the fact, and of the conclusions to be drawn from it. There is, therefore, nothing to surprise us if it should be found that the Zeus Meilichios of the Greeks had nothing to do with the mildness and gentleness which this epithet ascribed to him, and that the name Meilichios, although a genuine Greek word, was applied to him simply because it came nearest in sound to the Semitic Melekh or Moloch, much as the story of Whittington and his cat sprang up from the likeness, as seen on paper, between the English *cat* and the French *achat*. This Melekh or Moloch, whom we have seen in the form Melikertes, reappears probably in the name Bacchus. The first syllable of the word is seldom preserved entire. Seen in its full form in Hamil-car, it passes into the abraded forms Mocar, Macar, and Micar, for Molcar, Malcar, and Milcar. Mocar again appears in the form Bocar, Macar as Bacar, and so with the rest. So too Bokchus or Bocchus, the name of certain Mauretanian kings, is also written Bocus and Mocus, and is a contraction of Malchus or Malek; and so in the Greek Bacchus we have a variant form of Melkarth. But Bacchus is admittedly Dionysos; and thus Dionysos is himself Zeus Meilichios, the Moloch or king. If, however, we ask what the name Dionysos may itself mean, the answer is less clear and certain. Some have tried to explain it as a Greek equivalent for the Assyrian Daian-nisi or Dian-nisi, the judge of men. The name would thus correspond exactly to that of the Egyptian Rhot-amenti, the judge of the unseen world, who reappears in the Hellenised Rhadamanthys, the colleague of Minos and Aiakos (Æacus).[1]

The idea of Dionysos is, therefore, not a simple one; and the dislike shown at first to his worship sprang from a <small>Dionysos a cosmical deity. Zagreos.</small> disinclination for the mystic and intricate Semitic theology which was mixed up with it. Dionysos was, in fact, the mysterious mover and movement of the universe, the expression of the vast and mighty changes which go on within it; and the conception of the god thus became one of incomprehensible grandeur, but cumbrous and oppressive from its very greatness. In all this there was little to attract the genuine Greek, who was content to dwell on the simple image of the ivy-crowned son of Semelê. But the inroads of foreign beliefs could not be effectually resisted. In later Greek traditions Dionysos becomes identified with the horned Zagreos, whom his father Zeus places beside him on his throne. The jealousy of Hêrê is thus roused, and at her instigation the Titans slay Zagreos, and, cutting up his limbs, leave only his heart, which Athênê carries to Zeus. This heart is given to Semelê, who thus becomes the mother of Dionysos, in whom Zagreos springs to life again. In his earlier and, from the Aryan point of view, more genuine character, Dionysos is attended by the beautiful Charites, the ministers of the dawn-goddess Aphroditê, who give place in the later mythology to troops of raging Mainades or Bassarides, bearing in their hands the budding thyrsos, which marks the connexion of this worship with that of the great restoring or revivifying forces of the world.[2]

As a being concerned with the unceasing processes of reproduction going on in the world around us, Priapos holds a conspicuous place; but he exhibits the merely sen-

---

[1] Brown, *Great Dionysiak Myth.* ch. ix. sect. 6.
[2] The name Zagreos cannot probably be explained by a comparison with any Greek words, or by a reference to any Aryan languages. Nor have those who would wish to trace it to a Semitic source been thus far successful in their efforts.

suous idea in its grossest form;[1] and we need only say of him that he is spoken of as a son sometimes of Dionysos or Adonis, sometimes of Hermes or of Pan, while   Priapos. his mother is either Aphroditê or the Naiad Chionê. All these names denote simply the relation of the waters to the winds and the sun, and point to the yearly renewal which is carried on by all these powers in their due measure. Priapos is, in fact, Vishnu or Oannes, and, like them, he has the power of predicting things to come. The same idea was expressed by the Latin Mutinus or Muttunus, who was represented by the same symbol which was associated with the name of Priapos.

The true Hellenic earth-goddess, the mother and nourisher of all living things, is Dêmêtêr, the mother of the maiden whom, without his knowledge, Zeus   II. Dêmêtêr.— had promised to Hades as his wife. The lan-   Ceres. guage in which she would be addressed would necessarily exhibit a close likeness to the phrases in which the Vedic poet loves to speak of Ushas as the delight of all the children of men, so that it may even be hard to distinguish between the light which recalls all living things to life from the death of sleep, and the earth which answers to her kindly greeting and her genial warmth.[2] Like Hestia, Dêmêtêr is a daughter of Kronos and Rhea, and therefore a sister of Zeus, Poseidon, and Hades. In Greek mythical tradition she is especially the mother mourning for the loss of her summer child. By the Latin poets of the literary age, Ceres, as the producer of fruits, was identified with the mother of Persephonê; but the beautiful Eleusinian legend never grew up on Italian soil, and indeed could never take root there in the religious system of the people.[3]

[1] The name is probably akin to Fro and Friuja. See p. 48.
[2] Hence it matters little whether the name Dêmêtêr be referred to the root which gives us the names Gê and Gaia, or to that of Zeus, Dyaus, and Tyu, Tir, Tyr. Professor Max Müller, preferring the latter explanation, refers it to the Sanskr. Dyava-matar, the dawn-mother. *Myth. of Ar. Nat.* ii. 301.
[3] By some the word Ceres has been regarded as meaning the *maker*, and therefore as allied to the Greek κρείων, and the Latin *creo*, with many more.

The maiden, we are told, was playing with her companions on the plains of Enna, when far away across the meadow her eye caught the gleam of a narcissus flower. As she ran towards it a fragrance, which reached to the heaven and made the earth and sea laugh for gladness, filled her with delight. It was the stupifying odour of the plant of lethargy;[1] and when she stretched out her arms to seize the stalk with its hundred flowers, the earth gaped, and before her stood the immortal horses bearing the car of the king Polydegmon, who placed her by his side. In vain the maiden invoked the aid of Zeus, who was far away receiving the offerings and prayers of men in his holy places; and there was none to hear her save Hekatê, and Helios, the bright son of Hyperion, and one other, the loving mother, whose heart was pierced as with a sword when the cry of her child reached her ears, echoing mournfully over hills, valleys, and waters. Then Dêmêtêr threw a dark veil over her shoulders, and hastened like a bird over land and sea searching for her child. But neither god nor man could give her tidings, until, with torch in hand, she reached the cave of Hekatê, who knew only of the theft of the maiden, but could not tell whither she had been taken. From Helios, whom she addresses as the all-seeing, she learns that her child is the bride of Aidoneus, who reigns in the unseen land beneath the earth. The grief of the mourning mother is almost swallowed up in rage as she leaves the home of the gods and wanders along the fields and by the cities of men, so changed in form and so closely veiled that none could know the beautiful queen who had till then shed a charm of loveliness over all the wide world. At last she sat down by the wayside, near Eleusis, where the maidens of the city came to draw water from the fountain. Here,

---

It may, however, belong to the group of words akin to the Sanskrit *sarad*, autumn, for which we may assign a root *sri*, to cook or ripen.
[1] νάρκη, νάρκισσος. See p. 96.

on being questioned by the daughters of Keleos the king, the mourner tells them that her name is Dêô, and that, having escaped from Cretan kidnappers, she seeks a refuge and a home where she may nurse young children.[1]

Such a home she finds in the house of Keleos, which the poet makes her enter veiled from head to foot. But for a moment he forgets what he has said, when he tells us that at her entrance her head touched the roof, while a blaze of light streamed through the doors and filled the dwelling. Not a word does she utter in answer to the kindly greetings of Metaneira, the wife of the king; and the deep gloom is broken only by the jests and sarcasms of the serving-maid Iambe. When Metaneira offers her wine, she says that now she may not taste it, but asks for a draught of water mingled with flour and milk, and then takes charge of the new-born son of Keleos, whom she names Demophoôn. Under her care the babe thrives marvellously, though he has no nourishment either of bread or of milk. The kindly nurse designs, indeed, to make him immortal; and thus by day she anoints him with ambrosia, and in the night she plunges him, like a torch, into a bath of fire. But her purpose is frustrated by the folly of Metaneira, who, seeing the child thus basking in the flames, screams with fear, and is told by Dêmêtêr that, though her child shall ever receive honour because he has slumbered in her arms, still, like all the sons of men, and like Achilles himself, he must die. Nevertheless, though she cast the child away from her, she still remained in the house of Keleos, mourning and grieving for the maiden, so that all things in the heaven above and in the earth beneath felt the weight of her sorrow. In vain the plough turned up the soil; in vain was the barley seed scattered along the furrows. In Olympos itself the gloom and sadness was so great that Zeus bade Iris to go and summon Dêmêtêr to the palace of the gods. But neither her words nor

Dêmêtêr in the house of Keleos.

[1] *Hymn to Dêmêtêr*, 123 *et seq.*

those of the deities who follow her avail to lessen her grief, or to bend her will. The mourning mother will not leave the place of her exile till her eyes have looked upon her child once more. Then Hermes, at the bidding of Zeus, enters the dismal under-world, and Polydegmon consents to the return of Persephonê, who leaps with delight for the joy that is coming. Still he cannot altogether give up his bride, and Persephonê finds that, having eaten the pomegranate seed, she must come back to Aidoneus again. But even with this condition the joy of the meeting is scarcely lessened. For a third part only of the year must Persephonê be queen in Hades; through all the other months she is to be once more the beautiful maiden who sported with her comrades on the plains of Enna. The wrath of Dêmêtêr departs with her grief; the air is filled with fragrance, and the corn fields wave with the ripening grain.

Such was the story told by the poet who composed the hymn in honour of the goddess. But for many of the details there were different versions. Thus it is said that when Metaneira gave the alarm on seeing the babe bathed in the fire, Dêmêtêr suffered the child Demophoôn to be consumed by the flames; but that as an atonement for this she gave to his brother Triptolemos a chariot drawn by winged dragons, and taught him to plough the earth and to sow wheat, thus winning for herself the title of Dêmêtêr Thesmophoros, as the guardian of peace, order, and law.

Dêmêtêr and Demophoôn.

For the people of Eleusis her sojourn in the house of Keleos was an event of vast moment. Having bidden Keleos to build a temple for her worship, she instructed him and his subjects in the rites of the great Eleusinian mysteries, which were regularly celebrated there in her honour. The name Eleusis, which denotes a place of meeting, thus acquired a double meaning. It pointed to the reunion of the mother with her

Eleusis, the trysting place.

child, and to the concourse of Ionian pilgrims, which made Eleusis a rival of Delphi, Nemea, and Olympia itself. By the Eleusinians all the incidents of this legend, with their strong local colouring and their striking circumstantiality, were regarded as the history of events which had actually occurred at the place. But so clearly does the record explain itself, that it becomes almost superfluous to add that it grew up out of the old phrases which at first described the changes of summer and winter. The sorrow of Dêmêtêr is nothing but the gloom which falls on the earth during the cheerless months of winter; and the outburst of spring is the return of her child in all her radiant beauty.

It is a story found in all lands where the changes of the seasons are marked. Particular features may be different; but the spirit of the tale is everywhere the same. In some Persephonê appears as a beautiful maiden, who, while the earth without is cold and dead beneath its shroud of snow, lies wrapped in slumber, hidden away from all mortal eyes. But in all the stories we have the images of boundless wealth which the robbers have carried away, and for the time rendered useless. These robbers in the Teutonic legends are the Niflungs or Nibelungs, the children of the chill mists, who hide away the earth treasures, until they are compelled to yield them up again to one to whom they must submit, as Hades submits to the bidding of Hermes. In these tales generally the summer maiden is imprisoned in a subterranean palace, or in a stronghold surrounded by hedges of thorns or spears; and there she must remain until the arrival of her destined deliverer. But the powers of winter are not conquered in a day. Many a newly-risen sun after the winter solstice makes the attempt to throw down the icy barriers, and is compelled to retreat and sink below the horizon baffled and conquered. We have thus here the germ of those many tales in which a series of knights or heroes attempt a task in which one only is to succeed, and we can at once ac-

Teutonic versions of the myth of Persephonê.

count for the constant repetition of the incident which makes the father of the maiden proclaim that he will bestow her on the man who can pierce the hedge of thorns or leap over the wall of spears, death being the doom of those who fail. This is the story of Dornroschen or Briar-rose in the Teutonic tradition. In that of Rapunzel the maiden is shut up in a high tower, and her deliverer ascends on the long golden locks which stream to the earth from her head. In the legend of the Dwarf she eats a golden apple, which clearly reproduces the narcissus, and thereupon sinks a hundred fathoms deep in the earth, where the prince finds her with the nine-headed dragon resting on her lap. The palace of Polydegmon, in the Eleusinian myth, becomes in the German tale the House in the Wood, which in other stories is the case of ice in which the seemingly dead princess is laid. This house or case breaks up at the destined time. The sides crack, the story tells us, 'the doors were slammed back against the walls; the beams groaned as if they were being riven away from their fastenings; the stairs fell down, and at last it seemed as if the whole roof fell in.' The maiden on awakening from her slumber finds herself in a splendid palace, in which her eyes feast on beautiful forms. Persephonê has, in short, returned from the dungeons of Hades to her summer home. The gradual lengthening of the days, as bringing about the victory of the sun over the winter, is brought out with singular clearness in Grimm's story of the Nix[1] of the Mill Pond. Parted from her husband, the dawn-maiden in this tale betakes herself to an old woman, who bids her comb her hair by the water-side, and see what will come of it. As she plies her comb, a wave rolling to the bank carries it away. The waters now began to bubble, and the head of the huntsman is seen; but another wave rolled up and covered him. In place of the comb the old woman gives her a flute, and this time there appeared 'not only

[1] See p. 98.

the head, but half the body of the man, who stretched out his arms towards his wife; but at the same moment a wave came, and, covering his head, drew him down again.' The third time she comes with a spinning wheel of gold,[1] and the huntsman now succeeds in leaping out of the water, and in escaping with his wife from the demons who seek to seize him, as the Gorgons chase Perseus after the death of Medusa. In the Norse tale of the Old Dame and her Hen, the maiden falls down a cave within a mountain; and in the closest accordance with the spirit of the Eleusinian legend, her great grief is because 'her mother is hard pinched, she knows, for meat and drink, and has no one with her.'[2]

Another earth-goddess in German popular tradition is the benignant Holda, who reappears as Frau Berchta, or the bright lady. Holda fosters the life of the winter-bound earth under her genial mantle of snow. As the flakes fall she is said to be making her bed, the feathers of which are flying about, as in Herodotus we read that they fill the air in the Scythian land. The name of Frau Holda became Latinised in mediæval legends into Pharaildis, of whom a strange story is told in reference to St. John the Baptist.[3]

III. Holda and Berchta.

In the Eleusinian myth Dêmêtêr is the wife only of Zeus, and the mother of Persephonê. As the wife of Poseidon, in other myths, she is the mother of Despoina and Orion. She also loves Iasion, the son of Zeus and Hemera, the heaven and the day, and becomes the mother of Ploutôn or Ploutos, the god who guards the treasures of the earth, and who, as Pluto, was regarded by Latin writers as representing the Greek Hades. But Pluto was Latin neither in name nor in idea. The

Earth deities of the Latins.

---

[1] We can scarcely doubt that this is the wheel which comes before us in the myth of Ixion, p. 96.
[2] For the very remarkable Hindu story of Little Surya Bai (the Sun-child), and the significance of its minutest details, see *Myth. of Ar. Nat.* ii. 303 *et seq.* [3] *Myth. of Ar. Nat.* ii. 306.

notion that his true Latin name was Dis as a shortened form of *dives*, rich, is probably a mistake, the word being akin rather to Deus, Divus, and the Indian Dyaus. The name Proserpina, assigned to the wife of Pluto, seems to be nothing more than an adaptation of the Greek Persephonê.

But if Pluto and Proserpina are undoubtedly Greek, we have a group of earth deities in Italy which are not less certainly Latin. They are for the most part little more than names, and some of them merely denote processes of agriculture. Thus Saturnus,[1] identified by literary poets like Virgil with the Greek Kronos, whom he in no way resembles, is simply the sower of the seed, and answers, therefore, more nearly to the Eleusinian Triptolemos. With no better reason Ops, a goddess of wealth and fertility, who was assigned to him as his wife, and whose name corresponds in meaning with that of Ploutôn and Pluto, was identified with Rhea. At the end of his work Saturn is said to have vanished from the earth, as Persephonê disappears when the summer has come to an end; and the local tradition went, we are told, that Latium[2] was his lurking place.

IV. Saturnus and Ops.

In the Latin Genii we have beings closely akin to the Dryads and Hamadryads of the Greeks. Their life ceased, it was supposed, with that of the persons whom they guarded. The name Dii Indigetes was nothing more than a title for those mythical heroes of the land who after death were ranked among the gods.

The Latin Genii and Dii Indigetes.

With Saturn we may take Pilumnus, Picumnus, and Semo-Sancus. The first and second of these are said to have been brothers, and were worshipped as rural deities; but their names are mere epithets, Pilumnus being the

---

[1] We may compare the name with the Teutonic Sætere.

[2] From a supposed connexion with the verb *latere*, to lie hid. The explanation was undoubtedly wrong. Latium is the land of the Latini, a name which seems to assume a wonderfully large variety of forms, whatever may be the common source of them all.

grinder of corn, and Picumnus the tiller of the earth. The names Semo-Sancus are sometimes taken together to denote a single deity. They belong really to two gods, Sancus being, like the Zeus Pistios or Horkios of the Greeks, the ratifier of oaths and contracts; and Semo, like Saturnus, the sower of the seed. In the Palici we have twin deities worshipped in Sicily, of whom little more is known than the names, which may, perhaps, be connected with that of Pales, a rural deity worshipped especially by shepherds. *Pilumnus, Picumnus, and Semo-Sancus.*

Pomona was the Latin goddess of fruit trees and their fruits, as Flora was the guardian of flowering plants. As there was nothing answering exactly to her in Greek mythology, Pomona retained her Latin form, and is said to have been loved by Silvanus, a deity of the woods; by Picus, who, like Picumnus, is the tiller of the ground; and by Vertumnus, the god of the changing seasons. In these returning seasons the giver of plenty was known as Anna Perenna, of whom Virgil speaks as a sister of the Carthaginian queen, Dido. This name was naturally referred to the words *annus* and *perennis* by a people who had forgotten its original meaning; but the origin thus assigned is to the last degree unlikely. It is noteworthy that in Sanskrit we have a deity named Apna-purna, 'who gives subsistence, who is bent by the weight of her full breasts, and in whom all good is united.' The title Apna, which we have already met with in the Apsaras,[1] points to nourishment by water, while Purna belongs apparently to the same stem with the Latin *pario*, to produce. A similar idea is expressed in the title Bona Dea, or good goddess, who is described as a sister or daughter of Faunus, and who was worshipped only by women. She is herself called Fauna; but Fauna and Faunus seem to mean simply the favourers, and were rural deities of the old Latins. *Pomona and Anna Perenna.*

Of the Latin god Consus little more is known than that

[1] Note 3, p. 204.

the festival called Consualia was held in his honour. The name may be connected with that of the Consentes Dii; but it is by no means likely that even this name may be taken as indicating a divine council, both the notion and the thing being little congenial to the spirit of the Latin religion. There is, perhaps, an affinity of name between the Latin Consus and the Indian Ganesa, the lord of life and the reproductive powers of nature, the name reappearing in the Greek *genos* and our *kin*. Hence it is, perhaps, that when Romulus is in want of women for his new city, it is to Consus that he makes his vows and prayers. The Consualia would thus precisely correspond with the Eleusinian festival of Dêmêtêr.

<small>V. Consus.</small>

The story of the earth and her treasures, which the Eleusinians embodied in their myth of Dêmêtêr, the Athenians associated with the name of Erichthonios; and the rivalry of the two cities, which, if we may believe the tradition recorded by Herodotus, found expression in war, may have had something to do with the growth of the independent Athenian tale, which spoke of Erichthonios as a son of Atthis, daughter of Kranaos, another version calling him a child of Athênê herself. But Kranaos, as we have seen,[1] is a title of Athênê, and Atthis is probably only the dawn-goddess of Athens under a slight disguise. In the story related by Apollodoros, Athênê becomes his mother when she goes to Hephaistos to ask for a suit of armour. Soon after the birth of the child she places it in a chest, and giving it to the three sisters, Pandrosos, Hersê, and Agraulos,[2] charges them not to raise the lid. They disobey, and find the coils of a snake folded round the body of the babe. They throw themselves down the precipice of the Akropolis; and the dragon-bodied or snake-bound Erichthonios lives on under the special pro-

<small>VI. Erichthonios, and his kinsfolk.</small>

---

[1] See p. 71.
[2] Of these three Hersê is the mother of Prokris; and Pandrosos, the all-dewy, is but the reduplication of Hersê. Agraulos is simply the being whose abode is the open country.

tection of Athênê. But Erichthonios himself reappears in his grandson Erechtheus, who is said to have been killed by the thunderbolts of Zeus after his daughters had been sacrificed to atone for the slaughter of Eumolpos by the Athenians. But both these legends simply repeat the myth of the dragon-bodied Kekrops, who is said to have given his name to the land which till then had been called Akte, and who was the father of the faithless nurses of Erichthonios.

Like the Greek words Hersê, Selênê, and Helios, the Latin Tellus or Terra was a name the meaning of which was never either lost or weakened. It belongs to a group of words, all denoting dryness and comparative hardness; and the Latin *terra* is, in fact, the *dry* land; but it was otherwise with Mars, whom the Latin poets of the literary age identified with the Hellenic Arês. The two names contain, as we have seen, the same root; but the genuine Latin Mars was originally the reaper of fruits and grain, his name pointing to the softer and milder aspects of decay. Hence he is commonly known as Silvanus, the god of the woods, who softens the earth and prepares its harvests. As such, he was venerated as the father of all living things, Marspiter or Maspiter, the parent of the twin Romulus and Remus.

<small>Terra, Tellus, and Mars.</small>

As the child of Ouranos and Gaia, Rhea,[1] the mother of the great Olympian deities, is closely connected with the earth; and she became pre-eminently the great mother, worshipped under the names Mâ and Abbas, and perhaps more widely known as Kybele and Kybêbê.[2]

<small>VII. Rhea.</small>

There remain still certain groups of mysterious beings whose origin cannot perhaps be determined with any approach to absolute certainty, but who both in their names

---

[1] See p. 36.
[2] For the origin of the name Rhea, see *Myth. of Ar. Nat.* ii. 312. The names Kybele and Kybêbê are certainly not Greek; hence it is probable that, like Adonis, Melikertes, Bacchus, and many others, they may be Semitic.

and in their character seem to have little or nothing in common with the creations of genuine Aryan mythology.

The Kabeiroi and Idaian Daktyloi. Among these the most important are the Kabeiroi (Cabiri), the Korybantes, the Idaian Daktyloi, the Kouretes (Curetes), and the Telchines. The efforts made to explain these names by a comparison with Greek words, or with the words of any Aryan language, cannot be regarded as successful. At the utmost we can only say that in one or two instances the explanation is plausible, and no more. We have to note further that they belong to lands lying far to the east; and thus still further warrant is given for the surmise that both the names of these beings and the ideas expressed by them may be Semitic. The lightness, grace, and beauty of genuine Greek or Aryan mythical creations are absent from the forms of these strange beings, who are in some instances dwarfish, in others uncouth and repulsive. The Kabeiroi, whatever else they may be, are described as nourishers of the earth and its fruits, and as the givers of wine to the Argonauts; and if their name is only a Grecised form of the Semitic Gibbor and Gibborim,[1] they are the 'mighty ones' who carry on the great work of reproduction throughout the material world. The Telchines are pre-eminently forgers of iron, weapons, or instruments for the gods, and they resemble the metal-working Kyklôpes, not only in their work, but in their parentage, which exhibits them as sons of Poseidon, and may possibly imply that, like him, they had crossed the sea from Semitic lands. They are creatures without feet, they can pour down rain and snow on the earth, and they can change their form at will. According to Strabo, those of the Telchines who went with Rhea to Crete were there called Kourêtes, as guardians of Zeus, the child (Kouros); but the explanation is probably worth as much or as little as that which the Greeks could give of the name Prometheus.

[1] Brown, *Great Dionysiak Myth*, vol. ii. 133, 213.

NYMPHS AND SATYRS. 243

Among the inhabitants of the forests and waters are the Satyrs and Seilenoi, or children of Seilenos. Of these the former dwelt amongst woods and hills; the latter haunted streams, fountains, or marshy grounds, and are thus, like the Naiads, spirits of the waters. The grotesque form which Seilenos is made to assume may be an exaggeration of the Western Greeks, who saw in the ass which bore him a mere sign of his folly and absurdity, while it points rather to the high value set upon that animal by Eastern nations. It was, in fact, the symbol of his wisdom and of his prophetical powers, and not the mere beast of burden which in Western myths staggered along under the weight of an unwieldy drunkard. The story of his being caught in the rose gardens of Midas connects him with the myth of that Phrygian king who, as we have seen, is only Tantalos in another form.[1] The fancies which represented the children of Seilenos and the Satyrs as having human heads, arms, and breasts, with the lower parts of goats, are probably of comparatively late growth. But the name of Seilenos, as a water-sprite, may suggest a comparison with the Italian Silanus, a word for gushing or bubbling streams, and with the Seirens, who likewise haunt the waters.[2] Akin to these are the Oreads or spirits of the mountains, and the Dryads, or nymphs living in or with trees. The name Hamadryad expresses more fully the notion that the duration of their life was determined by that of the tree to which they were attached.

The Satyrs and Seilenoi.

[1] See p. 100.   [2] See p. 192.

CHAPTER VIII.

THE UNDER-WORLD AND THE DARKNESS.

AMONG the ideas earliest impressed on the mind of the primitive Aryans was the yearly stealing away of the treasures of the earth or dawn-mother by the greedy and pitiless winter. In the Teutonic story the serpent Fafnir lies coiled round the maiden Brynhild and her wealth of gold on the Glistening Heath. In the Eleusinian myth Dêmêtêr mourns for the beautiful child who has been taken away to the regions of darkness. These regions, therefore, become a prison or a storehouse, containing the germs of all future harvests; and thus, as the earth was regarded as a flat surface, the underworld became a land of unimaginable riches, although it was not on this account rendered less gloomy. The lord of this cheerless abode, according to Hellenic belief, was Hades or Aides, the third of the three Kronid brothers and children of Rhea. We might suppose that his name in some of its forms denotes his sovereignty over an unseen kingdom. The variations Ais, Aides, and Aidoneus seem at the least to indicate such a belief among the Greek tribes: but in this belief they may have been as much mistaken as in most of the explanations of names which they attempted to interpret without the knowledge of any language but their own. The helmet[1] given to him by the Cyclopes renders the wearer invisible. Thus Perseus, to whom it is given when he goes to the Gorgon land, cannot be seen so long as he has it on his head, but is again visible

Ἄϊδος κυνέη, Il. 5. 845.

I.
Hades.

when he takes it in his hand. It is, in short, the Tarnkappe of the popular German stories, and of the Nibelungenlied. But we may fairly doubt whether Hades and Aides are merely different forms of the same name, or whether they are not, rather, two distinct words. The name of Hödr, the slayer of Balder, can scarcely be left out of consideration, when we are dealing with a cognate being in Greek tradition.

As one of the Kronid gods, Hades is spoken of as Zeus Katachthonios, or the Zeus of the under-world. His bride is the maiden (Korê) for whom the earth-mother mourns during the months of winter, and who then returns to gladden gods and men with the sunshine and fruits of summer; but in later versions of the myth Hades himself never departs from his dark abode, and therefore he was never reckoned among the twelve Olympian gods. In the Iliad and Odyssey this distinction is not known; and there he has the power of going at will to Olympos. He appears before Zeus and the gods, when he is wounded by Herakles. *Hades and the Olympian gods.*

The home of Hades is the bourne to which all the children of men must come, and from which no traveller returns;[1] and thus he becomes the host who must receive all under his roof, and whom it is best therefore to invoke as one who will give them a kindly welcome—in other words, as Polydektes, Polydegmon, or Pankoites, the hospitable one, who will assign to every man his place of repose. Still none can forget the awful character of the Pylartes or gatekeeper of the lower world. He must be addressed, not as Hades the unseen, but as Ploutôn (Pluto) the wealthy; and the averted face of the man who offered sacrifice to him may remind us of the rites of the devil-worshippers of the Lebanon at the present day. His palace is guarded by the monstrous dogs Orthros and Kerberos (Cerberus), the latter of whom has three *Hades Polydegmon.*

[1] As such, it is Anostos.

heads. These are the Vritra and Çarvara of the Vedic mythology of India. On examining the myth generally, we can scarcely fail to see that there is little in the way of continuous story related of this god. We have a series of separate pictures, describing either his person, his character, or his abode. He is connected with the upper world chiefly through his wife Persephonê; and he comes on the field of Enna, just as she has plucked the deadly narcissus or lethargic plant, only to steal her away, and is noticed again only as suffering her to return to earth when the messenger of Zeus constrains him. In describing his shadowy kingdom poets might exercise their fancy; but their notions could only add to the separate features by which some idea might be imparted of the outlines of the unknown land. It had first, it would seem, one river running through it, the Acheron, whose name is probably only another form of the Achelôos, and of the many other words for running water which contain the same root with the Latin *aqua*. But to a Greek ear the name Acheron called up the idea of grief and pain, and the stream was therefore supposed to be laden with aches and woe. It became easy to multiply the number of such streams, and to place on its desolate wastes the gloomy Styx, at which men shudder, as the boundary which separates the world of the dead from the world of the living, and to lead through them the channels of Lethe, in which all things are forgotten, of Kokytos (Cocytus), which echoes only with groans of pain, and of Pyriphlegethon, whose waves are billows of fire.

The passage beyond which this gloomy region lies is guarded by Erebos, who in the Hesiodic Theogony is described as the offspring of Chaos. This name may perhaps be Aryan: it is more probably non-Aryan. To the Semitic tribes Arabia is not the eastern but the western land, and the Algarve of Portugal answers to the Estremadura of Spain. In the name of his son Charon we come back to a word which is perhaps both Aryan

<small>Erebos and Charon.</small>

THE HOME OF THE BLESSED.

and Greek. He is the grim and silent ferryman who bears the souls of the dead across the Stygian stream to the judgment seat of Minos, Rhadamanthys, and Aiakos (Æacus); but probably before the myth took this definite shape, he was, as his name seemingly denotes him to be, the ogre with gaping jaws always hungering to swallow any prey that may come within his reach. He would thus belong to the family of the Greek Lamyroi, or devourers, who reappear in the Latin Lemures or Manduci.

But a sojourn in the gloomy land of Hades is not the doom of all, or lasts but for a while. Those who are accepted as righteous by the three judges pass to the happy abodes of Elysion, far away in the west, where the sun goes down beyond the bounds of the earth. Here no grief or sorrow, no sickness or pain, can ever touch them. In the description of this blissful abode we have the same images of beauty which are seen in the pictures drawn of the palace of Alkinoös; and the source from which they spring is the same. The phrases bring before us the glories of the golden sea, in which the sun sinks to rest; and the thought of those who have passed away after having done great things and won themselves a place among the good and noble of mankind was naturally associated with the peace and rest of this unsullied home. Achilles is here and Hektor; but the hand of the Trojan hero is clasped in the hand of the man who slew him. Helen, too, is here 'pardoned and purified,' and is now the bride of him who left Phthia to fight in a quarrel which was not his own. It is, after all, only another version of the myth which reunites Iolê with Herakles, Urvasî with Purûravas, Psyche with Eros; but if the myth itself was in its origin purely physical, it led the mind of the primitive men on to the thought of trial and purification; and the human mind, having advanced thus far, could not fail to advance further. Hence we have in the later descriptions of the unseen world ideas which have passed from the region of mythology

II. Elysion.

into that of theology. The reprobate are conveyed to Tartaros, the name of which is akin to Thalassa, the heaving and restless sea; but Tartaros must at the first have been an epithet of Hades as strictly as Polydegmon or Ploutôn. In the Hesiodic Theogony, Tartaros and Gaia are the parents of the Gigantes, of Typhôeus, and Echidna; and thus Tartaros is placed in the same rank with Poseidon.

The land of Hades is essentially the land of darkness; but whether in that unseen region, or under the conditions of an existence here, it is impossible to get rid of the idea of an absolute antagonism between darkness and light. In the conflict so caused the Vedic hymns represent men as taking their part. Their sacrifices supply the steeds of Indra with food, and from them the god receives the Soma on which his own strength depends.[1] In the Rig Veda the idea of darkness is closely connected with that of drought, and the cows which nourish the sons of men with their milk are hidden away by the robbers in their gloomy caverns. On this theme the Vedic poets are never tired of dwelling. Clearly they found in it no monotony; and their language leaves on us no impression of forced and useless iteration. The battle between light and darkness, between drought and fertility, may assume a thousand forms; and in each we may have the germ of an epic poem. There is, therefore, absolutely no weight or force in the argument which urges this supposed monotony as a conclusive reason for asserting that in their plot and their materials the Iliad and Odyssey, the Ramayana and the Nibelungenlied, can have nothing in common. If we confine ourselves to the mere outlines of human life, birth, marriage, toil and death, that life has a wearisome, and indeed an intolerable monotony; but when we think of the colouring thrown over all the incidents of that life, the infinite play of motives, and the infinite variety of results involved in it, it is seen to be a drama of wonderful richness, of

The conflict of light and darkness.

[1] See p 8.

the most varied action, and of the most touching interest. We thus see that the phrases to which we owe the myth of Indra could not fail sooner or later to give birth to the Iliad. In the former the enemy of the sun-god imprisons the rain-giving clouds; in the other, Paris steals away the radiant Helen. In both there is a fierce struggle, which in both has the same issue. At first the fight of Indra with the demon of drought was simply a struggle to gain possession of the rain-clouds; but his enemy soon begins to assume a hateful moral character. We have thus two antagonistic powers facing each other in internecine war: on the one side the sun-god as beneficent as he is irresistible; on the other, the Vritra, or being who seeks to veil or cloud his splendours. In the earliest hymns this name is little more than an epithet denoting hostility; and the phrase, 'Vritra of the Vritras,' meant simply the most malignant of foes. He is Vritra, he is Ahi the throttler, he is Çarvara, he is Vala, who after a thousand transformations reappears in the English Wayland the Smith. He is also, as we have seen, Çushan, Çambara, Namuki; and lastly he is the Pani, or seducer, who entices the cows of Indra to leave their pastures, and then seeks to corrupt Saramâ, who is sent to bring them back. But Pani is Paris, and Saramâ is Helen;[1] and thus we have in the Vedic hymns the first preparation for the framework on which was reared afterwards the fabric of the great epic poems of the Greek world.

The battle between Indra and Vritra is waged, therefore, chiefly because the demon of drought and darkness has imprisoned the waters; and we have already had abundant evidence to show how strongly this idea was impressed on the mind of the Western Aryans. The Python at Delphi, the worm slain by Kadmos at Thebes, the Sphinx discomfited by Œdipus, all withhold from the earth the nourishment indispensably needed for

The shutting up of the waters.

---
[1] See note 4, p. 58.

it; and when they are slain, the dry land is refreshed with water. But in some passages in the Rig Veda the victims of Vritra are spoken of not as cows or clouds, but as women; and thus Sita, the bride of Rama, who is carried off by the giant Ravana, answers closely to Helen, who is borne away by Paris from Sparta. The story of the Odyssey does little more than reproduce that of Saramâ, the only difference between the Vedic goddess and Penelope being that the latter, unlike the former, is absolutely unswerving in her fidelity. Saramâ is tempted by an offer of a share in the Pani's booty. Penelope is told, also, that she shall share the treasures if she will become the wife of any one of the suitors for her hand. These men bring about their own ruin; and the issue in both cases is the same. 'I do not know that Indra is to be subdued,' says Saramâ, 'for it is he himself that subdues; you Panis will lie prostrate, killed by Indra.' In like manner Penelope points to a weapon which will bring the suitors to death if ever her lord returns home; and they are at length smitten down by the arrows of Odysseus as certainly as the Vritras are slain by the spear of Indra.

In the West, Vritra and his peers are represented by a host as numerous as are their followers in the hymns of the Rig Veda. Among the most prominent of these creations of the Western mind are Typhon and Typhoeus, the beings who, like the Vritra, vomit out smoke and flames—in other words, the lightnings which precede the fall of the pent-up rain. In the Hesiodic Theogony, Typhon is the father of those winds which bring ruin and havoc to mortals. By this devastating hurricane Echidna becomes the mother of Kerberos, of the Lernaian Hydra, of the Chimera, the Sphinx, and the Nemean lion, all of these being representatives of the dark powers who fight with and are overcome by the lord of day.

Typhon and Typhoeus.

One of the most noteworthy versions of the myth of Indra and the Panis is found in the story of Hercules and

Cacus, localised in Italy. The Latin god Hercules was connected, we cannot doubt, with boundaries and fences. He was, in fact, Jupiter Terminus, the Zeus Horios of the Greeks; and as such his name was Herclus or Herculus, as is shown by the popular exclamations Mehercule, Mehercle. But the similarity of the name furnished to the literary Romans an irresistible temptation to identify their Herculus or Hercules with the Greek Herakles. They were further strengthened in their conclusion by the fact that a hero named Garanus, or Recaranus, was said to have slain a great robber named Cacus, and that this hero closely resembled not only Herakles, but Perseus, Theseus, and all other destroyers of monsters and evil-doers. This story of Cacus is told in many ways; but the most popular version says that when Hercules reached the banks of the Tiber, Cacus, the three-headed son of Vulcan, stole some of his cattle, and, to avoid detection, dragged them backwards into his cave. But their lowing reached the ears of Hercules, who, forcing his way into the robber's den, recovered not only his cattle, but all the stolen treasures which he had stored within it. In vain Cacus vomited forth smoke and flame upon his enemy, who soon slew him with his unerring darts. This myth is only another form of the many tales which recount the conflict of the sun-god with the powers of night or darkness. Garanus, or Recaranus, who is called by Aurelius Victor the slayer of Cacus,[1] is, like Sancus, whose name was also inscribed on the Ara Maxima, or great altar, of Hercules, simply Jupiter— Garanus being so named as the maker or creator of things.[2] Recaranus must, therefore, be the god who makes again, or who, like Ushas, renders all things young. Recaranus would thus denote the Re-creator, and so the Recuperator or recoverer of the cattle stolen by Cacus or Vritra, for Cacus in the Latin story is a three-headed monster, answer-

---

[1] *Myth. of Ar. Nat.* ii. 340.
[2] The word contains the same root with Kreon, Lat. *creo*, &c.

ing to the Greek Geryon and Kerberos, the Indian Çarvara. As stealing the cows of Hercules, he is Vritra, who shuts up the rain in the thunder-cloud, and who is pierced by the lance of Indra. The flames which he sends forth from his cave are the lightning flashes preceding that downfall of the rain which is signified by the recovery of the cows from Cacus. When then the Roman, becoming acquainted with the Greek myths, found the word Alexikakos (as keeping off evil and mischief) among the epithets of Herakles, he naturally came to regard Recaranus as only another name for that hero. But the quantity of the name Cacus leaves no room for this explanation. The first syllable is long, and the word given by Diodorus under the form Kakios and reappearing in the Præenestine Cæculus seems to warrant the conclusion that the true Latin form was Cæcius, as Sæturnus answers to Saturnus. What then is Cæcius? The idea of the being who bears this name is clearly that of the Vedic Vritra, the being who steals the rain-clouds and blots out the light from the sky. Now, in a proverb cited by Aulus Gellius from Aristotle, a being of this name is mentioned as possessing the power of drawing the clouds towards him;[1] and thus we have the explanation of an incident which, translated into the conditions of human life, becomes a clumsy stratagem. In storms, when contrary currents are blowing at different elevations, the clouds may often appear from the earth to be going against or right towards the wind. Then it is that Cacus, Cæcius, is drawing the cattle of Herakles by their tails towards his cave.

The powers of drought and darkness have been brought before us already in many myths; and on some of these it is unnecessary to dwell longer now. We have traced the monster Belleros, slain by the Corinthian Hippoönos, to the far East; and of the Theban Sphinx

Belleros and the Sphinx.

[1] κἄκ' ἐφ' αὑτὸν ἕλκων, ὡς ὁ Καικίας νέφος. See further *Myth. of Ar. Nat.* ii. 341.

we need only say that some versions of the story made her a daughter of Laios. But Laios represents the Sanskrit *dasas* or enemies of the gods, and their slayer is Dasyuhan, which transliterated into Greek becomes Leophontes, a name by which Hipponoös is almost as much known as he is by that of Bellerophon. The coming of the Sphinx is ascribed in some stories to the wrath of Hêrê for the offence of Laios in carrying off Chrysippos from Pisa; in others to Arês, who wished to avenge himself on Cadmus for killing his offspring the dragon. The death of the Sphinx, like that of the dragon, is followed by the letting loose of the waters; and in the tradition of Northern Europe the same result follows the death of the dragon Fafnir, although the rain is here spoken of as his blood. Sigurd knows that the slaying of the monster will be followed by a deluge, and he is bidden to dig a pit in the dragon's pathway, and then getting into the pit to smite him to the heart. But his fears are not allayed; and Odin tells him therefore to dig many pits which may catch the (blood or) rain, and thus the streams are made to fertilise the earth, and the victory of the sun-god is accomplished. A character approaching to the more modern ghost or goblin stories is imparted to the legend related by Pausanias of the hero of Temessa, who is the demon of one of the companions of Odysseus slain for wrong done to a maiden of that city. The ravages of this demon, we are told, could be stayed only by the building of a temple in his honour, and by the yearly sacrifice of a maiden at his shrine. The demon, encountered by the wrestler Euthymos (the valiant-hearted), who is resolved to win the victim as his bride, sinks into the sea, this being the fate also of the demon Grendel, who ravages the country of king Hrothgar, and who is slain by Beowulf, the wolf-tamer. It may be well to notice, further, how accurately the mythical genealogies register the phenomena of the outward world. As the daughter of Laios, the Sphinx is the sister of Œdipus. The cloud in which the rain is imprisoned, and the clouds from which the refreshing waters are poured fourth, are alike produced in the air; and hence Phœbus Chrysaor and the beautiful nymph Kallirhoê are said to be the parents of the frightful Geryon. All these monsters, again, lurk in secret places, the access to which is difficult, if not impossible. Thus the Panis tell Saramâ that the way to their abode 'is far and leads tortuously away,' a phrase which points perhaps to the more fully developed myth of the Cretan labyrinth.

In all these myths the conflict between the light and the darkness has chiefly, if not wholly, a physical significance. It is the battle of the sun with the powers of the night or with the demons of drought; but the importation of a moral meaning into this struggle would convert the myth into a philosophy or a religion, and this conversion was brought about on Iranian soil. In the Rig Veda we have no clearer sign of the change which might pass over the spirit of the tale than the prayer that the wicked Vritra may not be suffered to reign or tyrannise over the worshippers of Indra. But in Persian mythology the antagonism between Indra and Vritra became the spiritual struggle between moral good and moral evil; and thus phrases suggested by a very common sight in the outward world became the foundation of a philosophical system known as Dualism—in other words, the conflict between two gods, one good, the other evil.

Persian dualism.

In not a few instances the myths thus spiritualised retained the old names. Thus Trita or Traitana[1] becomes the Persian Thraetana, while Verethragna, or the slayer of Verethra, the Feridun of later epic poetry, is the Vedic Vritrahan, the bane or slayer of Vritra. Feridun, again, is the slayer of Zohak (a name which was at first written Azidahaka, the choking or biting serpent), or Ahi, which carries us, as we have seen, to the Greek Echidna. This battle, dimly foreshadowed in the hymns of the Rig Veda,

III. Ormuzd and Ahriman.

---

[1] See p. 72.

becomes in Persian tradition the great conflict between Ormuzd and Ahriman, the former being the good, the latter the evil deity. In Ormuzd the devout Zoroastrian trusted with all the strength of spiritual conviction; but the idea of his enemy was as closely connected with his conception of the righteous God as the idea of Vritra in the mind of the Hindu was associated with that of Indra; and the exaltation of Ormuzd carried the greatness of Ahriman to a pitch which made him the creator and sovereign of an evil universe at war with the Kosmos of the spirit of light. Such was the origin of Iranian dualism, a system which has powerfully affected the religious belief of the world to the present time, dividing the universe between two opposing self-existent deities, while it professedly left to men the power of choosing whom they should obey. 'In the beginning there were two spirits, each of a peculiar activity, These are the Good and the Base in thought, word, and deed. Chose one of these two spirits. Be good, not base.' The name Ormuzd is not a Persian word, and it cannot be explained by the Persian language any more than Helen or Erinys can be explained from the Greek. In the Zend-Avesta, or Zoroastrian books, the name is given in the form Ahurô-Mazdâo, thus carrying us to the Sanskrit words Asuro-medhas, the wise spirit.[1] Ormuzd was also known as Spento-mainyus, or spirit of light, while his adversary became Angro-mainyus, Ahriman, the spirit of darkness.

The moral process which issued in this dualistic philosophy lowered the character of the Vedic Devas. These, with the Hindu, are the bright gods who fight on the side of Indra; but in the Avesta the word Devas and Asuras. has come to mean an evil spirit, and the Zoroastrian was bound to renounce them, and declare in his confession of faith, 'I cease to be a Deva-worshipper; I profess to be a Zoroastrian worshipper of Ahuramazda, an enemy of the Devas, and a devotee to Ahura.' Thus the bright gods of

---

[1] The word *medhas* is the Greek Metis, Polymetis; and the Asuras are the Teutonic Æsir or gods of Asgard.

the Rig Veda were placed side by side with Verethra or Vritra and all their other foes belonging to this class of malignant beings, and were branded with the common epithet, Drukhs,[1] deceitful. The Persian Aêshma-daêva is the Asmodeus, or unclean spirit, of the book of Tobit.[2]

The dualism of Persia found a thoroughly congenial soil in the Jewish mind; but it was not so readily received by the Teutonic nations. This, however, was not because they were strangers to the language which had furnished a foundation for the theology of Zoroaster; but because the beings introduced into his scheme were in the belief of the Western Aryans as of the Hindus overcome and conquered every year. Vritra and Ahi, the Sphinx and the Python, Belleros and Chimera, are all of them brought utterly to nought; and even the conquerors as well as the conquered are not always regarded in a perfectly serious light. Some of them, as Herakles in the myth of Alkestis, assume a burlesque aspect; and all such pictures tend to hinder the translation of phrases which have a purely physical meaning into others which are purely spiritual. Thus Hel had been simply, like Persephonê, the queen of the unseen land; but although she afterwards became not merely the sovereign of Niflheim, but Niflheim itself, her abode was not wholly comfortless. It is here that the old man in the Teutonic popular story hews wood for the Christmas fire, and that the devil, eager to buy the flitch of bacon, resigns for it the quern which is good to grind almost anything. But more particularly in the tales of the Western Aryans, the devil is a being who is perpetually outwitted, and who is regarded with no special horror or even dislike. His home was not so pleasant as the old Valhalla; but it was better to be there than to be thrust forth into the outer cold. The epithets

margin: The Teutonic devil.

---

[1] This word seems to have dropped out of the Western Aryan dialects, except the Greek, in which it is found seemingly only in the word ἀ-τρεκ-ής, *not deceitful*, and therefore accurate or true. *Myth of Ar. Nat.* ii. 353 *et seq.*

[2] For the effects of Persian or Zoroastrian theology on the religion and faith of the Jewish people, see *Myth. of Ar. Nat.* ii. 358.

applied in the Vedic hymns to Vritra are all, or almost all of them, addressed familiarly to the devil, whose name passes through an immense number of forms, every one of which furnishes proof that it belongs to the group of words containing the same root with the Latin *divus, djovis,* and the Sanskrit *deva.* He is the ealda deofol, or old devil, of Cædmon, the old Nick and old Davy of the language of English sailors.[1] He is Vâlant, the cheat; but the notion of his fall from heaven suggested that he must have been lamed by the descent, and so we have the devil upon two sticks, who resembles Hephaistos not only in his gait but in his office.[2] He is the Graumann, or Greyman, the dark and murky being of German popular tradition; and he is also known as the leviathan, or Valfish, in which we again have the deceiving Vala. His dwelling is Ovelgunne, or the Nobiskrug, a late word from the Greek Abyssos.[3] He is also a huntsman; but the mighty procession of Odin is degraded in the wretched throng of evil-doers, who are hurried along in his train. Lastly, he is not merely fooled, but killed through his folly. In one legend he asks a man who is moulding buttons, what he may be doing. The answer is that he is making eyes; and on hearing this, the devil asks if the man can give him a pair of new eyes. He is told that he may have them, but that the operation cannot be properly performed unless he is first tied on his back to a bench. Being thus fastened, he asks the man's name; and the reply is Issi (self). The melted lead poured on his eyes makes him start up in agony, bearing away the bench; and when he is asked who has thus maltreated him, he tells them ' Issi teggi ' (self did it). He is, of course, told to lie on the bed which he has made. His new eyes killed him, and he was never seen again. This is, clearly, a story which substantially agrees with that of Odysseus and Polyphemus; and this story is reproduced in the tale of

---

[1] See p. 46.   [2] This is Wayland the Smith. See p. 249.
[3] Through the Italian form *nabisso* for *in abysso.*

the Robber and his Sons in Grimm's collection. Here the robber, who is the only one not devoured by the giant who represents the Cyclops, blinds his enemy while pretending to heal his eyes. In the sequel, instead of clinging to the ram's fleece, he clings first to the rafters of the ceiling, and then wrapping himself in a ram's skin, escapes between the giant's legs. But no sooner is he out of the cave, than he turns round, like Odysseus, to mock at his enemy; and the giant, saying that so clever a man ought not to go unrewarded, offers him a ring which when he places it on his finger makes him cry out, 'Here I am! here I am!' But even then the giant stumbles and falls in his search, and the robber at last escapes by biting off his finger, and so getting rid of the ring.[1]

[1] For other versions of the story see *Myth. of Ar. Nat.* ii. 366. It has been urged that the behaviour of the hero in these tales, in turning round to mock the giant almost before he is out of his reach, points to a conception wholly different from that of the wise and circumspect hero of the *Odyssey*. This may not prove composite authorship for the poem; but it shows that different lines of thought have been brought into it, and that the poets did not care to remove the inconsistency.

CHAPTER IX.

THE EPICAL TRADITIONS AND POEMS OF THE ARYAN WORLD.

THE great epic poems of the Aryan nations have sprung from germs furnished by a mass of materials, of which the portions rejected are not proved by the fact of their rejection to have been inferior to the portions chosen. In the pages of the Greek mythographers, in German, Scottish, Hindu, or other popular stories, we have a vast number of traditions which, perhaps, never found their way beyond the hands of the story-tellers, but which might have been moulded into series of epics as magnificent as any which have been shaped by the highest human genius. The myths of Perseus and Theseus would have been as rich a mine for the imagination of the poet to work in, as those of Paris, Helen, and Penelope ; but the former, like those of Herakles, have not been used by epic poets as the groundwork of any consecutive story, and many others, not less rich, beautiful, and touching, they have left altogether unnoticed. But the essential character of the materials is the same in all ; and we may, therefore, expect to find in the Aryan epic poems the same conceptions which in a cruder form we find in the primary myths of Endymion and Prokris.

In the Hymns of the Rig Veda the morning brings health and wealth. She discovers hidden treasures which have been locked up in the darkness, and these treasures are seen again in the evening twilight only to be swallowed

Materials for epical poems.

up in the darkness again. But this recurring cycle may be regarded as beginning in the evening quite as easily as in the morning, and perhaps even more naturally, for the mind is more readily impressed by the sense of loss, and by the consequent need of action, in order to make it good. It is, therefore, this idea of treasures stolen by dark robbers, and recovered from them, which has become the root and groundwork of epic poetry, and has produced a harvest of wonderful luxuriance. In the Vedic hymns the action goes on between Indra, Saramâ, and the Panis; but in the Greek epical legends the actors are, as we should expect, human, and the events with which they are connected are put into a form which gave them the semblance of a continuous history of facts. The framework of all these traditions is in their main features the same; but the names and the local colouring are so far changed that they might easily be regarded as independent narratives; and thus a number of tales which really repeat each other, assumed the form of a consecutive series. In the Greek myths the taking away of precious things and the united search of armed hosts for their recovery come before us first in the story of the Argonautic voyage. The tale is repeated in the stealing away of Helen and her treasures [1] by Paris, and is once more told in the banishment of the Herakleids, and their efforts, at last successful, to recover their lost inheritance.

The stolen treasures.

The object of the Argonautic expedition was to recover the golden fleece, of which the following story was told.

I. *The Argonautic expedition.* Phrixos and his sister Hellê were children of Athamas[2] and Nephelê, or the cloud. On the death of Nephelê Athamas married Ino, and Phrixos with his sister lived in great unhappiness until a ram with a golden fleece carried them away. As it soared through the air, Hellê fell off its back and was drowned in

---

[1] They are constantly put together, 'Ελένη καὶ κτήμαθ' ἅμ' αὐτῇ.
[2] See p. 216.

the Hellespont, which bears her name. Her brother[1] was carried onwards to the palace of Aietes, king of Kolchis, and there he sacrificed to Zeus Phyxios, the guardian of fugitives, the ram which had borne him thither. The golden fleece was hung up in the house of Aietes, 'where,' in the words of the poet Mimnermos, 'the rays of Helios rest in a golden chamber;' and thither the Achaian chieftains, urged on by Athamas, came to claim it. The expedition, it is said, was thus planned. Pelias, the chief of Iolkos, the son of Salmoneus and Tyro,[2] had received a warning to be on his guard against a man with only one shoe; and when Iason (Jason), the pupil of the centaur Cheiron, appeared at a sacrifice, having lost one of his sandals in a stream, Pelias bade him go and fetch the golden fleece from Kolchis. Iason accordingly gathered all the great chieftains round about, and sailed away in the ship Argo, which was endowed with the powers of thought and speech, and which refused to descend into the water until it was charmed by the lyre of Orpheus.[3] Besides Orpheus there went with him Herakles, Meleagros, Amphiaraos, Admetos, and other heroes. Sailing eastwards, they passed through the dangerous rocks, called Symplegades, which opened and again closed continually with such quickness that a bird had scarcely time to fly through. The helmsman Tiphys steered the vessel safely through these rocks, which thenceforth became fixed—a tradition which seems to point manifestly to a time when the Black Sea was infested with icebergs brought down by a westerly current and stranded at the entrance to the Bosporos.

Having passed through the land of the Amazons, they at last reached Kolchis, where Iason demanded the fleece from Aietes, who refused to give it up until Iason had ploughed the land with the fire-breathing bulls, and sown it with the dragon's teeth. This he was enabled to

Iason and Medeia.

---

[1] For the reason of Helle's death, and the survival of Phrixos, see p. 216.
[2] See p. 130. [3] See p. 191.

do with the aid of Medeia, the wise daughter of Aietes, who anointed his body with an ointment which protected him against the fiery breath of the bulls, and told him to cast a stone amongst the armed men who would spring up from the dragon's teeth. When the stone was thrown, the men began to fight with each other, and fought on until all were slain. Then Medeia lulled to sleep the dragon which guarded the fleece, and Iason, slaying the monster, gained possession of the treasure and hurried away in the ship Argo. Aietes pursued the vessel in hot haste; but Medeia, who had fled with Iason, cut up her brother Absyrtos and threw his limbs one by one into the sea. Aietes stopped to pick them up, and the Argo thus passed beyond his reach. On the return of the Argonauts to Iolkos, Medeia persuaded the daughters of Pelias to cut up the body of their father and place the limbs in a caldron, saying that she would again restore him to life as in youth. They obeyed; but Medeia, pretending to be looking at the stars in order to learn the right moment for using her spells, allowed his limbs to be consumed, and thus the warning given to Pelias that his doom would come through Iason was fulfilled. From Iolkos Medeia took Iason in her dragon chariot to Argos, where he was smitten with the beauty of Glaukê, the daughter of the Argive king Kreon. So far as her words and gestures went, Medeia seemed to be well pleased, and she sent to Glaukê as a bridal gift the spendid robe which Helios, the sun, gave her before she left her father's house. No sooner had the maiden put it on than the robe began to burn her flesh, and Kreon, who tried to tear it off, died with his child. Having killed her two children, the sons of Iason, Medeia vanished from Argos in her dragon chariot.

This strange tale may be traced back to the myth in which Helios, Hyperion, the climbing sun, was said to go down in the evening into a golden cup or vessel, which carried him across the ocean stream to the abode of black night, where he found his mother, his wife,

<small>The materials of the myth.</small>

and his children, and from this cup he rose again in the morning. But in the oldest Vedic hymns we find the departure of the sun spoken of as leaving men in grief and fear, 'Our friend the sun is dead: will he return?' The idea of a search for the lost friend thus naturally suggested itsel'; and all the things which he had cherished with his warmth in the daytime were supposed to seek for him until they found him and brought him back again. The ship Argo is itself the symbol of the earth as a parent,[1] which contains in itself the germs of all living things. Hence it carries all the Achaian chieftains, who return with renewed strength and vigour when their mission is accomplished. The ship, therefore, is gifted with the powers of speech, because the earth as the parent of all things was regarded as a conscious being, endowed with the powers of thought, sight, and language. The golden fleece, it scarcely needs to be said, is the golden garment of solar light, which reappears as the robe given by the sun-god Helios to Medeia, and which may either warm or scorch and consume those whom it may touch. It is the same robe which Deianeira dipped in the blood of Nessos, and which eats into the body of Herakles himself. As having received this robe, Medeia is a being who possesses the wisdom which belongs to Phœbus Apollo as his birthright. This wisdom is inherited, as we have seen, by Asklepios and Tantalos, as representing the sun, who alone can see into the hidden secrets of Zeus, the sky. This notion, when applied to Medeia as a wise woman, grew into the idea of witchcraft or sorcery. In the story of the dragon's teeth, which is reproduced in the Theban myth of Cadmus, we have a legend which may also be compared with the turning of stones into men in the story of Deukalion, while in the chase of Aietes after the retreating Argo we have the pursuit of Perseus by the Gorgons, the dark powers which may be thought to chase the sun, who leaves them

[1] It is the Yoni of the Hindu. See p. 143. Dutt, *India Past and Present*, p. 42.

behind as he rises in the heavens. In Medeia, as we might expect, the power to destroy is combined with the power of giving or restoring life. The former is possessed by Tantalos or Lykaon, the latter by Asklepios and Herakles. Her dragon chariot is simply the chariot of Indra, Helios, and Achilles; and it is drawn by dragons because the word denoted simply beings of keen sight, and was naturally applied to the creatures which may be supposed to bear the sun across the heaven.

<small>11. The Tale of Troy.</small> The tale of Troy and Ilion is simply another tale of stolen treasure which is recovered after a fierce struggle from the powers of darkness, which had carried them away from the West. It consists of that series of legends which together make up the mythical history of Paris, Helen, Achilles, and Odysseus. Parts only of this tale—and, indeed, a very small part—are contained in the Iliad and Odyssey, to which almost exclusively we are in the habit of giving the name of Homer; but expressions and hints scattered throughout these poems prove clearly that the poets were acquainted with many incidents and episodes of the story, about which they did not care to speak in detail. The tale begins with the birth of Paris, whose mother Hekabê (Hecuba) dreamt that her son was a torch which would destroy the city of Ilion. Owing to this foreboding of evil, the child was exposed, we are told, on the heathy sides of Mount Ida; but, like other Fatal Children, he was rescued by a shepherd, and growing up beautiful, brave, and vigorous, was called Alexandros, the helper of men.[1] Supposing him to be dead, his father Priam ordered a sacrifice to be offered up for his repose in Hades, and his servants chose the favourite bull of Paris, who followed them and was conqueror in his own funeral games. Although no one else knew him, his sister Kasandra, to whom Phœbus had given the power of second sight,

---

[1] If the first part of the word be taken to mean what it evidently means in Alexikakos (see p. 252), the name is susceptible of another interpretation; but it seems unnecessary to resort to this alternative here.

under the penalty that her predictions should not be believed, told them who the victor was. Paris, however, refused to stay with those who had treated him so cruelly in his infancy, and in the dells of Ida he won as his bride Oinônê (Œnone), the beautiful daughter of the stream Kebren. With her he remained, until he departed for Sparta with Menelaos, an event brought about by incidents far away in the West, which were to lead to mighty issues.

At the marriage feast of Peleus and Thetis, Eris (strife), who had not been invited with the other deities, cast on the table a golden apple, which was to be given to the fairest of all the guests. It was claimed by Hêrê, Athênê and Aphroditê, and Zeus made Paris the umpire. By him, as we have seen, it was given to Aphroditê, who in return promised him Helen, the fairest of all women, as his wife. Some time after this there fell on Sparta a sore famine, from which the Delphian oracle said that they could be delivered only by bringing back the bones of the children of Prometheus. For this purpose Menelaos, the king, came to Ilion, and returned with Paris, who saw the beautiful Helen at Sparta, and carried her away with her treasures to Troy. Resolving to rescue her from Paris, Menelaos invited Agamemnon, king of Mykenai (Mycenæ), and other great chieftains to take part in the expedition which was to avenge his wrongs and to recover the wealth of which he had been despoiled. Among these chiefs were the aged Nestor, the wise ruler of Pylos; Aias (Ajax), the son of Telamon; Askalaphos and Ialmenos, sons of Arês; Diomedes, son of Tydeus; and Admetos of Pherai, the husband of Alkestis. But the greatest of all were Achilles, the son of Peleus and the sea-nymph Thetis, and Odysseus, the son of Laertes, chieftain of Ithaca.

The judgment of Paris.

The forces thus gathered went to Troy by sea; but the fleet was becalmed in Aulis, and Kalchas, the seer, affirming that this was caused by the anger of Artemis for the slaughter of a stag in her sacred grove, declared that she could be appeased only by the sacrifice

Agamemnon and Iphigeneia.

of Iphigeneia, the daughter of Agamemnon.[1] According to the story in the Iliad the sacrifice was made; but there was another version which said that Artemis herself rescued Iphigeneia, while others again said that Artemis and Iphigeneia were one and the same. If, however, her blood was shed, the penalty must be paid; and so in the terrible drama of Æschylus we find the Atê, whose office it is to exact this penalty to the last farthing, brooding on the house of Agamemnon, until she had brought about the death of the king by the hands of his wife Klytaimnestra (Clytemnestra), and the death of Klytaimnestra and her paramour Aigisthos by the hands of her son Orestes.

The hindrance to the eastward course of the Achaians was now removed, but the achievement of their task was still far distant. Nine years must pass in seemingly hopeless struggle; in the tenth, Ilion would be taken. So mighty was to be the defence of the city, maintained chiefly by Hektor, the son of Priam and brother of Paris, aided by the chiefs of the neighbouring cities, among whom were Aineias (Æneas), son of Anchises and Aphroditê; Pandaros, son of Lykaon, and bearer of the bow of Apollo; and Sarpêdôn, who with his friend Glaukos led the Lykians from the banks of the eddying Xanthos.[2] The legend of this brilliant hero is, as we have seen, one of the many independent myths which have been introduced into the framework of our Iliad. He is distinctly a being of the same order with Saranyû, Erinys, Iason, Helen, and many more; and the process which made him an ally of Paris is that which separated Odysseus from the eye of the Cyclops, whom he blinded.[3] Another episode of a like kind is that of Memnon, who, like Sarpêdôn, comes from a bright and glistering land; but instead of Lykia it is in this instance Ethiopia. The meaning of the name Sarpêdôn had been so far forgotten that the chief was regarded as a ruler of mortal Lykians, and we are told that his cairn was

Sarpêdôn and Memnon.

---

[1] See p. 159. [2] See p. 133. [3] See pp. 107, 179.

raised high to keep alive his name amongst his people, although there were versions of the myth which brought him back again to life. But Eôs, the mother of Memnon, is so transparently the morning, that her child must rise again as surely as the sun reappears to run his daily course across the heaven. Like Sarpêdôn, he is doomed to an early death; and when he is smitten by the hand of Achilles, the tears of Eôs are said to fall as morning dew from the sky. To comfort her Zeus makes two flocks of birds meet in the air and fight over his funeral sacrifice, until some of them fall as victims on the altar. But Eôs is not yet satisfied, and she not only demands but wins the return of her child from Hades. The thought of a later age becomes manifest in the tale that when Memnon fell in atonement for the slaughter of Antilochos, his comrades were so plunged in grief that they were changed into birds which yearly visited his tomb to water the ground with their tears.

The story of Achilles himself has many points of marked likeness to the myths of these two heroes; but his guardian Phenix actually recites to him the career of Meleagros as the very counterpart of his own. *The wrath of Achilles.* What the career of Meleagros really signifies we have already seen;[1] and we need only mark what the Iliad tells us, if we would trace the unconscious fidelity of the poet to the types of character sketched out for him in the old mythical phrases. Achilles is pre-eminently the irresistible hero who fights in a quarrel which is not his own. As Herakles served the mean Eurystheus, so Achilles is practically the servant of one on whom he looks down with deserved contempt. But he has his consolation in the love of Briseis, and when he is called upon to surrender the maiden, he breaks out into the passion of wrath which in the opening lines of the Iliad is said to be the subject of the poem. Although the fury of his rage is subdued by

[1] See p. 68.

the touch of the dawn-goddess Athênê, he yet vows a solemn vow that henceforth in the war the Achaians shall look in vain for his aid. But inasmuch as in many of the books which follow the first the Achaian heroes get on perfectly well without him, winning great victories over the Trojans,[1] and as no reference is made in them to his wrath or to its consequences, the conclusion seems to be forced upon us that these books belong to an independent poem which really was an Iliad, or a history of the struggle of the Achaians for the possession of Ilion or Troy; and that this Iliad, which begins with the second book, has been pieced together with the other poem, which relates to the wrath of Achilles and its results, and is therefore an Achillêis. Thus the poem which we call the Iliad would consist of two poems, into which materials from other poems may or may not also have been worked in. It is, of course, quite possible that these two poems, the Iliad and the Achillêis, may both be the work of one and the same poet, who chose thus to arrange his own compositions; and this is the opinion of some whose judgment on such points is worthy of respect. But although the question is one on which an absolute decision may be unattainable, the balance of likelihood seems to be in favour of the conclusion that these great epic poems grew up in the course of a long series of ages. We have already seen how the germs of a story full of human passion and feeling might be found in epithets, in words, or in phrases, which the forefathers of the Aryan tribes, while yet in their original home, applied consciously to the sights and sounds of the outward world, these sights and sounds being regarded as the work of beings who could feel, and suffer, and toil, and rejoice like ourselves. This language was, strictly, the language of poetry, literally revelling in its boundless powers of creation and development. In almost every word lay the material

---

[1] *Myth. of Ar. Nat.* i. 240. Mure, *Critical History of Greek Literature*, i. 256. Grote, *History of Greece*, Part I. ch. xxi.

of some epical incident; and it is the less wonderful, therefore, if each incident was embodied in a separate legend, or even reproduced in the independent tales of separate tribes. A hundred Homers may well have lit their torch from this living fire.[1]

In the ninth book we return to the subject of the wrath of Achilles. The victorious career of the Achaian chieftains is interrupted, and they are made to feel their need of the great hero, who keeps away from the strife. But the embassy which they send to him goes to no purpose, although Phenix holds up to him as a warning the doom of the Kalydonian Meleagros. There must be humble submission, and Briseis must be restored. But Agamemnon cannot yet bring himself to this abasement, and the struggle goes on with varying success and disaster, until their misfortunes so multiply as to excite the compassion of Patroklos, the friend who reflects the character of Achilles without possessing his strength, and who thus belongs to the class of Secondaries.[2] Melted by the tears of this friend, Achilles gave him his own armour, and bade him go forth to aid the Argives, adding a strict caution, which cannot fail to remind us of the story of Phaethon. As Phaethon is charged not to touch the horses of Helios with his whip, so Patroklos must not drive the chariot of Achilles, which is borne by the same undying steeds, on any other path than that which has been pointed out to him. But we are especially told that although Patroklos could wear his friend's armour, he could not wield his spear. The sword and lance of the sun-god may be used by no other hands than his own. As in the story of Phaethon, so here the command was disobeyed; and thus Patroklos, after slaying Sarpêdôn, was himself overpowered and killed by Hektor, who stripped off

<small>Achilles and Patroklos.</small>

---

[1] For a more full examination of the question of the composition of the Homeric poems, see *Myth. of Ar. Nat.* Book I. ch. ix.-xi. and the works there referred to.
[2] See p. 93.

from his body the glittering armour of his friend. In the heart of that friend the tidings of his death rekindled the fury of the passion which had long been only smouldering. Beneath 'the black cloud of his sorrow' his anguish was preparing an awful vengeance. The beauty of his countenance was marred; but the nymphs rose up from the sea to comfort him. To all consolation he replies that he must have revenge; and when Thetis, his mother, warns him that the death of Hektor must soon be followed by his own, his answer is that even Herakles, the dearest son of Zeus, had submitted to the same hard lot, and that he is ready to face it himself. He has still his unerring spear; and it only remains that he should wait for the glistening armour, wrought on the anvil of the fire-god Hephaistos. But although the hour of his vengeance is not yet come, his countenance still had its terrors, and the very sight of his form filled the Trojans with dismay, as they heard his well-known war cry. His work is in part done. The body of Patroklos is recovered, and Achilles makes a vow that the blood of twelve Trojans shall gush in twelve streams on the altar of sacrifice. But the old phrases which spoke of Herakles as subject to death, still spoke of both as coming forth conquerors of the power which had seemed to subdue them; and true to the ancient speech, the poet makes Thetis assure her son that no hurtful thing shall touch the body of Patroklos, and that, though it should be untended the whole year round, his face should wear at its close a more glorious and touching beauty.

The end now draws nigh. Agamemnon is so far humbled, that he promises to yield to him the maiden whom he had taken away; but with a persistency which except by thinking of the sources of the story we cannot understand, he asserts his own innocence. 'I am not guilty,' he said; 'the blame rests with Zeus and Moira,[1] and Erinys who wanders in the air.'[2]

Achilles and Agamemnon.

[1] See p. 68. [2] See p. 59.

So, again, although on the reappearance of Briseis, Achilles forgives the wrong, he repeats the riddle which lurked in the words of Agamemnon. There was nothing in the son of Atreus, he says, which could really call forth his wrath. 'He could never, in his utter helplessness, have taken the maiden from me against my will; but so Zeus would have it, that the doom of many Achaians might be accomplished.' So he bids them go and eat, and make ready for the fight; but when Agamemnon would have Achilles himself feast with him, he replies that he will touch neither food nor drink until he has won the victory which will give him his revenge.

The same truthfulness to the ideas furnished by the old mythical phrases runs through the magnificent passage which tells us of the arming of Achilles. The picture is more splendidly drawn and coloured; but we are taken back to the imagery of the Vedic hymns, to Indra or to Ushas, as we read that the helmets of the humbler warriors were like the cold snow clouds which gather in the north, but that when Achilles donned his armour, a glorious light flashed up to heaven, and the earth laughed at its dazzling radiance. His shield, we are told, gleamed like the blood-red morn, as it rises from the sea; his helmet glittered like a star; each hair on the plume glistened like burnished gold; and when he tried the armour to see whether it fitted him, it bore his limbs like a bird upon the wing. But when, having taken up his spear, he mounts his chariot, and bids his immortal horses bear him safe through the battle, and not leave him to die as they left Patroklos, he hears again the warning of his early death. The horse Xanthos bows his head, and tells him that, though their force is not abated, and their will is only to save the lord whom they serve and love, the will of Zeus is stronger yet, and Achilles must die. But he answers again, as he had answered before, that, whatever may follow, the work of vengeance must be accomplished.

The arming of Achilles.

Through the wild confusion of the fight which follows, Achilles hastens surely to his victory. His great enemy Hektor appears before him; but although Phœbus has forsaken him, yet Achilles cannot reach him through his own armour, which Hektor had stripped from the body of Patroklos, and which he was now wearing. The death-wound is given where an opening in the plates left the neck bare. The prayer of Hektor for mercy is dismissed with contempt, and in his boundless rage Achilles tramples on the body—a trait of savagery scarcely to be explained by a reference to the manners of the Greeks in any age, but quite intelligible when we compare it with the mythical language of the Eastern Vedic hymns, which speak of the sun as stamping mercilessly on his conquered enemies.

The story of the Iliad is completed with the narrative which tells us how the aged Priam, guided by Hermes, came to Achilles, and embracing his knees, begged for the body of his son, over which Phœbus Apollo had spread his golden shield to keep away all unseemly things, and how it was borne back to Ilion, where his wife, Andromache, bitterly bemoaned her loss, and all the Trojans wept for the hero who had fought for them so bravely.

Achilles and Priam.

At this point our Iliad comes to an end; but from the Odyssey we learn that Achilles was slain by Paris and Phœbus Apollo at the Skaian or western gates; that Thetis with her sea-nymphs rose from the water and wrapped his body in shining robes; that after many days the Achaians placed it on the funeral pile, and that his ashes were laid in a golden urn brought by Hephaistos, over which a great cairn was raised, that men might see it afar off as they sailed on the broad Hellespontos, an expression which seems to show that the Hellespont of the Iliad was not merely the narrow strait between Sestos and Abydos, but a wider sea, so-called probably from a

The death of Achilles.

people named Helloi or Selloi, who lived on its shores and crossed it in their migration from the east to the west.

Thus the whole Achilleis seems to be a magnificent solar epic, telling us of a sun rising in radiant majesty, and early separated from the beautiful twilight of the dawn, soon hidden by the clouds, yet abiding his time of vengeance, when from the dark veil he breaks forth at last in more than his early strength, scattering the mists and kindling the rugged clouds which form his funeral pyre nor caring whether the splendour of his victory shall be succeeded by a darker battle as the vapours close again over his dying glory. From other sources we learn that after the death of Achilles the Achaians took Ilion and burnt it, and that Priam and his people were slain. Paris himself, smitten with the poisoned arrows[1] of Philoktetes, fled to Mount Ida, where, as he lay dying, Œnônê appeared before him, beautiful and loving as ever. But though her love might soothe him, it could not heal a wound inflicted by the weapons of Herakles. So Paris died on Ida, and Œnônê also died upon his funeral pile which her own hands kindled.

The fall of Ilion.

This wonderful siege of Troy is, it has been well said,[2] simply a repetition of the daily siege of the east by the solar powers that every evening are robbed of their brightest treasures in the west. We have to mark that quite as much stress is laid on the stealing away of the treasures of Helen as on the stealing away of Helen herself, and that we have precisely the same feature in all the great epics of Northern Europe. Of the names of the actors in this great drama some certainly are found in the mythology of the East. The name Helen, we have seen, is that of the Indian Saramâ; and Paris is Pani, the deceiver, who, when Saramâ comes seeking the cows of Indra, beseeches her to remain with him. Although Saramâ refuses

Paris and the Panis.

[1] See p. 103.
[2] Max Müller, *Lectures on Language*, Second Series, p. 471.

T

to do so, she yet accepts from him a drink of milk; and this passing disobedience to the commands given to her may be the germ of that unfaithfulness of Helen which causes the Trojan war. Whether the name Achilles is that of the solar hero Aharyu, it may be unwise to determine; but it seems more certain that Briseis, who is one of the first captives taken by the Achaians, is the offspring of Brisaya, who in the Veda is conquered by the bright powers before they can recover the treasures stolen by the Panis.

A specially remarkable feature in this story of the Trojan war is the blending of different ideas. A hero may belong to the powers which represent the night and darkness; but the groundwork for the incidents of an heroic career were supplied by phrases which spoke of the toils, the battles, and the victories of the sun, and thus regarded, the heroes would reflect a splendour to which, in their relation to their enemies, they would have no right. Thus, as stealing Helen from the Western Sparta or as abetting in this theft, Paris and all the Trojans represent the dark powers who steal away the twilight from the western sky. But in the lives of many of the Trojan chiefs, as perhaps or possibly in that of Paris himself,[1] we have a repetition of the life of Meleagros, Perseus, and other solar heroes. As to Achilles, the points of likeness are beyond question. The key-note of the myth of Herakles, namely, subjection to an inferior, is the key-note of the myth of the great Phthiotic chieftain; and the parting from Briseis is an incident which we look for in all such tales. In the vow which follows his loss we see the veiling of the sun behind the dark clouds; and as the golden rays are no

Achilles and the Myrmidons.

---

[1] The beauty of Paris may have been from the first the beauty of the night, cloudless and still. This beauty is evidently signified by the myth of Medousa (see p. 221), as well as by the legends of Kalypso and the fairy queens who tempt Tanhäuser and True Thomas to their caves (see p. 160). Professor Goldziher has shown that in the mythology of the Hebrews the myths of the night are far more important than those of the day, and that they ascribe to the night not only a singular beauty, but a wonderful restorative power. The conditions of the Assyrian climate render this fact easily intelligible.

longer seen when his face is hidden, so his followers the Myrmidons no longer appear on the battle-field when their chief hangs up his spear and shield within his tent. These followers are in the Iliad persistently compared with wolves,[1] and we have seen how nearly the Greek name for wolves, given to them, we cannot doubt, from the glossiness of their skin, is allied to words denoting brightness. The rays of the sun would in the old mythical language of poetry be called Lukoi or Lykians; and as the meaning of the phrase became in part forgotten, the Myrmidons, who are simply the sun's rays, would be naturally compared to wolves with gleaming eyes and blood-red jaws. The conflict which precedes the death of Hektor is the mighty battle of the vapours and the sun, who seems to trample on the darkness, as Achilles tramples on the body of Hektor; and as this victory of the sun is gained just when he is sinking into the sea, so the death of Achilles is said to follow very soon after that of Hektor. So again the fight over the dead body of Achilles is the story of a stormy evening, when the clouds fight over the dead sun. The main conclusion is this, that the chief incidents of the story, and even the main features in the character of the chief heroes, were handed down ready-made for the Homeric poets. They might leave out this or that incident; but they were not free to alter the general character of any. Thus they must describe Achilles as fighting in a quarrel which was not his own—as robbed of Briseis—as furious with rage and grief at her loss—as hiding himself in his tent—as sending out Patroklos instead of appearing himself on the battle-field— as shedding the blood of human victims on the funeral pile of his friend, and as dying early after his bright but troubled career. This necessity seems to explain the whole character of Achilles, which, regarded as that of an Achaian chief, seems untrue not only to their national character but to human nature. His portrait, as drawn in the

[1] See note 1, p. 106.

Iliad, is not only not Achaian; it can scarcely be called human. There is no evidence that Achaian chiefs visited on those who were manifestly innocent the wrong doings of the guilty; that they had no sense of duty, and no sympathy for the sufferings of those who had never injured them; that they offered human sacrifices, or that they fought with poisoned arrows, or that they mangled the corpses of brave enemies whom they had slain. But although we have no evidence that Achaian chiefs ever did such things, it is easy to see that such stories could not fail to spring up, when phrases which had at first denoted the varying action of the sun were regarded as relating to the deeds and sufferings of human beings.

The return of the heroes from Troy is an event answering precisely to the return of Iason (Jason) and his comrades from Kolchis: as they bring back the golden fleece, so Menelaos returns with Helen and her treasures to Sparta. These legends are uniform and consistent only so far as they represent the heroes returning from the east to the west. Otherwise the incidents, and the names of persons and places, are changed almost at will. The tombs of Odysseus, Aineias (Æneas), and many others, were shown in many places, for it was as easy to take them to one country as to another.

III. The return of the heroes from Troy.

Of these returning chieftains, the most conspicuous is Odysseus, the tale of whose wanderings is given in the Odyssey, and whose story practically reproduces that of Herakles or Perseus, for the simple reason that the return from Ilion to Achaia represents the return journey of the day from east to west. His life, like that of all kindred heroes, is marked by strange changes of happiness and misery, by successes and reverses, ending in complete victory, as the lights and shadows of a stormy and gloomy day are often scattered

The Odyssey.

at sundown by the effulgence of the bright orb whose glory they have so long hidden. Thus Odysseus becomes a counterpart of Achilles, the main difference being that Achilles represents the action of the sun in his strength and his capricious fitfulness, while the character of Odysseus is that of Phœbus, Asklepios, Iamos, and Medeia, the possessors of a marvellous and superhuman wisdom. The desire ever present to his mind is an intense yearning to be united again with his wife, whom he left long ago at eventide in the bloom of her youthful beauty. Thus, although, as he journeys homewards, he is often tempted to tarry or turn aside in his course, he cannot be made to give up his purpose. It is impossible for Helios and Surya to deviate from the course marked out for them whether in their daily or their yearly round. The stone which Sisyphos rolls to the top of the hill must roll down again; and the blood of Sisyphos, we must remember, flows in the veins of Odysseus.

The first conflict of the wanderer, we are told, was with a people called the Kikones (Cicones) of Ismaros, who destroyed six men out of every ship in his fleet. Thence he came to the land of the Lotos-eaters, who spend their life in a delicious dream, feasting on the fruit which makes all who taste it forget their homes. Here he had to bind some of his men who disobeyed his warning not to touch the fruit, and to drag them away to their ships. A terrible storm next carried him to the land of the Kyklôpes (Cyclopes).[1] With some of his companions he entered a cave in which were stored large supplies of milk and cheese; but before they could make their escape, the giant Polyphemos came in and shut the entrance with a great rock which they could not move. The fire which he lit showed the forms of Odysseus and his men, two of whom Polyphemos cooked and devoured. After some

<small>Odysseus and Polyphemos.</small>

[1] See p. 179.

more had been thus eaten, Odysseus, with the survivors, blinded the giant by thrusting a burning pole into his eye,[1] and then tying his men under the rams of the giant, he made his escape with them when Polyphemos opened the door of the cave. The efforts of the latter to make his troubles known to his kinsfolk were defeated by a crafty device of Odysseus. When Polyphemos on first seeing him asked him his name, Odysseus told him that it was Outis, Nobody. Hence, when the other giants came to the entrance of the cave and asked why he roared so loud, he told them that Nobody, Outis, was doing him harm, and they, thinking that nothing was the matter, went away to their own homes. Of the name Kyklops, it is enough to say that it may be a Grecised form of a word which may be neither Greek nor even Aryan. We have seen that the Indian Pramantha suggested to the Greek a name which carried with it for him a perfectly clear meaning, although it happened to be a wrong one, and that this mistake suggested the corresponding name Epimetheus. In the same way it is possible that the name Kyklops may simply represent the Semitic Khouk-lobh, or Khouk-labh, 'Rulers of the flame or fire-worshippers,'[2] these Khouk-lobh being builders of those gigantic works which we still associate with their names.[3] But the giants with whom Odysseus was here brought into contact were not builders at all; and most certainly the Greek name could not have been given to them as a race of circle-builders. The word Kyklops ought rather to mean one with a round face than one with a round eye in the midst of his face; but one or other of those meanings the word must have, if it be Greek at all.

After the discomfiture of the one-eyed giant, the fate of Odysseus carries him to the land of the cannibal Laistrygones. Having with difficulty escaped from them, he sailed

---

[1] For other versions of the myth of the blinded giant or devil, see p. 257.
[2] Brown, *Poseidon*, 43.
[3] This explanation agrees with the character of those Kyklôpes who are described as the ministers of Hephaistos.

to Aiaia (Æaea).[1] Here the nymph or goddess Kirkê (Circe) turned many of his men into swine, but was compelled to restore them to their human shape by Odysseus, who had received from Hermes a herb which made the charms of Kirkê powerless. Kirkê is one of the beings who seeks to win the love of the hero [2] as he journeys homewards; and although her entreaties fail to change his purpose, he is ready to avail himself of such enjoyments as may not hinder him from reaching home at last. Before he left her abode, the goddess warned him against greater perils from the Seirens, who sat in their cool green caves, enticing the passing mariners to their destruction by the sweet singing with which they besought them to come and rest and forget all their toil and trouble.[3] These perils he escaped by stuffing his sailors' ears with wax, and by having himself bound to the mast as they passed by. The next enemies encountered were Skylla and Charybdis, the demons of the whirlpools, which sucked down many of his men. The rest were lost in a storm, after they had slain some of the cattle of Helios, whom Phaethousa and Lampetie, the *bright* and *glistering* daughters of Neaira, the early morning, tended in Thrinakia;[4] and Odysseus, after tossing about for hours on the heaving sea, was thrown half dead on the shore of Ogygia. Here the beautiful Kalypso tended him lovingly in her cave, and kept him there seven years, although he longed once more to be at home. At length Hermes commanded her to let him go, and she then helped him to build a raft which carried him some way across the sea; but another storm washed him off, and he was thrown bleeding and senseless on the shore of Phaiakia.

On coming to himself he heard the merry voices of girls who were playing on the beach, while the clothes which

Kirkê, the Seirens, Skylla, Charybdis, and Kalypso.

---
[1] On the impossibility of framing any geographical scheme out of the narrative of these wanderings, something has been already said, see p. 153.
[2] See p. 160.   [3] See p. 191.
[4] See p. 185; *Myth. of Ar. Nat.* i. 421.

they had washed were drying. They were maidens who had come with Nausikaa, the beautiful daughter of king Alkinoös and his wife Arêtê. Guided by her, Odysseus came to her father's palace, which stood in a glorious garden, where the leaves never faded, and the fruits glistened on the branches the whole year round. He was, in truth, in enchanted land, and we have already seen what this enchanted land must be.[1] Its name, we are told, was Scheria; but it seems useless to contend that by Scheria the poet meant Corfu.[2] The description given of it answers to no earthly region. The people had come from Hypereia, the upper regions of the sky, where they had been sorely vexed by the Cyclopean giants; and if these monsters represent, as they assuredly seem to do in the case of the Thrinakian Kyklôpes, the dark masses of storm-vapour through which a single angry eye glares down upon the earth and sea, we can well understand the fear which they would strike into the hearts of the bright and happy Phaiakians. As painted by the poet, their new home in Scheria is that ideal land far away in the west over which is spread the soft beauty of an everlasting twilight, and where the radiant processions which gladden the eyes of mortal men only when the heavens are clear, are ever passing through the streets and along the flower-clad hills. Dogs of gold and silver guard the house of the king, and busy maidens who have received their skill from Athênê, the goddess of the dawn, ply their golden distaffs. It is the land where trouble and sorrow are unknown, where the dancers are never weary, and the harp is never silent. The Phaiakians are not good boxers or wrestlers; but as mariners they are unrivalled. The mariners are in fact the ships, and the ships are the mariners. These vessels have the powers of thought, speech, and will. Without masts or tackling, without helmsmen or rowers, they go straight to their mark; and not one of

The land of the Phaiakians.

---

[1] See p. 217. [2] Bunbury, *History of Ancient Geography.* See also p. 153.

that goodly fleet, Alkinoös tells his guest, has ever been stranded, for so have the gods ordained for the blameless leaders and guides of all across the sounding seas. With these ships we have seen that the Teuton was as well acquainted as the Greek;[1] but, as we might expect, the poet contradicts himself when he relates the voyage of the Phaiakians as they carry Odysseus to Ithaka. Here the ship has oarsmen and oars, and these imply that the ships have the furniture which he has expressly denied to them before.[2]

Reaching his home at last as an unknown stranger, Odysseus learnt from his swineherd, Eumaios, who did not recognise him, that his father, Laertes, was living in squalid misery; that a crowd of chiefs who came as suitors to his wife Penelope, had taken up their abode in his house, where some of his servants were in league with them to devour his substance, and that Penelope, having promised to give them an answer when her web was finished, put them off continually by undoing at night that portion of the web which she had woven during the day. Odysseus now entered his own hall disguised as a beggar; and when provoked by some of the suitors, he challenged them to stretch a bow which hung upon the wall. This was his own bow, which, like Achilles and other heroes, he alone could stretch. In vain they strove to bend it; but when the beggar put forth his hand to take it, the thunder of Zeus was heard in the heaven, and presently the suitors began to fall under the unerring arrows; but his son Telemachos, who belongs, like Patroklos and Phaethon, to the class of Secondaries, had left the chamber door ajar, and many of the chiefs, seizing the weapons which they found there, pressed hard upon Odysseus. Odysseus himself they could not hurt; but Telemachos was wounded,

Odysseus and the suitors.

[1] See p. 3.
[2] For a more full examination of the Phaiakian myth, see *Myth. of Ar. Nat.* ii. 274.

though not mortally, like Patroklos. At this crisis Athênê came to his aid, and scared the suitors with her dazzling Aigis (Ægis). The corpses of the dead were thrust away like refuse; but on the body of Melanthios, the son of Dolios, Odysseus wreaked his full rage, as Achilles trampled on the body of Hektor. Lastly, he summoned all the women who had abetted the suitors, and hung them upon a beam across his great hall. He was then united again with Penelope, for whom he had made the beautiful bridal chamber long years ago; and in this chamber he rested after the great slaughter. This tale is manifestly the counterpart of the vengeance of Achilles. In both an excessive revenge is taken for a comparatively small wrong. Indeed, in the case of Odysseus, the wrong was confined to the intrusion of the suitors into his house. Of direct evidence which may justify us in regarding the character of Odysseus as true to that of the Achaians or the historical Greeks, we have none. As in the case of Achilles, we may more justly speak of his character as not merely not Achaian, but as inhuman. Odysseus uses poisoned arrows;[1] he shoots a man behind his back without warning; he lies whenever it suits his purpose to do so; he slays a whole band of chieftains who had done him no great injury, and whom he might have dismissed in utter abasement, and then he hangs up, 'like sparrows on a string,' a crowd of women, simply because they had not persistently resisted the demands of the suitors.[2]

The parallel between these two stories in the Iliad and the Odyssey may be traced down to the minutest particulars. Both heroes have weapons which they alone can wield; both are aided by Athênê; both have in Patroklos and Telemachos a reflexion of themselves; both make a vow to exact a deadly vengeance; both trample on and disfigure their slaughtered enemy; both are nearly overpowered at one part of their struggle, and

Parallel between the stories of the Iliad and the Odyssey.

---

[1] *Od.* i. 263; xii. 260. [2] *Myth. of Ar. Nat.* i. 265.

both have a time of quietness and rest after their fearful conflict. Of other details, some are easily explained, some are quite uncertain. Like Helios, in the story of Medeia, Penelope is the weaver: but her web, although begun, cannot be finished until Odysseus returns, because the web of morning clouds reappears only at sundown. For the name of Odysseus himself it is not so easy to account. When his old nurse Eurykleia recognises him in the bath by the mark left on his leg by the bite of a boar in his early youth, she tells him[1] that he received his name as expressing the hatred generally felt for his grandfather Autolykos. It is possible that the word may be connected with a Greek verb (odussomai) meaning 'to be angry;' but the way of accounting for it is worth nothing, and the presumption, as we have seen, lies against any such explanation. The name Eurykleia is, like Euryphassa, Euryanassa, and many others, simply a name for the being who goes before the sun at his rising. She may be spoken of as his mother, his sister, his bride, or his nurse; and the boar's wound is repeated in the story of Adonis with more terrible effect. The name Autolykos again, like that of Lykaon, denotes simply light. In the same way the dog of Odysseus is called Argos, the white or shining, and is in fact the hound which appears by the side of Artemis in the legend of Prokris. The servants who aid the suitors have such names as Melanthios and Melantho, the *black*, the children of Dolios, the *treacherous* darkness; and the name of Telemachos, like the names of Telephos and Telephassa, represents the far-shooting light of Phœbus Hekaergos, Hekatos, or Hekatebolos.

It thus becomes abundantly clear that the phrases which described the infinitely various aspects of the outer world would furnish inexhaustible materials for legends which might be expanded into splendid epic poems. The Homeric poets worked with marvellous success

<small>Materials of Aryan epic poems.</small>

[1] *Od.* xix. 419.

on these materials, which also supplied the framework for the great epic poems of other countries—this fact being proved by the astonishing coincidences in minute incidents, and in the sequence of these incidents, as well as in names and characters, between the Iliad and Odyssey, the Volsunga Saga, the Lay of the Nibelungs, the Persian epic of Firdusi, and many more. That some historical facts may be mixed up with these tales of Paris, Helen, Achilles, and Odysseus is, of course, quite possible, and it would be rash, as it is needless, to deny it; but we are not justified in affirming it. We know that most of the incidents belonging to these stories never could have taken place in the world of men and within the sphere of human action. We know that Aphroditê and Athênê never mingled in battles with mortal men, and that the armour of no Achaian chief was forged on the anvil of Hephaistos. We may, if we so please, strike out all the marvellous events in the story, and make up the account of a war without Thetis and Helen, or Sarpêdôn, or Memnon, or Xanthos and Balios, an account such as we have in the preface of Thucydides to his great history; but when we have done so, we shall have nothing more than a dry outline of events, which might have taken place, but which we have no warrant whatever for regarding as historical fact.

In another and a more complicated form the story of this battle between light and darkness, day and night, is brought before us again in the Saga of the Volsungs. The real hero of this story is Sigurd, the son of Sigmund, the son of Volsung, a descendant of Woden or Odin. The fatal children [1] are all destined not only to achieve greatness, but to destroy one or both of their parents.[2]

IV. The Volsung Tale.

---

[1] See p. 90.
[2] In this, as in many other Northern stories, the hero dies before his son, who is to take his place or to revenge him, is born. Macduff's birth, like that of Asklepios or Dionysos, marks the moment of his mother's death; and we are told of him, 'they say that the youngling kissed his mother or ever she died.' So uniform is the career of children thus born, that Grimm could say generally,

The story goes that the childless Rerir besought the aid of the All-father, who sent Freya, in the guise of a crow, with an apple which she dropped into his lap. Rerir took it and gave it to his wife, who then became the mother of Volsung; but before the child was born Rerir had gone home to Odin. The fortunes of his house turn on a sword which Odin thrusts to the hilt in the roof-tree of Volsung's hall, to be drawn forth only by him who has strength to wield it. The story is clearly the same as that of Theseus, who alone is able to lift the huge stone under which his father Aigeus had placed his sword and sandals. So here the sword Gram will yield to no hand but that of Volsung's son Sigmund, and at his touch it leaves the trunk as though it were a feather floating on the water.

For this sword, which is a weapon from the same armoury with the spears and arrows of Phœbus, Achilleus, and Philoktetes, and the brands of Arthur and of Roland, there is a deadly contest between Sigmund and his people and the men of king Siggeir, who has married Sigmund's sister Signy. The result is that Sigmund and his ten brothers are all bound; the deaths of these ten brothers being brought about in a way which will be familiar to all who are acquainted with Hindu folklore. As in the story of the wolf and the seven little goats, the wolf swallows six of the kids, but is ripped up before it has swallowed the seventh,[1] so here Sigmund alone escapes the she-wolf who each night devours one of the ten, and who is the mother of king Siggeir, the enemy of Volsung and his children. Being loosed from his bonds, Sigmund now dwells in the woods; and his sister Signy sends to him one of her children, the son of Siggeir, to whom Sigmund gives his meal bag, charging him to make bread. The boy fails to do so, being afraid to set hand to the meal-sack because somewhat quick lay in the meal; and at the bidding of

'Aus dem Mutter-leib geschnittene Kinder pflegen Helden zu werden.' For the devouring of his parents by Agni, see p. 164.

[1] *Myth. of Ar. Nat.* i. 358.

Signy Sigmund slays him. The same fate befalls her next child, and then Signy, changing forms with a witch woman whom she leaves with Siggeir, goes into the wood, and becomes, by her brother Sigmund, the mother of Sintjötli, who safely goes through the ordeal before which the children of Siggeir had failed. The child, when he is asked if he has found aught in the meal, answers: 'I misdoubted me that there was something quick in the meal when I first fell to kneading of it; but I have kneaded it all up together, both the meal and that which was therein, whatever it was.' Sigmund replies with a laugh: 'Nought wilt thou eat of this bread this night, for the most deadly of worms hast thou kneaded up therewith.' This worm is almost ubiquitous in Teutonic and Scandinavian myths; and we have already met with it in the myths of Phœbus, Cadmus, Œdipus, Herakles, and others. Its death is the slaying of the darkness, whether of the night or of the winter; and the weakly children who fail to slay it answer to the ill-fated knights who fail in their efforts to pierce the thorn hedge behind which sleeps Briar-rose, or to leap the barrier of spears which guards the sun maiden of Hindu fairy tales. When at length Siggeir is overcome, his wife Signy exults in the thought of her son Sinfjötli, and says to Sigmund: 'I let slay both my children, whom I deemed worthless for the revenging of our father, and I went into the wood to thee in a witch wife's shape, and now behold Sinfjötli is the son of thee and of me both, and therefore has he this so great hardihood and fierceness, in that he is the son of Volsung's son and Volsung's daughter, and for this and for nought else have I so wrought that King Siggeir might get his bane at last. And merrily now will I die with King Siggeir, though I was nought merry to wed with him.' Having thus said, she kisses her brother and her son, and going back into the fire dies with Siggeir and his men.[1]

---

[1] When a like idea was presented to the Greek mind in the marriage of Œdipus and Iokastê, a feeling of horror was roused directly by the thought of

Nothing is perhaps more remarkable in the legends of Northern Europe than the recurrence of the same myth in cycles, the series of narratives thus formed being regarded as a single continuous tradition. *Sigurd and Regin.*
No sooner are the adventures of one hero ended than another starts up to do the same things over again, or the same series of exploits is being achieved by two or more heroes at the same time. The objects of their career and the mode in which they seek to attain them are always the same, and in most cases tell their own tale with a clearness which it is impossible to misapprehend. The story of Sigmund is in its main features the story of the son who avenges him, and Sigurd's victory is won only with the sword which Odin himself had shattered in his father's hand. The broken bits are forged afresh by the smith Regin, who charges Sigurd to slay with it his kinsman Fafnir,[1] and thus to end their quarrel for the treasures which Fafnir had contrived to get into his own keeping. The mode by which this antagonism between the dragon and the dwarf was brought about is among the most significant features of the legend. The treasures are the ransom by which Odin, Loki, and Hœnir, the gods of the bright heaven, are compelled to purchase their freedom from the sons of Reidmar, whose brother, the otter, they have slain. By way of atonement they are not only to fill the otter's skin with gold, but so to cover it with gold that

its bearing on the conditions of human society; and in that tale there is throughout, on the part of the involuntary actors, nothing but grief of mind and agony of conscience. Here there is nothing but exultation as well for the incest as for the wild havoc wrought without any motives higher than those which might prompt the treacheries of the most truculent savages. But when in Greek myths we get away from the circle or what was supposed to be the circle of human affairs, and find ourselves among the inhabitants of Olympos, we discern precisely the same indifference to what we may fairly call Aryan morality in any of its forms; and in Zeus and Hêrê, Artemis and Apollon, sister and brother, wife and husband, we see the original forms of which Signy and Sigmund are the reflexions.

[1] Grimm regards this name as a cognate form of the Greek Python, the words standing to each other in the relation of θήρ and φήρ (*Deutsche Mythologie*, 345).

not a white hair upon it shall remain visible; in other words, they are to set the earth free from its fetters of ice, and so to spread over it the golden sunshine that not a single streak of snow shall be seen upon it. But the most precious of all the treasures hoarded by the elf Andvari, who appears as Alberich in the Nibelungenlied, is the golden ring from which other golden rings are constantly dropping. It is the source of all his wealth, for in fact it is the symbol of the reproductive powers of nature, which in a thousand myths is associated with the wealth-giving rod of Hermes or of Vishnu. On this treasure, whether it be the dower of Brynhild or of Helen, there rests the curse which leads to theft and betrayal, to vengeance and utter ruin; and the doom which Regin brings on Fafnir falls also on himself so soon as Sigurd learns that Regin seeks to cheat him of the dragon's wealth.

No sooner, again, is the story of Brynhild ended than the woeful tale is repeated in the sequel of the gloomy history of Gudrun. Brynhild is the peerless maiden who has slept in a charmed slumber caused by the thorn of winter thrust into her right hand by Odin, like the Raksha's claw which leaves Surya Bai, the sun-maiden, senseless in the Hindu story.[1] One knight alone can rouse her, and that knight is Sigurd, who, having slain the dragon, becomes possessed of the treasures lying within the mighty coils of his body, and by eating his heart, gains wisdom beyond that of mortal man. Wakened from her sleep, the maiden plights her troth to Sigurd, who afterwards rides on to the house of Giuki, the Niflung, who is determined that he shall marry his daughter Gudrun, and that Brynhild shall become the wife of his son Gunnar. But Gunnar cannot ride through the flames, and by magic arts Sigurd is made to assume the form and voice of Gunnar, and to hand Brynhild over to him. Discovering his treachery, Brynhild urges Gunnar

[1] Frere, *Deccan Tales*.

to slay Sigurd; but, as in the legend of Balder, he and his brothers had sworn not to lay hands on the hero. They, therefore, get Guttorm to do what they could not do themselves, and thus Sigurd is slain while he sleeps. His death re-awakens all the love of Brynhild, who dies heart-broken on his funeral pile. We can scarcely doubt that in earlier forms of the myth these bright beings are restored to life, as are Balder, Adonis, Memnon, Alkestis, and Sarpêdôn. In the Helgi Saga[1] Sigrun mourns the death of her lover Helgi, Hunding's bane,

O Helgi, thy hair	Is thick with death's rime:
With the dew of the dead	Is my love all dripping.
Dead cold are the hands	Of the son of Hogni.
How for thee, O my king,	May I win healing?

Her prayers avail so far that Helgi comes to her on the great mound, where she has dight a bed for him on which she will come, and rest as she was wont when her lord was living, and they remain together till the dawn comes, when Helgi must ride on the reddening paths, and his pale horse must tread the highway aloft. The Sagaman adds simply that 'in old time folk trowed that men should be born again, though the troth be now deemed but an old wife's doting; and so, as folk say, Helgi and Sigrun were born again, and at that tide was he called Helgi the scathe of Hadding, and she Kara the daughter of Halfdan.' When we reach the story of Sigurd, the bane of Fafnir, this old faith, which rested on the reappearance of Balder, Osiris, Tammuz, Zagreos, and Adonis, has grown weaker. Dire vengeance may be taken for his death, yet he himself is seen on earth no more, and Gudrun in her agony cries out, 'Oh! mindest thou not, Sigurd, the words we spoke that thou wouldest come and look on me, yea, even from thy abiding place among the dead?'

But Gudrun, who after the abandonment of Brynhild

---

[1] For some account of the three Sagas known by this name, see *Myth. of Ar. Nat.* i. 285, *et seq.*

to Gunnar, becomes the companion of the sun in his middle journey, has yet to be wedded to two husbands, the gloaming and the darkness, or the autumn and the winter's cold. She is, however, not the less resolved that Sigurd shall be avenged. The treasures won by him were in the hands of her brothers; and Atli, her second husband, bent on getting possession of them, invites them to a feast and receives them at the spear's point. Hogni and Gunnar are taken prisoners, and Atli insists on their yielding up Sigurd's wealth. Gunnar answers that he will do so, if Atli will bring him the heart of his brother Hogni, and on seeing it he tells the king that now the secret rests with himself alone and that it shall never be tortured from him. He is then thrown into a pit full of snakes, but with the help of Hermes or of Orpheus he charms the serpents, until one flies at his heart and kills him. The time for vengeance has now come. The Kolchian Medeia slew the children of Iason, after she had sent the death-dealing robe to Glaukê. With fiercer revenge Gudrun feasts Atli at the awful banquet to which Astyages in the old Greek story invited Harpagos,[1] and then having slain him with the aid of her brother Hogni's son, she makes the whole hall his funeral pile, and sends all Atli's men to bear their master company to the dwelling place of the dead. Gudrun's lot becomes darker, like the northern summer drawing to its close. The sea into which she plunges to end her misery bears her away to the land of King Jonakr, and the last act in the terrible drama begins. It is practically a repetition of the scenes which have gone before. Gudrun becomes the wife of Jonakr, the lord of the winterland, and mother of his three children, Saurli, Hamdir, and Erp. From her summer home she now summons Swanhild, Sigurd's daughter, whom Jormunrek would have as his wife. Jormunrek's son woes her for himself, and is slain by his father's command. The beautiful Swanhild is

[1] Herod. i. 119.

trodden down by the horses of his knights as she combs out her long golden locks, and Jormunrek himself is slain by two of the sons whom Gudrun had borne to him. The thoughts of Gudrun turn to the golden days when she dwelt with Sigurd, and she passes away from the land of living men, like the last expiring flicker of a dwindling autumn twilight.[1]

In this series of incidents, which belong to the great tragedy of the year as clearly as the most transparent Vedic descriptions of Ushas or the Maruts, we have more than the framework of the Nibelungenlied. That this epic poem virtually reproduces the Volsung tale, is disputed by none. The few points of difference lie in a mere change of names. In the Nibelung lay Gudrun becomes Kriemhild; but Kriemhild, like Gudrun, is the sister of Gunnar, who now becomes Gunther, king of the Burgundians, and (as in the Volsung story) she has to mourn the loss of Siegfried, whom Brynhild does to death by means of Hagen. But in its general spirit the story has undergone no change. Siegfried, like Sigurd, is the invincible hero with the sword which no enemy ever withstood. He has bathed his body in the dragon's blood, as Achilles and Demophoön were plunged into the bath of fire, and no weapon can hurt him except on one spot between his shoulders on which a linden leaf rested while he bathed, as Achilles could be wounded only in the heel, and Rustem slain only by the thorn, or Balder only by the mistletoe. On this spot he is pierced by the spear of Hagen, and from that time forth Kriemhild has no rest until she enacts a vengeance more fearful than that which Gudrun wreaked on the murderers of Sigurd, or Odysseus on the robber-suitors of Penelope. The great German epic may differ

v. The Nibelungenlied.

---

[1] For a more minute examination of this Saga, see *Myth. of Ar. Nat.* book i. ch. xii. and Dasent, *Popular Tales of the Norse*, introduction. A shorter summary, exhibiting most clearly the solar or physical character of the whole epic, may be found in Professor Max Müller's ' Essay on Comparative Mythology,' *Chips*, ii. 107 *et seq.*

from the Volsung tale, as carrying us from the rougher life of Norse sea-rovers to the elaborate pageants of kings and princes; but otherwise there is little change or none. Like all other kindred heroes, Sigurd and Siegfried are both doomed to be wanderers,[1] and Siegfried is hated by Hagen as the slayer of the Niblungs, or folk of the mist, the possessor of their magic sword Balmung, of the tarnkappe or cape of darkness, and of all their treasures. Here, as in the Volsung tale, we have the enmity between Kriemhild (Gudrun) and Brynhild, who insists that Siegfried is Gunther's man and must pay tribute. But Brynhild's girdle and ring have passed into the hands of Kriemhild, and the latter, holding them up, taunts the former with having been won by Siegfried, like the maiden of the older story. Hagen now resolves to avenge on the hero the wrong done by Brynhild to his sister, and learns from her the secret on which his life depends. He even takes the precaution of asking her to mark with a silver cross the spot on which alone he can be wounded. On this spot he is smitten by Hagen as he stoops to drink from a stream; and thus the death of the hero is connected with the water into which the orb of the sun sinks in the evening. In the spirting out of his blood on his murderer, and in the death-wrestle which covers the flowers all round with blood and gore, we have a reproduction of the blood-red sunset which looms out in the story of the death of Herakles. After Siegfried's death Hagen gains possession of Kriemhild's treasure and sinks it all in the Rhine.

With this incident the first of the series of mythical histories embodied in the Nibelung lay is brought to an end. This portion of the poem may or may not be older than the parts which follow it; but it is beyond doubt a narrative complete in itself, and indis-

<small>The vengeance of Kriemhild.</small>

---

[1] This doom is brought out with singular clearness in the story of the 'Dame of the Fine Green Kirtle.' Campbell, *Tales of the West Highlands*, ii. 345.

pensable to the general plan of the poem only as accounting for the hatred of Kriemhild for her brothers. The second part of the story begins with the death of Helche, the wife of Etzel, who takes the place of Atli in the saga of the Volsungs, and who thus marries Kriemhild, as Atli marries Gudrun. Kriemhild consents to the union only because it gives her the means of avenging the death of Hagen's victim. To get Hagen into her power she sends messengers to Gunther, bidding him bring all his friends whom Hagen can guide into the Huns' land. Hagen sees the trap laid for him, and is unwilling to go; but he cannot withstand the taunt of Gunther that, if he feels guilty on the score of Siegfried's death, he had better stay at home. With three thousand men Gunther, Hagen, and Dankwart set out on the fatal journey. Omens of coming disaster are not lacking on their path. Dietrich, who is sent to meet the Burgundians, tells Hagen that Kriemhild still weeps sore for the hero of the Niblungland; and when he is asked how he knows her mind, he answers, 'What shall I say? Every morning early I hear her, Etzel's wife, weep and wail full sadly to the God of heaven for strong Siegfried's body.' When Hagen appears before her, Kriemhild asks him what gifts he has brought. Hagen tries to evade the question by saying that one so wealthy needs no gifts; and then she asks him plainly, 'Where is the Niblung's hoard? It was my own, as ye well know.' But when the Burgundians are told that they must give up their arms before going into the hall, Hagen says that the honour is greater than he deserves, and that he will himself be chamberman. His caution only enables him to sell his life dearly. Sixty men are ready to slay Hagen and the harper Volker by his side, but Kriemhild says that so small a number can never do this work; and thus we see that we are dealing with beings beyond or above the conditions of humanity. Then, as in the Odyssey and in the Volsung tale, follows the vengeance in the great hall; and it is impossible to read the story without feeling that it relates to no struggle between mortal men. The Burgundians are full of misgivings, but Volker, the Phemios of the Odyssey, lulls to sleep with his music the sorrows of the men who are soon to die. The tragedy begins the next day with the accidental slaying of a Hun by Volker; and in the fight which follows Hagen strikes off the head of Ortlieb, which falls into the lap of his mother Kriemhild. The hall runs with blood. Seven thousand bodies are flung down the steps. Thousands and thousands more are brought up to take part in the bloody work, until Kriemhild sets fire to the hall. The burning rafters fall crashing round the Burgundians, of whom six hundred still survive. The Huns attack them two to one; and at last Hagen and Gunther are caught, bound, and brought before the woman who is thirsting for their blood. Placing them apart, Kriemhild goes to Hagen and tells him that even now he may go free if he will yield up the treasure which he stole from Siegfried. It is but a repetition of the Volsung story. Hagen answers that he cannot say where it is so long as any of his masters remain alive. When Kriemhild brings him the head of Gunther, Hagen tells her that she has slain the last man who knew the secret beside himself, and that from himself she should never learn it. In her fury she snatches from him Siegfried's sword Balmung, and with it she strikes off his head. Thus far Etzel has favoured the schemes of his wife; but the sight of the dead Hagen rouses his grief, and with the aid of Hildebrand he hews Kriemhild in pieces.[1]

These older epics, so massive in their outlines, so rich in their detail, could not fail to furnish materials for a thousand romances to writers who sat down in their closets to spin stories for a less robust and hardy generation. Thus the Nibelungenlied was watered down until it assumed the form of the legend of Walter of Aquitaine, who plays in it the part of Siegfried. Here, as

VI. Walter of Aquitaine.

[1] See Appendix II.

in the Lay, we have the names Gibicho, Gunther, and Etzel, and a possible historical element in the hostages taken to the country of the Huns from Basqueland and the banks of the Rhine, and perhaps also in the description of the life and court of the Hunnish chief, when he returns to his home and to his wife Helche, or, as some call her, Ospirin. But with these exceptions the tale exhibits the old incidents, to which the writer has given a more cheerful ending. Grani, the war-steed of Sigurd, appears here as Lion, who, like Grani, is able to carry from Etzel's house the heavy treasure which Walter bears away with Hildegund. He is returning to his home in the land where the sun goes down, with the golden hoard which has been the bane of Fafnir and Regin, of Brynhild and Gudrun, of Sigurd and Siegfried, of Helen and Menelaos. But Walter has to face and overcome dire perils in the greed and enmity of King Gunther. The lord of Worms resolves that the hoard shall not be carried through the land of the Franks, and with his knights he assails Walter on his journey. But Hagen, who accompanies him, has lost much of the dauntless courage which marks him in the Nibelung story; and his advice to Gunther is that he should feign a retreat, and thus withdraw Walter from the stronghold in which he had placed Hildegund and his treasure. This counsel, which is given after the death of many knights, is followed by Gunther, and in the combat which ensues Walter smites off a leg from Gunther's body, and is about to deal him the death-stroke, when Hagen interposes his helmet, and the blade of Walter's sword is shivered. In a moment of rashness Walter raises his arm to throw the hilt away, and Hagen, quick as lightning, strikes off his right hand. The penalty for this deed is soon exacted. Walter draws with his left hand his short Hunnish dagger, and tearing Hagen's right eye from its socket casts it on the ground; these incidents corresponding closely with the myths which make Zio or Tyr and

Indra Savitar lose each his right hand, and speak of Woden as leaving an eye in pledge at the fountain of Mimir.[1] The blood thus drawn is held to wipe away the old enmity, and Hildegund is summoned to perform the office of Asklepios, or Œnônê, or Helgi, the healers. From this point onwards all is smooth. The rivalry of courtesies follows the rivalry of swords and spears; and even Etzel is bidden to the feast, when, having reached the hero's home, Hildegund becomes the wife of Walter. More pure than Helen, but not less radiant, she returns from Helen's exile with Helen's wealth, to shed joy and gladness on all around her.[2]

In the story of Hugdietrich we have only another version of the tales in which a maiden is shut up in a lonely tower, and none can approach her except the knight who is destined to win her. Whether it be Danaê,[3] or Rapunzel,[4] or the Rose of the Alhambra,[5] all precautions are vain. Craft achieves what force vainly strives to hinder; and in the guise of the womanly Theseus, or Achilles, or Dionysos, Hugdietrich finds his way to the prison house of Hildeburg, where, like Odysseus, he shows his skill in weaving. The legend of the birth of his child[6] is a travesty of the myths of Cyrus, Romulus, Telephos, and many others. In all these the beast takes up the child from a kindly impulse; in the legend of Hugdietrich alone the babe is taken away to be devoured, and it becomes necessary that some one should discover him at once, instead of suffering him to remain like Romulus or Paris in the beast's lair.

VII. The Hugdietrich.

In the story of Gudrun, the daughter of Hettel,[7] the name Hagen is given to a child who is carried away, like Ganymedes or Surya Bai, by a griffin to his nest among the rocks, and who there grows up to the strength of manhood,

---
[1] See p. 46.   [2] *Popular Romances of the Middle Ages*, 315.
[3] See p. 111.   [4] See p. 236.   [5] *Myth. of Ar. Nat.* ii. 401.
[6] *Popular Romances of the Middle Ages*, p. 333.
[7] *Ibid.* p. 341.

his only companions being three maidens who like himself have been stolen away from their homes. One of these, on his return to his home in Iceland, becomes his wife, and with the birth of his daughter the story starts afresh in the path of the thousand myths which speak of a host of knights wooing a maiden to their own destruction until the destined hero comes to claim her. But Hilda is scarcely a more prominent person in this portion of the lay than the sweet singer Horant or Hjärrandi, who appears as Orendil or Aurentil in the Hamlet myths, and is no other than Orpheus or Amphion, Pan or Wäinämöinen. The fortunes of Gudrun, the daughter of Hilda and Hettel, are those of the fearless maidens who are born to be the cause of strife and warfare, and who after long suffering and shameful toil are raised to the glory which is their birthright. In vain Hartmuth of Normandy and Siegfried of Moorland ask her in marriage; in vain Herwig of Zealand seeks to have her as his wife. But, more bold than the others, Herwig marches with his knights to the walls of Hegelingen, and in a combat to which he challenges Hettel is well-nigh winning the day, when Gudrun rushes between them. To her prayer that the battle may cease Herwig assents, on condition that she will wed with him. The troth is pledged, the words being added that Gudrun never changes. The sequel of the story is a long comment on her invincible fidelity. In revenge for the slight put upon him Siegfried invades Denmark, and while Hettel besieges Siegfried in the fortress to which he has driven him, Hartmuth, with his father Ludwig, makes a raid on Hegelingen, and carries Gudrun with many of her maidens into Normandy. There Hartmuth seeks vainly to win the love which is pledged for life and death to Herwig; but the catastrophe of the Danish army, and the death of king Hettel, who comes to rescue his child, seem to leave to Gudrun no hope of escape from her bondage. Time goes on. Fair means and foul are alike employed to work a

VIII. The Gudrun Lay.

change in her mind, and the beautiful Gudrun is brought down to the low estate of the royal maidens who, like Cinderella or the Goose Girl of popular stories, are compelled to work among the ashes or the kine. But Girlinda, the mother of Hartmuth, who thinks thus to break her spirit, brings on herself a terrible vengeance when once more the Danish host comes, and Herwig with them, to rescue Gudrun from her long captivity.

The story of Frithjof and Ingebjorg[1] contains, perhaps, an amount of local history larger than that which may exist in the Nibelungenlied; but some of its most striking features it shares with confessedly solar legends. Frithjof himself is invested with the attributes of that large class of solar heroes, of whom Herakles may be taken as the most splendid representative. He is the man born to be great, but for a time others are placed at a vantage over him. He is, in short, the Boots of popular stories, who must not presume to wed the royal maiden on whom he has set his love. Nevertheless, he carries with him the earnest of his great inheritance. The rising of the bright sun-god, Balder, who comes back from the land of the dead to gladden earth and heaven, is the token of the high destiny which awaits him. He bears in his hand the invincible sword of Perseus; on his arm is the magic ring, which we have seen among the treasures of Andvari the dwarf; and the good ship Ellide does his bidding, like the Phaiakian barks and the marvellous ship of the Æsir.[2] But many a dark cloud must cast its shadow on his path before the sky may shine bright and clear above him. Like Herakles, he must pass through a time of madness. The doom of exile is also upon him, and he must be a wanderer over earth and sea, like Siegfried and Sigurd, like Wuotan and Indra, like Phœbus, Bellerophon, and Odysseus. Like these he achieves mighty exploits; like these he longs to see once more the maiden from whom he

IX. The Frithjof Saga.

[1] *Popular Romances of the Middle Ages*, p. 372.   [2] See p. 3.

has been parted; and at length, when his unwitting offence has been expiated, he wins her as his bride.

For the Icelandic Saga of Grettir something of an historical character has been claimed on grounds which seem scarcely to justify it. To a certain extent, especially in the love of litigation and the love of violence, it is a faithful picture of Icelandic manners; but we have already admitted in the case of the Iliad and other Aryan epics that the poet must throw over his work the colouring of the social life of his own time. But so far as the career of Grettir himself is concerned, it is not a picture of human life at all, for the narrative is little more than a string of sheer impossibilities. The horse Keingala from whom Grettir strips off the hide is seemingly none the worse for the loss. Not only do six men fall upon him without warning, and are beaten off; but when Grettir has slain Thorir Redbeard, Thorir of Garth assails him with eighty men. The solitary Grettir slays eighteen and wounds many more, and the rest take to flight.[1] Throughout his life, no one expects him to do anything, yet his exploits leave those of all other men far behind. His father, who shows him scant love, sets him to watch his geese: he does no work or spoils all that he takes in hand. When he puts forth his strength, the comment is, 'We wotted not that thou wert a man of such powers as we have now proved thee.' In short, he is Boots, or Cinderella, or the Goose Girl, or the disguised Odysseus waiting patiently until the time shall come for making himself known.

X. The Grettir Saga.

[1] In Scott's *Old Mortality*, ch. xi., old Major Bellenden takes his niece to task for believing that the heroes of romance fought single-handed with whole battalions. 'One to three,' he says, ' is as great odds as ever fought and won; and I never knew anybody that cared to take that, except old Corporal Raddlebanes. . . . I dare say you would think very little of Raddlebanes if he were alongside of Artamines.' But it is not to be supposed that the poets of the myth-making ages spent their time in multiplying tales which, if referred to the conditions of human life, are mere absurdities. There is a sense in which these stories are strictly true, and the myth-makers were well aware of their truth; but it is the sense in which the conflict between Indra and Vritra is true, and not any other.

There is scarcely an incident or a feature in the narrative which has not its parallel in other epics of the Aryan world;[1] but throughout his whole life there presses on him the doom which is never taken off from Herakles, Perseus, Achilles, and the rest—the doom of unremitting toil, for which he himself receives no recompense. As Olaf says, 'If ever a man has been cursed, of all men must thou have been;' and in strange accordance with the story of Ixion, his father says of him, 'Methinks over much on a whirling wheel his life turns.' But this invincible hero dreads darkness like a child, as we may well suppose that he should, if his character was moulded by phrases which spoke of the extinguishing of the sun's light when the dark hours have come. He is, of course, avenged, as are the three Helgis and Sigurd, and the avenging of all these is the avenging of Balder.[2]

According to the tale which relates the battle of Roncesvalles, Roland[3] and his comrades win a victory as splendid as that of Leonidas at Thermopylai, although at the same cost. But at best this is but a popular tradition; and another popular tradition is found in the magnificent Song of Attabiscar,[4] which gives a vivid picture of the utter defeat of the invaders. The one tradition is, perhaps, worth as much as the other, and no more; and the attempt to extract any history from them must be fruitless. Of the two, the popular Basque song is the more credible. Armies may be as utterly routed as that of the great Charles is there said to have been; but the exploits of Roland and his comrades are absolute impossibilities. Even when the ground is piled with the dead whom their swords have smitten down, Roland has not so much as a scratch upon his body, though his armour is pierced everywhere with spear points, and his death is

XI. The story of Roland.

[1] For the evidence of this see *Myth. of Ar. Nat.* book i. ch. xii.
[2] *Popular Romances of the Middle Ages*, p. 400.
[3] *Ibid.* p. 202.
[4] *Myth. of Ar. Nat.* i. 189.

caused not by any wound but by the excessive toil, which splits his skull and lets his brain ooze out at his temples. He is, in short, one of those invulnerable heroes, whom death must nevertheless be suffered somehow or other to lay low; and his sword Durandal is one of those magic weapons of which Excalibur, and Morglay, and Gram, are the fellows. If, when drawn from its sheath, it flashes like lightning and blinds the eyes of foemen, this may be put down to the licence of poetical fancy; but there must surely be some method in the madness of so many poets, when all describe the armour of their heroes in the like terms of hyperbole, absurd when the words are spoken of any weapons fashioned by human hands, but less than the reality when spoken of the spears of Indra or of Phœbus. Nay, Roland himself knows that it is no earthly weapon which he wields. It has been brought by angels from heaven, like the robe which came to Medeia from Helios; and when Roland feels that his death hour has come, even he is utterly unable to break it. In vain he tries to shiver it against marble, sardonyx, and adamant; and then he sinks down exhausted, but with the firm conviction that the angels who brought the sword will bear it away again, as Excalibur is drawn down beneath the waters from which it had arisen. Of the beautiful Hilda, to whom Roland is betrothed, it is enough to say that she belongs to that bright array of beings to whom death brings life and gladness, and among whom are seen the glorious forms of Kleopatra and Brynhild, of Daphnê and Arethousa, of Iolê and Brisêis, and that with this touching myth ends the lay of the hero, in whom some see the prefect of the Britannic march named in the pages of Eginhard.

But Roland appears again in Olger the Dane.[1] The name may be changed, and the incidents of his career may be somewhat different, but he is the same invincible hero, whose weapons have been forged on no earthly anvil. He

[1] *Popular Romances of the Middle Ages*, p. 223.

is the defender of the same land, a warrior in the same hosts which the mythical Roland led on to victory; and those points in which he seems to be unlike the mighty Paladin serve only to identify him with other heroes to whom both he and Roland stand in the relation of brothers. Like Arthur, and Tristram, and Macduff, like Telephos, Perseus, Cyrus, Romulus, Œdipus, he is one of the Fatal Children, whose greatness no earthly obstacles can hinder. At his birth the fairies appear to bestow on him their gift and their blessing, as the Moirai are seen round the cradle of Meleagros. His life on earth is to be spent in defending the realm of the great Karl; but he stands to him in the relation of Herakles to Eurystheus. He is a hostage placed in the emperor's hands by his father the king of Denmark, and is sentenced to a hard punishment because his father fails in his trust. He is rescued from death only by the sudden appearance of formidable enemies, against whom Karl sees that Olger may be as useful as Herakles was to his Argive master. In the cause of Karl Olger performs exploits as wonderful as those of the son of Alkmene; but a sense of wrongs suffered at the hands of the emperor sends him forth to be, like Indra, and Savitar, and Woden, and Phœbus, a wanderer over the wide earth. But Olger is also, like them, one whom all women love; and more especially he is the darling of Morgan le Fay, who at his birth had promised that when he had achieved his greatness she would take him to dwell with her in her fairy palace of Avilion. In her love for the Danish warrior we have simply a reflexion of the love of Eôs for Tithonos, of the goddess of the Horselberg for Tanhaüser, of the Fairy Queen for True Thomas of Ercildoune. But in this her delicious land, where he forgets the years which have passed away, Olger may not tarry for ever. The influence of the old faith still survives, which holds that Helgi the slayer of Hunding[1] must appear

<small>XII. Olger the Dane.</small>

---
[1] *Myth. of Ar. Nat.* i. 286.

again on earth in other guise, that Arthur must once more be king, that the slumber of the Ephesian Sleepers must come to an end, that Sarpêdôn must once again gladden his bright Lykian home, and the slain Memnon return to the courts of Olympos. While his days pass away in Avilion in a dream of delight, the land which he had guarded is overrun by foes, and in answer to the cry of the Franks Morgan le Fay lifts from his head the cap of forgetfulness, and instantly he is eager to hasten to the help of the people for whom he had fought in times past. But the years which have rolled by have had an effect which only the magic of Morgan has been able to counteract; and by a singular modification of the myth of Tithonos she gives him a ring which shall preserve his youth so long as he keeps it on his hand. If he parts with it he will be a wrinkled old man from whose fingers all strength will have passed utterly away. Thus defended, he appears again in the land of the Franks; and the scenes to which his strange questions and answers lead reflect the incidents which followed the visit of the Seven Sleepers to the Ephesus where they had spent the days of their youth. The old fortune of Olger pursues him still. Women cannot see him without loving him, and, more than all others, the princess of the land seeks to obtain him for a husband. But the strange rumours which had gone abroad about this redoubtable champion had reached her ears, and she determines to test their truth by taking away the ring from his hand. Instantly he becomes the withered old man which Odysseus appeared to be, when Athênê took away all beauty from his face and all brightness from his golden hair.[1] When it is replaced on his finger, he is seen again in all the vigour of early manhood; and in this lusty guise he is leading the daughter of the land to the altar, when he is once more taken away by the Fay Morgan to her beautiful home, from which, the popular tale still averred that, like Arthur, and

[1] *Od.* xiii. 431; xvi. 175.

Helgi, and Harold, and Sebastian, he would return once more.[1]

The story of Havelok is more curious and important, not so much in its own incidents, as in the strange modifications which it has undergone, and the wide range of myths with which, etymologically or otherwise, it is connected. The comparatively late date at which the English story, as we have it, was put together, may be taken for granted; but although from a certain point of view this fact has its significance, it has little to do with the nature of the materials out of which the legend has been evolved. Havelok is one of the Fatal Children who are born to be kings, and to destroy those who keep them out of their rightful inheritance; and there is, therefore, but one maiden in the world who may be his wife. Into the Havelok myth the story of this maiden is introduced independently; and thus we have in Denmark Havelok and his sisters entrusted to the care of Godard, and in England, Goldborough, the daughter of Æthelwald, entrusted to the care of Godric, the trust in both cases betrayed, and the treachery made to subserve the exaltation of the intended victims. Godard is resolved that he, not Havelok, shall bear rule in Denmark, and Godric that oldborough shall not stand in his way in England. But the Norns do not work in vain. Godard puts Havelok nto the hands of Grimm, the fisherman, with the strict

XIII. Havelok the Dane.

[1] In the infinite multiplicity of details introduced into the myth by French romance-makers it is possible that some may be really borrowed from history, while others are mere arbitrary fictions, as, from their stupidity, many of them may be fairly supposed to be. Others are as manifestly borrowed from the old familiar stores of mythical imagery. Ogier's horse, Broiefort, while his master is in the underground prison, is carried away, and made to serve in a lime-pit, where all his hair is burnt off his flanks, and his tail is shorn to the stump. But when Ogier, whose weight crushes all other beasts, leans against him, Broiefort, far from yielding, only strengthens himself against the weight. This is, plainly, only another version of the myths in which the sword or the cloak is useless except to the one man who is destined to draw the one or to put on the other, as in the stories of Arthur, Balin, Lancelot, and Orendil. When Ogier draws his sword, we have, as we might expect, the comparison with which the weapons of Achilles, of Arthur, and other heroes have rendered us familiar.

charge that he shall put him to death; and this trust is in its turn betrayed, as it is by Harpagos and the messengers of Amulius in the stories of Cyrus and Romulus. When at midnight Grim rises to do Godard's bidding, he sees streaming from the mouth of the child the bright light which, encircling the head of Servius Tullius, betokened the future greatness of the son of the slave Ocresia, and as it gleamed round the head of Asklepios, warned the shepherd Aristhanas that he saw before him a divine child. Havelok is thus recognised by him as the son of king Birkabeyn, and the fisherman, to avoid the wrath of Godard, hastens away from Denmark, and takes up his abode in the town which bears his name in England. But what is Havelok to do in the new land? His preserver is poor, he himself is meanly clad and without friends, and so, when he reaches Lincoln in search of work, he becomes the scullion-boy in Earl Godric's kitchen. But, as in the Gaelic legend, the Great Fool[1] is still the one to whom hosts yield, and it is he alone who is destined to be the husband of the young Fairfine, so Havelock alone can win the queenly daughter of Æthelwald.

Thus it comes to pass that at the games held by Earl Godric the kitchen-boy distances all his competitors in a way which renders all thought of coping with him impossible. In the victory of the scullion-lad Godric sees an opportunity for humiliating Goldborough. He has promised her father that he will wed her to the strongest man, and he will keep his word. The marriage is accordingly celebrated, and Goldborough finds herself in the hovel of Havelok with a feeling of disgust equal to that of the princess who in the Norse and German stories marries King Thrushbeard or King Hacon Grizzlebeard in their disguise as beggars. But like Grimm, Goldborough sees at night the flame which streams from Havelok's mouth, and she hears an angel say that she

Havelok and Goldborough.

[1] Campbell, *Tales of the West Highlands*, lxxiv.

is the wife of the man who is to be king of Denmark. Havelok, on waking, says that he, too, has seen a vision, which assured him that he was to sit upon king Birkabeyn's throne; and with his wife and the three sons of Grim he sets sail from England to fight for and to win back his inheritance. In Denmark his might is at once proved by the destruction of sixty-one thieves, who, when they assail the house in which he is sojourning, are all slain by him and the three sons of Grim. The next night Ubbe, his host, sees a great light streaming from his chamber, and going in, he beholds what Grim and Goldborough had beheld before him. The sequel of the story tells us of the discomfiture and death of Godard in Denmark, and the romance ends with a period of repose as profound as that which marks the close of the Odyssey.[1]

But the English story of Havelok does not stand by itself. In the French poem, put together probably in the latter half of the twelfth century, the heroine is not Goldborough, but Argentile (a name which looks as mere a translation as the Gaelic Fairfine from the Greek Chryseis), and Havelok has become Havelok Curan. Here, then, we have the story of the loves of Argentile and Curan, one of the narratives in Warner's poem, entitled 'Albion's England,' in which Curan, in order to win Argentile, becomes a scullion in the household of Ethil, who compels her to marry him from the same motives which led Godric to insist that Goldborough should wed Havelok. If we ask what or who is Curan, we are carried to the Danish hero whom the Angles call Anlaf-cwiran, and we are put on a track which ends in the identification of the name Anlaf with that of Havelok, whose story, as furnishing groundwork for the claim of the Danes through him to England, is connected with the myth of Guy of Warwick.[2]

The loves of Argentile and Curan.

---

[1] *Popular Romances of the Middle Ages*, 'Havelok.'
[2] The chronicle cited by Sir F. Madden gives to the kings of Denmark and Norway, who bring over Colbrand, the names Anclaphus and Conelaphus. In the metrical romance of Guy of Warwick these names appear in the forms

But Havelok further presents a link with the Saga of Beowulf, as bearing a name which is only a modification of that of Higelac, one of the heroes of that myth. Whether this name is further to be identified with the Danish Chochilaichus of Gregory of Tours, is a question which has an interest only in so far as it may tend to prove what is disputed by none, that the names of historical persons have found their way into popular legends. But when we find the name Anlaf, Anelaph, Hanelocke, in the Latinised Amlethus, we are brought at once to a name familiar to all English ears ; and when Hamlet is seen to stand to Havelok in the relation of *cloth* to *cloak*, we are compelled to ask what stories are told of Hamlet besides that which has been told by Shakespeare. On the very face of the Shakespearian play we have the same myth repeated more than once ; and it is known that other versions of the drama existed before Shakespeare took the subject in hand. If we look into the incidents of Shakespeare's play we find (apart from the connexion of Denmark with England, which marks the story of Havelok and Grim) that the method of Hamlet's death agrees precisely with that of his father. The latter is poisoned while sleeping in his orchard of an afternoon ; and the ghost tells Hamlet that the false report given out to cover his uncle's guilt, is that he had been stung by a serpent. But in either case, whether by accident or otherwise, we have the features common to a thousand mythical stories—the snake which appears in the myths of Eurydike and Arthur, the poison which plays a part in many a story of dawn-maidens, the afternoon slumber into which Endymion sinks in the land of Latmos.

When we go further back in the mythical genealogy of Hamlet, we find ourselves amongst a crowd of beings whose names are as transparent as those of Asterodia, Asteropaios,

Hanelocke and Conelocke, while the MS. English chronicle *Harl.* 63, referred to by Sir F. Madden, speaks of the Danes who 'had claimed before, by the title of King Havelocke that wedded Goldesburghe, the king's daughter of Northumbr.'

Narkissos, Aëthlios, Selênê, Chryseis, or Fairfine. We may take the story of his father Orendil, or Aurentil, who reappears in the Gudrun Lay as Hjarrandi, the being who, like Orpheus, Amphion, Hermes, or Pan, can charm all men with his sweet sounds, and whose name probably denotes nothing more than the hearing ear (ohr, auris). But Orendil is one of the three sons of Oygel, king of Treves, who with a slight change of name appears as Eigil, a counterpart of Tell, the shooting god, and is possibly the same as the Higelac of Beowulf. Like his son Havelok, Orendil can wed but one woman in the world, and she is queen of Jerusalem; but when he sets sail in search of her, the fleet is held windbound for three years in the Klebermeer, another Aulis, until the Virgin hears his prayers and lets them go, as Artemis at last sent a breeze to waft the Achaians to Ilion. The sequel of the story is a strange jumble of many myths. The fleet is wrecked when within sight of the Holy Sepulchre, and none escape but Orendil who, becoming servant to a fisherman, catches a whale, in the body of which is a grey coat. Although he wishes earnestly to possess this coat, and it is offered for sale at a very low price, he cannot meet the cost; but when anyone else tries to put it on, the garment splits. When Orendil dons it, it not only becomes as good as new, but makes him invulnerable—a myth which recalls not only the stories of Medeia and Nessos, but more especially those of Arthur, Balin, Lancelot, Tristram, and Galahad. The coat which will suffer only one man to put it on is but the sword which will yield only to one man's touch; and the scabbard of Arthur's Excalibur possesses precisely the power of the grey coat of making its owner invulnerable. Henceforth Orendil bears the name Graurock, the man with the grey or gleaming robe.[1] In a tournament, in which

The genealogy of Hamlet.

---

[1] The word *grey* denotes strictly not subdued but dazzling light. It is the Glaukos of the Sarpêdôn myth, and Athênê is Glaukôpis, the maiden with the flashing face.

he next takes part, he has to borrow a horse. He is miraculously provided with golden spurs, and he is, of course, the conqueror. The betrothal of Orendil with Queen Bride is followed by a war for the conquest of Jerusalem in which he outdoes Grettir, Herakles, or Rustem, by slaying single-handed sixteen thousand men, and by other exploits scarcely less marvellous. At length an angel forewarns Orendil and his wife of the hour in which they must die, and when that time has come, they are borne away to heaven. The grey frock becomes, it is scarcely necessary to say, the holy coat of Treves, where Orendil's father had been king.[1]

Through Higelac, the Wægmunding, the romance of Beowulf[2] is connected with that of Havelok, as through the myth of Sceaf it is connected with that of Arthur.[3] The saga itself is pre-eminent among the legends which describe the struggle of light with darkness. Grendel is the gloomy demon in one of his most awful forms; and we see in him the monstrous sphinx who strikes terror into the citizens of Thebes, the robber Cacus who breathes fire from his nostrils, the giant Ravana who steals away the beautiful Sita, or any other of the fearful beings who find their prototype in the thievish Panis and the throttling snake Ahi. When Grendel is killed, his fearful mother, the devil's dam, comes to avenge his death; but the second struggle, in which Beowulf is conqueror, is but a reflexion of the first, while both are repeated in the later

XIV.
The Saga of Beowulf.

---

[1] For these remarks on Hamlet I am indebted to the kindness of Dr. Latham; and I acknowledge my debt with the more gratitude, inasmuch as his inquiries have been instituted for purely historical purposes. It has been his object to ascertain how far Hamlet belongs to a family which existed in history; and the result of his search is that almost every name with which he is connected is the subject of myths of which it is impossible not to see the identity with the myths of other branches of the Aryan race.

[2] *Popular Romances of the Middle Ages*, 189.

[3] A further point of connexion is furnished by the name of King Birkabeyn, who is here the father of Havelok, and in the French poem is the father of Havelok Curan. Latham, 'Havelok the Dane,' *Transactions of the Royal Society of Literature*, vol. viii. new series.

encounter with the great dragon, which, like Vritra and the Panis, like Fafnir and Python, keeps guard over his priceless treasures, which he hides away greedily beneath the the earth. Like Hamlet or Havelok, again, or like Achilles and Herakles, Beowulf reaps no great harvest of his toil, although the king for whom he works is a more kindly master than Eurystheus. But in death as well as in life Beowulf is but a counterpart of the great son of Alkmene. The latter died by the blood of the Kentaur Nessos, whom he had smitten to death: the former dies by the blood of the fiery dragon whom he has slain. The venomed drops which remain on his hands burn and swell, until the poison comes through his limbs. In his agony the hero asks to look again upon the choice treasures which he has won for the people, before his eyes are closed in death; and thus having feasted once more on the dazzling vision of golden cups, jewelled bracelets, and gleaming coffers, he hastens from the land of the living to the unseen regions, whither the Wægmundings had gone before him. It may seem but a barbaric vision; yet the splendour which soothes the dying Beowulf is but the brilliancy of the golden doors and statues which shed their dazzling lustre on the palace of Alkinoös. So far as the conceptions differ, the contrast is but the result of impressions made by the phenomena of sunset on the mind of the Teuton beneath his harsher sky, and on that of the Greek in his more genial home.[1]

XV. The Romance of Arthur.

The very foundations of Comparative Mythology rest on the laws brought to light by the science of language; and without the guidance of etymology the analysis and classification of myths would be impossible. All primary myths must yield at once to the tests of language, or they must be excluded from the class of primary myths altogether. In the secondary myths

---

[1] The date at which the epic of Beowulf was composed is uncertain. It exists in a single manuscript of the tenth century. Craik, *History of English Literature*, i. 57.

we must have a certain proportion of names which tell their own tale philologically and point to the sources from which the materials for the myth were derived; and when we find such names in myths which are common to many or to all the branches of the Aryan race, we conclude without hesitation that we are dealing with traditions which have come down to us from a time when the forefathers of these peoples formed a single society. The stories of Endymion, of Prokris, of Sarpêdôn and Glaukos, of Dêmêtêr and Persephonê, are transparent; and their nature is determined by the most cogent philological evidence. This evidence is scarcely less cogent when we come to the myth of the Teutonic Iduna, of whom, as of Persephonê, we are told that Wuotan and all the Æsir mourned when she was stolen away, how the trees shed frozen tears, and the sun withdrew his face, until Loki brought her back in the form of a quail.[1]

But the case is altered only in degree when the stories furnish us with few names to which philological tests may be applied, or perhaps with none. We can be under no doubt as to the meaning of tales in which all things are held in a dreamless sleep, while a beautiful maiden slumbers either within a fortress of ice, or walls of flame, or an impenetrable hedge of briars, until the destined hero comes to wake her. When Dornroschen awakes from her slumber at the kiss of the brave knight who has found his way to her chamber, the scullion-boy receives the blow which the cook had raised his hand to inflict a hundred years ago, and the maid goes on with the process of basting the meat, in which she had been interrupted when the thorn pierced the hand of the Rose Maiden. It is but the familiar form which the myth is sure to receive at the hands of the common folk; but the transformation makes the task

[1] Bunsen asserts naturally that this myth is an exact counterpart of the earliest myth of Herakles, who falls into the sleep of winter, and lies, stiff and stark, until Iolaos wakes him by holding a quail to his nose. (*God in History*, ii. 483.) For Ortygia, the quail land, see p. 85.

a simple one for thousands of popular tales, the origin of which is determined by the character and sequence of their incidents. There is no etymological connexion, seemingly, between the Hindu story of Punchkin,[1] and the Teutonic tale of the giant who had no heart in his body;[2] yet it is impossible not to see that the death of the one, both in the mode of its infliction and in the whole train of incidents which led to it, is the precise counterpart of the catastrophe which overtakes the other. The names Sisyphos and Ixion may explain themselves, although in the case of the latter this has been disputed; but apart from this it cannot be questioned that wealth and wisdom and a terrible punishment are the characteristics of Sisyphos, Ixion, and Tantalos; that the stone which Sisyphos heaves to the summit of the hill only to see it roll down again, is but the blazing four-spoked wheel on which the body of Ixion is stretched as on a rack at noon-day, and that the effects of drought could scarcely be more vividly described than by the myth of the sun, who scorches the fruits which he has quickened into life, as he puts his face down close to the earth or makes the water flee away as he stoops to quench his thirst. The Ottawa tale of Iosco is a story of the antagonism between Ioskehi, the White One, with his brother Tawiseara, the Dark One.[3] We have seen these brothers in the correlative deities of the Aryan world, appearing sometimes as brothers, sometimes as sisters, as friends, or as enemies, sometimes as both brilliant, sometimes one light and one dark.

The evidence of language sets its seal on these myths of the two dawns, Ushasau, or the two Rudras (Rudrau), the morning and evening breezes, of Varuna and Mitra, of Eros and Anteros, of Phaethon and Helios, of Herakles and Iphikles, of Glaukos and Sarpêdôn, of Prometheus and Epimetheus, of Soma and Surya. But we cannot hesitate to place in their company the familiar forms of Romulus

---

[1] *Myth. of Ar. Nat.* i. 135.   [2] *Ib.* i. 138.
[3] Tylor, *Primitive Culture,* i. 314.

and Remus, of Pelias and Neleus, of Theseus and Peirithoös, of Achilles and Patroklos, of the Icelandic Grettir and Illugi, of Rama and Luxman, of Krishna and Arjuna, of Danaos and Aigyptos, or to recognise these under a different dress as the Two Brothers, the Two King's Children, the Two Sisters, the Two Wanderers, True and Untrue, and others who figure in Teutonic household stories. It follows that identity of idea and similarity in a marked train of incidents are sufficient evidence that any given stories belong to the same stock.

The conclusion is one which is, of course, quite independent of the further inquiry whether the stories stand to each other as brother and sister, or father and child, or as more distant kinsfolk who have grown to manhood without having ever seen each other or known each of the other's existence. The likeness may be the result of direct borrowing or importation, or it may be caused by independent growth as of plants from seeds which once came from a single tree; but whatever be the cause, the likeness is still there, and according to these points of likeness, these stories may be grouped and classified. These remarks apply with special force to the romance, or rather the body of romances, in which King Arthur is a more or less prominent figure. There can be no question that in the chronicle of Malory we have a number of stories, the connexion between some of which is very slender, and which have been pieced together with no great dexterity and skill. The whole story, as he gives it, resolves itself into cycles, the heroes of which had each his own separate legend or tradition, which probably at first made no reference to Arthur. Of the whole narrative it may be said that its general outlines and its special features may be traced not only in other mediæval romances, but in the traditions of almost every Aryan tribe. Nor can it be maintained that these resemblances are such as may be traced at the will of any who choose to find them in any two or more of modern novels, if these novels profess to relate incidents belonging to real life.¹ The incidents which mark the Arthur story are confessedly extraordinary, or miraculous, or impossible; and it is the recurrence of these features either in different portions of the story, or in other legends, which both shows how each romance has been brought into shape and determines its affinity with other versions of the same tale.

The story begins with an incident which recalls that of Alkmene and Amphitryon in the device by which Uther Pendragon obtains access to Igerne, the wife of Gorlois. The incidents which follow the birth of her child, Arthur,² carry us to the tales which tell us of the birth and early years of the Persian Cyrus, the Latin Romulus, or the Theban Œdipus. All these heroes are made known by doing something which others cannot do; but the mode in which Arthur is revealed is identical with that in which Sigmund is made known in the Volsung tale. In the Arthur story the sword is firmly fixed in an iron anvil; in the Volsung legend it is thrust into the roof-tree by the one-eyed stranger, who appears with a slouched hat and a spotted cloak.³ In the one case we have the inscription, that he who can pull the sword out of the stone and anvil is right wise born king of England; in the other, the one-eyed old man says: 'Whoso draweth this sword from this stock shall have the same as a gift from me, and shall find in good sooth that never bare he better sword in hand than is this.' The weapon yields to Arthur's touch, although all others strive in vain to stir it; and Sigmund, when he

Early years of Arthur.

---

[1] It would be impossible to explain Walter Scott's story of the *Antiquary*, or his *Legend of Montrose*, as nature-myths. As a picture of the times of which it professes to treat, *Ivanhoe* may be worthless; but the words and acts of Prince John and his followers, of Cedric and the Templar, may be the words and acts of real men. It is otherwise when we come to the exploits of Locksley at the tournament, for here Scott has chosen to insert a bit of popular legend belonging to the story of Robin Hood or William of Cloudeslee and Adam Bell; and the affinity of these stories with the myth of Tell will not be disputed. See p. 139.

[2] *Popular Romances of the Middle Ages*, p. 2.

[3] This is the heaven-god Odin or Woden himself. See p. 284.

sets hand to the sword Gram, 'pulls it from the stock, even as if it lay loose before him.' The Arthur version may be a direct copy from the Sigmund myth; it is far less likely, and is indeed to the last degree unlikely, that the latter was directly suggested by the myth of Theseus, who draws from beneath the mighty stone the sword and sandals of his father. The weapon reappears necessarily in the myths of all lands. It is the Morglay of Bevis of Hampton, the Durandal which flashes like the sun in the hands of Roland. When Arthur draws it from its sheath it gleams on the eyes of his enemies like the blaze of thirty torches; when Achilles holds it up, the splendour leaps to heaven like the lightning.

According to the later ideal, Arthur is the king or knight of spotless purity. With this notion the earlier traditions stand out in striking contrast. The inci- <small>The loves of</small> dents relating to the daughter of Earl Sanam and <small>King Arthur.</small> the wife of the king of Orkney are cardinal points in the story. As in the Theban tradition, the ruin of the hero or of his kingdom must be brought about by his own son or descendants; and Mordred and the wife of the king of Orkney stand to Arthur in the relation of Polyneikes and Iokastê to Œdipus. The queen of Orkney is Arthur's sister, the daughter of Igerne, although he knows it not, as Œdipus knows not that in wedding Iokastê he is wedding his mother. But in the Arthur story it must be remembered that he dallies with the queen of Orkney, though she comes to his court with her four sons, as he dallies with the daughter of Earl Sanam, for the mere attraction of her beauty. In neither case has he any misgivings of conscience. If his relations with the mother of Mordred cause him sadness, this sadness is not awakened until he has dreams which forbode the ruin to be one day wrought. But if Arthur really belong to the same heroic company with Herakles and Sigurd, with Phœbus, or Indra, or Agni, this sensuous characteristic is precisely what we should look for. All these must be lovers of the maidens. So it is with Paris; and so, too, Minos is the lover of Diktynna and of Prokris. So again the Vedic poet, addressing the sun as the horse, says: 'After thee is the chariot; after thee, Arvan, the man; after thee, the cows; after thee, the host of the girls,' who all seek to be wedded to him, and who, as we have seen, are all wedded at one and the same moment to Krishna. Nor may we pass over the incident which closes the first portion of the Arthur myth, and which tells us that Arthur, on hearing that his destroyer should be born on Mayday, orders that all the children born on that day shall be brought to him. With these Mordred is placed in a ship, which is wrecked, and, as we may suppose, Mordred is the only one saved.[1]

But the sword which Arthur draws out of the stone is not the weapon by which his greatest deeds are wrought. It is snapped in conflict with the knight Pellinore. Precisely the same is the fortune of the sword Gram which Odin thrusts into the roof-tree of the Volsungs. The sword of Arthur, whether it be Excalibur, or, as some versions have it, Mirandoise, is bestowed on him by the Lady of the Lake; just as the shards of the sword Gram, welded together by Regin the smith, are brought by the Fair Hjordis to Sigurd her son, who now stands in place of his father Sigmund. But the Lady of the Lake and the mother of Sigurd are simply counterparts of Thetis, the nymph of the sea, who brings from the smith Hephaistos the armour which is to serve for her child Achilleus, in place of that which Hektor had taken from the body of Patroklos. The parallel is complete, and its significance cannot be mistaken.

The scabbard of this sword is even more marvellous

Arthur's sword.

[1] With this we may compare the myth which represents Kamsa as ordering the slaughter of the new-born children, amongst whom he hopes that Krishna will meet his death: see p. 147. The only difference is that Kamsa represents the darkness, while Arthur is the light; but the night destroys the day, and the day destroys the night, and what is said of the one holds good of the other.

than the weapon itself: nay, the sage Merlin tells Arthur that it is worth ten of the sword, for so long as he bears the sheath about him, the sorest blow shall not cause him to lose a drop of blood; and thus Arthur is placed in the ranks of that large class of heroes who may be wounded only in one way, whether as being vulnerable only in one part of their body, like Achilles or Siegfried, or only by some particular weapon or instrument, as Balder by the mistletoe, or Ragnar Lodbrog by the viper. In all these stories a way is necessarily provided by which the catastrophe may be brought about. Arthur, invulnerable with the scabbard, as is Aurendil with the grey cloak,[1] must somehow or other be deprived of it; and here this is done by means of Arthur's sister, Morgan le Fay, to whom he entrusts it for safety, but who, loving Sir Accolon more than her husband Sir Uriens, gives it to him, making by enchantment a forged scabbard for her brother. In a fight which follows the king is well-nigh overcome; but though he regains the sheath, yet Morgan contrives once more to get it into her hands. Excalibur she cannot take from the grasp of Arthur as he sleeps; but she hurls the scabbard into the lake, and the death of the king at some time or other is insured.

The scabbard of Arthur's sword.

Nor is it here only in the Arthur cycle that this magic sword is seen. The whole story is repeated in the episode of the good Sir Galahad. When the day for filling up the Perilous Seat has come, a squire tells the king that he has seen a great stone floating down the river, and a sword fixed in it. Here again we have the inscription, by which the weapon is made to say that no man shall take it hence but he by whose side it ought to hang, and that he shall be the best knight in the world. At Arthur's bidding Lancelot, Gawaine, and Percivale strive to draw it forth; but it will yield only to the touch of the pure Sir Galahad, who, in full assurance of winning it, has come with a scabbard only.

[1] See p. 308.

The reluctance which Uther's nobles show to receive Arthur as their lord, on the ground that he is but a base-born boy, brings before us another familiar feature in this whole class of legends. Without exception the Fatal Children, as Grimm calls them, have to spend their early years in banishment or disguise or humiliation; and when they come to claim their rightful inheritance, they are despised or jeered at by men of meaner birth, who can never be their match in strength and wit. The wise Odysseus is mocked for his beggarly garb as he stands on the day of doom in his own hall; and this passing shame before the great victory is reflected in countless popular stories which tell us of a degradation culminating in the Gaelic lay of the Great Fool. This story is repeated in the episode of Sir Tor, who is brought in by a cowherd. The herdsman, supposing him to be his own son, complains of his folly; but the wise Merlin, who happens to be present, declares that he is the son of King Pellinore. The same imputation of weakness is seen again in the demands made to Arthur for homage to his alleged sovereigns—demands which are in each case refused, and which lead to the discomfiture whether of King Ryons or of the Roman Cæsar.

Arthur and the Fatal Children.

The recurrence of precisely the same ideas in the story of the poor knight Balin,[1] throws light on the method in which a crowd of originally independent stories have been sorted and pieced together in order to produce the Arthur story of Jeffrey of Monmouth, and still more of Malory. In truth, the myth told of Arthur is now told all over again of Balin, and Arthur becomes altogether subordinate to the new protagonist. Here, as before, the first incident is that of the drawing of a sword; but in this case the weapon is attached not to an anvil or a stone, but to the side of a maiden who cannot be freed from

The story of Balin.

[1] *Popular Romances of the Middle Ages*, p. 7.

it save by a true knight guileless of treason. No knights of the court of King Ryons have been able to rid her of the burden; and Arthur himself is now not more successful. Hence, when Balin, the poor-clad knight, who has just been let out of prison, begs that he may be suffered to try, the maiden tells him that it is in vain for him to do so, when his betters have failed before him. To his hand, however, the weapon yields as easily as those which were drawn forth at the touch of Arthur or of Galahad.

With the death of Balin and his brother Balan the story returns to the myth of Arthur and his wedding with Guenevere, whose character approaches more nearly to that of the Helen of the Greek lyric and tragic poets, than to the Helen of our Iliad and Odyssey. As Helen is with Æschylus the ruin of ships, men, and cities, so is Arthur here warned by Merlin that Guenevere is not wholesome for him; and at a later time the knights who are besought to come forward as champions in her behalf demur to the request, on the ground that she is a destroyer of good knights. Their reluctance is fully justified. The real Guenevere of the Arthur story is sensual in her love and merciless in her vengeance; nor is Lancelot the austerely devoted knight which sometimes he declares himself to be. By equivocation or direct falsehood Lancelot contrives to avoid or rebut the charge brought against him by Sir Meliagrance; but when, in the encounter that follows, that knight goes down beneath the stroke of Sir Lancelot and yields him to his mercy, the latter is sorely vexed, because he wished to destroy the evidence of his guilt; and when he looks to Guenevere, she makes a sign which expressed the will of the Roman ladies in the amphitheatre, that the vanquished gladiator should die. It may, of course, be said that the incident which furnished grounds for the accusation of Meliagrance has been interpolated into the myth; but the process is perilous which rejects from a legend every portion that clashes

Arthur and Guenevere.

with our conceptions of the character of certain heroes. Assuredly it cannot be maintained that the acts which roused the suspicions of Meliagrance are consistent with any notion of merely Platonic affection; nor is it safe to impute the coarseness which characterises Lancelot and Guenevere, Tristram and Isolte, wholly to the coarseness of the mediæval storytellers. There is everything to support, and little or nothing to invalidate the conclusion, that the harsher and more repulsive portraits are the older; and if in the original myth Lancelot had been a man such as later poets have painted him, the quest of the Sangreal could not have been accomplished, for it is only by personating Guenevere that Elaine becomes the mother of Galahad.

But Guenevere, like Helen, has her treasures as well as the rich dower of beauty; and her special gift to Arthur is the Round Table. This table Merlin is said to have made in token of the roundness of the world; but no explanation can be received as adequate which is confined merely to its shape, and takes no notice of its marvellous powers. The quest of the Holy Grail may be to all appearance a narrative wholly distinct from that which tells us how the fellowship of the Round Table was formed; but in all essential characteristics the Round Table and the Sangreal do but reflect each other. Around the one Arthur and his knights hold high festival; the other makes its presence felt among the whole company of the Round Table, filling the air with exquisite fragrance and placing before each knight the viands which he would most wish to have. They are both, in short, different forms of the same vessel of plenty which carries us at length to the Egyptian lotus and the Yoni of the Hindu.[1] Appearing first as the sign of the earth, the fertilised mother, this symbol assumes the form of a ship, as in the Argo, or the ship of Isis, and then passes through all possible forms of

[1] See p. 143.

boat-shaped vessels from the great cosmic mixing-bowl of the Platonists to the Luck of Edenhall. Like the table of the Ethiopians, the Round Table may minister to the wants of the indifferent or the bad as well as of the good, while the Holy Grail may be seen by none but the purest of the pure.[1] If the mystic vessel of the Sangreal acts as a test of righteousness and purity, the same power is possessed by the horn which Sir Lamorak sends to King Mark; and this horn is manifestly the horn which Oberon gives to Huon of Bordeaux, and which yields the costliest wine in the hands of a good man only.[2] The story of the Sangreal is thus a reproduction merely of the story of the Round Table; and it is not here only that we shall find ourselves moving within the same magic circle.[3]

With his election as king begin the toils and the wanderings of Arthur. No sooner is one enemy overcome than another assails him from some other quarter. 'Alas!' he complains when he hears that the king of Denmark is ravaging his northern lands, 'never have I had one month's rest since I became king of the land.' It is but the doom which lies on the mythical heroes of all countries; and the reason is given in the Gaelic story which tells us that the spell laid by the Dame of the Fine Green Kirtle on the Fair Gruagach is that where he takes his breakfast, there he may not take his dinner, and where he takes his dinner he may not sup, till he finds out in what place she may be under the four brown quarters of

The wanderings of Arthur

---

[1] It must, however, be remembered that in the *Iliad* and *Odyssey* the Ethiopians are always 'blameless.' If we make this a condition of their feasting at their table, we have all the elements of the Christian myth of the Sangreal.
[2] *Myth. of Ar. Nat.* book i. ch. ii.
[3] The notion that *greal* is a welsh word, signifying a magazine, which passed into the Latinised form *gradalis*, may be safely dismissed as a mere *hysteron proteron*. The opinion that the Latin *gradalis* represents the Greek *kratêr*, a goblet or mixing bowl, is far more plausible; but the strange connexion of the vessel with the Holy Blood seems to justify the conjecture that to this we owe the name of the Sang-real.

Y

the world.[1] Of course, he wins her in the end, and her fine green kirtle is found to be a garment endowed with the magic properties of the robe which Medeia received or inherited from Helios. In short, there is but one being of whom this tale is eternally true, and that being is the sun, who can never rest until he joins in the evening the beautiful maiden from whom he was parted in the morning. The force of the evidence becomes irresistible, as we ascend from the wanderers of folklore stories to the great company of epical heroes, and beyond these to the divine persons whose real nature was closely known to those who spoke of them— to Dionysos, the wine god ; to Phœbus, who cannot rest in Delos, but who, having wandered far away to the west, ever comes back to his bright birth-place ; to Wuotan or Odin, who is Wegtam, the pilgrim of the road, and to Indra the wonderful, who, like all the rest, is a wanderer.

Nothing can grow without a root ; and the most grotesque fictions are not altogether unreasonable and absurd. Thus, when in these Arthur legends we come across men whose strength increases from nine to twelve o'clock, so that towards noon they become almost irresistible, while from the moment of noon their power begins slowly but steadily to decline, it becomes impossible to resist the conclusion that here, again, we are reading of heroes who have had transferred to them the properties which belong only to the one-eyed wanderer who daily performs his journey through the heavens. This power of growth until noon is possessed by Sir Gawaine, while his adversary, Marhaus, who here represents the opponent of the sun-god, waxes bigger and bigger at sundown, as the shades deepen. It is shared also by the Red Knight of the Red Lawns. This magical power in Gawaine (of which, with one of the many direct contradictions exhibited by the legends pieced together to form the Arthur story, we are told that Arthur alone was aware), is especially manifested

Gawaine and Lancelot.

[1] *Myth. of Ar. Nat.* i. 291.

in the last desperate struggle with Lancelot, which ends in the death of Gawaine.

If any doubt yet remained that these otherwise inexplicable characteristics of the Knights of the Round Table or their antagonists are remnants of nature-myth, these would be removed by the transparent scene in which the three fatal sisters[1] are brought before us by the stream side in the forest of Alroy. The images of the Past, the Present, and the Future with its budding hope, cannot be mistaken in the three maidens, of whom the eldest wears a circlet of gold on hair white with the snows of more than threescore winters, while the second has seen thirty years, and the third, whose head is crowned with flowers, is but in her fifteenth summer. These maidens sit where the roads parts, watching for errant knights, whom they may teach strange adventures. It is enough to say that Uwaine and Marhaus choose the more sober and discreet of the sisters; the youngest falls to the share of Gawaine, and by her early desertion of him illustrates the truth that the young and his hopes, like the fool and his money, are soon parted. *The weird sisters.*

In the Arthur legends there have been brought before us already two distinct mythical cycles, the one telling the story of Arthur himself, the other that of the poor knight Balin. We now reach a third, in which are related the adventures of Sir Lancelot du Lake. This cycle is interwoven with the Arthur myth, which is made to serve as a common framework for these and for two other cycles which are included with them. The main thread in the legend of Lancelot is the love which he bears to Guenevere, and which the queen fully returns. This love the mediæval story-teller has evidently sought to exhibit in the fairest light. When Morgan le Fay and three other queens bid him choose one of them for his lady-love, Lancelot's answer is a stern *Mythical cycles in the Arthur Romance: I. Arthur. II. Balin. III. Lancelot. IV. Gareth.*

[1] See p. 5.

refusal; and to the daughter of King Bagdemagus, who tells him that he lacks one thing, the love of a lady, and warns him of the rumours which are busy in connecting his name with that of Guenevere, Lancelot replies that he thinks not ever to be a wedded man, but that he wishes only to keep his hands clean and his heart pure. The story gives sufficient evidence that the love of Guenevere and Lancelot is not pure, and that if it had been pure, the quest of the Sangreal would not have been accomplished. But the narrator leaves, to be taken up hereafter, the threads which are to join the Lancelot story with those of Arthur and Tristram.

For the present he betakes himself to a fourth cycle of myth, which is concerned with the adventures of Gareth. The story of this knight, who is brought into Arthur's court unable to walk, and leaning on the shoulders of two men, is, throughout, one of that vast class of solar myths which speak of weakness issuing in victory. The first thing related of him carries us to the other tales which tell of great heroes whose lower limbs are not proportioned to the rest of their bodies. If Gareth seems unable of himself to walk, we must remember that Odysseus standing is comparatively insignificant, but that when he sits his presence is more dignified than that of Menelaos.[1] So, again, of the Icelandic Grettir it is said that he is right well ribbed about the chest, but few might think he would be so small of growth below. They are all, in truth, counterparts of the Shortshanks who figures in the folk-lore of Northern Europe.[2] But the destiny of Gareth, who, though the goodliest youth on whom the eyes of Arthur have ever rested, yet knows neither his name nor his parentage, is for the present the kitchen. Like Halvor in the story of Soria Moria Castle, he must grub among the ashes; like the Lad who knew not how to shiver, he cannot be placed far away from the living embers which are to reveal his future splendour. As he has no birth-name, Sir Kay con-

---

[1] *Iliad* iii. 211.   [2] *Myth. of Ar. Nat.* i. 325.

THE GARMENT OF HUMILIATION.

temptuously calls him Prettyhands, and bids him go to the kitchen and there have fat brose, so that at the year's end he may be fat as a pork hog. The time for action at length comes, when a maiden beseeches Arthur to send succour to a lady besieged in her castle by the Knight of the Red Lawns; but even now he must drink a bitter draught of humiliation. When he entreats Arthur that he may be sent on this service, the maiden asks indignantly if she is to be put off with a kitchen-knave, and hastens away in wrath. Sir Kay, who wishes to see how the ash-boy fares, speedily receives a stroke which compels him to believe that in his case discretion is the better part of valour; and even Lancelot, who ventures to parry lances with him, is constrained to own that their quarrel is not so great but they may fairly leave off.

This myth is repeated in the episode of the Knight with the Ill-shapen Coat, the ubiquitous garment of humiliation worn by the wanderer who owns the Knapsack, the Hat, and the Horn in the German story, by the Gold Child when he appears before the king in the guise of a bear-hunter, and by the soldier who is seen in the Boots of Buffalo Leather.[1] Here, too, the maiden reviles him, and tells him that, if he will follow her, his skin shall be as well hewn as his coat. The answer of the youth is that when he is so hewn, he will ask for no plaster wherewith to heal him. In the issue, the young knight becomes lord of the castle of Pendragon and the husband of the maiden who has reviled him.

Nor is this the only mythical incident, rendered familiar to us in the legends of many lands, which has been introduced into the story of Gareth. After the battle before the Perilous Castle, the youth thinks at once to win the lady of his love; but she tells him that though she will never love another, yet he must be tested by flood and field till twelve months should have passed by, before she can be his wife. The spirit of the old myth is so far weakened, that means are

[1] Grimm, *Household Stories*.

devised for cutting short the ordeal. But he has no sooner met again the lady of the Perilous Castle, than he becomes an actor in a series of astonishing scenes, in which the notion lying at the root of the story of the Snake-leaves [1] is extravagantly exaggerated. It assumes here a coarse form in the hands of a tale-teller, to whom the story conveys not a tittle of its orginal meaning. The head of the knight, who, approaching Gareth in the dark with a drawn sword, is beheaded by him, is made to grow on his body again by means of salve which the damsel Linet applies to it. When his enemy, thus restored to life, again attacks Gareth on the following night, the latter not only smites off his head, but hews it in pieces. But Linet is not to be thus baffled, and the murderer is again made to live. A like exaggeration is seen in the power of the ring which the lady of the Perilous Castle gives to Prettyhands. The owner of the ring of Gyges becomes invisible or visible according to the way in which he handles it; in the Arabian Nights story of the Wonderful Lamp the handling of the ring brings into sight the demon who is its slave. Here the ring has this power, that that which is green it will turn to red, red to green, blue to white, and so with all other colours, while he who wears it shall lose no blood. In other words, it will both disguise and guard him effectually; and this is the idea which lies at the root of the Gyges myth, in which the ring represents the circular emblem of wealth and fertility common to the mythology of the whole human race, and pre-eminent in the Arthur story both of the Round Table and the vessel of the Sangreal.

Having brought Gareth to the scene of his glory, the story now enters on a fifth cycle of myth, which retraces in the person of Tristram the threads of the tale relating the adventures of Lancelot. If there be a difference between them, it is that the Tristram story is more full of incidents common to all tales, the origin and

The fifth cycle—Tristram.

[1] See p. 5.

meaning of which cannot be questioned. But in their love and their madness, their bravery and their sufferings, their triumphs and their punishment, they are but shadows each of the other. So close, indeed, is the parallel, that Guenevere herself strikes the equation which makes herself and Lancelot on the one side the counterparts of Tristram and Isolte on the other. By his birth Tristram belongs to the number of those who are destined to greatness. He is the child of sorrow, born in the dark forest in which his mother seeks her lord who has been entrapped and shut up in a dungeon. Like Macduff and Sigurd, Tristram is scarcely seen by his mother who, before she dies, has only time to give him his ill-boding name; but, as with other heroes, the woes of his infancy are but clouds which are scattered before the splendour of his manhood. This story is repeated in the episode of Sir Alisander, whom king Mark of Cornwall, who is here represented in the darkest colours, orders Sir Sadok to slay. Alisander is, of course, saved by Sadok who pretends to the king that he has drowned the lad. On growing up he receives from his mother the blood-stained sark of his murdered father, and swears to take vengeance on king Mark, who on hearing that his intended victim is still alive seeks again to slay him by means of Morgan le Fay. But no woman can approach him without loving him, and Morgan le Fay enables him to overthrow all antagonists, until at length he wins the love of Alice the Fair Pilgrim. We have already had the counterpart of this tale in the story of Havelok the Dane.

Tristram[1] is pre-eminently the huntsman and the harper 'passing all other harpers that ever lived,' as are Hermes, Orpheus, Amphion, Pan, Sigurd, Volker, and many more. He is also a fearless knight, and alone ventures to encounter Sir Marhaus, whom the king of Ireland sends to demand tribute from the king of

Tristram and Marhaus.

[1] See Appendix III.

Cornwall. The combat is long and fierce; but at length Marhaus is smitten down by Tristram's sword, of which a piece is left sticking in his head. This piece is carefully stored away by the queen of Ireland, whose palace Marhaus reaches only to die. But Tristram, also, is sorely wounded by the arrows of Marhaus, which were poisoned. On this point it would be difficult to lay too great stress. Whatever may be said for African savages, it can never be maintained that the employment of poisoned weapons is a fit work for Christian chivalry, or that the fact of their being so used is credible. But what is to be said if we find this practice avowed without shame in the heroic legends of almost all lands? Poisoned arrows, as we have seen, are used by Herakles, and by him bequeathed to Philoktetes, who with one of them inflicts the death-wound of Paris. Nay they do not scruple to make use of poison in other forms. The poisoned robe of Medeia scorches to death the Corinthian Glaukê; the blood of Nessos seals the doom of Herakles; the messenger of Morgan le Fay is burnt to coals by the garment which she had been charged to lay at the feet of King Arthur. The significance of such incidents has been perhaps sufficiently pointed out already;[1] and we need not, therefore, perplex ourselves if the use of poisoned weapons is attributed to heroes of early or mediæval Christendom.

The relations which exist between Tristram, Isolte, and king Mark, precisely reproduce those which are found between Sigurd, Brynhild, and Gunnar in the Volsung tale. In Isolte Tristram finds the woman to whom he can give his whole heart, while Tristram is the only man who can win the love of Isolte, as Sigurd is the only hero who can wake the heart of Brynhild. But both are under the same doom. The bride is in each case, like Helen, the most beautiful of women, and she must in each case be wooed for another, and Mark of

_{Tristram and the two Isoltes.}

[1] See p. 103.

Cornwall in the Tristram story takes the place of Gunnar. The parallel may be traced even further. The naked sword which Sigurd places between himself and Brynhild, when he lies down to sleep by her side, is placed again by Tristram between himself and Isolte, and is used for the same purpose in the German story of the Two Brothers, the Norse legend of Big Bird Dan, and the Arabian Nights tale of Allah-ud-deen.[1] But if, like Sigurd, Tristram and Lancelot give their love to women who are, or must be, the wives of others, there yet remains in each case one whom each must wed, and as Gudrun is but a weaker reflexion of Brynhild, so is Elaine, the mother of Lancelot's child, a weakened image of Guenevere, and Isolte of the white hands a feeble likeness of Isolte the fair.[2] So, again, the enmity between Gudrun and Brynhild is reproduced in the antipathy of the two Isoltes and the ill-concealed dislike of Guenevere for Elaine. Yet more, as Brynhild, on learning that Sigurd has wedded her in the form of Gunnar, declares that she will bring about his death, so Isolte the Fair, on hearing that Tristram has married her namesake, warns him that henceforth she is his deadly foe.

As a warrior, Tristram belongs to the class of heroes who resemble Herakles or Samson. Like them, he is able single-handed to slay scores or hundreds. It matters not how many may assault him, or whether they do so secretly or openly. It makes no difference to Bellerophon whether the ambush into which he

Tristram as a warrior.

---

[1] These instances alone suffice to prove not only the common origin of these popular stories, but their nature, and justify the remark of Sir G. Dasent that 'these mythical deep-rooted germs, throwing out fresh shoots from age to age in the popular literature of the race, are far more convincing proofs of the early existence of these traditions than any mere external evidence.' See further *Myth. of Ar. Nat.* i. 281.

[2] If Guenevere is reflected in Elaine, the daughter of King Pelles, as Gudrun wears the likeness of Brynhild, so is the story of the daughter of Pelles manifestly reproduced in the exquisite episode of the Fair Maid of Astolat, who also bears the name Elaine, the only difference being that the one would be, while the other really is, the mother of a child of Lancelot. In either case the spell which lies on the maiden is irresistible, as with Isolte the Fair it was impossible to withstand the witchery of Tristram's harping.

falls hide twenty or fifty foes ; it matters not to the Icelandic Grettir whether he finds himself surrounded by forty or eighty enemies, or to the Knight of the Misshapen Coat whether he be assailed by a hundred knights at once, or to Tristram whether a whole troop of King Mark's men set upon him by himself. In each case the assailants are scattered as chaff before the wind, or smitten like a tree blasted by the thunderbolt. With men these things are absurd impossibilities. As narratives springing from phrases which tell us of the irresistible power of the sun, the lightning, or the hurricane, these stories become full of meaning ; and we can thus as readily understand the madness which comes over Tristram and Lancelot as we understand the frenzy which seized on Herakles.

We have seen that in the stories of Balin and Gareth Arthur himself becomes a subordinate personage, and that Tristram and Arthur. too in the very points in which in his own myth he is the peculiar hero. In each case a sword is to be drawn forth from a stone or an anvil ; and in each case it moves lightly as a feather at the touch of the one knight who is destined to draw it out. It follows that if this peerless hero is elsewhere secondary or defeated, we have passed out from the cycle of traditions immediately relating to him ; and thus we find Arthur unhorsed by Tristram in the legend which relates the career of the latter.[1] In a still more striking scene, the power of healing, which Arthur vainly strives to exercise on Sir Urre of Hungary, is made to depend on the touch of Lancelot, for here we are in that portion of the tale in which Lancelot is the bravest and best knight in all the world.

In the horn of Morgan le Fay we have another feature common to the myths of many ages and many lands. Talismanic tests. Except in the hands of the innocent the liquor of the horn is immediately spilt, just as in the so-called Orphic poem the testing-stone held in the husband's

[1] See Appendix IV.

hand hurls the faithless wife from her couch. The same marvellous power of discernment belongs to the horns of Bran, Ceridwen, and of Tegan Euroron. It is possessed also by the vessel of the Sangreal, which heals the guileless knight, while it may not be seen by Lancelot. In like manner the ship or barge of the dead tells the story of their lives or proclaims their wrongs. The same power which converted the horn of Amaltheia into a talismanic test as the horn of Oberon, has derived from this barge of the dead the ship of Faith, which warns all the mistrustful against entering it, and into which Galahad enters with Percivale and his sister in the quest of the Holy Grail. But the sister of Percivale, when, like Iphigeneia, she has yielded up her gentle life to heal the lady of the castle, is laid again in the same and yet another barge, which is to bear her to the city of Sarras, that there her body may be laid to rest in the Spiritual Place, in which that of the good Sir Galahad is to take its long sleep. Once again the ship reappears in the tale, when Arthur himself is to be borne away from the sight of men, and when the three queens, who have already been seen in different guise in the early career of Gawaine and his brothers, once more do their office as the weird sisters. A clearer light is thrown on the nature of this ship in the story of Sceaf, the father of Scild, in the myth of Beowulf. Here Sceaf comes, as he goes, in a ship, with a sheaf of corn at his head ; and when his work among men is done, he bids his people lay him in the ship, and in the ship he is laid accordingly with the goodliest weapons, and the most costly of ornaments, and with all things which may gladden his heart in the phantom land. Here we have in its fairer colours the picture which in many lands and ages has been realised with ruthless completeness. In all these instances we see the expression of the ancient and universal animistic conviction, which ascribed to the dead all the wants of the living, and which led men to slay beasts to furnish them with food, and to slaughter their wives or comrades, that they might journey to their new home with a goodly retinue.[1]

Another boat-shaped vessel is the Sangreal[2] itself, which imparts to the Arthur myth, or rather to that of Lancelot, its peculiar character. Whatever be the beauty which the influence of Christian sentiment has thrown over this legend, all that we have to do in the first instance is to mark closely the points of likeness between this and other myths. These points of likeness are to be found in its shape, its healing and life-giving properties, and its inexhaustible fertility. To these are added certain talismanic powers which, as we have already seen, it shares in common with some other circular or boat-shaped symbols of wealth and plenty. But elsewhere this oval emblem is most closely associated with the rod, the pillar, or the spear, the stauros or the pole, which became the special sign of the sun as the fertilising and fecundating power. Hence, even if the Grail vessel were not in this Arthur or Lancelot myth connected with any spear-shaped signs, we should be justified in placing this mysterious dish in the class to which belong the cups of Rhea and Dêmêtêr, of Serapis, of the milkwoman or gardener's wife in Hindu folklore, the lotus of Harpichruti (Harpocrates), the ivory ewer of Solomon, the goblet of Taliesin, the Luck of Edenhall, the horn of Amaltheia, and the Round Table of Guenevere. But the connexion of the Grail vessel with the spear-shaped emblem is not only not lacking in the Lancelot story; it is put forward with a prominence which is the more significant, if we assume that the romance-maker was utterly unconscious of the origin and nature of the materials on which he was working. If in other myths the upright emblem, the staff or rod of wealth and prosperity which Phœbus gives to Hermes,

The Sang-real.

---

[1] These ships move of their own will, without oars, rudders, or rigging, and never fail to reach the port for which they are making. They may thus be compared with the barks of the Phaiakians, and other mythical fleets. See p. 3.

[2] See note 3, p. 321.

becomes the *arbor vitæ*, and if in purely heathen models it is represented as shedding drops which denote the blood or the life, we have the whole framework of the myth, over which the introduction of Christian sentiment has shed a colouring of marvellous beauty. In the Lancelot story we are told that after seeing the Sangreal in the house of king Pelles, Bors, having laid himself down to sleep in his armour, beholds a light, in which he discerns a spear, great and long, coming straight towards him. This spear is seen again in the supreme vision vouchsafed to the pure Galahad and his two comrades, when, the holy Grail being manifested, four angels enter, two bearing candles, the third a towel, and the fourth a spear, from which fall three drops of blood, and which is finally placed upright on the holy vessel. But it was obviously inevitable that this imagery should to Christians convey another meaning; and thus the liquor, which in the horn of Oberon is the costliest wine, becomes the blood of the Saviour, which Joseph of Arimathea caught in the sacred dish in which He ate the lamb at the last passover with the disciples. That the achieving of the Sangreal should be confined to the pure Galahad is, as we have seen, no peculiarity in the Grail myth. It is the characteristic of a large number of legends relating to the signs or symbols of life, fertility, wealth, healing, and power.

But although almost all the closing scenes of the romance are lit up with the splendour of Christian feeling, there are features in it which we can no more regard as Christian, or even as human, than we can look on the narrative of certain events related in the Odyssey as in conformity with Achaian character. The high ascetic tone imparted to the close of Lancelot's relations with Guenevere may be and is probably due entirely to the force of Christian opinion; and this fact must clearly distinguish the earlier and later forms of the myth. Rather it must be said that the whole romance, as we have it, is

Guenevere and Elaine.

really built up on the assumption that the love of Lancelot and Guenevere is throughout sensual. The very achievement of the Sangreal depends on the birth of a child of Lancelot; and except on such an assumption the result is rendered impossible. Lancelot is entrapped by Elaine, because he supposes that he has been summoned to Queen Guenevere. But this is not a solitary instance. The same incident is repeated when the daughter of king Pelles visits the court of Arthur; nor is it possible to mistake the nature of the colloquy between Lancelot and Guenevere when the knight tears away the bars from her chamber window.

It may be urged that these are later additions which mar the ancient purity of the myth; but in favour of such a notion there is little indeed to be said. It cannot be supposed that the romance-maker, who has drawn a perfectly consistent character in Galahad, would have allowed a series of incidents which involve a monstrous contradiction between the career and the character of Lancelot and Guenevere as he has drawn them. Galahad before his birth is destined to be the pure and spotless knight, and such he remains always. Not less earnestly are Guenevere and Lancelot made to declare that their love has never been of a kind to reflect the least dishonour on king Arthur; yet this solemn asseveration, made again and again, is contradicted by a series of incidents which they are compelled to keep out of Arthur's knowledge by a long course of equivocation and lying. In short, we have here two stories—one in which Guenevere is faithful to her husband, and Lancelot looks on her as a man may look to his guardian angel, and another in which she is faithless, and responds to a sensual love on the part of Lancelot; and all that we have to determine is, which of these stories is the earlier. It seems almost self-evident that the idea which has necessarily commended itself to modern poets is but a thin coating of later Christian sentiment thrown over the earlier picture in which Guenevere not only seems to play but really plays the part of Helen, as she is drawn by the great tragic poets of Athens. When first Arthur thinks of wedding her, he is warned, as we have seen, by the wise Merlin that she will not be a wholesome wife for him; and from the circumstances already noticed it is clear that according to the conceptions of some one or other of the romance-makers her actual faithlessness began before Lancelot had seen the future mother of his child. It may be urged that the sensual fury displayed by Guenevere, when she finds that the very plan which she has laid to keep Lancelot by her side leads to his being again entrapped by Elaine while he sojourns in Arthur's court, is to be charged to the corrupt imagination of a later age; but it must be remembered that the very structure of the story which relates the career of Galahad utterly precludes this notion. Nay, Guenevere is not only a destroyer of many knights, as she might easily be on the hypothesis that though seemingly guilty she was really innocent: we have seen that in the case of Meliagrance she combines cruelty with her sensuality.[1] As to Lancelot, who thus commits murder at her bidding, he avoids in this instance the utterance of a direct falsehood, because the partial knowledge of Meliagrance makes it possible for him to employ the tricks of a dishonest pleader.

Thus, then, we have treachery on the one side, and faithlessness on the other; and the taking away of Guenevere from the court of Arthur, who had cherished him as his friend, answers to the taking away of Helen from Menelaos by the man in whom he had placed a perfect trust. In short, the character of Lancelot precisely reflects that of Paris; and the words of Menelaos before the walls of Ilion are echoed in those of Arthur before the gates of Joyous Gard. 'Fie on thy fair speech; I am now thy mortal foe, for thou hast slain my knights and dishonoured my queen.' But in spite of all his efforts, the Christian sentiment of the romance-maker cannot disguise the nature of the materials which he was handling. If Arthur was

[1] See p. 319.

the man so little extreme to mark what is done amiss, as he is here represented, so little disposed to think evil of another without due evidence, the persistence with which he follows up to the death a quarrel with his friend on a charge which, according to some portions of the story as we have it, is unproven, and even after the touching protestations of innocence which mark the restitution of Guenevere to her husband, becomes inexplicable. But if the character of Arthur here drawn is not Christian, it is because the portraits of Achilles and Odysseus in our Iliad and Odyssey are not Achaian.[1]

We have now reached the ending of the great drama. The victory of the snake Ahi is a victory of the great worm of darkness, which slays the light of day; and thus in the Arthur myths also visions of snakes bring the foreboding of the end. The king dreams that he sits in a chair, fastened to a wheel, beneath which lies a deep black water full of serpents and noisome things, and that suddenly the wheel turns round and he is plunged into the infernal stream, where the serpents seize him by all his limbs. From this dream he passes into a half-waking state, in which he thinks that he sees the form of the dead Gawaine, and hears his voice warning him not to fight on the morrow, but to make a month's truce with Mordred, whose name (although little can be said of the names in these later compositions) seems to betoken him as the murderer, biter, or crusher. The king follows Gawaine's advice; but his doom is not thus to be averted. It had been agreed that if during the conference between Arthur and Mordred a sword should be raised on either side, this should be the signal for mortal battle. But while they are yet speaking, the snake again plays its part. An adder bites the heel of one of Arthur's knights, who raises his weapon to slay the venomous beast; and Mordred's people, taking alarm, rush upon their adversaries. The prophecy of Merlin is well-nigh accomplished. The father and the son

Arthur and Mordred.

[1] See p. 276.

are to die, each by the other's hand. In vain Sir Lucan warns Arthur to remember his dream; Arthur will not hear. He sees the traitor who has done all the wrong, and betide him life or betide him death, he is resolved to slay him. But Mordred, writhing like a snake along the spear which has passed through his body, smites Arthur on the temples with the sword which he holds in both hands, and the king falls back in a swoon. It is the old tale of the Fatal Children, of children born to be great, born to slay their parents. There is death everywhere; and the phrases which described the death of the day and the night, of the sun and the darkness, of the dawn and the dew, explain every incident of the closing scenes in the lives of the heroes or maidens who represent them in mythical stories. One feature more remains. With the death of the sun his rays cease to shoot across the heaven. The great being is gone who could wield the unerring spear, or bow, or sword; and his weapon must go with him. Hence Arthur's sword must no more be profaned by the touch of mortal hand; and as the sun rises from the eastern waters when Phœbus springs to life on Delos, and plunges into his sleep like Endymion or Odysseus in the western sea, so the sword Excalibur must be restored to the waters from which it had arisen.

Arthur himself, as we have seen, is borne away in the barge in which the weird sisters have long waited for him; but he departs, not to die, but only to heal *Arthur in the* him of his grievous wound in the valley of *Vale of Avilion.* Avilion, the Latmian land in which Endymion takes his rest. Still, as the ages rolled on, and experience taught men more and more that there is no man who shall not see death, and as the belief grew that in telling Arthur's story they were speaking of a man who had really lived on the earth, so was the need felt more and more of saying plainly that he died. But the old myth still retained something of its old power; and the story-tellers who chanted the lays of the Helgis or of Arthur were each constrained to avow that according to the older faith neither Helgi the slayer of Hunding nor Arthur the peerless knight had ever died at all, and that he who had been king should yet be king again. Arthur was now, in short, one of that goodly company which numbers in its ranks the great Karl and Barbarossa, Sebastian of Portugal, the Tells of Rutli, the English Harold, and the Moor Boabdil. None of these is dead; for the sun, while men see him not, is but slumbering under that spell of night, whether in her beautiful or in her awful forms, which keeps True Thomas beneath the hills of Ercildoune, or Tanhaüser in the caves of the Horselberg or Odysseus in the grotto of Kalypso. Arthur does but sleep in the charmed slumber of the Cretan Epimenides or the Seven Sleepers of Ephesus; and under this spell lies not Arthur only, but the wise Merlin who had foretold his birth and destiny, had received him as a babe, and had witnessed his fame.[1]

In his wisdom and foresight, in his perfect knowledge of a coming fate, which yet to Arthur's surprise he makes no
Merlin. attempt to avoid, Merlin [2] strongly resembles the Hellenic Odysseus. But the point of the story told about him in its closing scenes is the besotted affection of the old sage for a damsel who, he knows, cares nothing for him. Yet he suffers the maiden, who is a water-nymph, to entice him into a cavern in which she imprisons him beneath a great stone. This is precisely the story of Tanhaüser and the goddess of the Horselberg; with very slight modification it is the story of Thomas of Ercildoune, and of Prince Ahmed and the Peri Banou in the Arabian Nights Tales. Here he is kept fast in an imprisonment from which none can deliver him except the woman who lured him into it; or, as the story avers, not a hundred men could lift the huge stone beneath

---

[1] The Arthur story has been shown by Mr. Campbell to be in all essential features the same as the Highland legend of the history of the Feinne. *Popular Tales of the West Highlands*, iv. 267.

[2] *Popular Romances of the Middle Ages*, 115. See Appendix V.

which Merlin made great dole. This is substantially the legend of the philosopher Abu Ajeeb, related by Washington Irving in the Legends of the Alhambra. It is true that here it is the sage who contrives to get the Gothic princess within the gate of his enchanted paradise ; but the besotted affection of the old man for the blooming maiden is precisely reproduced, and here again it is the sorceress only who can set him free. Whenever the sage shows symptoms of awakening from his charmed slumber, the tones of her magic harp speedily lull him to sleep again. As she is herself imprisoned by him, this is obviously the only way in which she can prolong his captivity. In the Merlin story she can leave him to himself, because she has enticed him to enter in, while she stands without.[1]

Romances like those of Bevis of Hampton and Guy of Warwick may be regarded rather as the arbitrary fictions of

[1] The notion of Merlin being a demon child is the result of the same degradation which converted Odin and the Æsir into devils. Neither in Teutonic nor in Hellenic lands did the Christian missionaries question the existence of the gods or heroes named in the mythologies of the tribes to whom they preached. The deities were allowed to live, but they lived on under a curse. But that these deified or supernatural beings might connect themselves with mortal women, was a belief unquestioned, whether by those who framed the story of the hero Astrabakos (Herod. vi. 69), or of the loves of the angels in Hebrew tradition. Hence the child of a deified hero or demigod and of a mortal woman would, in the estimation of Christian teachers, be the offspring of a diabolical incubus. The marvellous powers of the child would be the natural result of his extraordinary parentage ; and the same power which made Iamos acquainted with the language of birds would enable Merlin to vindicate the name of his mother, or at the least to convict her accusers of sins not less than those which were laid to her charge. Like most other mythical beings, Merlin has enemies who are bent on taking his life ; and his wisdom is specially proved by his power of revealing the reason why the walls of a castle fall down as soon as they are built, as a result due to the agency of dragons underneath a running water. This revelation of Merlin may be compared with that of the griffin or the giant in the German story of the Old Griffin (Grimm) and the Norse tale of Rich Peter the Pedlar (Dasent), and perhaps also with the problem on which depends the life of the giant or the sorcerer in the Hindu story of Punchkin (Frere, *Deccan Tales*), and the Teutonic tale of the Giant who had no heart in his body.

The Merlin story, which Jeffrey introduces into the life of Arthur, is found in Nennius (*History of the Britons*, p. 42), who, however, calls the child Ambrose, and having said that he was conceived by no mortal man, makes him assert that a Roman consul was his father. Whatever be the date of Nennius, his 'History' is probably two centuries earlier than that of Jeffrey.

a comparatively late age than the genuine growth of popular mythical tradition; but this very fact, if it be admitted, only makes more noteworthy the adherence of the romance-maker to the old models. When he could insert at will the fancies of his own mind, it is strange that he should still keep within the charmed circle of the oldest Aryan myths. Like Arthur, or Tristram, or Lancelot, Bevis is born to greatness:[1] like them and many others, he is in peril from those who wish to take his life, and the device which Saber hits upon to hide the fact that Bevis is not slain is one which we find far beyond the circle of Aryan folklore. The sequel of the story seems to be built on the model of that of Bellerophon. Like him, or like Grettir, Bevis is a match for any number of men who may assail him: like him he is the victim of treacherous letters which order his host to put him to death. Like him, he is subjected by his host to terrible dangers; but from the noisome pit full of reptiles, answering to the Iron Stove or the Glass Coffin of German tales, Bevis escapes as Bellerophon escapes from the ambuscade which is placed for his destruction. With this story are interwoven incidents which are common to the myth of Odysseus and the tale of Logedas Raja and other popular Hindu legends.[2] He returns to the home where he had left the lady of his love, clad in palmer's raiment, and is told that of all who come in such garb she, like Penelope, asks tidings of the man of many griefs and wanderings who has left her mourning. As Odysseus, again, is recognised by his dog Argos, so is Bevis known at once to his trusty steed Arundel. Like other kindred heroes, he is a slayer of dragons and a tamer of giants, and Ascapard plays the part of a Troll who may be made to do good service but is not altogether to be trusted. Doubtless the constant repetition of incidents proves a comparative lack of imagination on the part of

---

[1] There were versions which represented Bevis as a son of Olger the Dane. Frere, *Deccan Tales.*

the romance-maker; but it shows still more clearly the nature of the materials which he sought to bring into shape. Josian, who lulls her suitor to sleep on her lap in order to be rid of his importunities and then strangles him, is simply a more active Penelope avenging her own wrongs. In the disguise by which she makes herself like the Loathly Lady, she assumes a form which the brilliant hero or the beautiful maiden of Eastern and Western tradition can alike put on, and which, passing through the phase exhibited by the ugly frog or toad in German folklore, carries us to the myth of Bheki the frog sun. Of the battle in Cheapside it is enough to say that it is as sheer an impossibility as the most marvellous exploits attributed to Grettir or to Herakles. The great strife is followed by a long period of peace and happy love, until at last Bevis, and his horse Arundel, and the devoted Josian all pass away from earth together.[1]

The idea which runs through the earlier portions of the story of Guy of Warwick has found expression in the Arthur story in the contempt shown by the maiden who serves as guide to Gareth in his disguise as Pettyhands, and in the ordeal to which he is subjected by the lady of the castle. But not only is Guy a knight-errant and a slayer of dragons and noisome beasts; the doom of the wanderer presses on him still more heavily. He toils hard and he achieves great glory, that he may win the maiden whom he loves; and when he has won her, forty days only pass before he feels that he must go from her side, and putting on a pilgrim's dress he wanders away to the Holy Land. But he has still mighty works to do; and the Ethiopian giant and other foes fall beneath his hands. In his later wanderings he comes across his friend Thierry, of whom an incident is recorded which is found in other legends, and illustrates the old animistic belief of the the separable soul which can go out from the body and

[1] *Popular Romances of the Middle Ages*, 140.

return to it again. In the story of King Gunthram the soul goes forth in the form of a snake; but the movement of the weasel which creeps from Thierry's throat differs not much from that of the snake.[1] Of the closing scenes in the life of Guy all that needs to be noted is the slight modification which here also Christian sentiment has introduced into a legend otherwise repeating the old tale of Odysseus and Penelope. They must be united after the weary wandering and the hard strife: but like Odysseus, like the Old Soldier of German folklore, and like a thousand others, he returns in the form of a pilgrim or a beggar, and the wife whom he has forsaken prays him, if he can, to give her tidings of her love. The sight of her gentle care of the poor and needy makes him shrink from the thought of breaking in upon her works of mercy, and turning away, he takes up his abode in a hermit's cell. When he feels that he has but a few hours to live, he sends her a ring by a herdsman; and the wife instantly knows that the poor pilgrim is her husband the great Guy of Warwick. Like Kleopatra, she clasps the hero in her arms, as he gently breathes his life away; and as Kleopatra lingers not long upon earth after Meleagros is gone, so Guy[2] has been but

[1] *Myth. of Ar. Nat.* i. 402-404. Of this incident Mr. Tylor (*Primitive Culture*, i. 397) says: 'This is one of those instructive legends which preserve for us, as in a museum, relics of an early intellectual condition of our Aryan race, in thoughts which to our modern minds have fallen to the level of quaint fancy, but which still remain sound and reasonable philosophy to the savage. A Karen at this day would appreciate every point of the story; the familiar notion of spirits not crossing the water, which he exemplifies in his Burmese forests by stretching threads across the brook for the ghosts to pass along; the idea of the soul going forth embodied in an animal; and the theory of the dream being a real journey of the sleeper's soul.' It is possible that this idea may be faintly traced in that scene in the wanderings of Vicram Maharaja (Frere, *Deccan Tales*, 129), in which the cobra emerges at will from his throat. But the connexion cannot go beyond the mere suggestion of the imagery; for the story of Vicram makes it evident that the cobra, which enters into his throat is the snake of winter, which makes the raja miserable until he can be freed from it; nor can he be freed from it except by the maiden who returns in spring from the cheerless land. If any doubt still remained as to the nature of this myth, it would be set at rest by the fact that the slaying of the cobra is followed by the recovery of the treasure which he had stolen, as it is recovered from the dragon Fafnir by Sigurd.

[2] *Popular Romances of the Middle Ages*, 162.

a fortnight dead when the sorrow of Felice is ended by her union with him in the land where there is no more parting. The beautiful hues of Eôs cannot linger long in the sky, when the Sun-god has gone to his rest.

The longest epic poems in the world are those of the Hindus; but for Western readers their interest is not in proportion with their length. Of their origin and growth we know no more than is known of [XVIII. The Mahâbhârata.] the growth of the Iliad and the Odyssey; and their composite character is scarcely questioned by any, perhaps by none. In the case of the Mahâbhârata the original poem, whatever it may have been, has been literally buried under the mass of accretions which have gathered round it; and we have to remember that in India the temptations to introduce new matter into old poems were far stronger than in Hellas. The institution of caste must be defended; and, more particularly, no opportunity must be lost for maintaining the ascendency of the Brahmans, and of enforcing the precepts by which they sought to regulate the religious life of the people. Hence the narrative is interlarded with episodes of asceticism, and the original framework of the story put out of sight by the cumbrous Brahmanic fancies which have been thrust into it. A poem so put together can have only a comparatively slight interest except for Asiatics; but there is, nevertheless, little doubt as to the nature of the foundation on which this huge superstructure has been reared. In its present shape the poem may be somewhat more recent than the Ramayana, but its framework is almost certainly older. It was seemingly unknown to Megasthenes, who was in India towards the close of the fourth century before the Christian era; it was known in the second half of the first century of our era. It has been inferred, therefore, that it took shape at some time between these two dates. But, however this may be (and the question is one of the greatest uncertainty), it may be safely said that the war between the Pandavas and the Kauravas, which forms its main subject, is one version of the Achaian or Hellenic myth which relates the wars of the Herakleids. The Mahâbhârata and the Ramayana are each ascribed to an individual poet; but the personality of the poet is as shadowy as that of Homer. The former is attributed to Krishna Dwaipayana Vyâsa, who is also the forefather of the most prominent actors in the story. He is the son of the nymph Satyavati, who calls on him after the death of his half-brother Chitrangâda to receive his two widows as his wives. These women become the mothers of Dhritarashtra and Pandu. Of these two Pandu is elected king on the death of Santanu, a descendant of Bharata; but owing either to a curse or to the disease of leprosy, he betakes himself to a hermit life in the forest, and Dhrita-rashtra, who is blind, takes his place. The sons of Pandu, or the Pandavas, are Yudhi-shthira, Bhima or Bhima-sena, Arjuna, who reappears in the Khrisna legend, Nakula, and Sahadeva. They are called children of Pandu, because they are said to have been acknowledged by him; but they are also called children of different gods: Bhima, for instance, being the son of Vayu, the god of the wind,[1] and Nakula and Sahadeva being a twin whom Madri bore to the Asvins,[2] the children of Surya, the sun. The children of Dhritarashtra, who is a descendant of Kuru, are known as the Kauravas. The eldest of these is Dur-yodhana, who is throughout represented in the character of Eurystheus, the enemy of Herakles. The Pandavas, being brought to the court of Dhrita-rashtra, are treated by him with great kindness, and brought up with the Kauravas; but the jealousy of the latter is roused when the latter names Yudhi-shthira his Vira-raja, or heir apparent. This act brings about the first expulsion of the Pandavas, answering to the first banishment of the Herakleids.

The Pandavas now live in the forest; but while they are there the king of the Panchalas proclaims that his

---

[1] See p. 182. [2] See p. 59.

daughter Draupadi would select as her husband the worthiest among the suitors who might present themselves. The condition imposed was the bending of a bow, which remains stiff in the hands of all except Arjuna, who thus answers to Sigurd, Arthur, Theseus, and other Western heroes. Hastening home to their mother, the Pandavas tell her that they have won a great prize, and she, not knowing what it was, bids them share it between them. On this follows the polyandrous marriage of Draupadi; an incident not explicable, it would seem, by any reference to Aryan manners or customs.[1] *The Pandavas and Draupadi.*

The victory of Arjuna led to the recall of the Pandavas by Dhrita-rashtra, who now placed them as rulers in Indraprastha, while he allotted Hastina-pura as the portion of his own sons. In the former Yudhi-shthira reigns with consummate wisdom and justice; but the announcement of his intention to perform the Rajasuya sacrifice, which would give him supremacy over other kings, again arouses the wrath of the Kauravas, who invite him to Hastina-pura, and there tempt him to gamble. Yudhi-shthira loses everything—his palace, his kingdom, his brothers, himself, and his wife. Through the influence of the blind old father of the Kauravas they are all restored to him, but in vain; Yudhi-shthira is again enticed into gambling, and his loss is as complete as it was before. But this time he had played under the condition that, if he lost, the Pandavas should spend twelve years as hermits in the forest. This compact may be compared with the covenant which binds the Herakleids not to attempt the recovery of their inheritance for fifty or for a hundred years. The sequel corresponds in substance with that of the Hellenic myth. The Pandavas at the end of this time resolve to recover what they had lost. To them and to their enemies *Yudhi-shthira and the Kauravas.*

---

[1] It is excused in the poem on the plea that the five Pandavas were all portions of one deity, and might therefore be regarded as one person. If the incident is to be taken as in any sense historical, it points to the polyandrous marriages still common among certain non-Aryan tribes of India.

Krishna offered the choice of himself armed as an ally, or the aid of a large army. The Kaurava chief Dur-yodhana eagerly took the army; Arjuna attached himself to the god, who agrees to be his charioteer.[1] The result was that at length three Kauravas alone remained alive with Dur-yodhana, who was mortally wounded; but these three made a raid into the land of the Pandavas, and left none remaining except the five brothers, who go to Hastina-pura, where Yudhi-shthira is crowned king. The sequel is, from a merely human point of view, both pathetic and touching, but it has nothing to do with the original myth, which ended with the triumph of the Pandavas in Hastina-pura.[2]

The Mahâbhârata has been swollen to its enormous size by the intrusion of a number of episodes which are themselves as bulky as the Iliad or Odyssey. In addition to the Bhagavadgita the Harivansa, besides its other themes, relates the life and adventures of Krishna, as an incarnation of Hari, the dwarf, that is of Vishnu,[3] while the story of Nala and Damayanti substantially repeats that of Yudhi-shthira and Draupadi. In each case the king loses his wife and all his treasures by gambling, and is obliged to leave his kingdom for a hermit's life in the forest; but like Yudhi-shthira, he recovers all that he has lost, and he not

Nala and Damayanti.

---

[1] As thus serving Arjuna, Krishna sings the Bhagavadgita before the rival armies, who are about to fight the battle of Kuru-kshetra. The poem, which is certainly later than most parts of the Mahâbhârata, is really an exposition of Brahmanic theology, assigning to Krishna the functions of the highest Vedic deities.

[2] This sequel relates the journey of the Pandavas with Draupadi to the Himalayas, for the purpose of reaching the heaven of Indra on Mount Meru. It is remarkable chiefly for the firmness with which Yudhi-shthira refuses to enter the gates of heaven, unless his brothers and Draupadi, and his dog, are admitted also. Entering it on this condition, he finds that they are not there, and not only refuses to remain without them, but resolves to share their sufferings in hell rather than be separated from them. The trial turns out to be the result of Mâyâ, or illusion, and all live thereafter happily with Indra.

[3] See p. 140.

only forgives his adversary, but sends him home loaded with gifts.[1]

The Ramayana, as its name implies, relates the adventures of Rama, and is ascribed to the sage Valmîkî. Its age is a matter of uncertainty; but if in its present form it is somewhat older than the Mahâ-bhârata in its latest shape, the original framework of the latter poem is, as we have seen, probably much older. The action of the Mahâbhârata belongs to Northern India; that of the Ramayana extends from Ayodhya (Oude) to Lanka (Ceylon), and this would point, therefore, to a decidedly later period of the history of the Aryan conquerors of India. Rama himself is the seventh incarnation of Vishnu; and the story of his career is given at less length in the Vana Parva episode of the Mahâbhârata.[2] His earthly father is Dasa-ratha, and his mother Kausalya, and in Lakshmana, the son of Sumitra, another wife of Dasa-ratha, he has a secondary as devoted to himself as Patroklos is to Achilles. He obtains the beautiful Sita, the daughter of Janaka, king of Videha, by breaking the bow of Siva, which no one else could even bend.[3] As heir to the throne of Ayodhya, he first wins the love, and then awakens the jealousy of Kaikeyi, the second wife of Dasa-ratha. Rama is expelled, and her son Bharata, being chosen king on the death of his father, refuses to usurp the place which belongs to Rama; but as the latter will not return until his allotted time of exile is past, Bharata consents to act as regent during his absence. Rama is now induced to go southwards into the country of the Rakshasas, one of whom inspires Ravana, the Rakshasa king of Lanka, with a passion for Sita, whom he carries off by force to his island home. With the aid of

XIX.
The Rama-yana.

[1] Dowson, *Classical Dictionary of Hindu Mythology*, articles 'Bhagavad-gita,' 'Harivansa,' 'Mahâbhârata,' 'Nala.' For the alleged historical substratum of the 'Mahâbhârata,' see *Myth. of Ar. Nat.* i. 180, note 2.
[2] Dowson, *Classical Dictionary of Hindu Mythology*, article 'Rama.'
[3] For the reference here made to Parasu-rama, see Dowson, *Classical Dictionary of Hindu Mythology*, p. 257.

the monkey-king Su-griva, and of his general Hanuman, son of the wind, whose powers of leaping and flying made his alliance invaluable, Rama succeeds in killing Ravana and rescuing Sita. But although he is assured of Sita's purity, he refuses to receive her, until she has submitted herself to the ordeal of fire, out of which she is safely brought by Agni. With the happy time which follows the return of Rama with Sita to Ayodhya the sixth section of the poem comes to an end. The remainder is a later addition, which tells us that Rama's suspicions impelled him to send his wife to the hermitage of Valmiki, where her twin sons were born. Going to Ayodhya when they were yet youths, these children of Rama were recognised by their father, who summons Sita to prove her innocence. Sita asserts it earnestly, and bids the earth show the truth of her words. A chasm opens in the ground, and Rama is deprived of his wife, without whom, he says, that he cannot live. He walks, therefore, into the river Sarayu, and enters 'into the glory of Vishnu.'[1] The connexion of the rising and setting sun with water has been brought before us in a vast number of myths; and in the stealing away of Sita by Ravana we have the counterpart of the seduction of Helen by Paris, the only difference being that Sita is faithful, while Helen is guilty of the offence the germs of which are seen in the dalliance of Saramâ with the Panis.[2]

These epics and romances of the Eastern and Western world differ, it is unnecessary to say, very widely both in their value and their interest; but whatever may be their merits or defects as works of art, the results of the analysis to which they have been submitted leave no room for reasonable doubt as to the origin and nature of the materials out of which they have been shaped. The processes by which they have been brought into their present form may seem to be somewhat

Results of the analysis of Aryan mythical tradition.

---

[1] Dowson, *Classical Dictionary of Hindu Mythology*, p. 260.
[2] See p. 59.

monotonous; yet it may be very safely asserted that the keenness with which we may spy out repetitions, or trace the substantial identity of any given story with other tales with which at first sight it might seem to have little in common, will detract nothing from the charm of the tales themselves. Rather, it may be said, that our knowledge of the source whence the stream flows will add indefinitely to the interest with which we trace its wanderings, until by the confluence of its tributary waters it swells into the great ocean of national epic poetry, while incidents which, regarded as events in the lives of human beings, must appear absurd, or impossible, or disgusting, will not unfrequently be invested with a touching truth and beauty.

APPENDIX.

I.

MYTHOLOGY AND PRIMITIVE REVELATION.

THE theory that the mythical system of the Greeks, and more especially the theology of the Iliad and Odyssey, is the corrupted form of a Divine revelation imparted to man in his infancy, has been maintained with great earnestness and force by Mr. Gladstone in his 'Homeric Studies,' and more recently in 'Juventus Mundi.' This revelation Mr. Gladstone formulates in a series of propositions which are, he asserts, contained inferentially in the early chapters of Genesis. (*See* 'Mythology of the Aryan Nations,' i. 11.) The scope and method of the inquiry are enforced in the following question:

'If we produce out of the Olympian system, from its Apollo, its Athênê, its Leto, its Iris, and its various other persons and particulars, ideas identical in substance with those that are embodied in the first chapter of Genesis, how can we avoid the conclusion, in parity of reasoning, that those ideas, marked and peculiar as they are, which are found existing alike in the poems of the Aryan Greeks and in the sacred books of the Semitic Hebrews, were common to those Aryans and those Semites before the epoch of their separation?'

Mr. Gladstone asks that this proposition may be examined, and equitably judged, without any premature view to consequences; and he justly insists that 'we have no right to import the consideration of results, which we may dislike, into the examination of questions of evidence.' The question is, indeed, strictly one of fact. But there are certain preliminary considerations which, although they must not be allowed to bias us unduly, may yet fairly be taken into account. The supposition that the Greek or any other myths embody a number of theological truths imparted by

Divine revelation, and that these beliefs were implanted in men centuries or millenniums before they could be realised in fact, seems to involve us at the outset in a maze of painful difficulties; and the question is surely justified, which would ask a reason why a series of propositions should be laid before men which they could not fail to misunderstand, from which, as so misunderstood, they could derive no possible benefit, and which, as Mr. Gladstone himself admits, are contained in the earliest records only by a dim and feeble foreshadowing. We seem, therefore, scarcely free to resort to the theory of a primitive revelation, unless other methods of explanation fail us altogether; and on the other hand we seem to be well within the bounds of truth in asserting that all the important characteristics of the Olympian gods in the Iliad and Odyssey are explained with the clearness of demonstration by the method of comparative mythology. It is, of course, necessary for the maintenance of Mr. Gladstone's theory that the theology of the Iliad and Odyssey should be entirely dissevered from what is called nature-worship. In other words, it is impossible for him to admit that the conceptions of deities named in those poems were at the outset obtained from impressions left on the mind by the phenomena of the outward world. If these deities are simply embodiments of ideas suggested by sensible objects, the question is answered before we enter into it: but the case is altered if there be a never-baffled Athênê, and an Apollo 'who is alone and always in absolute harmony with the will of the eternal Zeus.' Hence he draws 'broad and deep' a distinction between Homeric and post-Homeric mythology, by which terms he means the mythology of the Iliad and Odyssey and that of all other Greek poems, epic, lyric, or dramatic.

If this distinction should turn out to be an arbitrary assumption, the controversy is at an end; and the question will be soonest settled by a reference to what the Iliad and Odyssey really tell us of the deities of which they make mention. At the outset we are confronted with the fact that these poems speak of Zeus, Apollo, Hermes, Dêmêtêr, Aphroditê, without making any reference to incidents in their mythical history which do not fall within the scope of the poet's purpose. This purpose was to stir the minds of men by the relation of certain events in a momentous and memorable struggle; and in doing this the poets refer incidentally to a vast number of narratives which they do not care even to summarise. We have, therefore, no excuse for supposing them to be ignorant of traditions relating to the Olympian gods, merely because they happen to take no notice of them.

The gods of the Olympian hierarchy are, Mr. Gladstone contends, strictly anthropomorphic, or, as he prefers to call them, theanthropic. In other words, the Apollo and the Athênê of the Iliad and Odyssey are beings with human bodies, who speak and act in some sort like human beings, and exhibit the working of human feelings and passions, and thus no room is left for deities like the Vedic Agni, the child of two sticks rubbed together, who comes into the world puny and deformed, but soon acquires a terrible power by devouring all that lies in his path, and dies when his food fails him. But if the essence of the anthropomorphic idea lies in the power of appealing to or exciting human sympathy, then this anthropomorphic or humanitarian character belongs to many other deities or beings whose claim to it Mr. Gladstone rejects.

Among these is Dêmêtêr, who, we are told, 'is but a sleeping partner in the thearchy, and has no practical share whatever in the conduct of affairs.' But this remark applies to her, obviously, only as she is spoken of in the Iliad or the Odyssey; and it is not easy to see why without the most cogent evidence we should allow that the Achaian conception of Dêmêtêr is to be gathered from those poems only. If in these we read little about it, we have an exquisite picture of the mourning mother and her beautiful child in the so-called Homeric Hymn—a picture in which the relation of marvels and wonders nowhere interferes with the current of genuine human feeling, and of human feeling for the most part in its tenderest and most attractive forms. From the moment when the bright maiden is dragged away by the chariot of Hades from the plains of Enna to the hour when the bitter grief of the mother is changed into radiant joy by the sight of her child at the trysting-place Eleusis, the whole hymn appeals to our common human feeling with a force altogether beyond that of the ordinary records of Olympian doings in the Iliad or the Odyssey.

The story exhibits, it is true, a chain of cause and effect which lies beyond the range of ordinary human experience. The sun and moon are actors or speakers in the great drama; the grieving mother is a being who can appear before Zeus in Olympos as a peer of his celestial hierarchy; and of her sorrow all living things are partakers. But while even for Achaians the tale must have been transparent, although even for them the goddess must have been the image of the earth refusing to yield its fruits while her summer child is in the deadly abode of winter, there was nothing in it to check the warm current of purely human feeling in them, there is nothing to chill it in us. The form bowed down in sorrow by the side of the fountain, the gentle tenderness of the daughters of Keleos, the matronly dignity of Metaneira, are not rendered less human, and excite our sympathy none the less, because we see the child Demophoön plunged daily into his bath of fire,

A A

or because the eating of the pomegranate by the maiden must be followed by her return to the land of shadows.

Hermes, again, in the Odyssey is a purely anthropomorphic god, whose acts and words are marked for the most part by great gravity and decorum ; but Hermes is also the hero of the hymn which bears his name, and we may fairly ask on what grounds we are justified in asserting that the poet of the Odyssey knew nothing of the story embodied in that hymn. There, too, the interest is human throughout ; but it is difficult, if not impossible, to believe that the hymn-writer had not some consciousness of the materials with which he was dealing. His birth in the morning, his soft harping at midday, the huge strides with which in the evening he hurries after the cattle of Phœbus, the grinding of the forest branches until they burst into flame, the sacrifice which Hermes prepares, but of which he cannot taste, though sorely pressed by hunger, the wearied steps with which he returns to his cradle, passing through the opening of the bolt 'like the sigh of a summer breeze or mist on a hill-side,' must, with all the other incidents of the tradition, have taught the poet that the mysterious being who was to bear for ever the title of the master-thief was the wind which drives the clouds of Phœbus across the heaven, which takes counsel with the Thriai in the coverts of the mountain glens, and receives from the sun-god the solemn charge which makes him the guide of human souls to Hades.

Of this wonderful story, which has delighted the East and the West for hundreds or thousands of years, we hear nothing in the Odyssey, for the simple reason that the poet had no motive for introducing it. Like the Iliad, the Odyssey is a poem dealing with only a few of the incidents connected with or arising out of the war of Troy. Scant references or passing allusions attest his knowledge of a vast number of other incidents or traditions which did not fall within the scope of his plan : nor have we, seemingly, anything in the poem to show that he wished to assign a different origin to the messenger of Zeus. Whether before he put on his human form Hermes was worshipped by the forefathers of the Achaians simply as the wind, is a question which perhaps it is not very necessary to answer. Thinkers whose authority should carry great weight have doubted whether any worship was ever offered to any elemental god unless some idea of the bodily form of that deity was present to the mind of the worshipper. In most cases the two thoughts would probably be blended in a way which would almost defy analysis ; and such a blending we may notice especially in the idea of Ushas, as we have it in the hymns of the Rig Veda. Nothing is more certain than that for the writers of these hymns Ushas was veritably the Dawn which each morning spread her rosy flush across the heaven, which re-

APPENDIX I.

vealed the bright cows feeding in the pastures of the sky, and which in the long series of her visits brings to all living things old age, decay, and death. But the warm and genuine feeling of human affection with which she was regarded is not less beyond all doubt.

Ushas, in short, is in these hymns the beautiful being, who is the forerunner, the mother, the sister, or the wife of the brilliant sun-god whom, nevertheless, she must not look upon in his unclothed splendour, and who can tarry with his bride only during the time of twilight. It is the simple framework of the touching story of Eros and Psyche, and the framework also of the tale, perhaps even more touching, of Urvasi and Pururavas in the beautiful drama of Kalidasa. If it be said that the story of their loves is to the later poet a story simply of human joy and sorrow, of the origin of which he had not the faintest suspicion, the position is one which we need not greatly care to disturb, although much of the language of Kalidasa, like that of the poets of the Iliad and the Odyssey, would seem to warrant a different conclusion. It seems well-nigh impossible to suppose that the author of the hymn to Hermes was wholly unaware of the nature of the god whose story he was telling. Leave out all names, and put the tale before a child in the form of a riddle, asking him who it is that sings sweetly when he is born, that stalks with giant strides when only a few hours old over mountain and moor, dashing the trees of the forest together till their branches burst into flame, roasting meat which he cannot eat though he longs to do so, and when tired of doing mischief steals back wearily to his cave and lies down to sleep like an infant in his cradle. The child will readily answer, 'It is the wind;' and with this key he will be able to unlock the legend of Orpheus, who could by his voice charm the Argo into the water when the efforts of the heroes were powerless to move it, and whose harping stirred trees and rocks into motion. He will see the same legend in another form in the soft whisperings of Pan, whose gentle pipings wake the slumbering echoes at the same moment on the mountain-top and in the hidden glen; and in the song of Hermes, which sounded sweeter in the ears of Phœbus than any strain ever heard in the halls of Olympus, he will recognise the magic melody of the piper of Hameln, which drew the happy troop of children to the paradise which they saw far down in the depths of the blue river.

Of all these beings, Hermes, Phœbus, Orpheus, and the rest, some might be the objects of a greater, some of a lesser worship, and they might be so to a people who had acquired a marked dislike for deities of a nakedly elemental character, such as, in some at least of the descriptions given of him, is the Vedic Agni. It would become, therefore, the object of such a people to invest them, so far as might be possible, with an exclusively human personality; but this would not make the origin of the idea from which these beings had taken shape to be anything but what it was. Their anthropomorphic or humanitarian character had arisen from conceptions suggested by the sights or sounds of the outward world; and the evidence of the change, although it might be placed in the background, could not be obliterated. It has not been obliterated in any one instance. The Zeus who is described to us as ruling in Olympus and as exhibiting in himself some of the worst vices of humanity, and the absolutely righteous Zeus whom the worshipper approached in times of trouble and sorrow, were two distinct beings. But of the origin of the ideas which have given shape to the Olympian Zeus and other gods we are left in no doubt. Mr. Gladstone argues that, if the original meaning of the name Zeus be the material heaven, 'we are no more justified in determining herefrom that the Achaian Greeks worshipped that material heaven, than we should be justified in holding that because a divine object is worshipped under the name *spiritus* in Latin and *pneuma* in Greek, therefore the material thing we call breath was ever the object of adoration.' There is no need of making such an assertion with reference to the worship of the Achaian Greeks; but it is certainly a fact that Pan and Favonius, to say nothing of Hermes and Orpheus, are, if such phrases must be used, humanised embodiments of the air which breathes through the sky.

Whether the embodiment thus obtained becomes an object of adoration is quite a secondary question. The result might or might not be such: the main point to be determined is the originating idea, and this idea in the case of some of the deities of the Iliad is seen with unmistakable clearness. Pieces of meat, we are told by the poet, may be roasted over Hephaistos, who in such passages is the elemental fire as strictly as is Agni in any of the hymns of the Rig Veda. In like manner when we say that the relation of the Olympian Zeus to the material heaven is that of a ruler, we only say of him what may be said with not less truth of the Vedic Dyaus. His character is still so closely in harmony with the old conception, that he must remain in the region of which he is the king. The other gods can visit the earth and take part in the quarrels of mortal men; he alone descends not from the clear heaven, whence he looks down on all that is being done beneath him; and when the last hour of Sarpêdôn is come, his grief takes the form of rain which falls in blood-red drops upon the earth. In the multiplying of his loves we have simply the fertilising power of the heaven, and in legends like that of Danaê the mode by which his will is accomplished points to the action of light upon the outward world. As in the Vedic hymn

Aditi is praised as at once 'father, mother, and son,' so is Zeus both the brother and the husband, and his own daughters through many generations become the mothers of his children. This is the language, not of a poet who is determined to keep out of sight, or to get rid of, the elemental origin or characteristics of his gods, but of one whose expressions are influenced, perhaps without his knowing it, by the thoughts and ideas of earlier ages which had not learnt to draw a distinction between the visible heaven and the deity who dwelt within it.

Still less equivocal is the parentage of Phœbus Apollo, the glorious god, whose locks are never shorn, who is born in Delos, the land of light, and rules in Lykia, another land of light, through which flows the golden stream Xanthos. Unscathed himself, he is the destroyer of the dragon, the rotting of whose body in the sun is said to have suggested the name of his Pythian sanctuary ; but as the dragon-slayer, he is simply one of a large band of gods and heroes. He does no more than is done by Kadmos (Cadmus) or Herakles, Theseus or Œdipus ; nor is the battle described with the wealth of incident which is lavished on the great conflict between Indra and the throttling snake Ahi. These dragons, again, have nothing in common with the subtle serpent in Genesis. They offer no temptations to sin, they hold out no delusive promises, they cannot harm their conquerors. They are, in short, simply demons of drought, who shut up the waters needed to refresh the thirsting earth, and their death is followed at once by the outpouring of the life-giving flood. The Hydra slain by Herakles is a monster of a different kind ; and its connexion with water is manifested by its name. Here we have a myth in which the sun is described as causing drought by drying up the rivulets; but until the main source which feeds the multitude of springs in marshy or swampy land is dried up, the attempt to cut off these lesser streams is vain. Hence Herakles assails the Hydra's neck, and when the head is severed, his task is done.

But for the general character of Apollo, the appeal must lie to the hymns which embody the traditions of the Delian and Delphian god ; and, as in the case of Hermes, we must have very cogent evidence before we can allow that this appeal is inadmissible. Unquestionably, its meaning would even to a child be not less obvious than that of the hymn to Hermes. If Leto, the mother of Phœbus, is, in Mr. Gladstone's words, 'wholly functionless, wholly inactive,' and 'without a purpose,' except in so far as she is his mother, so also is the night which is the parent of the day or of the god who banishes the darkness. It was, in fact, impossible that the original idea could be developed into a much more definite personality.

It may, therefore, be fairly questioned whether an Olympian system, to be found in the Iliad and Odyssey exclusively, has any existence. Regarding these poems apart from any preconceived theories as to the time or the mode in which they grew up, we have in them the narrative of certain incidents in a well-known struggle in which certain superhuman beings take part. These beings are, in their general character, anthropomorphic, or theanthropic, or humanitarian, for all these words may be needed to express the desired meaning; but in every one of them there are features which point unmistakably to the ideas of earlier times, when men were content to express the feelings awakened in them by the objects or phenomena of the outward world. This is a change which was not confined to the mythology of the Achaian people. We find it carried out to a large extent in that of the Rig Veda; nor is it easy to discern any radical difference between the Olympian gods as portrayed in the Iliad and Odyssey, and the same gods as they appear in the works of the great lyric and dramatic poets of ancient Hellas, unless, indeed, it be in certain features which would seem to indicate that priority in point of time belongs to the latter rather than to the former.

In his 'Homeric Studies' Mr. Gladstone laid great stress on the degradation of certain actors in the Iliad and Odyssey as they appear in Greek lyric poems and dramas. Thus the wisdom and prudence of Odysseus become mere selfish cunning and trickiness, and the Helen who is more sinned against than sinning, and in the Odyssey is restored to her home pardoned and even glorified, appears in the drama of Æschylus as the bane of all amongst whom she is thrown. There is no doubt that the pictures of these actors are in the Iliad and Odyssey more graceful, refined, and attractive; but in the order of thought these more delicate conceptions are always rather of later than of earlier growth, and the arguments based on their greater antiquity may be reversed.

It would appear, then, that we have no grounds for drawing that distinction between what is called Homeric and post-Homeric mythology on which Mr. Gladstone lays special stress. Into the Homeric controversy it is unnecessary to enter, because the characteristics of the Olympian or Homeric hierarchy are, as we have seen, far more easily and more completely explained by referring them to the forms of thought and speech prevalent in the mythopœic ages than to any other causes. It can, however, by no means be taken for granted that our Iliad and Odyssey constitute the Homer of Solon and Peisistratos, of the lyric and tragic poets, of Herodotus and Thucydides. The evidence at our command seems all to point in another direction; and this evidence is derived from the whole character of the Greek lyric and tragic poetry, and of the illustrations of Greek myths to be seen on the vase paintings. In a still higher degree, perhaps, it is furnished by the poems themselves, which from beginning to end assume in their hearers a familiar knowledge with a multitude of incidents and mythical traditions, to which they make merely a passing reference or allusion.

It must not, however, be forgotten that the theories, which question the great age of the text of these poems, in no way question the antiquity of the materials used in their composition. They do but assert that the Homer of Plato was not identical with the Homer of Herodotus and Thucydides, and therefore could not have been the Homer of the lyric and tragic poets ; and the inferences involved in them are simply those which may be reached by comparing the treatment of subjects in our Homer, which seems to be the Homer of Plato, with the treatment of the same subjects in the dramas of Æschylus and Sophokles. At the same time, these are questions which must be settled before we can even enter on the examination of arguments which assume the vastly higher antiquity of our Iliad and Odyssey, and assign to them a place wholly different from that of all other products of Greek literature. The great changes which Homeric language underwent down to the age of the Alexandrine grammarians are clearly exhibited by Mr. Sayce, who, in his 'Introduction to the Science of Language,' ii. 104, following Mr. Paley's method and accepting his conclusions, asserts that 'the Atticisms which occur on every page, and caused Aristarchus to consider Homer as an Athenian, as well as words and phrases which seem to belong to the Periklean era, are witnesses to more than one Attic recension after the poems had been transferred to the mainland of Europe.'

But if from the text we turn to the contents or matter of the poems, it is certainly not easy to discern a form of religious thought radically different, or even differing largely, from that which we meet with elsewhere ; nor if we confine ourselves to internal evidence, can we shake off the suspicion, if not the conviction, that the mythology of the Achaian or Greek people had very little to do with their religion. The course of the people generally is from the lower to the higher, while the myths, which, when translated into the conditions of human existence, were at the outset startling and shocking, become mere sources of corruption and impurity. The Iliad and Odyssey exhibited to the people a sensual and lying Zeus ; the people themselves prayed to Zeus ; but it is a mere arbitrary and groundless assumption that the Zeus to whom the people prayed was the Zeus of the epic poems. The poems themselves answer the question in the negative. 'What,' asks Professor Max Müller, 'did the swineherd Eumaios know of the intricate Olympian theogony? Had he ever heard the name of the Charites or the Harpyias? Could he have told who was the father of Aphroditê, who were her husbands and her children? I doubt it; and when Homer introduces him to us, speaking of this life and of the higher powers that rule it, Eumaios knows only of just gods, who hate cruel deeds, but honour justice and the righteous works of men.'

In short, as the mythology grew more complicated, and in some parts more degrading, the ideas of morality and religion became more reasonable and more pure. If we turn to the Hesiodic 'Works and Days,' we find the poet bidding his friend to deal with all men according to the rule of righteousness which comes from Zeus, and telling him that justice and truth shall in the end prevail, that they who do evil to others inflict evil on themselves, that the eyes of God are in every place, that the way of evil is broad and smooth, and the path of good rough and narrow at first. But in the same poem we are told how Zeus bade the gods make Pandora fair to look upon, but evil within, and laughed at the thought of the miseries which should overtake mankind when all the evils snould be let loose from her box, while, to crush them utterly, hope should remain a prisoner within it. If in relating such tales the poet was not conscious that the Zeus who thus cheats and torments mankind is not the Zeus who commands them to do justice and mercy, how is it possible to explain the fact that he can use the same name without a thought seemingly that he is dishonouring the just and holy god whom he reverences?

In these poems, then, we have a religion, and we have a mythology; but between the two there is an absolute severance. What grounds have we, therefore, for asserting that the case stands otherwise with the mythology and theology of the Iliad and the Odyssey? Writing before Mr. Gladstone's 'Homeric Studies' were given to the world, Professor Max Müller had expressed his deliberate opinion that among the lowest tribes of Africa and America we hardly find anything more hideous and revolting than the stories told of Kronos and his offspring; and he had added that 'it seems blasphemy to consider these fables of the heathen world as corrupted and misinterpreted fragments of a divine revelation once granted to the whole race of mankind.' By Mr. Gladstone's admission the expressions or figures by which these beliefs were imparted were at best only adumbrations of things to come, while, to prove his hypothesis, there is need of a never baffled Athênê, and of an Apollo 'who is alone and always in absolute harmony with the will of the eternal Zeus;' nor can this conclusion in its turn be established except by severing that myth in the Iliad or Odyssey from the same myth as exhibited in Greek lyric or tragic poetry. That this severance cannot be justified or warranted by the facts of the case, has been shown conclusively. Even in the Iliad Athênê is signally baffled in the conspiracy to dethrone Zeus, in which she is an accomplice with Hêrê and Poseidon ; and if in the case of Apollo it was necessary to believe that there was an absolute harmony between himself and Zeus, of what practical avail would this belief be if it was confined to the author or authors of a single poem? This belief was certainly not shared by Euripides, who speaks of Zeus as smiting with his thunderbolt the son of Phœbus because he raised the dead. Elsewhere we are told that Phœbus, in his fierce wrath at the death of his son, smote the Kyklôpes (Cyclopes); that for this offence he was compelled to serve the Trojan Laomedon, who cheated him of his wages, and that then he found a more genial master, but a master still, in the Thessalian Admetos. That the dragon slain by him at Pytho had in the Achaian mind no connexion with the idea of human disobedience, and that it was simply one of the demons of drought slain by gods or heroes in all lands, we have already seen. So completely is the image of the Hellenic Phœbus opposed to the form which, confining his view to the Iliad and the Odyssey, Mr. Gladstone ascribes to it. But if the Olympian system falls to the ground, or if, rather, it would appear never to have had a substantial existence, the issue is one which surely brings into clearer light the action of the Divine Spirit on the soul of man. If Greek mythology was not the same thing as Greek religion, we can understand how the latter, as set forth in the Hesiodic poems and in the teaching of the great dramatists, rose steadily to a higher standard, while the former became more cumbrous, arbitrary, and repulsive in its complications. We can see in the one the working of the Spirit from whom all holy desires, all good counsels, and all just works proceed ; in the other a necessary growth from forms of thought and language which had reference to the incessantly changing phenomena of the sensible world.

I may refer the reader who wishes to examine the subject more in detail, to the 'Mythology of the Aryan Nations.'

II.

THE HISTORICAL VALUE OF THE NIBELUNGENLIED.

COMPARATIVE mythologists have made no attempt to conceal the conclusion that the Volsunga Saga is mythical, or, in other words, that its chief, if not indeed all its incidents, can be traced to phrases which spoke originally of the phenomena of the outward world, and of these only ; that these incidents are found in the myths of all Aryan lands ; and that as the Volsung tale is itself a development of the Helgi Sagas, so the Nibelung story has grown up in the same way from that of the Volsungs, the later growth being in its incidents not a whit more historical than the earliest. These inferences or conclusions are, it is now asserted, altogether upset, and the results of comparative mythology generally impugned, by the fact that some half-dozen names in the Nibelungenlied sound like the names of persons who lived in the fifth or sixth centuries of the Christian era. 'The story of Sigurd, the hero of the Edda,' we are told, 'with all the accessory characters, and all the adventures—a favourite example of the solar myth with the new school—is so closely imitated to all appearance in the Nibelungenlied, the great German epic composed centuries after it, that here if anywhere comparative mythology appears to have won a great victory. The names are the same, and the adventures very like. It would then follow necessarily that the later poem at all events (if not both) was mythical and not historical. But, strange to say, there is an historical basis for this later poem—an historical basis so certain, that not even the mythologers can gainsay it. Closely as the names appear to correspond to those of the Edda, they correspond just as closely to historical personages who lived after the Edda was known and referred to in literature. Sigurd represents Siegbert, king of Austrasia, 561-75 A.D. Gunther represents Gundicarius, king of Burgundy, in 435 A.D. So Brynhild, Irenfried, Dietrich, and Atli, are the reflexions of Brunehault, Hermannfried (Irminfried?), Theodoric, and Attila. Here then, where comparative mythology might possibly have explained everything ; here, where, in default of other evidence, we should all have been quite content to accept its explanation, it is shown to be a false and delusive guide.' Mahaffy, ' Prolegomena to Ancient History,' p. 89.

What is the meaning of these propositions? The assertion that the Nibelung song has a sure historical basis would seem to justify the supposition that the song contained a certain amount of history—in other words, that it recorded a number of facts which were done by the men or women to whom they were attributed, and that these persons were known to be and can be proved to be historical. But these sentences are, beyond doubt, not intended to convey this meaning. It is admitted that the actors in the Nibelung tale were, speaking generally, the same as those of the men and women who play their part in the Volsung story, and that the adventures attributed to the former are very like those of the heroes of the latter. The historical basis (astonishing as it seems) is limited to the names. These correspond closely, we are told, to the names of some persons who lived about the fifth or sixth century, and as this resemblance of names cannot be denied, therefore the poem is historical. This is really equivalent to asserting that the Arthur romance would become an historical poem of the nineteenth century, if a version of it were published which for the name of Arthur the British king should substitute that of Arthur Duke of Wellington. It would not be pretended that the actions of the duke were those of the Celtic chief; but if with his name a few other names should be given of contemporaries of the Duke of Wellington which correspond to those of the Arthur romance, the story would have an historical basis so certain that not even the mythologers could gainsay it. The argument is even more ridiculous, and, in the strict sense of the word, impertinent. Sigurd, or rather Siegfried, is said to represent the Austrasian king Siegbert; but he is the lover of Brynhild, who is the sister of Gunther or Gundicar, king of the Burgundians. They belong therefore to the same generation; but the Siegbert and Gundicar with which Mr. Mahaffy identifies them were separated by an interval of nearly a century and a half. If this throwing of dust into our eyes is to be suffered, probably no poem has ever been written which might not lay claim to a strictly historical character. The truth is that, in spite of the fancied resemblance of a few names which is not nearly so close as he represents it to be, Mr. Mahaffy puts no more trust in the narrative of the poem, as a history, than if these names were not found in it at all. He does not believe, nor does he pretend to believe, that the historical Gundicar or Siegbert or Attila did any of the things which in the poem they are said to have done. He merely wishes, on the strength of a certain resemblance of a very few amongst a multitude of names occurring in the same poem, to discredit the method and the conclusions of a science which has laid its foundations on the laws of language and on the analysis of a vast mass of myths which are the common inheritance of all the Aryan nations. The argument is scarcely ingenuous, nor can it be regarded as prompted by a disinterested love of truth.

We might therefore be justified in saying that further reply is uncalled for. But it may be well to show that Mr. Mahaffy's assertions have not even the poor significance which he claims for them. The question, beyond doubt, turns less on the names of the actors than on their careers; and of this fact it cannot be questioned that Mr. Mahaffy is well aware. If the series of deeds attributed to Sigurd and Etzel, Jörmunrek, and Gunnar, were done by Siegbert and Attila, Hermanric, and Gundicar, the tradition would certainly become historical; but, of course, Mr. Mahaffy does not pretend that this is the case. The resemblance and indeed the close correspondence of the Nibelung names to those which occur in the Saga of the Volsungs, is not denied; but it has been remarked that Jornandes, who wrote long before the murder of the Austrasian Siegbert, already knew the daughter of the mythic Sigurd, Swanhild, who was born, according to the Edda, after the murder of her father, and who was afterwards killed by Jörmunrek, 'whom the poem has again historicised in Hermanicus, a Gothic king of the fourth century.' (Max Müller, 'Chips from a German Workshop,' ii. 112.) If we had no other warrant for the inference, this resemblance of names would justify the surmise that popular tradition is tempted to assimilate the names of ancient heroes to those of persons living at the time when the tradition takes shape ; and this surmise would not be weakened by the fact that the character of Etzel in the Nibelungenlied is utterly unlike that of the historical Attila. But this temptation was not confined to names. The epic poems of a nation may be regarded as giving a tolerably faithful picture of the society of the age in which they are composed; but the age of the Nibelungenlied was in manner and form of thought separated from the age of the Volsung story by no gulf which would render the task of adapting the poem to a later time a matter of any special difficulty. If any names in the Nibelungenlied reflect the names of historical persons of the fifth or later centuries of the Christian era (and even this is in a high degree doubtful), the utmost that can be said is that the names of some kings and queens and warriors of those times lent themselves easily to the purpose of the more modern poet ; but this facility (even if we admit the fact) was purely accidental, and thus the resemblances of name impart no historical character to the poem, if by this term we mean a claim to credibility for the incidents related in the narratives. (Max Müller, 'Chips,' ii. 113.) That the colouring thrown over the poem should be made, so far as it was possible, to suit the political and social conditions of the age when it was composed, is in no way surprising : but so far as the incidents are concerned, it is no more than a colouring, and writers who would willingly trace the historical elements of the tale have found themselves compelled to admit that the real events noticed in the poem are very few in number.

The historical Attila had a brother whose name is given as Bleda. The Etzel of the Nibelung lay is the son of Bludi, or Budli, not his brother; and Bunsen has acknowledged the difficulty of making an expedition of Attila himself to the Rhine fit in with what we know of the history of those years. ('God in History,' ii. 478. See also 'Mythology of the Aryan Nations,' i. 289, note.) All that can be said is that the poet or poets of the Nibelung lay have adapted the names of the older legend to names of living or recently living persons, whenever it was possible to do so ; that they have introduced some fresh names which were likewise borne by historical persons, and that they have further imparted to the story some appearance of agreement with great events of their own or of a recent age. Nor can the fidelity with which the poet adheres to the manners of his time be ascribed necessarily to the narrative of the acts of the several personages of the drama. The subordinate or unimportant details are probably described with exactness and care. There would be no temptation to depart from existing customs with regard to dress, weapons, food, the precedence of ranks in the state, religious worship, or the usages of war. But the care of the poets to represent these things aright imparts no credibility to narratives of events which are in themselves impossible ('Mythology of Aryan Nations,' i. 289); and when we find that these impossible events form the groundwork of a thousand other stories, whether Greek, or Teutonic, or Scandinavian, we are at once justified in asserting that in the common element thus found we discover the real character of these tales; that in the Helgi and Volsung stories this common element is, in Bunsen's words, 'purely mythological, namely, the combat of the sun-god, who is slain by his brother and avenged by a younger brother' ('God in History,' ii. 474); and that this element must also pervade the Nibelung lay, in which, substantially, neither the names nor the incidents are changed. Thus the final conclusion is that, although a certain (and this a very small) amount of historical material may have been introduced into a story with which, until it was so introduced, it had nothing to do, the Nibelung romance has no historical character. It is simply and absolutely impossible that Siegfried should 'represent' the Austrasian Siegbert, or Gunther the Burgundian Gundicar, unless the poets who first introduced these names into the traditions intended that they should represent those chieftains or kings—in other words, unless the poets of the Edda knew that centuries after their day these kings would rule over Austrasia and Burgundy, and would do moreover precisely those acts which they described as the deeds of the Sigurds and Gunnars of long past ages. The utter absurdity of such a supposition surely needs not to be pointed out.

III.

THE TRISTRAM STORY.

IN the 'Popular Romances of the Middle Ages' the reader will find two versions of the Tristram story, the one occurring in the body of the Arthur legend, the other given separately. The points of difference between the two are not uninstructive. In both Tristram is the child of sorrow. In the one he is born while his father still lives, in the other the death of the father precedes the birth of the child. But in both the wife is left alone and forsaken. The story of the Norwegian merchant ship, the captain of which orders sail to be set in order to beguile Tristram, who is on board playing at chess with him, points to an incident in the German tale of Faithful John, and to the version of the myth of Io, generally taken to be a piece of Euemerism, as given by Herodotus. Tristram, like the heroes of all these tales, is the slayer of worms or dragons; but the narrative which relates Tristram's special exploit is manifestly identical with the story related in Grimm's tale of the Two Brothers. The lying steward of the Tristram myth is the lying marshal of the other; and the mode in which each is convicted is precisely the same. For the connexion of this tale with other legends, see 'Mythology of Aryan Nations,' i. 162 *et seq.*

The difference to all appearance most noteworthy between the two stories of Tristram is that which relates to the character of king Mark of Cornwall, who in the version of Thomas the Rimer is genial and faithful, while in the other he is an embodiment of falsehood and treachery. Such contradictions, if the story be regarded as in any way a narrative of historical facts, would suffice to deprive it of all credibility; but in the old myths the beings whom the sun has to supplant are not always malignant; and the two phases of Mark's character are reproduced in the Ring of the Frithjof Saga, and the Rinkrank of Grimm's popular German tale. In all these narratives, the good and the bad king Mark, the kindly Ring and the hard Rinkrank, each deprive the young and beautiful hero of his bride : in each case the maiden is united with her lover either in life or in death. Sir Henry Strachey ('Morte d'Arthur,' xiii.) regards the fact that Mark appears in his more genial form in the older romance as evidence that the later romance-writer found in the king's treachery some sort of palliation for what Sir Walter Scott calls the extreme ingratitude and profligacy of the hero. The charge of ingratitude seems but scantily borne out, or rather even according to Malory's story it has no foundation at all. The truth is, that if we judge the story from the standard of our human morality, we shall find profligacy everywhere. Tristram pledges his faith to Isolte in Ireland ; but when he returns to Cornwall, he and king Mark quarrel not for her, but about the wife of the Earl Segwarides. Rather it may be said that in the relations of Mark with Isolte Tristram displays a singular fidelity ; but the multiplication of theories is really not needed to explain variations which are common to the myths of the Aryan nations generally. Here, as elsewhere, the method of comparative mythology makes it unnecessary to enter into controversies which can have an interest only on the supposition that we are dealing with powers and persons which are in some degree historical. Hence we need not take into account the conclusion of Mr. Price (Introduction to 'Warton's History of English Poetry,' 1824) that Sir Walter Scott had wholly failed to prove any connexion between this romance and the Rimer of Ercildoune. It might rather be doubted whether Thomas the Rimer was a poet at all, for of the man himself we can scarcely be said to know anything, and by Sir Walter Scott's admission the name existed at the time as a proper name in the Merse, John Rymour, a freeholder of Berwickshire, being among those who did homage to Edward I. in 1296 ('Tristram,' p. 6). But even if the poet's existence be proved, Sir Walter Scott admits further that the romance existed before him; and we are concerned chiefly with the materials on which he worked.

IV.

COMPOSITION OF THE ARTHUR ROMANCE. (P. 330.)

NOTHING can show more clearly or convincingly than this fact the artificial process by which the Arthur romance as we have it has been brought into shape. But this assertion cannot be twisted into a charge that unity of authorship is denied for compositions which have manifestly proceeded from a single poet or story-teller. The whole myth of Arthur might have been first put into its present form by Malory, although we know that it was not; but it would be none the less a fact that the stories of Arthur, Balin, Lancelot, Gareth, Tristram, of the Isoltes, and the Elaines, and Guenevere, repeat each other; that this likeness is inherent in the materials on which the romance writer worked; and that he was compelled in each episode to give the supremacy to the hero of that episode. If then into this episode the heroes of other tales be introduced, it follows inevitably that they must play in it a subordinate part. If the whole legend of the Trojan war has grown up on a framework supplied by phrases which spoke of the struggle of the solar powers in the east to recover the dawn goddess who with her treasures of light and beauty had been stolen from the west, it is a self-evident fact that Sarpedôn, the creeping light, who comes from Lykia, the brilliant land, through which flows the golden stream of Xanthos, is a solar hero, along with his friend Glaukos, the gleaming day, which survives the death of the young sun of the morning. But it is not less clear that this piece of genuine solar myth is misplaced in the later structure of the Iliad, for Paris as stealing away Helen from the west represents the robber Panis who seek to detain Saramâ in their strongholds, and that they who take part with him are defending the citadel of night and darkness against the children of the sun who are come to take away the dawn-maiden from the east and lead her to her western home. Hence, in mythical congruity, Sarpêdôn ought to be fighting by the side of Achilles; but to the old story-tellers such inconsistencies were matters of little moment; and not only

Sarpêdôn, but Memnon, the very child of Eôs, the dawn, is arrayed on the side of Hektor, and therefore also of Paris. Yet the real spirit of the myth is in no case violated, for to Sarpêdôn Ilion is a spot far to the west of his bright Lykia; and no sooner is he slain than the old phrases assert their supremacy, and Phœbus himself wraps in a pure white robe of evening mist the body which Sleep and Death bear through the still night hours to the gleaming portals of the dawn. These inconsistencies, which are surely unavoidable when independent myths are woven together, illustrate precisely the changes which pass over Lancelot or Arthur in those parts of the tale which bear no immediate relation to themselves.

V.

THE HISTORICAL ARTHUR.

THE most earnest defence of the historical character of King Arthur is perhaps that of Lappenberg in his History of England. It amounts practically to little more than this, that the rapid spread of Jeffrey's legend over a great part of Europe proves that the belief in the hero of it was deeply rooted: and this argument, it is clear, may be urged with equal force in favour of the stories of Valentine and Orson or Jack the Giant-killer. William of Malmesbury, writing seven centuries ago, speaks of the many fables told about him by the Britons. William, it is true, mentions Arthur as a man who deserves to be celebrated not by idle fiction, but by genuine history; but he has no other mode of constructing or reconstructing that history than that which had been applied by Euêmeros before him and has been applied by Lappenberg after him. On the other hand, Dr. Lingard has no hesitation in asserting that 'if we divest his memory of the fictitious glory which has been thrown round it by the imagination of the bards and minstrels, he will sink into equal obscurity with his fellows. We know neither the period when he lived, nor the district over which he reigned.' ('History of England,' i. 72.) Mr. Freeman, having insisted on the totally different character of the story of the English conquest as told by the English Chronicles and by Jeffrey of Monmouth, has not thought it worth while to take any notice of the Arthur legend. Dr. Lingard adds that 'when the reader has been told that Arthur was a British chieftain, that he fought many battles, that he was murdered by his nephew and was buried at Glastonbury, where his remains were discovered in the reign of Henry II., he will have learned all that can be ascertained at the present day of that celebrated warrior.' It is very doubtful whether he can ascertain or learn nearly so much. In the case of a chieftain with whose life mythology has by universal consent been busy, the twelve victories which he wins provoke comparison with the twelve labours of Herakles, while the chronology which marks the result of the battle of Mount Badon is as little to be trusted as any other part of the legend. The annals of the Æscingas of Kent are constructed on an eight times recurring cycle of eight years ; and Lappenberg, who upholds the historical character of Arthur, traces this number through every stage in the career of the English conquerors. ('England under the Anglo-Saxon Kings,' i. 75.) The remaining incidents which Dr. Lingard is content that the reader should believe if he likes to do so, are, of course, perfectly possible ; but if our knowledge of them be derived solely from the legendary narrative of his exploits, it is worth neither more nor less than the chronology of the events which took place in the House that Jack Built. We may learn the truth of these facts, if they be facts, from other sources, as we learn from Eginhand that Hruodland, Roland, the prefect of the British march, fell at Roncesvalles. From the legend we learn nothing.

INDEX.

ABB	AIG	ARE
ABBAS, 241	Aiglaer, 90	Amykos, 34
Absyrtos, 262	Aineias, 76, 266	Ananke, 89, 123
Acca Larentia, 130	Aiolos, 197	Anchises, 76, 266
Acheron, 247	Ais, 244	Androgeos, 117
Achilleis, 268	Aisa, 62	Andromache, 272
Achilleus, Achilles, 15, 18, 265, 272, 276	Ajax, 265	Andromeda, 15, 16, 113
	Akersekomes, 89	Andvari, 288
Aditi, 145	Akrisios, 14, 16, 111, 114	Angiras, 58
Admetos, 15, 91, 106, 265	Akshanah, 98	Anna Perenna, 50, 239
Adonai, 67	Aktaion, 163	Anteia, 118, 126, 156
Adonis, 67, 76, 159	Alberich, 288	Antigone, 23, 121, 126, 132
Adrasteia, 61	Aleian plain, 157	
Ægis, 73, 114	Aleos, 127	Antikleia, 126
Æneas, 76, 77, 276	Alexandros, 129	Antilochos, 267
Æolus, 197	Alexikakos, 252	Antiope, 118, 126, 195
Aero, 163	Alkestis, 89	Anubis, 150
Aerth, 143	Alkinoös, 3, 217, 280	Anupu, 150
Æsculapius [Asklepios]	Alkmaion, 93	Aphaia, 159
Æsir, 3, 44, 45	Alkmênê, 101	Aphrodite, 28, 55, 74, 170
Æthra, 116, 119	Allah-ud-deen, 144	
Agamedes, 86	Allekto, 61	— Anadyomene, 74
Agamemnon, 279	All-father, 28, 35	— Enalia and Pontia, 75
Agave, 67, 227	Aloadai, 48, 197	— Ourania and Pandemos, 75
Agenor, 66	Alpheios, 92	
Ages, The, 172	Althaia, 68	Apis, 149
Agni, 164, 167	Amaltheia, 225	Apna-purna, 239
Agraulos, 240	Amazons, 118, 153	Apollon, 8, 15, 84
Ahanâ, 58	Ambrosia, 43	— Delphinios, 87
Ahi, 34, 127	Amen-ra, 148	— Nomios, 147
Ahriman, 172, 255	American Indian legends, 178	— Thyrxis, 144
Aia, 197		Apollon and Hermes, 184 et seq.
Aiakos, Æacus, 247	Ammon, 148	
Aias, 265	Amoun, 148	Apsaras, 204
Aides, 244	Amphiaraos, 87, 92	Ara, 60
Aidoneus, 244	Amphion, 195	Arbhu, 191
Aietes, 197, 261	Amphitrite, 72, 205, 210	Arcadia, 40,
Aigeus, 116	Amphitryon, 135	Areiopagos, 199
Aigisthos, 266	Amulius, 14. 130	Ares, 15, 67, 170 198

ARE	ATR	CLO
Arêtê, 102, 280	Atropos, 61	Brahm, 45
Arethusa, 203	Attabiscar, Song of, 300	Brahma, 34
Argeiphontes, 115	Atthis, 240	Bran, 144
Argentile, 306	Audhumla, 44	Briseis, 267, 274
Argiope, 127	Augé, 13, 127	Britomartis, 159
Argo, 119, 191	Augeias, 105	Broiefort, 304
Argonautic expedition, 92, 260	Aun, 210	Brond, 137
	Aurentil, 297	Bronte, 36, 80, 170
Argos, 11	Aurora, 29	Brynhild, 5, 17, 288
Argos Panoptes, 152	Ausera, 30	Buri, 44
Argos, the dog, 340	Aushasî, 140	
Argynnis, 11, 75	Autolykos, 102, 283	
Ariadne, 18, 118	Autonoê, 163	CABIRI [Kabeiroi]
Arion, 192	Avilion, 70	Cacus, 58, 106, 251
Aristaio s,205	Azidahaka, 131, 210	Cadmus [Kadmos]
Aristodemos, 110		Cæcius, 252
Arjuni, 11, 75		Cæculus, 252
Arnis, 196	BAAL HAMON, 67	Caia, Caius, 35
Artemis, 22, 53, 106, 134, 158, 212	Baal-peor, 144	Calliope, 64
	Bacchus, 76, 229	Camenœ, 64
— Tauropola, 158	Bala, 34	Carmenæ, 64
Arthur, 116, 310 et seq.	Balarama, 148	Carmentes, 64
Arusha, 63	Baldur, 42, 43, 113, 137, 190	Çarvara, 31
Arushi, 63		Cassandra [Kasandra]
Ascapard, 340	Bali, 140	Castor [Kastor]
Asgard, 44	Balin, 318	Cattle of the Sun, 7
Ashera, 142	Balmung, 292	Cecrops, 134
Askalaphos, 265	Barbarians, 155	Centaur [Kentaur]
Asklepios, 18, 43, 90	Barbarossa, 338	Cerberus [Kerberos]
Asmodeus, 256	Bassarides, 230	Ceres, 48, 231
Asphaliaios, 209	Bearer of God, 44	Ceridwen, 144
Asterion, 65, 152	Bellerophon, 15, 115, 153	Chalybes, 153
Asterodia, 11, 12, 95, 151	Belleros, 115, 155	Chandragupta, 132
Asteropaios, 160	Bellona, 200	Chaos, 28, 44
Astraios, 51, 194	Beowulf, 253, 310	Charis, 64, 75
Astyages, 14, 131	Berchta, Frau, 237	Charites, 63
Asuras, 255	Besla, 44	Charles the Great, 131
Asvins, 59, 62, 82, 341	Bettla, 44	Charles's Wain, 42
Atalante, 69, 99	Bevis of Hampton, 340	Charon, 246
Ate, 60, 101, 266	Bhagavadgita, 346	Charybdis, 205
Atergatis, 210	Bhava, Bhavani, 84, 146	Chatumerus, 137
Athamas, 67, 216	Bheki, 87	Cheiron, 102, 163
Athem, 45	Bhowanee, 146	Chemosh, 211
Athênê, 26, 58, 70, 73, 208	Bhuranyu, 11, 66	Children, the Fatal, 14, 90
	Bjelbog, 137	
— Akria, 71	Blarney, 45	Chimera, 15, 105, 156
— Glaukopis, 72	Boabdil, 338	Chione, 218
— Koryphasia, 71	Bölthorn, 44	Chnas, 67
— Optiletis, 72	Bona Dea, 239	Chrysaor, 85, 104, 221
— Tritogeneia, 71	Bor, 44	Chumuri, 34
Athens, 109	Boreas, 182, 194	Cicones, 277
Atlas, 99, 112	Bori, 192	Circe [Kirkê]
Atli, 290 et seq.	Bospoios, 153	Cleo, 64
Atman, 45	Bragi 11, 49	Clotho [Klotho]

INDEX. 373

CLO	DIA	FOL
Cloudeslee, 139	Dia, 96	Enyo, 200
Clym of the Clough, 139	Diana, 32, 53	Eos, 11, 22, 29, 65, 134
Clytemnestra, 220	Dianus, 32, 53	Epaphos, 149, 153
Cocles, 133	Dii Consentes, 239	Ephialtes, 198
Cocytus, 246	Dii Indigetes, 238	Epimenides, 162, 338
Cœlian hill, 49	Dikte, 36	Epimetheus, 175
Consus, 50, 239	Diktynna, 159, 160	Erato, 64
Cornucopiæ, 330 et seq.	Diktys, 111, 115	Ercildoune, 160
Correlative deities, 59, 83, 157, 312, 313	Diomedes, 199, 265	Erebos, 246
	Dionê, 74, 77	Erechtheus, 134, 171
Curetes, 69	Dioscuri [Dioskouroi]	Erichthonios, 134, 170, 240
Cybele [Kybele]	Dioskouroi, 59	
Cyclops, Cyclopes [Kyklops, Kyklôpes]	Dis, 238	Erinys, 11, 59
	Dodona, 40	Eriphyle, 93
Cynosarges [Kynosarges]	Dolios, 282	Eris, 60, 76
Cynossema [Kynossema]	Donar, 47	Eros, 45, 55, 63
Cynosure [Kynosoura]	Doris, 203	Erp, 290
Cyrus, 14, 127, 131	Dragon, Libyan, 15	Eteokles, 93, 126
	Drakon, 92	Ethiopians, Table of the, 144, 321
	Draupadi, 345	
DACTYLS [Daktyloi]	Drukhs, 256	Etzel, 293
Dædalus [Daidalos]	Dryads, 204, 238	Eumaios, 37, 281
Dagon, 87, 210	Dryope, 194	Eumenides, 59, 121, 125
Dahak, 132	Dualism, 255 et seq.	Eunomos, 94, 107
Dahana, 53	Duhita-divah, 75	Europa, 13, 65
Daidalos, 118, 171	Durandal, 301	Euryale, 112
Daktyloi, 242	Durga, 166	Euryanassa, 14, 98
Damayanti, 346	Dyaus, 31, 58	Eurybates, 14
Danae, 111	— Pitar, 32	Eurydike, 14, 95, 190
Danaides, 214	Dyava-matar, 59	Euryganeia, 14
Danaos, 213	Dyava-prithivi, 82	Eurykleia, 14, 233
Dankwart, 293	Dyonysos, 67, 77, 118, 163, 225 et seq.	Eurymedousa, 14
Daphne, 18, 53, 58, 89		Euryphassa, 14
Dasyu, 123	Dyu, 71	Eurystheus, 15, 60, 301
Davy Jones's locker, 46		Eurytos, 14, 102
Dawn maiden, 54		Euterpe, 64
Dawn, Myths of the, 53	EARTH, 143, 231	Evadne, 92
Deianeira, 107	Echemos, 109	Excalibur, 301, 317
Deimos, 76	Echidna, 34, 78, 105	
Deiokes, 132	Echis, 34	
Delos, 13, 40, 85	Echo, 95	FAFNIR, 5, 17, 287
Delphi, 66	Eckesax, 49	Fafnirbana, 156
Demeter, 7, 43, 231 et seq.	Eërophoitos, 125	Fata, 62
Demodokos, 170	Egeria, 64, 119	Fatal Children, The, 14, 90, 319
Demophoon, 233	Egyptus, 213	
Deo, 233	Eileithyia, 146	Fauna, 239
Derketo, 210	Elaine, 329	Faunus, 44
Despoina, 48, 237	Elektra, 60, 197	Faustulus, 130
Deukalion, 37, 132, 176	Eleusis, 232	Favonius, 44
Devaki, 146	Elfland, 161	Fenris, 172
Devas, 255	Elysion, 67, 247	Feridun, 254
Devil on two sticks, 257	Endymion, 12, 95	Fleece, Golden, 15, 63
Dew, Myths of the, 22	Enosichthon, 200	Flora, 239
Dharma, 145	Enyalios, 200	Folklore and Folkrede, 7

FRE	GRE	HYA
Freki, 46	Greyman, 257	Heosphoros, 65
Freya, 44, 48	Grimm, 304	Hephaistos, 26, 65, 66,
Freyr, 44	Gudrun, 288 et seq.	75. 165, 169
Friday, 48	Guenevere, 319 et seq.	Herakleids, 109
Frithjof, 298	Gunadhya, 193	Herakles, 15, 101
Fro, Friuja, 48	Gunnar, 288 et seq.	— labours of, 102
Frodi, wishing queen of, 144	Gunther, 293	Hercules, Herculus, 110, 251
	Guttorm, 289	
	Guy of Warwick, 341	Hêrê, 39, 43, 73, 78, 102, 170
	Gyges, ring of, 326	
Gaia, 28		Hermeias, 11
Gaieochos, 208		Hermes, 8, 25, 91, 113,
Galahad, 317 et seq.	Hades, 31, 37, 113, 244 et seq.	133 et seq.
Gandharva, 55, 97		Heroic Age, 173
Ganesa, 240	Hadufians, 137	Hersê, 22, 240
Ganymêdê, 65	Hagen, 291	Hertha, 144
Ganymedes, 65	Hahnir, 287	Herwig, 297
Garanus, 251	Haimon, 126	Hesioneus, 96
Gareth, 324	Halirrhothios, 199	Hesperides, 96, 107
Gari, 46	Hamadryads, 238, 243	Hesperos, 94, 96
Gawaine, 322	Hamar, 48	Hestia, 39, 91, 166
Gê, 35	Hamdir, 290	Hialprek, 170
Gemini, 83	Hamelin, Piper of, 189, 192	Hilda, 142
Genii, 238		Hildebrand, 294
Geography, Mythical, 153	Hamlet, 307 et seq.	Hildeburg, 296
Gerairai, 169	Hanuman, 348	Hildegund, 295
Geryon, 106, 252, 254	Hari, 140	Himeros, 74
Gibborim, 242	Harits, 33, 62	Himinbiorg, 49
Gibicho, 45, 295	Harivansa, 346	Hippokrênê, 221
Gigantes, 179	Harmonia, 67	Hippolochos, 138
Girlinda, 298	Harpagos, 132	Hippolytos, 118
Giuki, 288	Har-pi-chruti, 150	Hipponoös, 155
Glaukê, 15, 262	Harpies, 60, 65, 197	Hippotes, 197
Glaukos, 6, 72, 133, 266	Harpokrates, 149, 150	Hjarrandi, 297
Glistening Heath, 5, 17	Hartmuth, 297	Hjordis, 103, 170
Godard, 304	Havelok, 304, 307	Hnikar, 46
Godric, 304	Hebe, 65, 80, 108	Hoard, the Golden, 295
Gokala, 146	Hekabe, Hecuba, 264	Hödr, 43, 113, 137, 245
Goldborough, 304	Hekaergos, 91	Hogni, 290 et seq.
Golden Fleece, 15	Hekate, 66, 157	Holda, 237
— Shower, 16, 111	Hekatebolos, 66	Holy coat of Treves, 309
Goose-girl, the, 298	Hekatoncheires, 37, 179	Hope, 176
Gopias, 147	Hekatos, 66, 91	Horai, 78
Gorgons, 15, 16, 221	Hektor, 76, 79, 272	Horant, 297
Govinda, 145	Hel, 44, 256	Horos, 150
Graces, 63	Helche, 293	Horselberg, 129, 160
Graiai, 16, 112	Helen, 40, 76, 113, 319	Hrim-thursen, 44
Grail, the holy, 320	Helenê, 11, 58	Hrungnir, 43
Gram, 117, 285, 301	— Kunôpis, 40, 59	Hugdietrich, 296
Grani, 295	Helgi Sagas, 289	Huginn, 46
Grant, 172	Helios, 11, 15, 65, 88, 94	Huon of Bordeaux, 144, 320
Gratiæ, 63	Hellê, 4, 216	
Grendel, 172, 253 309	Hellen, 177	Hvar, 78
Grettir, 299	Hemera, 74, 237	Hyades, 220

INDEX. 375

HYD
Hydra, 105, 250
Hyllos, 109
Hyperborean Gardens, 59, 113
Hypereia, 280
Hyperion, 36, 65
Hypermnestra, 213
Hypnos, 134
Hyrieus, Treasury of, 87, 162

IALMENOS, 265
Iamos, 90, 92
Iapetos, 36
Iasion, 237
Iason, 130, 261
Ida, 36, 41
Iduna, 310
Ikaros, 171
Ikmenos Ouros, 45
Ilia, 200
Iliad, component parts of the, 267
Ilion, 104, 264
Inachos, 151
Indra, 14, 17, 33
— Parjanya, 34, 46
— Savitar, 46
Indus, 33
Ingebjorg, 298
Ino, 67, 217
Io, 151
Iobates, 156
Iokaste, 16, 24, 120
Iolaos, 104, 109
Iolê, 104, 108
Iphianassa, 95
Iphigeneia, 61, 159, 266
Iphikles, 104
Iphimedousa, 197
Iris, 49, 233
Isandros, 138
Isis, 149
— ship of, 143
Ismene, 121
Isolte, 328
Issi, 257
Ixion, 41, 80, 96

JANUS, 32, 53
Jáson [Iason]
Jemshid, 144

JOC
Jocasta [Iokastê]
Jonakr, 290
Jormunrek, 290
Joseph of Arimathea, 144
Jötun, 44
Jötunheim, 48
Juno, 32, 52
— Moneta and Jugalis, 53, 74, 80
Jupiter, 33, 38, 50
— Elicius, 52
— Pluvius, 46, 52
— Terminus, 52, 110

KABEIROI, 163, 242
Kadmos, 13, 15, 67
Kakia, 102
Kalchas, 265
Kali, 166
Kalinak, 148
Kalliope, 64, 190
Kallirrhoe, 254
Kalos, 171
Kalydonian boar, 68, 107
Kalypso, 160, 279
Kama, 45
Kamsa, 145
Karali, 166
Karmê, 159
Kasandra, 264
Kastor, 59, 102
Kauravas, 343
Kebren, 265
Kedalion, 163
Kedem, 67
Keingala, 299
Kekrops, 134, 241
Keleos, 233
Kentaur, 15, 97
Kephalos, 18, 22, 95, 134
Kepheus, 115
Kephisos, 95
Kerberos, 31, 104, 245
Kerdo, 167
Keto, 111
Kikones, 277
Kilix, 66
Kipicho, 45
Kirkê, 4, 160, 279
Kleio, 64
Kleitos, 65
Kleopatra, 69

LIB
Klotho, 61
Klymene, 94
Klytaimnestra, 220
Kneph, 148
Kokytos, 246
Korônis, 18, 90
Korybantes, 242
Korythos, 127
Kosmos, 44
Kouretes, 69, 163, 242
Kranaos, 240
Kreon, 126
Kresphontes, 110
Kretea, 40
Kriemhild, 291
Krishna, 22, 145 et seq.
Kronion, 78
Kronos, 35, 174, 179
Kumara, 140
Kyanean rocks, 191
Kybele, Kybêbê, 241
Kyklôpes, 36, 37, 40
Kyknos, 199
Kynopis, 40
Kynosarges, 40
Kynosoura, 40
Kynossêma, 40

LABYRINTH, 171
Lachesis, 61
Laertes, 265, 281
Laios, 14, 16
Laistrygones, 278
Lampetie, 13
Lamyroi, 247
Lance of, 319 et seq.
Laodameia, 138
Laomedon, 15, 91, 104, 209
Lares, 52, 74, 169
Larvæ, 169
Latin gods, 50
Latmos, 12, 84
Laverna, 190
Leda, 85
Legends, Tribal, 16
Lemures, 169, 247
Leophontes, 123
Lethe, 84, 246
Leto, 13, 73
Leukothea, 217
Liber, 48
Libera, 48

INDEX.

LIC
Lichas, 108
Lif, 43
Lightning, myths of the, 180
Linga, 143
Linos, 102, 196
Logi, 172
Loki, 42, 48, 136, 171
Lotus, 143
Lucerius, 52, 91
Luck of Edenhall, 332
Luck-flower, the, 180
Lycæus [Lykaios]
Lychnos, 73
Lycosura [Lykosoura]
Lykaios, 40
Lykaon, 42
Lykastos, 133
Lykegenes, 13, 85
Lykomedes, 119
Lykos, 195
Lykosoura, 40, 86
Lykourgos, 92
Lyktos, 36
Lympha, 204
Lynkeus, 213
Lyrkeios, 214

Mâ, 241
Macduff, 14
Magni, 43
Mahâbhârata, 343
Mahâdeva, 34
Maia, 184
Mainades, 230
Mamers, 200
Mana, 50, 169
Mandane, 131
Manduci, 247
Manes, 169
Mania, 74
Manu, 132
Marhaus, 322
Mars, 200, 241
Marspiter, Maspiter, 241
Marsyas, 100
Maruts, 34, 182
Master Thief, 18, 188
Matarisvan, 166
Matuta, 74
Mavers, 200
Maypole, 143
Medeia, 15, 175, 262

MED
Medusa, 15, 112, 221
Megaira, 61
Megapenthes, 114
Megara, 104
Melanthios, 282
Meleagros, 18, 68, 267
Melikertes, 67
Melkarth, 67
Melpomene, 64
Memnon, 65, 79, 134, 266
Menelaos, 276
Menestheus, 119
Mercury, Mercurius, 189
Merlin, 31
Merope, 120
Meru, mount, 346
Metaneira, 233
Metis, 71, 175
Midas, 100, 243
Midgard, 44
Milky Way, 147
Mimir, 46, 134
Minerva, 53, 74
— Capita, 71
Minos, 6, 66, 116, 132
Minotauros, 105, 171
Mithras, 33
Mitra, 33
Mœræ, 68
Moirai, 61, 68
Molion, 52
Molionids, 48, 197
Moloch, 67, 105, 211, 229
Monotheism, 38
Mordred, 315, 336
Mördur, 44
Morgan le Fay, 70, 302
Morglay, 301
Mulciber, 171
Muninn, 46
Muses, 63, 64
Mutinus, Muttunus, 50, 231
Myrmidons, 42, 106, 275
Mysteries, 144
— Eleusinian, 234
Mythology and Folklore, distinction between, 7
— Comparative, 8
— Egyptian, 149
— Hebrew, 274
— Latin, 50
— Semitic, 223 et seq.

ODI
Myths, Organic and Inorganic, 9
— Transmission and dispersion of, 9, 21
— of the Dawn, 29
— — Dew, 22, 23

NAIADS, 46, 76, 203
Nala, 346
Namuki, 34
Nanda, 146
Naraka, 22, 23
Narcissus [Narkissos]
Narkissos, 95
Naubandhana, 162
Nausikaa, 280
Necessity, doctrine of, 60
Nectar, 43
Neis, 95
Neith, 150
Neleus, 130
Nemesis, 60, 95
Neoptolemos, 103
Nephele, 216, 260
Neptunus, 212
Nereids, 46, 203
Nereus, 202
Nessos, 15, 107
Nestor, 265
Nibelungenlied, 5, 248, 291 et seq.
Nibelungs, 235
Nick, Old, 46
Nicor, 46
Niflheim, 77, 256
Niflungs, 235
Niobe, 66, 98, 218
Nisos, 177, 206
Nix, 46
Nixes, 46
Nobiskrug, 257
Norns, 61
Numa, 64
Nykteus, 195
Nymphs, 16
Nysa, Mount, 226

OANNES, 210
Oberon, 321
Ocean, 49
Odin, 42, 45
— Biblindi, 46

INDEX. 377

ODI
Odin Hakol-berend, 46
— Harbard, 46
— Rune Song of, 44
Odysseus, 103, 171, 265, 283
Œdipus, 14, 15, 16, 120 et seq.
Œgir, 49
Oegishialm, 49
Œneus, 68, 94
Œnone, 265
Ogen, 49
Ogier, 304
Ogyges, 49
Ogygia, 279
Oiagros, 190
Oidipous [Œdipus]
Oinopion, 162
Okeanos, 49, 78
Olger the Dane, 70, 301
Olympia, 40
Olympian gods, 25, 39
Olympian System of the Iliad and Odyssey, 351
Olympos, 25
Omphale, 107
On, 210
Onnes, 87
Ops, 238
Oreads, 204, 243
Oreithyia, 195
Orendil, 297, 308
Orestes, 266
Orion, 65, 162, 237
Ormuzd, 255
Orpheus, 95, 189, 261
Orthia, 212
Orthros, 31, 105, 243
Ortlieb, 294
Ortygia, 66, 85
Osci, Oski, 45
Osiris, 142, 144, 148
Oska-byrr, 45
Osk-mayjar, 45
Oska-stein, 45
Otos, 198
Ourania, 64
Ouranos, 31, 32
Ovelgunne, 257

PAIEON, 90
Palaimon, 67, 211
Palici, 239

PAL
Pallas, 72
Pan, 151, 194
Pandareos, 98
Pandaros, 266
Pandavas, 343 et seq.
Pandora, 73, 175
Pandrosos, 240
Pani, 34, 58
Parasurama, 347
Parcæ, 61
Paris, 128, 264
— Judgment of, 78
Parjanya, 34
Parnassos, 176
Pasiphae, 171
Patroklos, 79, 94, 269
Pavana, 193
Pegasos, 156, 221
Peirithoos, 119
Pelasgos, 42
Peleus, 76, 265
Pelias, 130, 261
Pelops, 98
Penates, 52, 169
Penelope, 194, 281, 283
Pentheus, 67, 105, 227
Peplos, 142
Periphetes, 117, 170
Persephone, 7, 77, 234
Perseus, 14, 15, 110 et seq.
Phaethon, 65, 69, 94
Phaethousa, 13
Phaiakians, 3, 217, 280
Phaidra, 118
Phallos, 143
Phanaios, 93
Pharaildis, 237
Phemios, 294
Phenicia, 40, 66
Phenician worship, 224
Phenix, 150, 267
Philoktetes, 103
Philomela, 196
Phineus, 113
Phix, 124
Phlegyas, 96
Phobos, 76
Phœbus, 36, 84
— Akersekomes, 43
Phœnix, 66, 68
Phol, 137
Phorkos, 111, 219
Phoroneus, 11, 66, 167

POP
Phrixos, 4, 217
Phthah, 151
Picumnus, 238
Picus, 239
Pierides, 64
Pieros, 64
Pilumnus, 238
Pirys, 194
Pleiades, 220
Plouton, 237
Pluto, 237, 245
Podarge, 197
Poias, 108
Polybos, 120
Polydegmon, 111, 234
Polydektes, 111
Polydeukes, 55, 59, 83, 102
Polyidos, 6
Polymetis, 171
Polymnia, 64
Polyneikes, 92, 126
Polyonymy, 10, 13
Polyphemos, 219, 257
Pomona, 239
Pontos, 35, 203
Popular stories:—
  Ahmed and the Peri Banou, 181, 338
  Ali Baba and the Forty Thieves, 4, 87, 181
  Alla-ud-deen, 181, 329
  Big Bird Dan, 2, 329
  Boots of Buffalo Leather, 324
  Briar-rose, 236, 314
  Champa Ranee, 18
  Cinderella, 4
  Dame of the fine Green Kirtle, 292, 321
  Dapplegrim, 83
  Dog and the Sparrow, 18
  East of the Sun and West of the Moon, 56
  Farmer Weathersky, 203
  Frog Prince, 87
  Giant who had no heart in his body, 339
  Glass Coffin, 340
  Gold Child, 324
  Golden Bird, 56

Popular stories :—
  Great Fool, 305
  Hacon Grizzlebeard, 305
  Handless Maiden, 46
  House in the Wood, 236
  Iron Stove, 96, 340
  Jew among the Thorns, 192
  Karpara and Gata, 3
  Knapsack, the Hat, and the Horn, 324
  Lad who knew not how to shiver, 324
  Master-smith, 170
  Master Thief, 318
  Maurice Connor, 193
  Moor's Legacy, 181
  Nix of the Mill Pond, 98, 236
  Nuad of the Silver Hand, 46
  Old Dame and her Hen, 237
  Old Griffin, 339
  Old Soldier, 342
  Panch Phul Ranee, 4
  Pilgrim of Love, 4
  Punchkin, 312, 339
  Queen Bee, 56
  Rapunzel, 236
  Rhampsinitos, Treasures of, 3, 87
  Rich Peter the Pedlar, 339
  Robber and his Sons, 258
  Shifty Lad, 4, 87
  Shortshanks, 3, 324
  Sick Queen, 87
  Snake Leaves, 5
  Snow-white and Rose-red, 63, 90
  Soaring Lark, 56
  Sodewa Bai, 4
  Suria Moria Castle, 324
  Surya Bai, 288
  The Dwarf, 236
  Three Wishes, 192
  Thrushbeard, 305
  True and Untrue, 313
  Twelve Brethren, 56
  Two Brothers, 313, 329

Popular stories :—
  Two Sisters, 313
  Vicram Maharaja, 19
  White Snake, 56
  Widow and her Daughters, 96
  Wolf and the Seven little Goats, 36, 285
Poseidon, 37, 73, 172, 206, 209
Pradyumna, 88
Prajâpati, 83, 139
Pramantha, 175
Priam, 79, 264, 273
Priapos, 76, 230
Primary and Secondary Myths, 9
Prithivî, 31
Procrustes, 117
Prœtos, 156
Prokne, 196
Prokris, 18, 22
Prokroustes, 117
Prometheus, 37, 42, 73, 137, 152, 165
Proteus, 83, 87, 202
Protogeneia, 12
Psyche, 55
Psychopompos, 47
Pururavas, 55
Putana, 147
Pylaochos, 172
Pyrakmon, 170
Pyriphlegethon, 246
Pyrrha, 176
Pytho, 87
Python, 287

QUIRINUS, 201
Qvasir, 43

RA, 148
Ramayana, 248, 347
Ravana, 250, 347
Recaranus, 251
Regin, 117, 287
Reidartyr, 47
Reidmar, 287
Remus, 14, 127, 130
Reris, 285
Rhadamanthys, 66, 149
Rhampsinitos, 3

Rhea, 36, 241
Rhea Silvia, 200
Rhodopis, 4
Rhot-amenti, 150
Ribhu, 191
Rig Veda, 29
Rind, 43
Ring, the magic, 303
Rishis, 42
Rohits, 62
Roland, 300 et seq.
Roman religion, 52
Romulus, 14, 127, 130, 201
Roncesvalles, 300
Roots in language, 28
Round Table, the 320
Rudra, 145, 182
Rustam, 17, 291

SACTI, 144
Saga, 47
Salmoneus, 130
Sambara, 34, 87
Sammuramit, 210
Sangreal, 144, 321
Saramâ, 11, 58
Sarameyas, 11, 185
Saranyû, 11, 59
Sarpedon, 11, 58, 66, 72, 79, 133, 266
Sassafras, 180
Sâtavâhana, 193
Saturnus, 238
Satyrs, 243
Saurli, 290
Savitar, 81
Sceaf, 331
Schamir, 180
Scheria, 280
Schœneus, 69
Secondaries, 93
Seilenos, 100, 243
Seirens, 191, 205
Seirios, 163
Seistron, 142
Selene, 11, 151
Semele, 67, 77, 226
Semiramis, 210
Semitic influence on Greek religion, 225
Semo Sancus, 50, 238
Serapis, 151

INDEX.

SER
Serpents in mythology, 92, 106
Servius Tullius, 305
Sesame, 180
Set, Sethi, 150
Seven Champions of Christendom, 162
— Manes of Leinster, 162
— Rishis, 162
— Sages of Hellas, 162
— Sleepers of Ephesus, 162
Shemesh, 211
Sibylline books, 193
Sidêro, 131
Siegfried, 291 et seq.
Siggeir, 285
Sigmund, 117, 284'
Signy, 285
Sigrun, 289
Sigtyr, 47
Sigurd, 5, 14, 17, 117, 192, 284, 288
Silanus, 192, 243
Silvanus, 239
Sinfjötli, 286
Sinis, 117
Sisyphos, 7, 8, 9, 98
Sita, 250, 347
Siva, 34, 166
Skambha, 82, 164
Skeiron, 117
Skidbladnir, 3, 48
Skuld, 61
Skylla, 177, 205
Sleipnir, 47
Snake leaves, the, 5
Solomon, Carpet of, 4
Solymoi, 156
Soma, 43, 81
Sphinx, 15, 24, 120, 124, 219, 253
Steropé, 36, 80, 170
Stheino, 112
Styx, 246
Sun, cattle of the, 7
— rays of the, 62
Surya, 34, 81
Sushna, 34
Sutala, 84
Svar, 63, 78
Svayambhu 162
Swanhild, 290

SWA
Swan-maidens, 204
Symplegades, 191, 261
Syrinx, 191
Syrma, 195

TAMLANE, ballad of, 203
Tammuz, 67, 142
Tanhaüser, 129, 160, 161, 274
Tantalos, 26, 41, 98
Tara Bai, 160
Tarnkappe, 37, 113
Tarquin, 193
Tartaros, 36, 64, 248
Telchines, 242
Telemachos, 94, 281
Telephassa, 13, 66
Telephos, 13, 127
Tell, 138
Tellus, 241
Telodike, 167
Telphoussa, 86
Temenos, 110
Tereus, 196
Terminus, 110
Terpsichore, 64
Terra, 241
Tethys, 78, 212
Teutamidas, 114
Teuthras, 127
Thalia, 64
Thanatos, 106, 109, 133
Thaumas, 60, 197, 203
Thebes, 67
Theogony, Hesiodic, 28
—, Orphic, 34
Theseus, 18, 105, 116, 122
Thetis, 76, 85, 170, 204, 270
Thomas the Rimer, 129, 160, 274
Thoôsa, 179
Thor, 42, 43
—, Hammer of, 47
— Miölnir, 48
Thorir Redbeard, 299
— of Garth, 299
Thraetana, 210, 254
Thriai, 61, 64, 185
Thrym, 48
Thunor, 47
Thursday, 47

VEN
Tiphys, 261
Tisiphone, 61
Titans, 37, 178
Tithonos, 65, 95
Tiu, 33
Treasure, the lost, 292 et seq.
Trimurtti, 34, 81
Triptolemos, 234
Tristram, 14, 326 et seq.
Trita, 72, 210, 254
Tritogeneia, 71
Triton, 72
Tritopatores, 72
Trophonios, 86
Troy, tale of, 264, 273
Tuesday, 33
Tuisco, 36
Twilight of the gods, 137
Tydeus, 48
Tyndareus, 48, 220
Typhaon, 78
Typhoeus, 250
Typhon, 250
Tyr, 36, 46
Tyro, 130

UASAR, 150
Uma, 82
Uokesahs, 49
Uranus [Ouranos]
Ursel, 160
Ursula, 95, 129, 160
Urukî, 55
Urvasi, 55
Ushapati, 63
Ushas, 29, 57

VAHNI, 81
Valant, 27, 257
Valhalla, 45
Vali, 43
Valkyries, 45
Vanaheim, 44
Vanen, 44
Varuna, 31, 60
Varvara, 155
Vasistha, 55
Vasus, 145
Vayu, 34, 81, 182
Venus, 50, 77, 171
— Cloacina, 77

INDEX.

VER
Verdhandi, 61
Vertumnus, 239
Vessels of plenty, 321
Vesta, 52, 166, 168
Vikramaditya, 14
Vikramorvasî, 55
Vilkina Saga, 49
Virbius, 118
Vishnu, 34, 48, 85, 139
Völa, 138
Volker, 293
Volsung, 14, 90, 284, 293
—, Saga of, 116
Völuspa Saga, 43
Vritra, 17, 31
Vritrahan, 115, 156
Vulcan, 171
Vurdh, 61

Wäinämöinen, 189
Walter of Aquitaine, 294
Wayland the Smith, 170, 249

WEA
Weapons, mythical, 86, 301, 314, 316
—, poisoned, 103, 328
Wegtam, 138, 322
Weird Sisters, 61, 323
Wind, Myths of the, 187 et seq.
Wish-god, 43
Wishing-stone, 45
Wish-maidens, 45
Witchcraft, 263
Wunsch, 45
Wuotan, 44
Wuth, 45

Xanthos, the horse, 79, 94, 271
— the river, 128
Xisuthros, 179

Yama, 83, 104
Yami, 83
Yavishtha, 166
Yggdrasil, 44, 49, 61

ZOI
Ymir, 44
Yoni, 143
Yudishthira, 344

Zagreos, 148, 230
Zaleukos, 92
Zephyros, 65, 196
Zethos, 195
Zeus, 26, 32, 174
— Ephestios, 41
— Herkeios, 110
— Horios, 52
— Horkios, 41, 239
— Meilichios, 229
— Nephelegerctes, 46
— Olympios, 37
— Ombrios, 46
— Patêr, 32
— Phyxios, 264
— Pistios, 41, 239
— Xenios, 41
Zio, 36
Zohak, 131, 210

A LIST OF
KEGAN PAUL, TRENCH & CO.'S
PUBLICATIONS.

1.83.

1, *Paternoster Square*,
London.

A LIST OF
KEGAN PAUL, TRENCH & CO.'S PUBLICATIONS.

CONTENTS.

	PAGE		PAGE
GENERAL LITERATURE	2	POETRY	34
INTERNATIONAL SCIENTIFIC SERIES	29	WORKS OF FICTION	43
MILITARY WORKS	31	BOOKS FOR THE YOUNG	44

GENERAL LITERATURE.

ADAMS, F. O., F.R.G.S.—**The History of Japan.** From the Earliest Period to the Present time. New Edition, revised. 2 vols. With Maps and Plans. Demy 8vo, 21s. each.

ADAMSON, H. T., B.D.—**The Truth as it is in Jesus.** Crown 8vo, 8s. 6d.

The Three Sevens. Crown 8vo, 5s. 6d.

The Millennium; or, the Mystery of God Finished. Crown 8vo, cloth, 6s.

A. K. H. B.—**From a Quiet Place.** A New Volume of Sermons. Crown 8vo, 5s.

ALLEN, Rev. R., M.A.—**Abraham: his Life, Times, and Travels,** 3800 years ago. With Map. Second Edition. Post 8vo, 6s.

ALLEN, Grant, B.A.—**Physiological Æsthetics.** Large post 8vo, 9s.

ALLIES, T. W., M.A.—**Per Crucem ad Lucem.** The Result of a Life. 2 vols. Demy 8vo, 25s.

A Life's Decision. Crown 8vo, 7s. 6d.

ANDERDON, Rev. W. H.—**Fasti Apostolici;** a Chronology of the years between the Ascension of our Lord and the Martyrdom of SS. Peter and Paul. Crown 8vo, cloth, 2s. 6d.

ANDERSON, R. C., C.E.—Tables for Facilitating the Calculation of Every Detail in connection with Earthen and Masonry Dams. Royal 8vo, £2 2s.

ARCHER, Thomas.—About my Father's Business. Work amidst the Sick, the Sad, and the Sorrowing. Cheaper Edition. Crown 8vo, 2s. 6d.

ARMSTRONG, Richard A., B.A.—Latter-Day Teachers. Six Lectures. Small crown 8vo, 2s. 6d.

ARNOLD, Arthur.—Social Politics. Demy 8vo, 14s.

Free Land. Second Edition. Crown 8vo, 6s.

AUBERTIN, J. J.—A Flight to Mexico. With Seven full-page Illustrations and a Railway Map of Mexico. Crown 8vo, 7s. 6d.

BADGER, George Percy, D.C.L.—An English-Arabic Lexicon. In which the equivalent for English Words and Idiomatic Sentences are rendered into literary and colloquial Arabic. Royal 4to, £9 9s.

BAGEHOT, Walter.—The English Constitution. Third Edition. Crown 8vo, 7s. 6d.

Lombard Street. A Description of the Money Market. Seventh Edition. Crown 8vo, 7s. 6d.

Some Articles on the Depreciation of Silver, and Topics connected with it. Demy 8vo, 5s.

BAGENAL, Philip H.—The American-Irish and their Influence on Irish Politics. Crown 8vo, 5s.

BAGOT, Alan, C.E.—Accidents in Mines: their Causes and Prevention. Crown 8vo, 6s.

The Principles of Colliery Ventilation. Second Edition, greatly enlarged. Crown 8vo, 5s.

BAKER, Sir Sherston, Bart.—Halleck's International Law; or, Rules Regulating the Intercourse of States in Peace and War. A New Edition, revised, with Notes and Cases. 2 vols. Demy 8vo, 38s.

The Laws relating to Quarantine. Crown 8vo, 12s. 6d.

BALDWIN, Capt. J. H.—The Large and Small Game of Bengal and the North-Western Provinces of India. With numerous Illustrations. Second Edition. 4to, 21s.

BALLIN, Ada S. and F. L.—A Hebrew Grammar. With Exercises selected from the Bible. Crown 8vo, 7s. 6d.

BARCLAY, Edgar.—Mountain Life in Algeria. With numerous Illustrations by Photogravure. Crown 4to, 16s.

BARLOW, James H.—The Ultimatum of Pessimism. An Ethical Study. Demy 8vo, cloth, 6s.

BARNES, William.—An Outline of English Speechcraft. Crown 8vo, 4s.

BARNES, William.—continued.
   Outlines of Redecraft (Logic). With English Wording. Crown 8vo, 3s.

BARTLEY, G. C. T.—Domestic Economy: Thrift in Every-Day Life. Taught in Dialogues suitable for children of all ages. Small crown 8vo, 2s.

BAUR, Ferdinand, Dr. Ph.—A Philological Introduction to Greek and Latin for Students. Translated and adapted from the German, by C. KEGAN PAUL, M.A., and E. D. STONE, M.A. Second Edition. Crown 8vo, 6s.

BAYNES, Rev. Canon R. H.—At the Communion Time. A Manual for Holy Communion. With a preface by the Right Rev. the Lord Bishop of Derry and Raphoe. 1s. 6d.

BELLARS, Rev. W.—The Testimony of Conscience to the Truth and Divine Origin of the Christian Revelation. Burney Prize Essay. Small crown 8vo, 3s. 6d.

BELLINGHAM, Henry, M.P.—Social Aspects of Catholicism and Protestantism in their Civil Bearing upon Nations. Translated and adapted from the French of M. le Baron de Haulleville. With a preface by His Eminence Cardinal Manning. Second and Cheaper Edition. Crown 8vo, 3s. 6d.

BENN, Alfred W.—The Greek Philosophers. 2 vols. Demy 8vo, cloth, 28s.

BENT, J. Theodore.—Genoa: How the Republic Rose and Fell. With 18 Illustrations. Demy 8vo, 18s.

BLOOMFIELD, The Lady.—Reminiscences of Court and Diplomatic Life. With three portraits and six illustrations by the Author. Third edition. 2 vols. Demy 8vo, cloth, 28s.

BLUNT, The Ven. Archdeacon.—The Divine Patriot, and other Sermons. Preached in Scarborough and in Cannes. Crown 8vo, 6s.

BLUNT, Wilfred S.—The Future of Islam. Crown 8vo, 6s.

BONWICK, J., F.R.G.S.—Pyramid Facts and Fancies. Crown 8vo, 5s.
   Egyptian Belief and Modern Thought. Large post 8vo, 10s. 6d.

BOUVERIE-PUSEY, S. E. B.—Permanence and Evolution. An Inquiry into the Supposed Mutability of Animal Types. Crown 8vo, 5s.

BOWEN, H. C., M.A.—Studies in English. For the use of Modern Schools. Third Edition. Small crown 8vo, 1s. 6d.
   English Grammar for Beginners. Fcap. 8vo, 1s.

BRIDGETT, *Rev. T. E.*—History of the Holy Eucharist in Great Britain. 2 vols. Demy 8vo, 18s.

BRODRICK, *the Hon. G. C.*—Political Studies. Demy 8vo, 14s.

BROOKE, *Rev. S. A.*—Life and Letters of the Late Rev. F. W. Robertson, M.A. Edited by.
  I. Uniform with Robertson's Sermons. 2 vols. With Steel Portrait. 7s. 6d.
  II. Library Edition. With Portrait. 8vo, 12s.
  III. A Popular Edition. In 1 vol., 8vo, 6s.

The Spirit of the Christian Life. A New Volume of Sermons. Second Edition. Crown 8vo, 7s. 6d.

The Fight of Faith. Sermons preached on various occasions. Fifth Edition. Crown 8vo, 7s. 6d.

Theology in the English Poets.—Cowper, Coleridge, Wordsworth, and Burns. Fourth and Cheaper Edition. Post 8vo, 5s.

Christ in Modern Life. Sixteenth and Cheaper Edition. Crown 8vo, 5s.

Sermons. First Series. Twelfth and Cheaper Edition. Crown 8vo, 5s.

Sermons. Second Series. Fifth and Cheaper Edition. Crown 8vo, 5s.

BROOKE, *W. G., M.A.*—The Public Worship Regulation Act. With a Classified Statement of its Provisions, Notes, and Index. Third Edition, revised and corrected. Crown 8vo, 3s. 6d.

Six Privy Council Judgments.—1850-72. Annotated by. Third Edition. Crown 8vo, 9s.

BROWN, *Rev. J. Baldwin, B.A.*—The Higher Life. Its Reality, Experience, and Destiny. Fifth Edition. Crown 8vo, 5s.

Doctrine of Annihilation in the Light of the Gospel of Love. Five Discourses. Third Edition. Crown 8vo, 2s. 6d.

The Christian Policy of Life. A Book for Young Men of Business. Third Edition. Crown 8vo, 3s. 6d.

BROWN, *J. Croumbie, LL.D.*—Reboisement in France; or, Records of the Replanting of the Alps, the Cevennes, and the Pyrenees with Trees, Herbage, and Bush. Demy 8vo, 12s. 6d.

The Hydrology of Southern Africa. Demy 8vo, 10s. 6d.

BROWN, *S. Borton, B.A.*—The Fire Baptism of all Flesh; or, the Coming Spiritual Crisis of the Dispensation. Crown 8vo, 6s.

BROWNE, *W. R.*—The Inspiration of the New Testament. With a Preface by the Rev. J. P. NORRIS, D.D. Fcap. 8vo, 2s. 6d.

BURCKHARDT, *Jacob.*—The Civilization of the Period of the Renaissance in Italy. Authorized translation, by S. G. C. Middlemore. 2 vols. Demy 8vo, 24s.

BURTON, Mrs. Richard.—**The Inner Life of Syria, Palestine, and the Holy Land.** With Maps, Photographs, and Coloured Plates. Cheaper Edition in one volume. Large post 8vo, 10s. 6d.

BUSBECQ, Ogier Ghiselin de.—**His Life and Letters.** By CHARLES THORNTON FORSTER, M.A., and F. H. BLACKBURNE DANIELL, M.A. 2 vols. With Frontispieces. Demy 8vo, 24s.

CARPENTER, Dr. Phillip P.—**His Life and Work.** Edited by his brother, Russell Lant Carpenter. With Portrait and Vignettes. Second Edition. Crown 8vo, 7s. 6d.

CARPENTER, W. B., LL.D., M.D., F.R.S., etc.—**The Principles of Mental Physiology.** With their Applications to the Training and Discipline of the Mind, and the Study of its Morbid Conditions. Illustrated. Sixth Edition. 8vo, 12s.

CERVANTES.—**The Ingenious Knight Don Quixote de la Mancha.** A New Translation from the Originals of 1605 and 1608. By A. J. DUFFIELD. With Notes. 3 vols. Demy 8vo, 42s.

CHEYNE, Rev. T. K.—**The Prophecies of Isaiah.** Translated with Critical Notes and Dissertations. 2 vols. Second Edition. Demy 8vo, 25s.

CLAIRAUT.—**Elements of Geometry.** Translated by Dr. KAINES. With 145 Figures. Crown 8vo, 4s. 6d.

CLAYDEN, P. W.—**England under Lord Beaconsfield.** The Political History of the Last Six Years, from the end of 1873 to the beginning of 1880. Second Edition, with Index and continuation to March, 1880. Demy 8vo, 16s.

CLODD, Edward, F.R.A.S.—**The Childhood of the World:** a Simple Account of Man in Early Times. Sixth Edition. Crown 8vo, 3s.
A Special Edition for Schools. 1s.

The Childhood of Religions. Including a Simple Account of the Birth and Growth of Myths and Legends. Ninth Thousand. Crown 8vo, 5s.
A Special Edition for Schools. 1s. 6d.

Jesus of Nazareth. With a brief sketch of Jewish History to the Time of His Birth. Small crown 8vo, 6s.

COGHLAN, J. Cole, D.D.—**The Modern Pharisee and other Sermons.** Edited by the Very Rev. H. H. DICKINSON, D.D., Dean of Chapel Royal, Dublin. New and Cheaper Edition. Crown 8vo, 7s. 6d.

COLERIDGE, Sara.—**Phantasmion.** A Fairy Tale. With an Introductory Preface, by the Right Hon. Lord Coleridge, of Ottery St. Mary. A New Edition. Illustrated. Crown 8vo, 7s. 6d.

Memoir and Letters of Sara Coleridge. Edited by her Daughter. With Index. Cheap Edition. With one Portrait. 7s. 6d.

Collects Exemplified. Being Illustrations from the Old and New Testaments of the Collects for the Sundays after Trinity. By the Author of "A Commentary on the Epistles and Gospels." Edited by the Rev. JOSEPH JACKSON. Crown 8vo, 5s.

COLLINS, Mortimer.—**The Secret of Long Life.** Small crown 8vo, 3s. 6d.

CONNELL, A. K.—**Discontent and Danger in India.** Small crown 8vo, 3s. 6d.

COOKE, Prof. J. P.—**Scientific Culture.** Crown 8vo, 1s.

COOPER, H. J.—**The Art of Furnishing on Rational and Æsthetic Principles.** New and Cheaper Edition. Fcap. 8vo, 1s. 6d.

CORFIELD, Prof., M.D.—**Health.** Crown 8vo, 6s.

CORY, William.—**A Guide to Modern English History.** Part I.—MDCCCXV.-MDCCCXXX. Demy 8vo, 9s. Part II.—MDCCCXXX.-MDCCCXXXV., 15s.

CORY, Col. Arthur.—**The Eastern Menace.** Crown 8vo, 7s. 6d.

COTTERILL, H. B.—**An Introduction to the Study of Poetry.** Crown 8vo, 7s. 6d.

COURTNEY, W. L.—**The Metaphysics of John Stuart Mill.** Crown 8vo, 5s. 6d.

COX, Rev. Sir George W., M.A., Bart.—**A History of Greece from the Earliest Period to the end of the Persian War.** New Edition. 2 vols. Demy 8vo, 36s.

The Mythology of the Aryan Nations. New Edition. Demy 8vo, 16s.

A General History of Greece from the Earliest Period to the Death of Alexander the Great, with a sketch of the subsequent History to the present time. New Edition. Crown 8vo, 7s. 6d.

Tales of Ancient Greece. New Edition. Small crown 8vo, 6s.

School History of Greece. New Edition. With Maps. Fcap. 8vo, 3s. 6d.

The Great Persian War from the History of Herodotus. New Edition. Fcap. 8vo, 3s. 6d.

A Manual of Mythology in the form of Question and Answer. New Edition. Fcap. 8vo, 3s.

An Introduction to the Science of Comparative Mythology and Folk-Lore. Crown 8vo, 9s.

COX, Rev. Sir G. W., M.A., Bart., and JONES, Eustace Hinton.—**Popular Romances of the Middle Ages.** Second Edition, in 1 vol. Crown 8vo, 6s.

COX, Rev. Samuel.—**Salvator Mundi; or, Is Christ the Saviour of all Men?** Seventh Edition. Crown 8vo, 5s.

COX, Rev. Samuel.—continued.
  The Genesis of Evil, and other Sermons, mainly expository. Second Edition. Crown 8vo, 6s.
  A Commentary on the Book of Job. With a Translation. Demy 8vo, 15s.

CRAUFURD, A. H.—Seeking for Light: Sermons. Crown 8vo, 5s.

CRAVEN, Mrs.—A Year's Meditations. Crown 8vo, 6s.

CRAWFURD, Oswald.—Portugal, Old and New. With Illustrations and Maps. New and Cheaper Edition. Crown 8vo, 6s.

CROZIER, John Beattie, M.B.—The Religion of the Future. Crown 8vo, 6s.

Cyclopædia of Common things. Edited by the Rev. Sir GEORGE W. COX, Bart., M.A. With 500 Illustrations. Third Edition. Large post 8vo, 7s. 6d.

DALTON, Rev. John Neale, M.A., R.N.—Sermons to Naval Cadets. Preached on board H.M.S. "Britannia." Second Edition. Small crown 8vo, 3s. 6d.

DAVIDSON, Rev. Samuel, D.D., LL.D.—The New Testament, translated from the Latest Greek Text of Tischendorf. A New and thoroughly revised Edition. Post 8vo, 10s. 6d.
  Canon of the Bible: Its Formation, History, and Fluctuations. Third and revised Edition. Small crown 8vo, 5s.
  The Doctrine of Last Things contained in the New Testament compared with the Notions of the Jews and the Statements of Church Creeds. Small crown 8vo, cloth, 3s. 6d.

DAVIDSON, Thomas.—The Parthenon Frieze, and other Essays. Crown 8vo, 6s.

DAVIES, Rev. J. L., M.A.—Theology and Morality. Essays on Questions of Belief and Practice. Crown 8vo, 7s. 6d.

DAWSON, Geo., M.A.—Prayers, with a Discourse on Prayer. Edited by his Wife. Eighth Edition. Crown 8vo, 6s.
  Sermons on Disputed Points and Special Occasions. Edited by his Wife. Third Edition. Crown 8vo, 6s.
  Sermons on Daily Life and Duty. Edited by his Wife. Third Edition. Crown 8vo, 6s.
  The Authentic Gospel. A New Volume of Sermons. Edited by GEORGE ST. CLAIR. Second Edition. Crown 8vo, 6s.
  Three Books of God: Nature, History, and Scripture. Sermons edited by George St. Clair. Crown 8vo, cloth, 6s.

DE REDCLIFFE, Viscount Stratford.—Why am I a Christian? Fifth Edition. Crown 8vo, 3s.

DESPREZ, Phillip S., B.D.—Daniel and John; or, the Apocalypse of the Old and that of the New Testament. Demy 8vo, 12s.

Kegan Paul, Trench & Co.'s Publications. 9

DIDON, Rev. Father.—Science without God. Conferences by. Translated from the French by ROSA CORDER. Crown 8vo, cloth, 5s.

DOWDEN, Edward, LL.D.—Shakspere: a Critical Study of his Mind and Art. Sixth Edition. Post 8vo, 12s.

Studies in Literature, 1789-1877. Second and Cheaper Edition. Large post 8vo, 6s.

DREWRY, G. O., M.D.—The Common-Sense Management of the Stomach. Fifth Edition. Fcap. 8vo, 2s. 6d.

DREWRY, G. O., M.D., and BARTLETT, H. C., Ph.D.—Cup and Platter; or, Notes on Food and its Effects. New and Cheaper Edition. Small 8vo, 1s. 6d.

DUFFIELD, A. J.—Don Quixote: his Critics and Commentators. With a brief account of the minor works of MIGUEL DE CERVANTES SAAVEDRA, and a statement of the aim and end of the greatest of them all. A handy book for general readers Crown 8vo, 3s. 6d.

DU MONCEL, Count.—The Telephone, the Microphone, and the Phonograph. With 74 Illustrations. Second Edition. Small crown 8vo, 5s.

EDGEWORTH, F. Y.—Mathematical Psychics. An Essay on the Application of Mathematics to Social Science. Demy 8vo, 7s. 6d.

EDIS, Robert W., F.S.A., etc.—Decoration and Furniture of Town Houses: a Series of Cantor Lectures, delivered before the Society of Arts, 1880. Amplified and Enlarged. With 29 Full-page Illustrations and numerous Sketches. Second Edition. Square 8vo, 12s. 6d.

Educational Code of the Prussian Nation, in its Present Form. In accordance with the Decisions of the Common Provincial Law, and with those of Recent Legislation. Crown 8vo, 2s. 6d.

Education Library. Edited by PHILIP MAGNUS:—

An Introduction to the History of Educational Theories. By OSCAR BROWNING, M.A. Second Edition. 3s. 6d.

John Amos Comenius: his Life and Educational Work. By Prof. S. S. LAURIE, A.M. 3s. 6d.

Old Greek Education. By the Rev. Prof. MAHAFFY, M.A. 3s. 6d.

Eighteenth Century Essays. Selected and Edited by AUSTIN DOBSON. With a Miniature Frontispiece by R. Caldecott. Parchment Library Edition, 6s.; vellum, 7s. 6d.

ELSDALE, Henry.—Studies in Tennyson's Idylls. Crown 8vo, 5s.

ELYOT, Sir Thomas.—**The Boke named the Gouernour.** Edited from the First Edition of 1531 by HENRY HERBERT STEPHEN CROFT, M.A., Barrister-at-Law. With Portraits of Sir Thomas and Lady Elyot, copied by permission of her Majesty from Holbein's Original Drawings at Windsor Castle. 2 vols. Fcap. 4to, 50s.

Eranus. A Collection of Exercises in the Alcaic and Sapphic Metres. Edited by F. W. CORNISH, Assistant Master at Eton. Crown 8vo, 2s.

EVANS, Mark.—**The Story of Our Father's Love,** told to Children. Fifth and Cheaper Edition. With Four Illustrations. Fcap. 8vo, 1s. 6d.

A Book of Common Prayer and Worship for Household Use, compiled exclusively from the Holy Scriptures. Second Edition. Fcap. 8vo, 1s.

The Gospel of Home Life. Crown 8vo, 4s. 6d.

The King's Story-Book. In Three Parts. Fcap. 8vo, 1s. 6d. each.

*** Parts I. and II. with Eight Illustrations and Two Picture Maps, now ready.

"Fan Kwae" at Canton before Treaty Days 1825-1844. By an old Resident. With frontispiece. Crown 8vo, cloth, 5s.

FELKIN, H. M.—**Technical Education in a Saxon Town.** Published for the City and Guilds of London Institute for the Advancement of Technical Education. Demy 8vo, 2s.

FLOREDICE, W. H.—**A Month among the Mere Irish.** Small crown 8vo, 5s.

Folkestone Ritual Case: the Arguments, Proceedings, Judgment, and Report. Demy 8vo, 25s.

FORMBY, Rev. Henry.—**Ancient Rome and its Connection with the Christian Religion:** An Outline of the History of the City from its First Foundation down to the Erection of the Chair of St. Peter, A.D. 42-47. With numerous Illustrations of Ancient Monuments, Sculpture, and Coinage, and of the Antiquities of the Christian Catacombs. Royal 4to, cloth extra, £2 10s.; roxburgh half-morocco, £2 12s. 6d.

FRASER, Donald.—**Exchange Tables of Sterling and Indian Rupee Currency,** upon a new and extended system, embracing Values from One Farthing to One Hundred Thousand Pounds, and at rates progressing, in Sixteenths of a Penny, from 1s. 9d. to 2s. 3d. per Rupee. Royal 8vo, 10s. 6d.

FRISWELL, J. Hain.—**The Better Self.** Essays for Home Life. Crown 8vo, 6s.

GARDINER, Samuel R., and J. BASS MULLINGER, M.A.—Introduction to the Study of English History. Large Crown 8vo, 9s.

GARDNER, Dorsey.—Quatre Bras, Ligny, and Waterloo. A Narrative of the Campaign in Belgium, 1815. With Maps and Plans. Demy 8vo, 16s.

GARDNER, J., M.D.—Longevity : The Means of Prolonging Life after Middle Age. Fourth Edition, revised and enlarged. Small crown 8vo, 4s.

GEDDES, James.—History of the Administration of John de Witt, Grand Pensionary of Holland. Vol. I. 1623-1654. With Portrait. Demy 8vo, 15s.

GENNA, E.—Irresponsible Philanthropists. Being some Chapters on the Employment of Gentlewomen. Small crown 8vo, 2s. 6d.

GEORGE, Henry.—Progress and Poverty : an Inquiry into the Causes of Industrial Depressions, and of Increase of Want with Increase of Wealth. The Remedy. Second Edition. Post 8vo, 7s. 6d. Also a cheap edition. Sewed, price 6d.

GILBERT, Mrs.—Autobiography and other Memorials. Edited by Josiah Gilbert. Third and Cheaper Edition With Steel Portrait and several Wood Engravings. Crown 8vo, 7s. 6d.

GLOVER, F., M.A.—Exempla Latina. A First Construing Book, with Short Notes, Lexicon, and an Introduction to the Analysis of Sentences. Fcap. 8vo, 2s.

GODWIN, William.—The Genius of Christianity Unveiled. Being Essays never before published. Edited, with a Preface, by C. Kegan Paul. Crown 8vo, 7s. 6d.

GOLDSMID, Sir Francis Henry, Bart., Q.C., M.P.—Memoir of. With Portrait. Second Edition, revised. Crown 8vo, 6s.

GOODENOUGH, Commodore J. G.—Memoir of, with Extracts from his Letters and Journals. Edited by his Widow. With Steel Engraved Portrait. Square 8vo, 5s.

*** Also a Library Edition with Maps, Woodcuts, and Steel Engraved Portrait. Square post 8vo, 14s.

GOSSE, Edmund W.—Studies in the Literature of Northern Europe. With a Frontispiece designed and etched by Alma Tadema. New and cheaper edition. Large crown 8vo, 6s.

GOULD, Rev. S. Baring, M.A.—The Vicar of Morwenstow : a Memoir of the Rev. R. S. Hawker. With Portrait. Third Edition, revised. Square post 8vo, 10s. 6d.

Germany, Present and Past. New and Cheaper Edition. Large crown 8vo, 7s. 6d.

GOWAN, Major Walter E.—A. Ivanoff's Russian Grammar. (16th Edition.) Translated, enlarged, and arranged for use of Students of the Russian Language. Demy 8vo, 6s.

GRAHAM, William, M.A.—The Creed of Science, Religious, Moral, and Social. Demy 8vo, 12s.

GRIFFITH, Thomas, A.M.—The Gospel of the Divine Life: a Study of the Fourth Evangelist. Demy 8vo, 14s.

GRIMLEY, Rev. H. N., M.A.—Tremadoc Sermons, chiefly on the Spiritual Body, the Unseen World, and the Divine Humanity. Third Edition. Crown 8vo, 6s.

GRÜNER, M.L.—Studies of Blast Furnace Phenomena. Translated by L. D. B. GORDON, F.R.S.E., F.G.S. Demy 8vo, 7s. 6d.

GURNEY, Rev. Archer.—Words of Faith and Cheer. A Mission of Instruction and Suggestion. Crown 8vo, 6s.

HAECKEL, Prof. Ernst.—The History of Creation. Translation revised by Professor E. RAY LANKESTER, M.A., F.R.S. With Coloured Plates and Genealogical Trees of the various groups of both Plants and Animals. 2 vols. Second Edition. Post 8vo, 32s.

The History of the Evolution of Man. With numerous Illustrations. 2 vols. Post 8vo, 32s.

Freedom in Science and Teaching. With a Prefatory Note by T. H. HUXLEY, F.R.S. Crown 8vo, 5s.

HALF-CROWN SERIES :—

Sister Dora : a Biography. By MARGARET LONSDALE.

True Words for Brave Men : a Book for Soldiers and Sailors. By the late CHARLES KINGSLEY.

An Inland Voyage. By R. L. STEVENSON.

Travels with a Donkey. By R. L. STEVENSON.

A Nook in the Apennines. By LEADER SCOTT.

Notes of Travel : being Extracts from the Journals of Count VON MOLTKE.

Letters from Russia. By Count VON MOLTKE.

English Sonnets. Collected and Arranged by J. DENNIS.

Lyrics of Love. From Shakespeare to Tennyson. Selected and Arranged by W. D. ADAMS.

London Lyrics. By F. LOCKER.

Home Songs for Quiet Hours. By the Rev. Canon R. H. BAYNES.

HALLECK'S International Law; or, Rules Regulating the Intercourse of States in Peace and War. A New Edition, revised, with Notes and Cases by Sir SHERSTON BAKER, Bart. 2 vols. Demy 8vo, 38s.

HARTINGTON, The Right Hon. the Marquis of, M.P.—Election Speeches in 1879 and 1880. With Address to the Electors of North-East Lancashire. Crown 8vo, 3s. 6d.

HAWEIS, Rev. H. R., M.A.—**Current Coin.** Materialism—The Devil—Crime—Drunkenness—Pauperism—Emotion—Recreation—The Sabbath. Fourth and Cheaper Edition. Crown 8vo, 5s.

Arrows in the Air. Fourth and Cheaper Edition. Crown 8vo, 5s.

Speech in Season. Fifth and Cheaper Edition. Crown 8vo, 5s.

Thoughts for the Times. Twelfth and Cheaper Edition. Crown 8vo, 5s.

Unsectarian Family Prayers. New and Cheaper Edition. Fcap. 8vo, 1s. 6d.

HAWKINS, Edwards Comerford.—**Spirit and Form.** Sermons preached in the Parish Church of Leatherhead. Crown 8vo, 6s.

HAYES, A. H., Junr.—**New Colorado, and the Santa Fé Trail.** With Map and 60 Illustrations. Crown 8vo, 9s.

HELLWALD, Baron F. Von.—**The Russians in Central Asia.** A Critical Examination, down to the Present Time, of the Geography and History of Central Asia. Translated by Lieut.-Col. THEODORE WIRGMAN, LL.B. With Map. Large post 8vo, 12s.

HENRY, Philip.—**Diaries and Letters of.** Edited by Matthew Henry Lee, M.A. Large crown 8vo, cloth, 7s. 6d.

HIDE, Albert.—**The Age to Come.** Small crown 8vo, cloth, 2s. 6d.

HIME, Major H. W. L., R.A.—**Wagnerism : A Protest.** Crown 8vo, cloth, 2s. 6d.

HINTON, J.—**The Place of the Physician.** To which is added Essays on the Law of Human Life, and on the Relations between Organic and Inorganic Worlds. Second Edition. Crown 8vo, 3s. 6d.

Philosophy and Religion. Selections from the MSS. of the late JAMES HINTON. Edited by CAROLINE HADDON. Crown 8vo, 5s.

Physiology for Practical Use. By Various Writers. With 50 Illustrations. Third and Cheaper Edition. Crown 8vo, 5s.

An Atlas of Diseases of the Membrana Tympani. With Descriptive Text. Post 8vo, £10 10s.

The Questions of Aural Surgery. With Illustrations. 2 vols. Post 8vo, 12s. 6d.

Chapters on the Art of Thinking, and other Essays. With an Introduction by SHADWORTH HODGSON. Edited by C. H. HINTON. Crown 8vo, 8s. 6d.

The Mystery of Pain. New Edition. Fcap. 8vo, 1s.

Life and Letters. Edited by ELLICE HOPKINS, with an Introduction by Sir W. W. GULL, Bart., and Portrait engraved on Steel by C. H. JEENS. Fourth Edition. Crown 8vo, 8s. 6d.

HOOPER, Mary.—**Little Dinners: How to Serve them with Elegance and Economy.** Seventeenth Edition. Crown 8vo, 2s. 6d.

Cookery for Invalids, Persons of Delicate Digestion, and Children. Third Edition. Crown 8vo, 2s. 6d.

Every-Day Meals. Being Economical and Wholesome Recipes for Breakfast, Luncheon, and Supper. Fifth Edition. Crown 8vo, 2s. 6d.

HOPKINS, Ellice.—**Life and Letters of James Hinton,** with an Introduction by Sir W. W. GULL, Bart., and Portrait engraved on Steel by C. H. JEENS. Fourth Edition. Crown 8vo, 8s. 6d.

Work amongst Working Men. Fourth edition. Crown 8vo, cloth, 3s. 6d.

HORNER, The Misses.—**Walks in Florence.** A New and thoroughly Revised Edition. 2 vols. Crown 8vo. Limp cloth. With Illustrations.
VOL. I.—Churches, Streets, and Palaces. 10s. 6d.
VOL. II.—Public Galleries and Museums. 5s.

HOSPITALIER, E.—**The Modern Applications of Electricity.** Translated and Enlarged by JULIUS MAIER, Ph.D. With 170 Illustrations. Demy 8vo, 16s.

Household Readings on Prophecy. By a Layman. Small crown 8vo, 3s. 6d.

HUGHES, Henry.—**The Redemption of the World.** Crown 8vo, 3s. 6d.

HULL, Edmund C. P.—**The European in India.** With a Medical Guide for Anglo-Indians. By R. S. MAIR, M.D., F.R.C.S.E. Third Edition, Revised and Corrected. Post 8vo, 6s.

HUNTINGFORD, Rev. E., D.C.L.—**The Apocalypse.** With a Commentary and Introductory Essay. Demy 8vo, 9s.

HUTTON, Arthur, M.A.—**The Anglican Ministry:** Its Nature and Value in relation to the Catholic Priesthood. With a Preface by His Eminence Cardinal Newman. Demy 8vo, 14s.

HUTTON, Rev. C. F.—**Unconscious Testimony;** or, the Silent Witness of the Hebrew to the Truth of the Historical Scriptures. Crown 8vo, cloth, 2s. 6d.

JENKINS, E., and RAYMOND, J.—**The Architect's Legal Handbook.** Third Edition, Revised. Crown 8vo, 6s.

JENKINS, Rev. R. C., M.A.—**The Privilege of Peter,** and the Claims of the Roman Church confronted with the Scriptures, the Councils, and the Testimony of the Popes themselves. Fcap. 8vo, 3s. 6d.

JERVIS, Rev. W. Henley.—**The Gallican Church and the Revolution.** A Sequel to the History of the Church of France, from the Concordat of Bologna to the Revolution. Demy 8vo, 18s.

JOEL, L.—**A Consul's Manual and Shipowner's and Shipmaster's Practical Guide in their Transactions Abroad.** With Definitions of Nautical, Mercantile, and Legal Terms; a Glossary of Mercantile Terms in English, French, German, Italian, and Spanish; Tables of the Money, Weights, and Measures of the Principal Commercial Nations and their Equivalents in British Standards; and Forms of Consular and Notarial Acts. Demy 8vo, 12s.

JOHNSTONE, C. F., M.A.—**Historical Abstracts:** being Outlines of the History of some of the less known States of Europe. Crown 8vo, 7s. 6d.

JOLLY, William, F.R.S.E., etc.—**The Life of John Duncan, Scotch Weaver and Botanist.** With Sketches of his Friends and Notices of his Times. Large crown 8vo, with etched portrait, cloth, 9s.

JONCOURT, Madame Marie de.—**Wholesome Cookery.** Crown 8vo, 3s. 6d.

JONES, C. A.—**The Foreign Freaks of Five Friends.** With 30 Illustrations. Crown 8vo, 6s.

JONES, Lucy.—**Puddings and Sweets:** being Three Hundred and Sixty-five Receipts approved by experience. Crown 8vo, 2s. 6d.

JOYCE, P. W., LL.D., etc.—**Old Celtic Romances.** Translated from the Gaelic. Crown 8vo, 7s. 6d.

JOYNES, J. L.—**The Adventures of a Tourist in Ireland.** Second edition. Small crown 8vo, cloth, 2s. 6d.

KAUFMANN, Rev. M., B.A.—**Socialism:** its Nature, its Dangers, and its Remedies considered. Crown 8vo, 7s. 6d.

Utopias; or, Schemes of Social Improvement, from Sir Thomas More to Karl Marx. Crown 8vo, 5s.

KAY, Joseph.—**Free Trade in Land.** Edited by his Widow. With Preface by the Right Hon. JOHN BRIGHT, M.P. Sixth Edition. Crown 8vo, 5s.

KEMPIS, Thomas à.—**Of the Imitation of Christ.** Parchment Library Edition, 6s.; or vellum, 7s. 6d. The Red Line Edition, fcap. 8vo, red edges, 2s. 6d. The Cabinet Edition, small 8vo, cloth limp, 1s.; cloth boards, red edges, 1s. 6d. The Miniature Edition, red edges, 32mo, 1s.

*** All the above Editions may be had in various extra bindings.

KENT, C.—**Corona Catholica ad Petri successoris Pedes Oblata. De Summi Pontificis Leonis XIII. Assumptione Epigramma.** In Quinquaginta Linguis. Fcap. 4to, 15s.

KERNER, Dr. A.—**Flowers and their Unbidden Guests.** Translation edited by W. OGLE, M.A., M.D. With Illustrations. Square 8vo, 9s.

KETTLEWELL, Rev. S.—**Thomas à Kempis and the Brothers of Common Life.** 2 vols. With Frontispieces. Demy 8vo, 30s.

KIDD, Joseph, M.D.—**The Laws of Therapeutics**; or, the Science and Art of Medicine. Second Edition. Crown 8vo, 6s.

KINAHAN, G. Henry, M.R.I.A.—**The Geology of Ireland,** with numerous Illustrations and a Geological Map of Ireland. Square 8vo, 15s.

KINGSFORD, Anna, M.D.—**The Perfect Way in Diet.** A Treatise advocating a Return to the Natural and Ancient Food of our Race. Small crown 8vo, 2s.

KINGSLEY, Charles, M.A.—**Letters and Memories of his Life.** Edited by his Wife. With two Steel Engraved Portraits, and Vignettes on Wood. Eleventh Cabinet Edition. 2 vols. Crown 8vo, 12s.

All Saints' Day, and other Sermons. Edited by the Rev. W. HARRISON. Third Edition. Crown 8vo, 7s. 6d.

True Words for Brave Men. A Book for Soldiers' and Sailors' Libraries. Eighth Edition. Crown 8vo, 2s. 6d.

KNIGHT, Professor W.—**Studies in Philosophy and Literature.** Large Post 8vo, 7s. 6d.

KNOX, Alexander A.—**The New Playground**; or, Wanderings in Algeria. New and cheaper edition. Large crown 8vo, 6s.

LAURIE, S. S.—**The Training of Teachers,** and other Educational Papers. Crown 8vo, 7s. 6d.

LEE, Rev. F. G., D.C.L.—**The Other World**; or, Glimpses of the Supernatural. 2 vols. A New Edition. Crown 8vo, 15s.

LEWIS, Edward Dillon.—**A Draft Code of Criminal Law and Procedure.** Demy 8vo, 21s.

LINDSAY, W. Lauder, M.D.—**Mind in the Lower Animals in Health and Disease.** 2 vols. Demy 8vo, 32s.
Vol. I.—Mind in Health. Vol. II.—Mind in Disease.

LLOYD, Walter.—**The Hope of the World:** An Essay on Universal Redemption. Crown 8vo, 5s.

LONSDALE, Margaret.—**Sister Dora:** a Biography. With Portrait. Twenty-fifth Edition. Crown 8vo, 2s. 6d.

LORIMER, Peter, D.D.—**John Knox and the Church of England.** His Work in her Pulpit, and his Influence upon her Liturgy, Articles, and Parties. Demy 8vo, 12s.

John Wiclif and his English Precursors. By GERHARD VICTOR LECHLER. Translated from the German, with additional Notes. New and Cheaper Edition. Demy 8vo, 10s. 6d.

Kegan Paul, Trench & Co.'s Publications. 17

LOWDER, Charles.—**A Biography.** By the Author of "St. Teresa." New and Cheaper Edition. Crown 8vo. With Portrait. 3s. 6d.

MACHIAVELLI, Niccoli. **The Prince.** Translated from the Italian by N. H. T. Small crown 8vo, printed on hand-made paper, bevelled boards, 6s.

MACKENZIE, Alexander.—**How India is Governed.** Being an Account of England's work in India. Small crown 8vo, 2s.

MACNAUGHT, Rev. John.—**Cœna Domini:** An Essay on the Lord's Supper, its Primitive Institution, Apostolic Uses, and Subsequent History. Demy 8vo, 14s.

MAGNUS, Mrs.—**About the Jews since Bible Times.** From the Babylonian Exile till the English Exodus. Small crown 8vo, 6s.

MAIR, R. S., M.D., F.R.C.S.E.—**The Medical Guide for Anglo-Indians.** Being a Compendium of Advice to Europeans in India, relating to the Preservation and Regulation of Health. With a Supplement on the Management of Children in India. Second Edition. Crown 8vo, limp cloth, 3s. 6d.

MANNING, His Eminence Cardinal.—**The True Story of the Vatican Council.** Crown 8vo, 5s.

Many Voices. Crown 8vo, cloth extra, red edges, 6s.

MARKHAM, Capt. Albert Hastings, R.N.—**The Great Frozen Sea:** A Personal Narrative of the Voyage of the *Alert* during the Arctic Expedition of 1875-6. With 6 Full-page Illustrations, 2 Maps, and 27 Woodcuts. Fifth and Cheaper Edition. Crown 8vo, 6s.

A Polar Reconnaissance: being the Voyage of the *Isbjörn* to Novaya Zemlya in 1879. With 10 Illustrations. Demy 8vo, 16s.

Marriage and Maternity; or, Scripture Wives and Mothers. Small crown 8vo, 4s. 6d.

MARTINEAU, Gertrude.—**Outline Lessons on Morals.** Small crown 8vo, 3s. 6d.

McGRATH, Terence.—**Pictures from Ireland.** New and Cheaper Edition. Crown 8vo, 2s.

MEREDITH, M.A.—**Theotokos, the Example for Woman.** Dedicated, by permission, to Lady AGNES WOOD. Revised by the Venerable Archdeacon DENISON. 32mo, limp cloth, 1s. 6d.

MILLER, Edward.—**The History and Doctrines of Irvingism;** or, the so-called Catholic and Apostolic Church. 2 vols. Large post 8vo, 25s.

The Church in Relation to the State. Large crown 8vo, 7s. 6d.

MILNE, James.—**Tables of Exchange** for the Conversion of Sterling Money into Indian and Ceylon Currency, at Rates from 1s. 8d. to 2s. 3d. per Rupee. Second Edition. Demy 8vo, £2 2s.

MINCHIN, J. G.—**Bulgaria since the War:** Notes of a Tour in the Autumn of 1879. Small crown 8vo, 3s. 6d.

c

MIVART, St. George.—**Nature and Thought:** An Introduction to a Natural Philosophy. Demy 8vo, cloth, 10s. 6d.

MOCKLER, E.—**A Grammar of the Baloochee Language,** as it is spoken in Makran (Ancient Gedrosia), in the Persia-Arabic and Roman characters. Fcap. 8vo, 5s.

MOLESWORTH, Rev. W. Nassau, M.A.—**History of the Church of England from 1660.** Large crown 8vo, 7s. 6d.

MORELL, J. R.—**Euclid Simplified in Method and Language.** Being a Manual of Geometry. Compiled from the most important French Works, approved by the University of Paris and the Minister of Public Instruction. Fcap. 8vo, 2s. 6d.

MORSE, E. S., Ph.D.—**First Book of Zoology.** With numerous Illustrations. New and Cheaper Edition. Crown 8vo, 2s. 6d.

MURPHY, John Nicholas.—**The Chair of Peter;** or, the Papacy considered in its Institution, Development, and Organization, and in the Benefits which for over Eighteen Centuries it has conferred on Mankind. Demy 8vo, cloth, 18s.

MUNRO, Major-Gen. Sir Thomas, Bart., K.C.B., Governor of Madras.—SELECTIONS FROM HIS MINUTES AND OTHER OFFICIAL WRITINGS. Edited, with an Introductory Memoir, by Sir ALEXANDER ARBUTHNOT, K.C.S.I., C.I.E. 2 vols. Demy 8vo, 30s.

NELSON, J. H., M.A.—**A Prospectus of the Scientific Study of the Hindû Law.** Demy 8vo, 9s.

NEWMAN, J. H., D.D.—**Characteristics from the Writings of.** Being Selections from his various Works. Arranged with the Author's personal Approval. Sixth Edition. With Portrait. Crown 8vo, 6s.

*** A Portrait of Cardinal Newman, mounted for framing, can be had, 2s. 6d.

New Werther. By LOKI. Small crown 8vo, 2s. 6d.

NICHOLSON, Edward Byron.—**The Gospel according to the Hebrews.** Its Fragments Translated and Annotated with a Critical Analysis of the External and Internal Evidence relating to it. Demy 8vo, 9s. 6d.

A New Commentary on the Gospel according to Matthew. Demy 8vo, 12s.

The Rights of an Animal. Crown 8vo, 3s. 6d.

NICOLS, Arthur, F.G.S., F.R.G.S.—**Chapters from the Physical History of the Earth:** an Introduction to Geology and Palæontology. With numerous Illustrations. Crown 8vo, 5s.

NOPS, Marianne.—**Class Lessons on Euclid.** Part I. containing the First two Books of the Elements. Crown 8vo, cloth, 2s. 6d.

Notes on St. Paul's Epistle to the Galatians. For Readers of the Authorised Version or the Original Greek. Demy 8vo, 2s. 6d.

Nuces: EXERCISES ON THE SYNTAX OF THE PUBLIC SCHOOL LATIN PRIMER. New Edition in Three Parts. Crown 8vo, each 1s.
∗ The Three Parts can also be had bound together, 3s.

OATES, Frank, F.R.G.S.—Matabele Land and the Victoria Falls. A Naturalist's Wanderings in the Interior of South Africa. Edited by C. G. OATES, B.A. With numerous Illustrations and 4 Maps. Demy 8vo, 21s.

OGLE, W., M.D., F.R.C.P.—Aristotle on the Parts of Animals. Translated, with Introduction and Notes. Royal 8vo, 12s. 6d.

O'MEARA, Kathleen.—Frederic Ozanam, Professor of the Sorbonne: His Life and Work. Second Edition. Crown 8vo, 7s. 6d.

Henri Perreyve and his Counsels to the Sick. Small crown 8vo, 5s.

OSBORNE, Rev. W. A.—The Revised Version of the New Testament. A Critical Commentary, with Notes upon the Text. Crown 8vo, cloth, 5s.

OTTLEY, H. Bickersteth.—The Great Dilemma. Christ His Own Witness or His Own Accuser. Six Lectures. Second Edition. Crown 8vo, cloth, 3s. 6d.

Our Public Schools—Eton, Harrow, Winchester, Rugby, Westminster, Marlborough, The Charterhouse. Crown 8vo, 6s.

OWEN, F. M.—John Keats: a Study. Crown 8vo, 6s.

OWEN, Rev. Robert, B.D.—Sanctorale Catholicum; or, Book of Saints. With Notes, Critical, Exegetical, and Historical. Demy 8vo, 18s.

An Essay on the Communion of Saints. Including an Examination of the Cultus Sanctorum. 2s.

OXENHAM, Rev. F. Nutcombe.—What is the Truth as to Everlasting Punishment. Part II. Being an Historical Inquiry into the Witness and Weight of certain Anti-Origenist Councils. Crown 8vo, 2s. 6d.
∗ Parts I. and II. complete in one volume, 7s.

OXONIENSES.—Romanism, Protestantism, Anglicanism. Being a Layman's View of some questions of the Day. Together with Remarks on Dr. Littledale's "Plain Reasons against joining the Church of Rome." Crown 8vo, cloth, 3s. 6d.

PALMER, the late William.—Notes of a Visit to Russia in 1840–1841. Selected and arranged by JOHN H. CARDINAL NEWMAN, with portrait. Crown 8vo, cloth, 8s. 6d.

Parchment Library. Choicely Printed on hand-made paper, limp parchment antique, 6s.; vellum, 7s. 6d. each volume.

French Lyrics. Selected and Annotated by GEORGE SAINTSBURY. With a minature frontispiece designed and etched by H. G. Glindoni.

Parchment Library.—*continued*.

The Fables of Mr. John Gay. With Memoir by AUSTIN DOBSON, and an etched portrait from an unfinished Oil Sketch by Sir Godfrey Kneller.

Select Letters of Percy Bysshe Shelley. Edited, with an Introduction, by RICHARD GARNETT.

The Christian Year. Thoughts in Verse for the Sundays and Holy Days throughout the Year. With Miniature Portrait of the Rev. J. Keble, after a Drawing by G. Richmond, R.A.

Shakspere's Works. Now publishing in Twelve Monthly Volumes.

Eighteenth Century Essays. Selected and Edited by AUSTIN DOBSON. With a Miniature Frontispiece by R. Caldecott.

Q. Horati Flacci Opera. Edited by F. A. CORNISH, Assistant Master at Eton. With a Frontispiece after a design by L. ALMA TADEMA, etched by Leopold Lowenstam.

Edgar Allan Poe's Poems. With an Essay on his Poetry by ANDREW LANG, and a Frontispiece by Linley Sambourne.

Shakspere's Sonnets. Edited by EDWARD DOWDEN. With a Frontispiece etched by Leopold Lowenstam, after the Death Mask.

English Odes. Selected by EDMUND W. GOSSE. With Frontispiece on India paper by Hamo Thornycroft, A.R.A.

Of the Imitation of Christ. By THOMAS À KEMPIS. A revised Translation. With Frontispiece on India paper, from a Design by W. B. Richmond.

Tennyson's The Princess: a Medley. With a Miniature Frontispiece by H. M. Paget, and a Tailpiece in Outline by Gordon Browne.

Poems: Selected from PERCY BYSSHE SHELLEY. Dedicated to Lady Shelley. With a Preface by RICHARD GARNETT and a Miniature Frontispiece.

Tennyson's "In Memoriam." With a Miniature Portrait in *eau-forte* by Le Rat, after a Photograph by the late Mrs. Cameron.

PARKER, Joseph, D.D.—The Paraclete: An Essay on the Personality and Ministry of the Holy Ghost, with some reference to current discussions. Second Edition. Demy 8vo, 12*s*.

PARR, Capt. H. Hallam, C.M.G.—A Sketch of the Kafir and Zulu Wars: Guadana to Isandhlwana. With Maps. Small crown 8vo, 5*s*.

PARSLOE, Joseph.—Our Railways. Sketches, Historical and Descriptive. With Practical Information as to Fares and Rates, etc., and a Chapter on Railway Reform. Crown 8vo, 6*s*.

Kegan Paul, Trench & Co.'s Publications. 21

PATTISON, Mrs. Mark.—**The Renaissance of Art in France.** With Nineteen Steel Engravings. 2 vols. Demy 8vo, 32*s.*

PEARSON, Rev. S.—**Week-day Living.** A Book for Young Men and Women. Second Edition. Crown 8vo, 5*s.*

PENRICE, Maj. J., B.A.—**A Dictionary and Glossary of the Ko-ran.** With Copious Grammatical References and Explanations of the Text. 4to, 21*s.*

PESCHEL, Dr. Oscar.—**The Races of Man and their Geographical Distribution.** Large crown 8vo, 9*s.*

PETERS, F. H.—**The Nicomachean Ethics of Aristotle.** Translated by. Crown 8vo, 6*s.*

PIDGEON, D.—**An Engineer's Holiday**; or, Notes of a Round Trip from Long. 0° to 0°. New and cheaper edition. Large crown 8vo, 7*s.* 6*d.*

PLAYFAIR, Lieut.-Col.—**Travels in the Footsteps of Bruce in Algeria and Tunis.** Illustrated by facsimiles of Bruce's original Drawings, Photographs, Maps, etc. Royal 4to cloth, bevelled boards, gilt leaves, £3 3*s.*

POLLOCK, Frederick.—**Spinoza, his Life and Philosophy.** Demy 8vo, 16*s.*

POLLOCK, W. H.—**Lectures on French Poets.** Delivered at the Royal Institution. Small crown 8vo, 5*s.*

POOR, Laura E.—**Sanskrit and its Kindred Literatures.** Studies in Comparative Mythology. Small crown 8vo, 5*s.*

PRICE, Prof. Bonamy.—**Currency and Banking.** Crown 8vo, 6*s.*

Chapters on Practical Political Economy. Being the Substance of Lectures delivered before the University of Oxford. New and Cheaper Edition. Large post 8vo, 5*s.*

Proteus and Amadeus. A Correspondence. Edited by AUBREY DE VERE. Crown 8vo, 5*s.*

Pulpit Commentary, The. (Old Testament Series.) Edited by the Rev. J. S. EXELL and the Rev. Canon H. D. M. SPENCE.

 Genesis. By the Rev. T. WHITELAW, M.A.; with Homilies by the Very Rev. J. F. MONTGOMERY, D.D., Rev. Prof. R. A. REDFORD, M.A., LL.B., Rev. F. HASTINGS, Rev. W. ROBERTS, M.A. An Introduction to the Study of the Old Testament by the Rev. Canon FARRAR, D.D., F.R.S.; and Introductions to the Pentateuch by the Right Rev. H. COTTERILL, D.D., and Rev. T. WHITELAW, M.A. Seventh Edition. 1 vol., 15*s.*

 Exodus. By the Rev. Canon RAWLINSON. With Homilies by Rev. J. ORR, Rev. D. YOUNG, Rev. C. A. GOODHART, Rev. J. URQUHART, and the Rev. H. T. ROBJOHNS. Third Edition. 16*s.*

Pulpit Commentary, The.—*continued*.
> **Leviticus.** By the Rev. Prebendary MEYRICK, M.A. With Introductions by the Rev. R. COLLINS, Rev. Professor A. CAVE, and Homilies by Rev. Prof. REDFORD, LL.B., Rev. J. A. MACDONALD, Rev. W. CLARKSON, Rev. S. R. ALDRIDGE, LL.B., and Rev. McCHEYNE EDGAR. Third Edition. 15s.
>
> **Numbers.** By the Rev. R. WINTERBOTHAM, LL.B.; with Homilies by the Rev. Professor W. BINNIE, D.D., Rev. E. S. PROUT, M.A., Rev. D. YOUNG, Rev. J. WAITE, and an Introduction by the Rev. THOMAS WHITELAW, M.A. Fourth Edition. 15s.
>
> **Deuteronomy.** By the Rev. W. L. ALEXANDER, D.D. With Homilies by Rev. C. Clemance, D.D., Rev. J. Orr, B.D., Rev. R. M. Edgar, M.A., Rev. D. Davies, M.A. Second edition. 15s.
>
> **Joshua.** By Rev. J. J. LIAS, M.A.; with Homilies by Rev. S. R. ALDRIDGE, LL.B., Rev. R. GLOVER, REV. E. DE PRESSENSÉ, D.D., Rev. J. WAITE, B.A., Rev. F. W. ADENEY, M.A.; and an Introduction by the Rev. A. PLUMMER, M.A., D.D. Fourth Edition. 12s. 6d.
>
> **Judges and Ruth.** By the Right Rev. Lord A. C. HERVEY, D.D., and Rev. J. MORRISON, D.D.; with Homilies by Rev. A. F. MUIR, M.A., Rev. W. F. ADENEY, M.A., Rev. W. M. STATHAM, and Rev. Professor J. THOMSON, M.A. Fourth Edition. 10s. 6d.
>
> **1 Samuel.** By the Very Rev. R. P. SMITH, D.D.; with Homilies by Rev. DONALD FRASER, D.D., Rev. Prof. CHAPMAN, and Rev. B. DALE. Fifth Edition. 15s.
>
> **1 Kings.** By the Rev. JOSEPH HAMMOND, LL.B. With Homilies by the Rev. E. DE PRESSENSÉ, D.D., Rev. J. WAITE, B.A., Rev. A. ROWLAND, LL.B., Rev. J. A. MACDONALD, and Rev. J. URQUHART. Third Edition. 15s.
>
> **Ezra, Nehemiah, and Esther.** By Rev. Canon G. RAWLINSON, M.A.; with Homilies by Rev. Prof. J. R. THOMSON, M.A., Rev. Prof. R. A. REDFORD, LL.B., M.A., Rev. W. S. LEWIS, M.A., Rev. J. A. MACDONALD, Rev. A. MACKENNAL, B.A., Rev. W. CLARKSON, B.A., Rev. F. HASTINGS, Rev. W. DINWIDDIE, LL.B., Rev. Prof. ROWLANDS, B.A., Rev. G. WOOD, B.A., Rev. Prof. P. C. BARKER, LL.B., M.A., and the Rev. J. S. EXELL. Fifth Edition. 1 vol., 12s. 6d.

Pulpit Commentary, The. (New Testament Series.)
> **St. Mark.** By Very Dean BICKERSTETH, D.D.; with Homilies by Rev. Prof. THOMSON, M.A., Rev. Prof. GIVEN, M.A., Rev. Prof. Johnson, M.A., Rev. A. ROWLAND, B.A., LL.B., Rev. A. MUIR, and Rev. R. GREEN. 2 vols. Second Edition. 21s.

Punjaub, The, and North-Western Frontier of India. By an Old Punjaubee. Crown 8vo, 5s.

Rabbi Jeshua. An Eastern Story. Crown 8vo, 3s. 6d.

Kegan Paul, Trench & Co.'s Publications. 23

RADCLIFFE, Frank R. Y.—The New Politicus. Small crown 8vo, 2s. 6d.

RAVENSHAW, John Henry, B.C.S.—Gaur: Its Ruins and Inscriptions. Edited by his Widow. With 44 Photographic Illustrations, and 25 facsimiles of Inscriptions. Royal 4to, £3 13s. 6d.

READ, Carveth.—On the Theory of Logic: An Essay. Crown 8vo, 6s.

Realities of the Future Life. Small crown 8vo, 1s. 6d.

RENDELL, J. M.—Concise Handbook of the Island of Madeira. With Plan of Funchal and Map of the Island. Fcap. 8vo, 1s. 6d.

REYNOLDS, Rev. J. W.—The Supernatural in Nature. A Verification by Free Use of Science. Second Edition, revised and enlarged. Demy 8vo, 14s.

The Mystery of Miracles. New and Enlarged Edition. Crown 8vo, 6s.

RIBOT, Prof. Th.—English Psychology. Second Edition. A Revised and Corrected Translation from the latest French Edition. Large post 8vo, 9s.

Heredity: A Psychological Study on its Phenomena, its Laws, its Causes, and its Consequences. Large crown 8vo, 9s.

ROBERTSON, The late Rev. F. W., M.A.—Life and Letters of. Edited by the Rev. Stopford Brooke, M.A.
   I. Two vols., uniform with the Sermons. With Steel Portrait. Crown 8vo, 7s. 6d.
   II. Library Edition, in Demy 8vo, with Portrait. 12s.
   III. A Popular Edition, in 1 vol. Crown 8vo, 6s.

Sermons. Four Series. Small crown 8vo, 3s. 6d. each.

The Human Race, and other Sermons. Preached at Cheltenham, Oxford, and Brighton. Large post 8vo, 7s. 6d.

Notes on Genesis. New and Cheaper Edition. Crown 8vo, 3s. 6d.

Expository Lectures on St. Paul's Epistles to the Corinthians. A New Edition. Small crown 8vo, 5s.

Lectures and Addresses, with other Literary Remains. A New Edition. Crown 8vo, 5s.

An Analysis of Mr. Tennyson's "In Memoriam." (Dedicated by Permission to the Poet-Laureate.) Fcap. 8vo, 2s.

The Education of the Human Race. Translated from the German of Gotthold Ephraim Lessing. Fcap. 8vo, 2s. 6d.

The above Works can also be had, bound in half morocco.

*** A Portrait of the late Rev. F. W. Robertson, mounted for framing, can be had, 2s. 6d.

RODWELL, G. F., F.R.A.S., F.C.S.—**Etna: A History of the Mountain and its Eruptions.** With Maps and Illustrations. Square 8vo, 9s.

ROLLESTON, T. W. H., B.A.—**The Encheiridion of Epictetus.** Translated from the Greek, with a Preface and Notes. Small crown 8vo, 3s. 6d.

Rosmini's Origin of Ideas. Translated from the Fifth Italian Edition of the Nuovo Saggio *Sull' origine delle idee*. 3 vols. Demy 8vo, cloth. Vol. I. now ready, price 16s.

Rosmini's Philosophical System. Translated, with a Sketch of the Author's Life, Bibliography, Introduction, and Notes by THOMAS DAVIDSON. Demy 8vo, 16s.

RULE, Martin, M.A.—**The Life and Times of St. Anselm, Archbishop of Canterbury and Primate of the Britains.** 2 vols. Demy 8vo, cloth, 21s.

SALTS, Rev. Alfred, LL.D.—**Godparents at Confirmation.** With a Preface by the Bishop of Manchester. Small crown 8vo, limp cloth, 2s.

SALVATOR, Archduke Ludwig.—**Levkosia, the Capital of Cyprus.** Crown 4to, 10s. 6d.

SAMUEL, Sydney M.—**Jewish Life in the East.** Small crown 8vo, 3s. 6d.

SAYCE, Rev. Archibald Henry.—**Introduction to the Science of Language.** 2 vols. Large post 8vo, 25s.

Scientific Layman. The New Truth and the Old Faith: are they Incompatible? Demy 8vo, 10s. 6d.

SCOONES, W. Baptiste.—**Four Centuries of English Letters:** A Selection of 350 Letters by 150 Writers, from the Period of the Paston Letters to the Present Time. Second Edition. Large crown 8vo, 9s.

SCOTT, Robert H.—**Weather Charts and Storm Warnings.** Second Edition. Illustrated. Crown 8vo, 3s. 6d.

SHAKSPEARE, Charles.—**Saint Paul at Athens.** Spiritual Christianity in relation to some aspects of Modern Thought. Five Sermons preached at St. Stephen's Church, Westbourne Park. With a Preface by the Rev. Canon FARRAR. Crown 8vo, 5s.

SHELLEY, Lady.—**Shelley Memorials from Authentic Sources.** With (now first printed) an Essay on Christianity by Percy Bysshe Shelley. With Portrait. Third Edition. Crown 8vo, 5s.

SHILLITO, Rev. Joseph.—**Womanhood: its Duties, Temptations, and Privileges.** A Book for Young Women. Third Edition. Crown 8vo, 3s. 6d.

SHIPLEY, Rev. Orby, M.A.—**Church Tracts: or, Studies in Modern Problems.** By various Writers. 2 vols. Crown 8vo, 5s. each.

SHIPLEY, Rev. Orby, M.A.—continued.
Principles of the Faith in Relation to Sin. Topics for Thought in Times of Retreat. Eleven Addresses delivered during a Retreat of Three Days to Persons living in the World. Demy 8vo, 12s.

SKINNER, the late James.—A Synopsis of Moral and Ascetical Theology. With a Catalogue of Ancient and Modern Authorities. Arranged according to Centuries. With a prefatory Note by Rev. T. T. CARTER. Demy 4to, cloth, 10s. 6d.

Sister Augustine, Superior of the Sisters of Charity at the St. Johannis Hospital at Bonn. Authorised Translation by HANS THARAU, from the German "Memorials of AMALIE VON LASAULX." Second Edition. Large crown 8vo, 7s. 6d.

SMITH, Edward, M.D., LL.B., F.R.S.—Health and Disease, as Influenced by the Daily, Seasonal, and other Cyclical Changes in the Human System. A New Edition. Post 8vo, 7s. 6d.

Tubercular Consumption in its Early and Remediable Stages. Second Edition. Crown 8vo, 6s.

SPEDDING, James.—Reviews and Discussions, Literary, Political, and Historical not relating to Bacon. Demy 8vo, 12s. 6d.

Evenings with a Reviewer; or, Bacon and Macaulay. With a Prefatory Notice by G. S. VENABLES, Q.C. 2 vols. Demy 8vo, 18s.

STAPFER, Paul.—Shakspeare and Classical Antiquity: Greek and Latin Antiquity as presented in Shakspeare's Plays. Translated by EMILY J. CAREY. Large post 8vo, 12s.

ST. BERNARD.—A Little Book on the Love of God. Translated by MARIANNE CAROLINE and COVENTRY PATMORE. Extra, gilt top, 4s. 6d.

STEPHENS, Archibald John, LL.D.—The Folkestone Ritual Case. The Substance of the Argument delivered before the Judicial Committee of the Privy Council on behalf of the Respondents. Demy 8vo, 6s.

STEVENSON, Rev. W. F.—Hymns for the Church and Home. Selected and Edited by the Rev. W. Fleming Stevenson.
The Hymn Book consists of Three Parts:—I. For Public Worship.—II. For Family and Private Worship.—III. For Children.
₊ Published in various forms and prices, the latter ranging from 8d. to 6s.
Lists and full particulars will be furnished on application to the Publishers.

STEVENSON, Robert Louis.—Travels with a Donkey in the Cevennes. With Frontispiece by Walter Crane. Small crown 8vo, 2s. 6d.

STEVENSON, Robert Louis.—continued.
    An Inland Voyage. With Frontispiece by Walter Crane. Small Crown 8vo, 2s. 6d.
    Virginibus Puerisque, and other Papers. Crown 8vo, 6s.

STRACHEY, Sir John, G.C.S.I., and *Lieut.-Gen. Richard STRACHEY, R.E., F.R.S.*—**The Finances and Public Works of India, from 1869 to 1881.** Demy 8vo, 18s.

STRECKER-WISLICENUS.—**Organic Chemistry.** Translated and Edited, with Extensive Additions, by W. R. HODGKINSON, Ph.D., and A. J. GREENAWAY, F.I.C. Demy 8vo, 21s.

SULLY, James, M.A.—**Sensation and Intuition.** Demy 8vo, 10s. 6d.
    Pessimism : a History and a Criticism. Second Edition. Demy 8vo, 14s.

SYME, David.—**Outlines of an Industrial Science.** Second Edition. Crown 8vo, 6s.
    Representative Government in England. Its Faults and Failures. Second Edition. Large crown 8vo, 6s.

TAYLOR, Algernon.—**Guienne.** Notes of an Autumn Tour. Crown 8vo, 4s. 6d.

THOM, J. Hamilton.—**Laws of Life after the Mind of Christ.** Crown 8vo, cloth, 7s. 6d.

THOMSON, J. Turnbull.—**Social Problems;** or, An Inquiry into the Laws of Influence. With Diagrams. Demy 8vo, 10s. 6d.

TIDMAN, Paul F.—**Gold and Silver Money.** Part I.—A Plain Statement. Part II.—Objections Answered. Third Edition. Crown 8vo, 1s.

TIPPLE, Rev. S. A.—**Sunday Mornings at Norwood.** Prayers and Sermons. Crown 8vo, cloth, 6s.

TODHUNTER, Dr. J.—**A Study of Shelley.** Crown 8vo, 7s.

TREMENHEERE, Hugh Seymour, C.B.—**A Manual of the Principles of Government,** as set forth by the Authorities of Ancient and Modern Times. New and enlarged Edition. Crown 8vo, 5s.

TUKE, Daniel Hack, M.D., F.R.C.P.—**Chapters in the History of the Insane in the British Isles.** With 4 Illustrations. Large crown 8vo, 12s.

TWINING, Louisa.—**Workhouse Visiting and Management during Twenty-Five Years.** Small crown 8vo, 3s. 6d.

UPTON, Major R. D.—**Gleanings from the Desert of Arabia.** Large post 8vo, 10s. 6d.

VACUUS, Viator.—**Flying South.** Recollections of France and its Littoral. Small crown 8vo, 3s. 6d.

VAUGHAN, H. Halford.—**New Readings and Renderings of Shakespeare's Tragedies.** 2 vols. Demy 8vo, 25s.

VILLARI, Professor.—**Niccolò Machiavelli and his Times.** Translated by Linda Villari. 2 vols. Large post 8vo, 24s.

VOLCKXSOM, E. W. V.—**Catechism of Elementary Modern Chemistry.** Small crown 8vo, 3s.

VYNER, Lady Mary.—**Every Day a Portion.** Adapted from the Bible and the Prayer Book, for the Private Devotion of those living in Widowhood. Collected and Edited by Lady Mary Vyner. Square crown 8vo, 5s.

WALDSTEIN, Charles, Ph.D.—**The Balance of Emotion and Intellect;** an Introductory Essay to the Study of Philosophy. Crown 8vo, 6s.

WALLER, Rev. C. B.—**The Apocalypse,** reviewed under the Light of the Doctrine of the Unfolding Ages, and the Restitution of All Things. Demy 8vo, 12s.

WALPOLE, Chas. George.—**History of Ireland from the Earliest Times to the Union with Great Britain.** With 5 Maps and Appendices. Crown 8vo, 10s. 6d.

WALSHE, Walter Hayle, M.D.—**Dramatic Singing Physiologically Estimated.** Crown 8vo, 3s. 6d.

WATSON, Sir Thomas, Bart., M.D.—**The Abolition of Zymotic Diseases,** and of other similar Enemies of Mankind. Small crown 8vo, 3s. 6d.

WEDMORE, Frederick.—**The Masters of Genre Painting.** With Sixteen Illustrations. Crown 8vo, 7s. 6d.

WHEWELL, William, D.D.—**His Life and Selections from his Correspondence.** By Mrs. STAIR DOUGLAS. With a Portrait from a Painting by SAMUEL LAURENCE. Demy 8vo, 21s.

WHITE, A. D., LL.D.—**Warfare of Science.** With Prefatory Note by Professor Tyndall. Second Edition. Crown 8vo, 3s. 6d.

WHITE, F. A.—**English Grammar.** Small crown 8vo, cloth, 2s.

WHITNEY, Prof. William Dwight.—**Essentials of English Grammar,** for the Use of Schools. Crown 8vo, 3s. 6d.

WICKSTEED, P. H.—**Dante : Six Sermons.** Crown 8vo, 5s.

WILLIAMS, Rowland, D.D.—**Psalms, Litanies, Counsels, and Collects for Devout Persons.** Edited by his Widow. New and Popular Edition. Crown 8vo, 3s. 6d.

WILLIAMS, Rowland D.D.—continued.
Stray Thoughts Collected from the Writings of the late Rowland Williams, D.D. Edited by his Widow. Crown 8vo, 3s. 6d.

WILLIS, R., M.D.—**Servetus and Calvin :** a Study of an Important Epoch in the Early History of the Reformation. 8vo, 16s.

William Harvey. A History of the Discovery of the Circulation of the Blood : with a Portrait of Harvey after Faithorne. Demy 8vo, 14s.

WILSON, Sir Erasmus.—**Egypt of the Past.** With Chromo-lithograph and numerous Illustrations in the text. Second Edition, Revised. Crown 8vo, 12s.

WILSON, H. Schütz.—**The Tower and Scaffold.** A Miniature Monograph. Large fcap. 8vo, 1s.

WOLLSTONECRAFT, Mary.—**Letters to Imlay.** New Edition, with a Prefatory Memoir by C. KEGAN PAUL. Two Portraits in *eau-forte* by Anna Lea Merritt. Crown 8vo, 6s.

WOLTMANN, Dr. Alfred, and WOERMANN, Dr. Karl.—**History of Painting.** Edited by Sidney Colvin. Vol. I. Painting in Antiquity and the Middle Ages. With numerous Illustrations. Medium 8vo, 28s. ; bevelled boards, gilt leaves, 30s.

WOOD, Major-General J. Creighton.—**Doubling the Consonant.** Small crown 8vo, 1s. 6d.

Word was Made Flesh. Short Family Readings on the Epistles for each Sunday of the Christian Year. Demy 8vo, 10s. 6d.

WREN, Sir Christopher.—**His Family and His Times.** With Original Letters, and a Discourse on Architecture hitherto unpublished. By LUCY PHILLIMORE. With Portrait. Demy 8vo, 14s.

WRIGHT, Rev. David, M.A.—**Waiting for the Light,** and other Sermons. Crown 8vo, 6s.

YORKE, J. F.—**Notes on Evolution and Christianity.** Crown 8vo, cloth, 6s.

YOUMANS, Eliza A.—**An Essay on the Culture of the Observing Powers of Children,** especially in connection with the Study of Botany. Edited, with Notes and a Supplement, by Joseph Payne, F.C.P., Author of "Lectures on the Science and Art of Education," etc. Crown 8vo, 2s. 6d.

First Book of Botany. Designed to Cultivate the Observing Powers of Children. With 300 Engravings. New and Cheaper Edition. Crown 8vo, 2s. 6d.

YOUMANS, Edward L., M.D.—**A Class Book of Chemistry,** on the Basis of the New System. With 200 Illustrations. Crown 8vo, 5s.

THE INTERNATIONAL SCIENTIFIC SERIES.

I. **Forms of Water:** a Familiar Exposition of the Origin and Phenomena of Glaciers. By J. Tyndall, LL.D., F.R.S. With 25 Illustrations. Eighth Edition. Crown 8vo, 5s.

II. **Physics and Politics;** or, Thoughts on the Application of the Principles of "Natural Selection" and "Inheritance" to Political Society. By Walter Bagehot. Sixth Edition. Crown 8vo, 4s.

III. **Foods.** By Edward Smith, M.D., LL.B., F.R.S. With numerous Illustrations. Seventh Edition. Crown 8vo, 5s.

IV. **Mind and Body:** the Theories of their Relation. By Alexander Bain, LL.D. With Four Illustrations. Seventh Edition. Crown 8vo, 4s.

V. **The Study of Sociology.** By Herbert Spencer. Tenth Edition. Crown 8vo, 5s.

VI. **On the Conservation of Energy.** By Balfour Stewart, M.A., LL.D., F.R.S. With 14 Illustrations. Sixth Edition. Crown 8vo, 5s.

VII. **Animal Locomotion;** or Walking, Swimming, and Flying. By J. B. Pettigrew, M.D., F.R.S., etc. With 130 Illustrations. Second Edition. Crown 8vo, 5s.

VIII. **Responsibility in Mental Disease.** By Henry Maudsley, M.D. Fourth Edition. Crown 8vo, 5s.

IX. **The New Chemistry.** By Professor J. P. Cooke. With 31 Illustrations. Sixth Edition. Crown 8vo, 5s.

X. **The Science of Law.** By Professor Sheldon Amos. Fifth Edition. Crown 8vo, 5s.

XI. **Animal Mechanism:** a Treatise on Terrestrial and Aerial Locomotion. By Professor E. J. Marey. With 117 Illustrations. Second Edition. Crown 8vo, 5s.

XII. **The Doctrine of Descent and Darwinism.** By Professor Oscar Schmidt. With 26 Illustrations. Fifth Edition. Crown 8vo, 5s.

XIII. **The History of the Conflict between Religion and Science.** By J. W. Draper, M.D., LL.D. Seventeenth Edition. Crown 8vo, 5s.

XIV. **Fungi:** their Nature, Influences, Uses, etc. By M. C. Cooke, M.D., LL.D. Edited by the Rev. M. J. Berkeley, M.A., F.L.S. With numerous Illustrations. Third Edition. Crown 8vo, 5s.

XV. **The Chemical Effects of Light and Photography.** By Dr. Hermann Vogel. Translation thoroughly revised. With 100 Illustrations. Third Edition. Crown 8vo, 5s.

XVI. **The Life and Growth of Language.** By Professor William Dwight Whitney. Third Edition. Crown 8vo, 5s.

XVII. **Money and the Mechanism of Exchange.** By W. Stanley Jevons, M.A., F.R.S. Fifth Edition. Crown 8vo, 5s.

XVIII. **The Nature of Light.** With a General Account of Physical Optics. By Dr. Eugene Lommel. With 188 Illustrations and a Table of Spectra in Chromo-lithography. Third Edition. Crown 8vo, 5s.

XIX. **Animal Parasites and Messmates.** By Monsieur Van Beneden. With 83 Illustrations. Second Edition. Crown 8vo, 5s.

XX. **Fermentation.** By Professor Schützenberger. With 28 Illustrations. Third Edition. Crown 8vo, 5s.

XXI. **The Five Senses of Man.** By Professor Bernstein. With 91 Illustrations. Third Edition. Crown 8vo, 5s.

XXII. **The Theory of Sound in its Relation to Music.** By Professor Pietro Blaserna. With numerous Illustrations. Second Edition. Crown 8vo, 5s.

XXIII. **Studies in Spectrum Analysis.** By J. Norman Lockyer, F.R.S. With six photographic Illustrations of Spectra, and numerous engravings on Wood. Crown 8vo. Second Edition. 6s. 6d.

XXIV. **A History of the Growth of the Steam Engine.** By Professor R. H. Thurston. With numerous Illustrations. Second Edition. Crown 8vo, 6s. 6d.

XXV. **Education as a Science.** By Alexander Bain, LL.D. Fourth Edition. Crown 8vo, 5s.

XXVI. **The Human Species.** By Professor A. de Quatrefages. Third Edition. Crown 8vo, 5s.

XXVII. **Modern Chromatics.** With Applications to Art and Industry. By Ogden N. Rood. With 130 original Illustrations. Second Edition. Crown 8vo, 5s.

XXVIII. **The Crayfish:** an Introduction to the Study of Zoology. By Professor T. H. Huxley. With 82 Illustrations. Third Edition. Crown 8vo, 5s.

XXIX. **The Brain as an Organ of Mind.** By H. Charlton Bastian, M.D. With numerous Illustrations. Third Edition. Crown 8vo, 5s.

XXX. **The Atomic Theory.** By Prof. Wurtz. Translated by G. Cleminshaw, F.C.S. Third Edition. Crown 8vo, 5s.

XXXI. **The Natural Conditions of Existence as they affect Animal Life.** By Karl Semper. With 2 Maps and 106 Woodcuts. Second Edition. Crown 8vo, 5s.

XXXII. **General Physiology of Muscles and Nerves.** By Prof. J. Rosenthal. Second Edition. With Illustrations. Crown 8vo, 5s.

XXXIII. **Sight:** an Exposition of the Principles of Monocular and Binocular Vision. By Joseph le Conte, LL.D. With 132 Illustrations. Crown 8vo, 5s.

XXXIV. **Illusions:** a Psychological Study. By James Sully. Second Edition. Crown 8vo, 5s.

XXXV. **Volcanoes: what they are and what they teach.** By Professor J. W. Judd, F.R.S. With 92 Illustrations on Wood. Second Edition. Crown 8vo, 5s.

XXXVI. **Suicide:** an Essay in Comparative Moral Statistics. By Prof. E. Morselli. With Diagrams. Crown 8vo, 5s.

XXXVII. **The Brain and its Functions.** By J. Luys. With Illustrations. Second Edition. Crown 8vo, 5s.

XXXVIII. **Myth and Science:** an Essay. By Tito Vignoli. Crown 8vo, 5s.

XXXIX. **The Sun.** By Professor Young. With Illustrations. Second Edition. Crown 8vo, 5s.

XL. **Ants, Bees, and Wasps:** a Record of Observations on the Habits of the Social Hymenoptera. By Sir John Lubbock, Bart., M.P. With 5 Chromo-lithographic Illustrations. Fifth Edition. Crown 8vo, 5s.

XLI. **Animal Intelligence.** By G. J. ROMANES, LL.D., F.R.S. Second Edition. Crown 8vo, 5s.

XLII. **The Concepts and Theories of Modern Physics.** By J. B. STALLO. Second Edition. Crown 8vo, 5s.

XLIII. **Diseases of the Memory**; An Essay in the Positive Psychology. By Prof. Th. RIBOT. Second Edition. Crown 8vo, cloth, 5s.

XLIV. **Man before Metals.** By N. JOLY, with 148 Illustrations. Second Edition. Crown 8vo, 5s.

XLV. **The Science of Politics.** By Prof. SHELDON AMOS. Crown 8vo, cloth, 5s.

MILITARY WORKS.

Army of the North German Confederation : a Brief Description of its Organisation, of the Different Branches of the Service and their *rôle* in War, of its Mode of Fighting, etc. Translated from the Corrected Edition, by permission of the Author, by Colonel Edward Newdigate. Demy 8vo, 5s.

BARRINGTON, Capt. J. T.—**England on the Defensive**; or, the Problem of Invasion Critically Examined. Large crown 8vo, with Map, 7s. 6d.

BLUME, Major W.—**The Operations of the German Armies in France,** from Sedan to the end of the War of 1870-71. With Map. From the Journals of the Head-quarters Staff. Translated by the late E. M. Jones, Maj. 20th Foot, Prof. of Mil. Hist., Sandhurst. Demy 8vo, 9s.

BOGUSLAWSKI, Capt. A. von.—**Tactical Deductions from the War of 1870-1.** Translated by Colonel Sir Lumley Graham, Bart., late 18th (Royal Irish) Regiment. Third Edition, Revised and Corrected. Demy 8vo, 7s.

BRACKENBURY, Col. C. B., R.A., C.B.—**Military Handbooks for Regimental Officers.** I. Military Sketching and Reconnaissance, by Col. F. J. Hutchison, and Major H. G. MacGregor. Fourth Edition. With 15 Plates. Small 8vo, 6s. II. The Elements of Modern Tactics Practically applied to English Formations, by Lieut-Col. Wilkinson Shaw. Fourth Edition. With 25 Plates and Maps. Small crown 8vo, 9s.

BRIALMONT, Col. A.—**Hasty Intrenchments.** Translated by Lieut. Charles A. Empson, R.A. With Nine Plates. Demy 8vo, 6s.

CLERY, C., Lieut.-Col.—**Minor Tactics.** With 26 Maps and Plans. Fifth and revised Edition. Demy 8vo, 16s.

DU VERNOIS, Col. von Verdy.—**Studies in Leading Troops.** An authorised and accurate Translation by Lieutenant H. J. T. Hildyard, 71st Foot. Parts I. and II. Demy 8vo, 7s.

GOETZE, Capt. A. von.—**Operations of the German Engineers during the War of 1870-1.** Published by Authority, and in accordance with Official Documents. Translated from the German by Colonel G. Graham, V.C., C.B., R.E. With 6 large Maps. Demy 8vo, 21s.

HARRISON, Lieut.-Col. R.—**The Officer's Memorandum Book for Peace and War.** Third Edition. Oblong 32mo, roan, with pencil, 3s. 6d.

HELVIG, Capt. H.—**The Operations of the Bavarian Army Corps.** Translated by Captain G. S. Schwabe. With 5 large Maps. In 2 vols. Demy 8vo, 24s.

Tactical Examples: Vol. I. The Battalion, 15s. Vol. II. The Regiment and Brigade, 10s. 6d. Translated from the German by Col. Sir Lumley Graham. With nearly 300 Diagrams. Demy 8vo.

HOFFBAUER, Capt.—**The German Artillery in the Battles near Metz.** Based on the Official Reports of the German Artillery. Translated by Captain E. O. Hollist. With Map and Plans. Demy 8vo, 21s.

LAYMANN, Capt.—**The Frontal Attack of Infantry.** Translated by Colonel Edward Newdigate. Crown 8vo, 2s. 6d.

Notes on Cavalry Tactics, Organisation, etc. By a Cavalry Officer. With Diagrams. Demy 8vo, 12s.

PARR, Capt. H. Hallam, C.M.G.—**The Dress, Horses, and Equipment of Infantry and Staff Officers.** Crown 8vo, 1s.

SCHAW, Col. H.—**The Defence and Attack of Positions and Localities.** Second Edition, revised and corrected. Crown 8vo, 3s. 6d.

SCHELL, Maj. von.—**The Operations of the First Army under Gen. von Goeben.** Translated by Col. C. H. von Wright. Four Maps. Demy 8vo, 9s.

The Operations of the First Army under Gen. von Steinmetz. Translated by Captain E. O. Hollist. Demy 8vo, 10s. 6d.

SCHELLENDORF, Major-Gen. B. von.—**The Duties of the General Staff.** Translated from the German by Lieutenant Hare. Vol. I. Demy 8vo, 10s. 6d.

SCHERFF, Maj. W. von.—**Studies in the New Infantry Tactics.** Parts I. and II. Translated from the German by Colonel Lumley Graham. Demy 8vo, 7s. 6d.

SHADWELL, Maj.-Gen., C.B.—**Mountain Warfare.** Illustrated by the Campaign of 1799 in Switzerland. Being a Translation of the Swiss Narrative compiled from the Works of the Archduke Charles, Jomini, and others. Also of Notes by General H. Dufour on the Campaign of the Valtelline in 1635. With Appendix, Maps, and Introductory Remarks. Demy 8vo, 16s.

SHERMAN, Gen. W. T.—**Memoirs of General W. T. Sherman,** Commander of the Federal Forces in the American Civil War. By Himself. 2 vols. With Map. Demy 8vo, 24s. *Copyright English Edition.*

STUBBS, Lieut.-Col. F. W.—**The Regiment of Bengal Artillery.** The History of its Organisation, Equipment, and War Services. Compiled from Published Works, Official Records, and various Private Sources. With numerous Maps and Illustrations. 2 vols. Demy 8vo, 32s.

STUMM, Lieut. Hugo.—**Russia's Advance Eastward.** Based on Official Reports. Translated by Capt. C. E. H. VINCENT. With Map. Crown 8vo, 6s.

VINCENT, Capt. C. E. H.—**Elementary Military Geography, Reconnoitring, and Sketching.** Compiled for Non-commissioned Officers and Soldiers of all Arms. Square crown 8vo, 2s. 6d.

Volunteer, the Militiaman, and the Regular Soldier. By a Public Schoolboy. Crown 8vo, 5s.

WARTENSLEBEN, Count H. von.—**The Operations of the South Army in January and February, 1871.** Compiled from the Official War Documents of the Head-quarters of the Southern Army. Translated by Colonel C. H. von Wright. With Maps. Demy 8vo, 6s.

WARTENSLEBEN, Count H. von.—continued.
The Operations of the First Army under Gen. von Manteufel. Translated by Col. C. H. von Wright. Uniform with the above. Demy 8vo, 9s.

WICKHAM, Capt. E. H., R.A.—Influence of Firearms upon Tactics: Historical and Critical Investigations. By an OFFICER OF SUPERIOR RANK (in the German Army). Translated by Captain E. H. Wickham, R.A. Demy 8vo, 7s. 6d.

WOINOVITS, Capt. I.—Austrian Cavalry Exercise. Translated by Captain W. S. Cooke. Crown 8vo, 7s.

POETRY.

ADAMS, W. D.—Lyrics of Love, from Shakspeare to Tennyson. Selected and arranged by. Fcap. 8vo, extra, gilt edges, 3s. 6d.

ADAM OF ST. VICTOR.—The Liturgical Poetry of Adam of St. Victor. From the text of Gautier. With Translations into English in the Original Metres, and Short Explanatory Notes, by Digby S. Wrangham, M.A. 3 vols. Crown 8vo, printed on hand-made paper, boards, 21s.

Antiope: a Tragedy. Large crown 8vo, 6s.

AUBERTIN, J. J.—Camoens' Lusiads. Portuguese Text, with Translation. Map and Portraits. 2 vols. Demy 8vo, 30s.

Seventy Sonnets of Camoens. Portuguese Text and Translation, with some original Poems. Dedicated to Capt. Richard F. Burton. Printed on hand-made paper, bevelled boards, gilt top, 7s. 6d.

AUCHMUTY, A. C.—Poems of English Heroism: From Brunanburh to Lucknow; from Athelstan to Albert. Small crown 8vo, 1s. 6d.

AVIA.—The Odyssey of Homer. Done into English Verse by. Fcap. 4to, 15s.

BANKS, Mrs. G. L.—Ripples and Breakers: Poems. Square 8vo, 5s.

BARNES, William.—Poems of Rural Life, in the Dorset Dialect. New Edition, complete in one vol. Crown 8vo, 8s. 6d.

BAYNES, Rev. Canon H. R.—Home Songs for Quiet Hours. Fourth and cheaper Edition. Fcap. 8vo, cloth, 2s. 6d.
*** This may also be had handsomely bound in morocco with gilt edges.

BENNETT, Dr. W. C.—Narrative Poems and Ballads. Fcap. 8vo, sewed in coloured wrapper, 1s.

BENNETT, Dr. W. C.—continued.
Songs for Sailors. Dedicated by Special Request to H.R.H. the Duke of Edinburgh. With Steel Portrait and Illustrations. Crown 8vo, 3s. 6d.
An Edition in Illustrated Paper Covers, 1s.
Songs of a Song Writer. Crown 8vo, 6s.

BEVINGTON, L. S.—**Key Notes.** Small crown 8vo, 5s.

BILLSON, C. J.—**The Acharnians of Aristophanes.** Crown 8vo, 3s. 6d.

BOWEN, H. C., M.A.—**Simple English Poems.** English Literature for Junior Classes. In Four Parts. Parts I., II., and III., 6d. each, and Part IV., 1s.

BRYANT, W. C.—**Poems.** Red-line Edition. With 24 Illustrations and Portrait of the Author. Crown 8vo, extra, 7s. 6d.
A Cheap Edition, with Frontispiece. Small crown 8vo, 3s. 6d.

BYRNNE, E. Fairfax.—**Milicent:** a Poem. Small crown 8vo, 6s.

Calderon's Dramas: the Wonder-Working Magician — Life is a Dream — the Purgatory of St. Patrick. Translated by Denis Florence MacCarthy. Post 8vo, 10s.

Chronicles of Christopher Columbus. A Poem in 12 Cantos. By M. D. C. Small crown 8vo.

CLARKE, Mary Cowden.—**Honey from the Weed.** Verses. Crown 8vo, 7s.

COLOMB, Colonel.—**The Cardinal Archbishop:** a Spanish Legend. In 29 Cancions. Small crown 8vo, 5s.

CONWAY, Hugh.—**A Life's Idylls.** Small crown 8vo, 3s. 6d.

COPPÉE, Francois.—**L'Exilée.** Done into English Verse, with the sanction of the Author, by I. O. L. Crown 8vo, vellum, 5s.

David Rizzio, Bothwell, and the Witch Lady. Three Tragedies by the author of "Ginevra," etc. Crown 8vo, cloth, 6s.

DAVIE, G. S., M.D.—**The Garden of Fragrance.** Being a complete translation of the Bostán of Sádi from the original Persian into English Verse. Crown 8vo, cloth, 7s. 6d.

DAVIES, T. Hart.—**Catullus.** Translated into English Verse. Crown 8vo, 6s.

DE VERE, Aubrey.—**The Foray of Queen Meave,** and other Legends of Ireland's Heroic Age. Small crown 8vo, 5s.
Alexander the Great: a Dramatic Poem. Small crown 8vo, 5s.
The Legends of St. Patrick, and other Poems. Small crown 8vo, 5s.

DE VERE, Aubrey.—continued.
> **St. Thomas of Canterbury:** a Dramatic Poem. Large fcap. 8vo, 5s.
>
> **Legends of the Saxon Saints.** Small crown 8vo, 6s.
>
> **Antar and Zara:** an Eastern Romance. **Inisfail,** and other Poems, Meditative and Lyrical. Fcap. 8vo, 6s.
>
> **The Fall of Rora, The Search after Proserpine,** and other Poems, Meditative and Lyrical. Fcap. 8vo, 6s.
>
> **The Infant Bridal,** and other Poems. A New and Enlarged Edition. Fcap. 8vo, 7s. 6d.

DILLON, Arthur.—**River Songs and other Poems.** With 13 autotype Illustrations from designs by Margery May. Fcap. 4to, cloth extra, gilt leaves, 10s. 6d.

DOBELL, Mrs. Horace.—**Ethelstone, Eveline,** and other Poems. Crown 8vo, 6s.

DOBSON, Austin.—**Vignettes in Rhyme,** and Vers de Société. Third Edition. Fcap. 8vo, 5s.
> **Proverbs in Porcelain.** By the Author of "Vignettes in Rhyme." Second Edition. Crown 8vo, 6s.

Dorothy: a Country Story in Elegiac Verse. With Preface. Demy 8vo, 5s.

DOWDEN, Edward, LL.D.—**Poems.** Second Edition. Fcap. 8vo, 5s.
> **Shakspere's Sonnets.** With Introduction. Large post 8vo, 7s. 6d.

DOWNTON, Rev. H., M.A.—**Hymns and Verses.** Original and Translated. Small crown 8vo, 3s. 6d.

DUGMORE, Rev. Ernest Edward.—**From the Mountains of the East:** A Quasi-Dramatic Poem on the Story of the Prophet-Soothsayer Balaam. Crown 8vo, cloth, 3s. 6d.

DUTT, Toru.—**A Sheaf Gleaned in French Fields.** New Edition, with Portrait. Demy 8vo, 10s. 6d.
> **Ancient Ballads and Legends of Hindustan.** With an Introductory Memoir by Edmund W. Gosse. Small crown 8vo, printed on hand-made paper, 5s.

EDWARDS, Rev. Basil.—**Minor Chords**; or, Songs for the Suffering: a Volume of Verse. Fcap. 8vo, 3s. 6d.; paper, 2s. 6d.

ELDRYTH, Maud.—**Margaret,** and other Poems. Small crown 8vo, 3s. 6d.

ELLIOTT, Ebenezer, The Corn Law Rhymer.—**Poems.** Edited by his son, the Rev. Edwin Elliott, of St. John's, Antigua. 2 vols. Crown 8vo, 18s.

English Odes. Selected, with a Critical Introduction by EDMUND W. GOSSE, and a miniature frontispiece by Hamo Thornycroft, A.R.A. Elzevir 8vo, limp parchment antique, 6s.; vellum, 7s. 6d.

Epic of Hades, The. By the Author of "Songs of Two Worlds." Thirteenth Edition. Fcap. 8vo, 7s. 6d.

* Also an Illustrated Edition, with 17 full-page designs in photo-mezzotint by George R. Chapman. 4to, extra, gilt leaves, 25s.; and a Large Paper Edition, with Portrait, 10s. 6d.

EVANS, Anne.—**Poems and Music.** With Memorial Preface by ANN THACKERAY RITCHIE. Large crown 8vo, 7s.

GOSSE, Edmund W.—**New Poems.** Crown 8vo, 7s. 6d.

GROTE, A. R.—**Rip van Winkle:** a Sun Myth; and other Poems. Small crown 8vo, printed on hand-made paper, limp parchment antique, 5s.

GURNEY, Rev. Alfred.—**The Vision of the Eucharist,** and other Poems. Crown 8vo, 5s.

Gwen: a Drama in Monologue. By the Author of the "Epic of Hades." Third Edition. Fcap. 8vo, 5s.

HAWKER, Robt. Stephen.—**The Poetical Works of.** Now first collected and arranged. With a Prefatory Notice by J. G. Godwin. With Portrait. Crown 8vo, 12s.

HELLON, H. G.—**Daphnis:** a Pastoral Poem. Small crown 8vo, 3s. 6d.

HICKEY, E. H.—**A Sculptor,** and other Poems. Small crown 8vo, 5s.

HOLMES, E. G. A.—**Poems.** First and Second Series. Fcap. 8vo, 5s. each.

Horati Opera. Edited by F. A. CORNISH, Assistant Master at Eton. With a Frontispiece after a design by L. Alma Tadema, etched by Leopold Lowenstam. Parchment Library Edition, 6s.; vellum, 7s. 6d.

INGHAM, Sarson, C. J.—**Cædmon's Vision, and other Poems.** Small crown 8vo, 5s.

JENKINS, Rev. Canon.—**The Girdle Legend of Prato.** Small crown 8vo, 2s.

Alfonso Petrucci, Cardinal and Conspirator: an Historical Tragedy in Five Acts. Small crown 8vo, 3s. 6d.

KING, Mrs. Hamilton.—**The Disciples.** Fourth Edition, with Portrait and Notes. Crown 8vo, 7s. 6d.

Aspromonte, and other Poems. Second Edition. Fcap. 8vo, 4s. 6d.

LANG, A.—**XXXII Ballades in Blue China.** Elzevir 8vo, parchment, 5*s*.

LEIGH, Arran and Isla.—**Bellerophon.** Small crown 8vo, 5*s*.

LEIGHTON, Robert.—**Records**, and other Poems. With Portrait. Small crown 8vo, 7*s*. 6*d*.

Living English Poets MDCCCLXXXII. With Frontispiece by Walter Crane. Second Edition. Large crown 8vo. Printed on hand-made paper. Parchment, 12*s*., vellum, 15*s*.

LOCKER, F.—**London Lyrics.** A New and Revised Edition, with Additions and a Portrait of the Author. Crown 8vo, 6*s*.

*** Also a New and Cheaper Edition. Small crown 8vo, 2*s*. 6*d*.

Love Sonnets of Proteus. With Frontispiece by the Author. Elzevir 8vo, 5*s*.

LOWNDES, Henry.—**Poems and Translations.** Crown 8vo, 6*s*.

LUMSDEN, Lieut.-Col. H. W.—**Beowulf:** an Old English Poem. Translated into Modern Rhymes. Small crown 8vo, 5*s*.

MACLEAN, Charles Donald.—**Latin and Greek Verse Translations.** Small crown 8vo, 2*s*.

MAGNUSSON, Eirikr, M.A., and PALMER, E. H., M.A.—**Johan Ludvig Runeberg's Lyrical Songs, Idylls, and Epigrams.** Fcap. 8vo, 5*s*.

M.D.C.—**Chronicles of Christopher Columbus.** A Poem in Twelve Cantos. Small Crown 8vo, cloth, 7*s*. 6*d*.

MEREDITH, Owen, The Earl of Lytton.—**Lucile.** With 160 Illustrations. Crown 4to, extra, gilt leaves, 21*s*.

MIDDLETON, The Lady.—**Ballads.** Square 16mo, 3*s*. 6*d*.

MOORE, Mrs. Bloomfield.—**Gondaline's Lesson :** The Warden's Tale, Stories for Children, and other Poems. Crown 8vo, 5*s*.

MORICE, Rev. F. D., M.A.—**The Olympian and Pythian Odes of Pindar.** A New Translation in English Verse. Crown 8vo, 7*s*. 6*d*.

MORRIS, Lewis.—**Poetical Works of.** New and cheaper Edition, with Portrait. Complete in 3 vols., 5*s*. each.

Vol. I. contains "Songs of Two Worlds." Vol. II. contains "The Epic of Hades." Vol. III. contains "Gwen" and "The Ode of Life."

MORSHEAD, E. D. A.—**The House of Atreus.** Being the Agamemnon, Libation-Bearers, and Furies of Æschylus. Translated into English Verse. Crown 8vo, 7*s*.

NADEN, Constance W.—**Songs and Sonnets of Spring Time.** Small crown 8vo, 5*s*.

NEWELL, E. J.—**The Sorrows of Simona and Lyrical Verses.** Small crown 8vo, cloth, 3*s.* 6*d.*

NICHOLSON, Edward B.—**The Christ Child, and other Poems.** Crown 8vo, 4*s.* 6*d.*

NOAKE, Major R. Compton.—**The Bivouac**; or, Martial Lyrist. With an Appendix: Advice to the Soldier. Fcap. 8vo, 5*s.* 6*d.*

NOEL, The Hon. Roden.—**A Little Child's Monument.** Second Edition. Small crown 8vo, 3*s.* 6*d.*

NORRIS, Rev. Alfred.—**The Inner and Outer Life Poems.** Fcap. 8vo, 6*s.*

Ode of Life, The. By the Author of "The Epic of Hades," etc. Fourth Edition. Crown 8vo, 5*s.*

O'HAGAN, John.—**The Song of Roland.** Translated into English Verse. Large post 8vo, parchment antique, 10*s.* 6*d.*

PAUL, C. Kegan.—**Goethe's Faust.** A New Translation in Rhyme. Crown 8vo, 6*s.*

PAYNE, John.—**Songs of Life and Death.** Crown 8vo, 5*s.*

PENNELL, H. Cholmondeley.—**Pegasus Resaddled.** By the Author of "Puck on Pegasus," etc., etc. With 10 Full-page Illustrations by George Du Maurier. Second Edition. Fcap. 4to, elegant, 12*s.* 6*d.*

PFEIFFER, Emily.—**Glan Alarch**: His Silence and Song: a Poem Second Edition. Crown 8vo, 6*s.*

    Gerard's Monument, and other Poems. Second Edition. Crown 8vo, 6*s.*

    Quarterman's Grace, and other Poems. Crown 8vo, 5*s.*

    Poems. Second Edition. Crown 8vo, 6*s.*

    Sonnets and Songs. New Edition. 16mo, handsomely printed and bound in cloth, gilt edges, 4*s.*

    Under the Aspens: Lyrical and Dramatic. With Portrait. Crown 8vo, 6*s.*

PIKE, Warburton.—**The Inferno of Dante Allighieri.** Demy 8vo, 5*s.*

POE, Edgar Allan.—**Poems.** With an Essay on his Poetry by ANDREW LANG, and a Frontispiece by Linley Sambourne. Parchment Library Edition, 6*s.*; vellum, 7*s.* 6*d.*

RHOADES, James.—**The Georgics of Virgil.** Translated into English Verse. Small crown 8vo, 5*s.*

ROBINSON, A. Mary F.—**A Handful of Honeysuckle.** Fcap. 8vo, 3*s.* 6*d.*

    The Crowned Hippolytus. Translated from Euripides. With New Poems. Small crown 8vo, 5*s.*

SAUNDERS, John.—**Love's Martyrdom.** A Play and Poem. Small crown 8vo, cloth, 5s.

Schiller's Mary Stuart. German Text, with English Translation on opposite page by LEEDHAM WHITE. Crown 8vo, 6s.

Shakspere's Sonnets. Edited by EDWARD DOWDEN. With a Frontispiece etched by Leopold Lowenstam, after the Death Mask. Parchment Library Edition, 6s.; vellum, 7s. 6d.

Shakspere's Works. In 12 Monthly Volumes. Parchment Library Edition, 6s. each; vellum, 7s. 6d. each.

SHAW, W. F., M.A.—**Juvenal, Persius, Martial, and Catullus.** An Experiment in Translation. Crown 8vo, cloth, 5s.

SHELLEY, Percy Bysshe.—**Poems Selected from.** Dedicated to Lady Shelley. With Preface by Richard Garnett. Parchment Library Edition, 6s.; vellum, 7s. 6d.

Six Ballads about King Arthur. Crown 8vo, extra, gilt edges, 3s. 6d.

SKINNER, James.—**Cœlestia.** The Manual of St. Augustine. The Latin Text side by side with an English Interpretation in Thirty-six Odes with Notes, *and* a plea *for the* study *of* Mystical Theology. Large crown 8vo, 6s.

SLADEN, Douglas B.—**Frithjof and Ingebjorg, and other Poems.** Small crown 8vo, cloth, 5s.

Songs of Two Worlds. By the Author of "The Epic of Hades." Seventh Edition. Complete in One Volume, with Portrait. Fcap. 8vo, 7s. 6d.

Songs for Music. By Four Friends. Containing Songs by Reginald A. Gatty, Stephen H. Gatty, Greville J. Chester, and Juliana Ewing. Square crown 8vo, 5s.

STEDMAN, Edmund Clarence.—**Lyrics and Idylls,** with other Poems. Crown 8vo, 7s. 6d.

STEVENS, William.—**The Truce of God,** and other Poems. Small crown 8vo, 3s. 6d.

TAYLOR, Sir H.—Works Complete in Five Volumes. Crown 8vo, 30s.

TENNYSON, Alfred.—Works Complete:—
    The Imperial Library Edition. Complete in 7 vols. Demy 8vo, 10s. 6d. each; in Roxburgh binding, 12s. 6d. each.
    Author's Edition. In 7 vols. Post 8vo, gilt 43s. 6d.; or half-morocco, Roxburgh style, 52s. 6d.
    Cabinet Edition. 13 vols. Each with Frontispiece. Fcap. 8vo, 2s. 6d. each.
    Cabinet Edition. 13 vols. Complete in handsome Ornamental Case. 35s.

TENNYSON, Alfred.—continued.

The Royal Edition. In 1 vol. With 26 Illustrations and Portrait. Extra, bevelled boards, gilt leaves, 21*s*.

The Guinea Edition. Complete in 13 vols. neatly bound and enclosed in box, 21*s*. ; French morocco or parchment, 31*s*. 6*d*.

Shilling Edition. In 13 vols. pocket size, 1*s*. each, sewed.

The Crown Edition. Complete in 1 vol. strongly bound, 6*s*. ; extra gilt leaves, 7*s*. 6*d*. ; Roxburgh, half-morocco, 8*s*. 6*d*.

*** Can also be had in a variety of other bindings.

In Memoriam. With a Miniature Portrait in *eau-forte* by Le Rat, after a Photograph by the late Mrs. Cameron. Parchment Library Edition, 6*s*. ; vellum, 7*s*. 6*d*.

The Princess. A Medley. With a Miniature Frontispiece by H. M. Paget, and a Tailpiece in Outline by Gordon Browne. Parchment Library Edition, 6*s*. ; vellum, 7*s*. 6*d*.

Songs Set to Music by various Composers. Edited by W. J. Cusins. Dedicated, by express permission, to Her Majesty the Queen. Royal 4to, extra, gilt leaves, 21*s*. ; or in half-morocco, 25*s*.

Original Editions :—

Ballads, and other Poems. Small 8vo, 5*s*.

Poems. Small 8vo, 6*s*.

Maud, and other Poems. Small 8vo, 3*s*. 6*d*.

The Princess. Small 8vo, 3*s*. 6*d*.

Idylls of the King. Small 8vo, 5*s*.

Idylls of the King. Complete. Small 8vo, 6*s*.

The Holy Grail, and other Poems. Small 8vo, 4*s*. 6*d*.

Gareth and Lynette. Small 8vo, 3*s*.

Enoch Arden, etc. Small 8vo, 3*s*. 6*d*.

In Memoriam. Small 8vo, 4*s*.

Harold : a Drama. New Edition. Crown 8vo, 6*s*.

Queen Mary : a Drama. New Edition. Crown 8vo, 6*s*.

The Lover's Tale. Fcap. 8vo, 3*s*. 6*d*.

Selections from the above Works. Super royal 16mo, 3*s*. 6*d*. ; gilt extra, 4*s*.

Songs from the above Works. 16mo, 2*s*. 6*d*. ; extra, 3*s*. 6*d*.

Idylls of the King, and other Poems. Illustrated by Julia Margaret Cameron. 2 vols. folio, half-bound morocco, £6 6*s*. each.

Tennyson for the Young and for Recitation. Specially arranged. Fcap. 8vo, 1s. 6d.

The Tennyson Birthday Book. Edited by Emily Shakespear. 32mo, limp, 2s. ; extra, 3s.

*** A superior Edition, printed in red and black, on antique paper, specially prepared. Small crown 8vo, extra, gilt leaves, 5s. ; and in various calf and morocco bindings.

Horæ Tennysonianæ sive Eclogæ e Tennysono Latine Redditæ Cura A. J. Church, A.M. Small crown 8vo, 6s.

THOMPSON, Alice C.—Preludes : a Volume of Poems. Illustrated by Elizabeth Thompson (Painter of "The Roll Call "). 8vo, 7s. 6d.

TODHUNTER, Dr. J.—Laurella, and other Poems. Crown 8vo, 6s. 6d.

Forest Songs. Small crown 8vo, 3s. 6d.

The True Tragedy of Rienzi : a Drama. 3s. 6d.

Alcestis : a Dramatic Poem. Extra fcap. 8vo, 5s.

A Study of Shelley. Crown 8vo, 7s.

Translations from Dante, Petrarch, Michael Angelo, and Vittoria Colonna. Fcap. 8vo, 7s. 6d.

TURNER, Rev. C. Tennyson.—Sonnets, Lyrics, and Translations. Crown 8vo, 4s. 6d.

Collected Sonnets, Old and New. With Prefatory Poem by ALFRED TENNYSON ; also some Marginal Notes by S. T. COLERIDGE, and a Critical Essay by JAMES SPEDDING. Fcap. 8vo, 7s. 6d.

WALTERS, Sophia Lydia.—The Brook : a Poem. Small crown 8vo, 3s. 6d.

A Dreamer's Sketch Book. With 21 Illustrations by Percival Skelton, R. P. Leitch, W. H. J. BOOT, and T. R. PRITCHETT. Engraved by J. D. Cooper. Fcap. 4to, 12s. 6d.

WATERFIELD, W.—Hymns for Holy Days and Seasons. 32mo, 1s. 6d.

WAY, A., M.A.—The Odes of Horace Literally Translated in Metre. Fcap. 8vo, 2s.

WEBSTER, Augusta.—Disguises : a Drama. Small crown 8vo, 5s.

In a Day : a Drama. Small crown 8vo, cloth, 2s. 6d.

Wet Days. By a Farmer. Small crown 8vo, 6s.

WILKINS, William.—Songs of Study. Crown 8vo, 6s.

WILLOUGHBY, The Hon. Mrs.—On the North Wind—Thistledown : a Volume of Poems. Elegantly bound, small crown 8vo, 7s. 6d.

WOODS, James Chapman.—A Child of the People, and other Poems. Small crown 8vo, 5s.

YOUNG, Wm.—Gottlob, etcetera. Small crown 8vo, 3s. 6d.

YOUNGS, Ella Sharpe.—Paphus, and other Poems. Small crown 8vo, 3s. 6d.

WORKS OF FICTION IN ONE VOLUME.

BANKS, Mrs. G. L.—God's Providence House. New Edition. Crown 8vo, 3s. 6d.

BETHAM-EDWARDS, Miss M.—Kitty. With a Frontispiece. Crown 8vo, 6s.

Blue Roses; or, Helen Malinofska's Marriage. By the Author of "Véra." New and Cheaper Edition. With Frontispiece. Crown 8vo, 6s.

FRISWELL, J. Hain.—One of Two; or, The Left-Handed Bride. Crown 8vo, 3s. 6d.

GARRETT, E.—By Still Waters: a Story for Quiet Hours. With 7 Illustrations. Crown 8vo, 6s.

HARDY, Thomas.—A Pair of Blue Eyes. Author of "Far from the Madding Crowd." New Edition. Crown 8vo, 6s.

The Return of the Native. New Edition. With Frontispiece. Crown 8vo, 6s.

HOOPER, Mrs. G.—The House of Raby. Crown 8vo, 3s. 6d.

INGELOW, Jean.—Off the Skelligs: a Novel. With Frontispiece. Second Edition. Crown 8vo, 6s.

MACDONALD, G.—Malcolm. With Portrait of the Author engraved on Steel. Sixth Edition. Crown 8vo, 6s.

The Marquis of Lossie. Fourth Edition. With Frontispiece. Crown 8vo, 6s.

St. George and St. Michael. Third Edition. With Frontispiece. Crown 8vo, 6s.

MASTERMAN, J.—Half-a-Dozen Daughters. Crown 8vo, 3s. 6d.

MEREDITH, George.—Ordeal of Richard Feverel. New Edition. Crown 8vo, 6s.

The Egoist: A Comedy in Narrative. New and Cheaper Edition, with Frontispiece. Crown 8vo, 6s.

PALGRAVE, W. Gifford.—Hermann Agha: an Eastern Narrative. Third Edition. Crown 8vo, 6s.

Pandurang Hari; or, Memoirs of a Hindoo. With an Introductory Preface by Sir H. Bartle E. Frere, G.C.S.I., C.B. Crown 8vo, 6s.

PAUL, Margaret Agnes.—**Gentle and Simple**; a Story. New and Cheaper Edition, with Frontispiece. Crown 8vo, 6s.

SHAW, Flora L.—**Castle Blair**; a Story of Youthful Lives. New and Cheaper Edition. Crown 8vo, 3s. 6d.

STRETTON, Hesba.—**Through a Needle's Eye**: a Story. New and Cheaper Edition, with Frontispiece. Crown 8vo, 6s.

TAYLOR, Col. Meadows, C.S.I., M.R.I.A.—**Seeta**: a Novel. New and Cheaper Edition. With Frontispiece. Crown 8vo, 6s.

Tippoo Sultaun: a Tale of the Mysore War. New Edition, with Frontispiece. Crown 8vo, 6s.

Ralph Darnell. New and Cheaper Edition. With Frontispiece. Crown 8vo, 6s.

A Noble Queen. New and Cheaper Edition. With Frontispiece. Crown 8vo, 6s.

The Confessions of a Thug. Crown 8vo, 6s.

Tara: a Mahratta Tale. Crown 8vo, 6s.

THOMAS, Moy.—**A Fight for Life.** Crown 8vo, 3s. 6d.

Within Sound of the Sea. New and Cheaper Edition, with Frontispiece. Crown 8vo, 6s.

BOOKS FOR THE YOUNG.

Aunt Mary's Bran Pie. By the Author of "St. Olave's." Illustrated. 3s. 6d.

BARLEE, Ellen.—**Locked Out**: a Tale of the Strike. With a Frontispiece. Royal 16mo, 1s. 6d.

BONWICK, J., F.R.G.S.—**The Tasmanian Lily.** With Frontispiece. Crown 8vo, 5s.

Mike Howe, the Bushranger of Van Diemen's Land. New and Cheaper Edition. With Frontispiece. Crown 8vo, 3s. 6d.

Brave Men's Footsteps. A Book of Example and Anecdote for Young People. By the Editor of "Men who have Risen." With 4 Illustrations by C. Doyle. Seventh Edition. Crown 8vo, 3s. 6d.

Children's Toys, and some Elementary Lessons in General Knowledge which they teach. Illustrated. Crown 8vo, 5s.

COLERIDGE, Sara. — **Pretty Lessons in Verse for Good Children,** with some Lessons in Latin, in Easy Rhyme. A New Edition. Illustrated. Fcap. 8vo, 3s. 6d.

COXHEAD, Ethel.—**Birds and Babies.** Imp. 16mo. With 33 Illustrations. Cloth gilt, 2s. 6d.

D'ANVERS, N. R.—**Little Minnie's Troubles:** an Every-day Chronicle. With 4 Illustrations by W. H. Hughes. Fcap. 8vo, 3s. 6d.

Parted: a Tale of Clouds and Sunshine. With 4 Illustrations. Extra fcap. 8vo, 3s. 6d.

Pixie's Adventures; or, the Tale of a Terrier. With 21 Illustrations. 16mo, 4s. 6d.

Nanny's Adventures: or, the Tale of a Goat. With 12 Illustrations. 16mo, 4s. 6d.

DAVIES, G. Christopher.—**Rambles and Adventures of our School Field Club.** With 4 Illustrations. New and Cheaper Edition. Crown 8vo, 3s. 6d.

DRUMMOND, Miss.—**Tripp's Buildings.** A Study from Life, with Frontispiece. Small crown 8vo, 3s. 6d.

EDMONDS, Herbert.—**Well Spent Lives:** a Series of Modern Biographies. New and Cheaper Edition. Crown 8vo, 3s. 6d.

EVANS, Mark.—**The Story of our Father's Love,** told to Children. Fourth and Cheaper Edition of Theology for Children. With 4 Illustrations. Fcap. 8vo, 1s. 6d.

FARQUHARSON, M.
  I. **Elsie Dinsmore.** Crown 8vo, 3s. 6d.
  II. **Elsie's Girlhood.** Crown 8vo, 3s. 6d.
  III. **Elsie's Holidays at Roselands.** Crown 8vo, 3s. 6d.

HERFORD, Brooke.—**The Story of Religion in England:** a Book for Young Folk. Crown 8vo, 5s.

INGELOW, Jean.—**The Little Wonder-horn.** With 15 Illustrations. Small 8vo, 2s. 6d.

JOHNSON, Virginia W.—**The Catskill Fairies.** Illustrated by ALFRED FREDERICKS. 5s.

KER, David.—**The Boy Slave in Bokhara:** a Tale of Central Asia. With Illustrations. New and Cheaper Edition. Crown 8vo, 3s. 6d.

The Wild Horseman of the Pampas. Illustrated. New and Cheaper Edition. Crown 8vo, 3s. 6d.

LAMONT, Martha MacDonald.—**The Gladiator:** a Life under the Roman Empire in the beginning of the Third Century. With 4 Illustrations by H. M. Paget. Extra fcap. 8vo, 3s. 6d.

LEANDER, Richard.—**Fantastic Stories.** Translated from the German by Paulina B. Granville. With 8 Full-page Illustrations by M. E. Fraser-Tytler. Crown 8vo, 5s.

LEE, Holme.—Her Title of Honour. A Book for Girls. New Edition. With a Frontispiece. Crown 8vo, 5s.

LEWIS, Mary A.—A Rat with Three Tales. New and Cheaper Edition. With 4 Illustrations by Catherine F. Frere. 3s. 6d.

MAC KENNA, S. J.—Plucky Fellows. A Book for Boys. With 6 Illustrations. Fifth Edition. Crown 8vo, 3s. 6d.

At School with an Old Dragoon. With 6 Illustrations. New and Cheaper Edition. Crown 8vo, 3s. 6d.

Mc CLINTOCK, L.—Sir Spangle and the Dingy Hen. Illustrated. Square crown 8vo, 2s. 6d.

MALDEN, H. E.—Princes and Princesses: Two Fairy Tales. Illustrated. Small crown 8vo, 2s. 6d.

Master Bobby. By the Author of "Christina North." With 6 Illustrations. Fcap. 8vo, 3s. 6d.

NAAKE, J. T.—Slavonic Fairy Tales. From Russian, Servian, Polish, and Bohemian Sources. With 4 Illustrations. Crown 8vo, 5s.

PELLETAN, E.—The Desert Pastor, Jean Jarousseau. Translated from the French. By Colonel E. P. De L'Hoste. With a Frontispiece. New Edition. Fcap. 8vo, 3s. 6d.

REANEY, Mrs. G. S.—Waking and Working; or, From Girlhood to Womanhood. New and Cheaper Edition. With a Frontispiece. Crown 8vo, 3s. 6d.

Blessing and Blessed: a Sketch of Girl Life. New and Cheaper Edition. Crown 8vo, 3s. 6d.

Rose Gurney's Discovery. A Book for Girls. Dedicated to their Mothers. Crown 8vo, 3s. 6d.

English Girls: Their Place and Power. With Preface by the Rev. R. W. Dale. Third Edition. Fcap. 8vo, 2s. 6d.

Just Anyone, and other Stories. Three Illustrations. Royal 16mo, 1s. 6d.

Sunbeam Willie, and other Stories. Three Illustrations. Royal 16mo, 1s. 6d.

Sunshine Jenny, and other Stories. Three Illustrations. Royal 16mo, 1s. 6d.

ROSS, Mrs. E. ("Nelsie Brook")—Daddy's Pet. A Sketch from Humble Life. With 6 Illustrations. Royal 16mo, 1s.

SADLER, S. W., R.N.—The African Cruiser: a Midshipman's Adventures on the West Coast. With 3 Illustrations. New and Cheaper Edition. Crown 8vo, 2s. 6d.

Kegan Paul, Trench & Co.'s Publications. 47

Seeking his Fortune, and other Stories. With 4 Illustrations. New and Cheaper Edition. Crown 8vo, 2s. 6d.

Seven Autumn Leaves from Fairy Land. Illustrated with 9 Etchings. Square crown 8vo, 3s. 6d.

STOCKTON, Frank R.—**A Jolly Fellowship.** With 20 Illustrations. Crown 8vo, 5s.

STORR, Francis, and TURNER, Hawes.—**Canterbury Chimes;** or, Chaucer Tales retold to Children. With 6 Illustrations from the Ellesmere MS. Second Edition. Fcap. 8vo, 3s. 6d.

STRETTON, Hesba.—**David Lloyd's Last Will.** With 4 Illustrations. New Edition. Royal 16mo, 2s. 6d.

The Wonderful Life. Sixteenth Thousand. Fcap. 8vo, 2s. 6d.

Sunnyland Stories. By the Author of "Aunt Mary's Bran Pie.' Illustrated. Second Edition. Small 8vo, 3s. 6d.

Tales from Ariosto Re-told for Children. By a Lady. With 3 Illustrations. Crown 8vo, 4s. 6d.

WHITAKER, Florence.—**Christy's Inheritance.** A London Story. Illustrated. Royal 16mo, 1s. 6d.

ZIMMERN, H.—**Stories in Precious Stones.** With 6 Illustrations. Third Edition. Crown 8vo, 5s.

www.ingramcontent.com/pod-product-compliance
Lightning Source LLC
Chambersburg PA
CBHW032137010526
44111CB00035B/595